New Revised

P9-DNN-307

Over 6 million in print!

Webster's
Classic
Reference
Library

ENGLISH/SPANISH
DICTIONARY

McGraw-Hill
Children's Publishing

A Division of The McGraw·Hill Companies

Send all inquiries to:
McGraw-Hill Children's Publishing
8787 Orion Place
Columbus, Ohio 43240-4027

00735-1590

This is an abridged dictionary, containing a useful selection of words in English and Spanish. It is a portable reference tool for those at all levels of fluency in both languages and is intended as a general guide. To keep this volume's convenient size, we have excluded proper nouns, place names, and historical events, all of which are far more suited to research of greater depth.

ABBREVIATIONS

abbr.—abbreviation

adj.—adjective

adv.—adverb

Amer.—American

coll.—colloquial

conj.—conjunction

contr.—contraction

def. art.—definite article

f.—feminine

indef. art.—indefinite article

infin.—infinitive

interj.—interjection

m.—masculine

n.—noun

obj.—object

pl.—plural

poss.—possessive

prep.—preposition

pron.—pronoun

Español—Inglés
Spanish—English

A

a *prep.* at; to
a•ba•ce•rí•a *f.* grocery
a•ba•ce•ro *m.* grocer
á•ba•co *m.* abacus
a•bad *m.* abbot
a•ba•de•sa *f.* abbess
a•ba•dí•a *f.* abbey
a•ba•jo *adv.* beneath; down; below; *prep.* down
a•ba•lan•zar *v.* to hurl
a•ban•de•ra•mien•to *m.* registration (nautical)
a•ban•de•rar *v.* to register
a•ban•do•na•do, a *adj.* derelict; careless
a•ban•do•nar *v.* to desert; to forsake; to abandon; to give up
a•ban•do•no *m.* abandonment; neglect
a•ba•ni•car *v.* to fan
a•ba•ni•co *m.* fan
a•ba•ra•jar *v.* to catch
a•ba•ra•tar *v.* to lower; to become cheaper
a•bar•car *v.* to embrace; to comprise; to encompass
a•ba•ti•do, a *adj.* downcast; dejected; despondent; glum
a•ba•ti•mien•to *m.* dejection
a•ba•tir(se) *v.* to knock down; to depress; to discourage
ab•di•car *v.* to abdicate
ab•do•men *m.* abdomen
ab•do•mi•nal *adj.* abdominal

a•be•dul *m.* birch
a•be•ja *f.* bee
a•be•jo•rro *m.* bumblebee
a•be•jón *m.* hornet
a•be•rra•ción *f.* aberration
a•ber•tu•ra *f.* aperture; gap
a•be•to *m.* fir
a•bier•ta•men•te *adv.* outright
a•bier•to, a *adj.* open; clear
a•bi•ga•rra•do, a *adj.* many-colored, variegated; motley
a•bis•mal *adj.* abysmal
a•bis•mo *m.* abyss
ab•ju•rar *v.* to abjure
a•blan•dar(se) *v.* to soften; to mollify
a•bla•ti•vo *m.* ablative
a•blu•ción *f.* ablution
ab•ne•ga•ción *f.* abnegation
ab•ne•gar *v.* to renounce; to abnegate
a•bo•car *v.* to mouth
a•bo•car•dar *v.* to ream
a•bo•chor•na•do, a *adj.* flushed, put to shame
a•bo•fe•tear *v.* to slap
a•bo•ga•cí•a *f.* bar; law; advocacy
a•bo•ga•do *m.* attorney; counsel; lawyer
a•bo•gar *v.* to plead; to advocate
a•bo•len•go *m.* ancestry
a•bo•li•ción *f.* abolition
a•bo•li•cio•nis•ta *m., f.* abolitionist
a•bo•lir *v.* to abolish
a•bo•lla•du•ra *f.* dent
a•bo•llar *v.* to emboss; to dent
a•bo•mi•na•ble *adj.* abominable
a•bo•mi•na•ción *f.* abomination
a•bo•mi•nar *v.* to abominate; to loathe

a·bo·nar v. to fertilize; to give credit

a·bo·no m. manure; fertilizer; subscription; guarantee

a·bo·ri·gen adj. m. aboriginal

a·bo·rre·cer v. to hate; to abhor

a·bo·rre·ci·ble adj. detestable; abhorrent; loathsome; hateful

a·bo·rre·ci·mien·to m. hate; hatred; abhorrence; loathing

a·bor·tar v. to abort

a·bor·ti·vo, a adj. abortive

a·bor·to m. abortion

a·bo·to·nar v. to button up

a·bo·za·lar v. to muzzle

a·bra f. cove

a·bra·sión adj. abrasion

a·bra·si·vo adj. abrasive

a·bra·za·de·ra f. clamp; brace

a·bra·zar(se) v. to hug; to cuddle; to embrace

a·bre·car·tas m. letter opener

a·bre·var v. to soak; to water

a·bre·via·ción f. abbreviation

a·bre·viar v. to abridge; to abbreviate; to curtail; to condense

a·bri·gar(se) v. to shelter; to harbor; to protect

a·bri·go m. shelter; coat; overcoat

a·bril m. April

a·bri·llan·tar v. to polish; to brighten

a·brir(se) v. to open up; to spread out; to open

a·bro·char v. to button up; to fasten; to buckle

a·bro·ga·ción f. abrogation

a·bro·gar v. to abrogate; to repeal

a·bru·ma·dor, a adj. crushing

a·bru·mar v. to overwhelm

a·brup·to, a adj. abrupt; steep; blunt

a·bru·ta·do, a adj. bestial

abs·ce·so m. abscess

ab·so·lu·ción f. absolution

ab·so·lu·to, a adj. complete; absolute

ab·sol·ven·te adj. absolving

ab·sol·ver v. to acquit; to clear; to absolve

ab·sor·ben·cia f. absorbence

ab·sor·ben·te m. absorbent

ab·sor·ber v. to soak up; to engross; to absorb

ab·sor·ción f. absorption

ab·sor·to, a adj. absorbed; intent

abs·ten·ción f. abstention

abs·te·ner·se v. to abstain; to refrain

abs·ti·nen·cia f. abstinence

abs·trac·to, a adj. abstract

abs·tra·er v. to abstract

abs·tru·so, a adj. abstruse

ab·sur·di·dad f. absurdity

ab·sur·do, a adj. silly; preposterous; absurd

a·bue·la f. grandmother

a·bue·lo m. grandfather; grandparent

a·bun·da·mien·to m. abundance

a·bun·dan·te adj. plentiful; abundant; ample

a·bun·dar v. to abound

a·bun·do·so adj. abundant

a·bu·rri·do adj. boring; bored

a·bu·rri·mien·to m. boredom

a·bu·rrir v. to bore

a·bu·sar v. to misuse; to maltreat; to abuse

a·bu·si·vo, a adj. abusive

a·bu·so m. encroachment; abuse

ab·yec·ción f. abjectness

ab·yec·to, a adj. abject

a·cá adj. here

a·ca·ba·do, a adj. end; conclusion

a·ca·bar v. to accomplish; to end; to fail

a·ca·de·mia f. academy

a·ca·dé·mi·co, a adj. academic

al·ca·li·zar v. to alkalize

a·cam·par v. to camp

a·ca·ri·ciar v. to pet; to pat

a·ca·rrear v. to cart

a·ca·rreo m. cartage

ac·ce·der v. to accede

ac·ce·si·ble adj. accessible

ac·ce·so m. approach; access

ac·ce·so·rio, a m. accessory

ac·ci·den·ta·do, a adj. uneven; broken; eventful

ac·ci·den·te *m.* casualty; accident

ac·ción *f.* movement; action

a·ce·bo *m.* holly

a·ce·char *v.* to lurk; to watch for

a·cei·te *m.* oil

a·cei·tu·na *f.* olive

a·ce·le·rar(se) *v.* to speed; to accelerate

a·cen·to *m.* stress; emphasis; accent

a·cen·tuar(se) *v.* to emphasize; to accent; to stress

a·cep·tar *v.* to adopt; to accept; to agree to something

a·cer·car(se) *v.* to bring near; to get close

a·ce·ro *m.* steel

a·cer·ti·jo *m.* riddle

a·cé·ti·co *adj.* acetic

a·ce·to·na *f.* acetone

á·ci·do *m.* acid

á·ci·do bó·ri·co *m.* boric acid

á·ci·do cí·tri·co *m.* citric acid

á·ci·do sul·fú·ri·co *m.* sulfuric acid

a·cla·ma·ción *f.* acclaim

a·cla·ra·ción *f.* clarification

a·cla·rar *v.* to clear; to clarify; to rinse

a·cli·ma·tar *v.* to acclimate

ac·ne *m.* acné

a·co·bar·dar(se) *v.* to flinch; to unnerve; to cringe

a·co·gi·da *f.* welcome

a·col·char *v.* to pad

a·có·li·to *m.* altar boy; acolyte

a·co·me·ter *v.* to attempt; to undertake; to cover; to come; attack

a·co·mo·da·di·zo *adj.* easygoing

a·co·mo·da·dor *m.* usher *f.* usherette

a·co·mo·dar *v.* to suit; to accommodate; to put up

a·com·pa·ñan·te *m.* escort, accompanist

a·com·pa·ñar *v.* to escort; to attend; to go with; to accompany

a·con·di·cio·na·dor de ai·re *m.* air conditioner

a·con·se·jar(se) *v.* to advise; to counsel

a·con·te·cer *v.* to chance: to happen

a·con·te·ci·mien·to *m.* occasion; event; occurrence; happening

a·cor·dar(se) *v.* to agree on; to remember; to agree

a·cor·de *m.* chord; in tune; harmony; in accord

a·cor·deón *m.* accordion

a·cor·near *v.* to gore

a·co·rra·lar *v.* to round up; to corral; to intimidate; to pen

a·cor·tar(se) *v.* to clip; to shorten; to lessen; to obstruct

a·co·sar *v.* to harass; to pursue; to beset

a·cos·tar(se) *v.* to lie down; to go to bed

a·cos·tum·brar(se) *v.* to be accustomed to; to be used to; to habituate

a·cre *adj.* acrid; sour

a·cre *m.* acre

a·cre·cen·tar *v.* to advance; to increase

a·cree·dor *m.* creditor

a·cri·mo·nia *f.* acridity

a·cró·ba·ta *m., f.* acrobat

ac·ti·tud *f.* pose; position; attitude

ac·ti·var *v.* to activate

ac·ti·vi·dad *f.* movement; nimbleness; activity

ac·ti·vo, a *adj.* alive; brisk; active; quick

ac·to *m.* event; act; function

ac·tor *m.* actor

ac·triz *f.* actress

ac·tual *adj.* instant; actual

ac·tual·men·te *adv.* at present; now; actually

ac·tuar *v.* to perform; to act; to set in action

a·cua·rio *m.* aquarium

a·cuá·til *adj.* aquatic

a·cu·chi·llar *v.* to slash; to hack; to knife

a·cue·duc·to *m.* aqueduct, waterworks

á·cueo, a *adj.* watery

a·cuer·do *m.* resolution; agreement; accord

a·cu·mu·lar *v.* to amass; to stockpile; to accumulate; to congest

a·cu·ña·ción *f.* coinage

a·cu·ñar *v.* to coin; to mint

a·cu·sar *v.* to impeach; to charge; to indict; to accuse

a·cús·ti·ca *f.* acoustics

a·chi·car *v.* to diminish; to humble; to bail

a·chis·pa·do, a *adj.* tipsy

a·da·gio *m.* proverb; adage

a·da·lid *m.* commander

a·dap·ta·ble *adj.* adaptable; versatile

a·dap·ta·ción *f.* adaptation

a·dap·tar *v.* to fit; to adapt; to adapt oneself to; to adjust

a·de·cua·do, a *adj.* fit; suitable; adequate

a·de·fe·sio *m.* something gaudy; extravagance

a·de·ha·la *f.* tip; bonus

a·de·lan·ta·do, a *adj.* fast; advanced

a·de·lan·tar(se) *v.* to further; to proceed; to overtake

a·de·lan·te *adv.* forwards; forward

a·de·lan·to *m.* progress; advance

a·del·ga·zar(se) *v.* to lose weight; to taper; to make thin; to attenuate; to slim down

a·de·mán *m.* attitude; gesture

a·de·más *adv.* besides; moreover; in addition

a·den·tro *adv.* inside; within

a·dep·to *m.* adept

a·de·re·zar *v.* to adorn; to garnish

a·de·re·zo *m.* finery; adornment; dressing

a·des·trar *v.* adiestrar

a·deu·dar *v.* to debit; to owe

ad·he·ren·cia *f.* bond; adherence

ad·he·ren·te *adj.* adherent; adhesive

ad·he·rir(se) *v.* to cling; to adhere; to stick

ad·he·sión *f.* adherence

ad·he·si·vo, a *adj.* adhesive

a·di·ción *f.* addition

a·di·cio·nal *adj.* more; extra; additional

a·dic·to, a *adj.* addicted

a·dies·trar(se) *v.* to exercise; to train; to practice

a·diós *m.* farewell; goodbye; good day

a·di·po·so, a *m.* fat; adipose

a·di·ta·men·to *m.* attachment; addition

a·di·ti·vo *m.* additive

a·di·vi·nar *v.* to foretell; to guess

ad·je·ti·vo *m.* adjective

ad·ju·di·ca·ción *m.* ward; adjudgement

ad·ju·di·car(se) *v.* to allot; to award

ad·jun·tar *v.* to annex, to attach

ad·mi·nis·tra·ción *f.* administration; management

ad·mi·nis·tra·dor, a *m.* administrator; steward; manager

ad·mi·nis·trar *v.* to manage; to dispense; to administer

ad·mi·nis·tra·ti·vo, a *adj.* administrative

ad·mi·ra·ble *adj.* fine; excellent; admirable

ad·mi·ra·ción *f.* admiration

ad·mi·rar(se) *v.* to wonder; to admire; to amaze

ad·mi·si·ble *adj.* acceptable; admissible

ad·mi·sión *f.* input; admission

ad·mi·tir *v.* to acknowledge; to permit; to admit

a·do·be *m.* adobe

a·do·les·cen·cia *f.* adolescence

a·dop·tar *v.* to embrace

a·dop·ti·vo, a *adj.* adoptive

a·do·ra·ble *adj.* adorable

a·do·ra·ción *f.* adoration

a·do·rar *v.* to worship; to adore

a·dor·me·cer(se) *v.* to fall asleep; to drowse

a·dor·mi·de·ra *f.* poppy

a·dor·na·mien·to *m.* adornment

a·dor·nar *v.* to adorn, to deck; to decorate; to grace

a·dor·no *m.* adornment; ornament; array

ad·qui·rir *v.* to obtain; to secure; to acquire

a·dre·na·li·na *f.* adrenaline

ads·cri·bir *v.* to assign; to ascribe

a·dua·na *f.* customs

a·dua·ne·ro *m.* customs

a·du·cir *v.* to cite; to adduce

a·du·ja·da *adj.* coiled

a·du·la·ción *f.* flattery; adulation

a·du·la·dor, a *m.* flatterer

a·du·lar *v.* to flatter; to adulate

a·dul·te·ra·ción *f.* adulteration

a·dul·te·ra·dor *m.* adulterator

a·dul·te·rar *v.* to adulterate

a·dul·te·rio *m.* adultery

a·dul·to, a *m.* adult

a·dul·zar *v.* to make sweet

ad·ver·bial *adj.* adverbial

ad·ver·bio *m.* adverb

ad·ver·sa·rio *m.* opponent; adversary

ad·ver·si·dad *f.* adversity

ad·ver·so, a *adj.* averse; unfavorable; adverse

ad·ver·ti·do, a *adj.* skillful; informed; intelligent; capable; sagacious

ad·ver·tir *v.* to notify; to advise; to caution; to take notice of something; to observe

ad·ya·cen·te *adj.* adjacent

ae·ra·ción *f.* aeration

aé·reo, a *adj.* aerial

ae·ro·di·ná·mi·co *adj.* aerodynamic

ae·ro·náu·ti·co, a *adj.* aeronautic

ae·ro·pla·no *m.* airplane

ae·ro·puer·to *m.* airport

a·fa·bi·li·dad *f.* affability

a·fa·ble *adj.* affable; genial; kind

a·fán *m.* anxiety; travail

a·fa·nar *v.* to urge; to toil; to strive

a·fa·no·so, a *adj.* anxious

a·fec·ción *f.* fondness; affection

a·fec·ta·ción *f.* pretense; affectation

a·fec·ta·do, a *adj.* affected

a·fec·tar *v.* to affect

a·fec·to *m.* affection

a·fec·tuo·sa·men·te *adv.* fondly, affectionately

a·fec·tuo·so,a *adj.* affectionate

a·fei·ta·do, a *m.* shave

a·fei·tar *v.* to shave

a·fei·te *m.* shave; cosmetic

a·fe·rrar(se) *v.* to grasp; to furl

a·fian·zar *v.* to bail; to clinch; to guaranty

a·fi·ción *f.* liking; affection; inclination

a·fi·cio·na·do, a *m.* fan; amateur; fancier

a·fi·jo, a *m.* affix

a·fi·lar(se) *v.* to sharpen

a·fi·liar(se) *v.* to join; to affiliate; to adopt

a·fín *adj.* related; contiguous; adjacent

a·fi·na·ción *f.* refining; tuning

a·fi·nar *v.* to refine; to polish; to complete; to tune

a·fi·ni·dad *f.* affinity; relationship

a·fir·mar(se) *v.* to secure; to assert; to contend; to affirm; to make fast

a·fir·ma·ti·vo *adj.* affirmative

a·flic·ción *f.* anxiety; bereavement; affliction

a·fli·gi·do *adj.* stricken

a·fli·gir(se) *v.* to afflict

a·flo·jar(se) *v.* to loosen; to slacken; to weaken

a·flo·rar *v.* to emerge; to sift

a·fluen·cia *f.* affluence; crowd; jam; fluency; abundance

a·fluen·te *adj.* affluent

a·fo·rar *v.* to appraise; to gauge; to measure

a·fo·ris·mo *m.* aphorism; maxim

a·for·tu·na·do, a *adj.* prosperous; lucky; fortunate

a·fren·ta *f.* insult; affront

a·fren·tar(se) *v.* to insult; to affront; to be affronted

a·fro·di·siá·co *adj.* aphrodisiac

a·fue·ra *adv.* outside; outskirts; suburbs

a·ga·char(se) *v.* to crouch; to squat; to bow down

a·ga·lla *f.* gill

a·ga·rrar(se) *v.* to grasp; to seize

a·ga·rre *m.* gripping

a·ga·rro *m.* grip; clutch; grab

a·ga·rro·tar *v.* to compress; to bind tightly

a·ga·sa·ja·dor *adj.* attentive

a·ga·sa·jar *v.* to entertain; to fondle; to welcome

a·gen·cia *f.* bureau; agency

a·gen·ciar *v.* to obtain

a·gen·cio·so *adj.* industrious

a·gen·da *f.* diary; notebook

a·gen·te *m.* officer; agent

á•gil *adj.* nimble; agile; lithe; active; lithesome

a•gi•li•dad *f.* agility

a•gi•ta•ción *f.* flurry; flutter; stir; excitement; agitation

a•gi•tar(se) *v.* to stir up; to churn; to flutter; to shake

a•glo•me•ra•ción *f.* agglomeration

a•glo•me•ra•do *adj.* agglomerate

a•glo•me•rar *v.* to agglomerate

a•glu•ti•na•ción *f.* agglutination

a•glu•ti•nan•te *m.* cement

a•glu•ti•nar *v.* to agglutinate

a•go•ní•a *f.* pain; agony

a•go•nio•so *adj.* persistent

a•go•rar *v.* to foretell

a•gos•tar *v.* to consume

a•gos•to *m.* August; harvest

a•go•ta•mien•to *m.* exhaustion; depletion

a•go•tar(se) *v.* to drain; to give out; to tire; to exhaust

a•gra•cia•do, a *adj.* graceful

a•gra•ciar *v.* to award; to grace

a•gra•da•ble *adj.* gracious; nice; pleasant; agreeable; delightful

a•gra•dar *v.* to please

a•gra•de•cer *v.* to appreciate; to acknowledge; to thank

a•gra•de•ci•do, a *adj.* thankful; grateful

a•gra•do *m.* liking; taste

a•gra•va•ción *f.* aggravation

a•gra•van•te *adj.* aggravating

a•gra•viar *m.* to harm; to wrong

a•gra•vio *m.* offense; injury; grievance; harm

a•gra•vio•so *adj.* injurious; offensive; insulting

a•gre•dir *v.* to assault

a•gre•sión *f.* aggression

a•gre•si•vo *adj.* aggressive

a•gre•sor, a *m.* aggressor

a•griar *v.* to annoy; to sour

a•gri•cul•tu•ra *f.* farming

a•grie•tar *v.* to split, to crack

a•gri•men•su•ra *f.* surveying

a•grio, a *adj.* acid; sour

a•gro *m.* farming

a•gro•nó•mi•co, a *adj.* agronomical

a•gru•pa•ción *f.* group

a•gru•par(se) *v.* to cluster; to group

a•gua *f.* water

a•gua•ca•te *m.* avocado

a•gua•do, a *adj.* diluted

a•gua•ma•ri•na *f.* aquamarine

a•guan•tar(se) *v.* to support; to endure; to hold

a•guan•te *m.* endurance

a•guar•dar *v.* to await

a•gu•de•za *f.* acuteness; keenness; sharpness; brightness

a•gu•di•zar *v.* to sharpen

a•gu•do, a *adj.* sharp

a•güe•ro *m.* omen

a•gue•rri•do, a *adj.* seasoned

á•gui•la *f.* eagle

a•gu•ja *f.* needle

a•gu•je•ro *m.* hole

a•guo•so, a *adj.* watery

a•gu•zar *v.* to sharpen

a•hí *adv.* there

a•hi•ja•da *f.* goddaughter

a•hi•ja•do *m.* godson

a•hi•jar *v.* to adopt

a•hi•la•do *adj.* faint; soft

a•hi•lar *v.* to faint

a•hi•to, a *adj.* stuffed

a•ho•gar *v.* to oppress; to drown; to choke

a•ho•ra *adv.* now

a•hor•ca•jar(se) *v.* to straddle

a•hor•mar *v.* to fit

a•ho•rrar *v.* to spare, to save

a•ho•rro *m.* savings

a•hue•va•do *adj.* egg-shaped

a•hu•ma•do, a *adj.* smoky; cured; smoked

a•hu•mar *v.* to cure; to smoke

ai•rar *v.* to annoy; to anger

ai•re *m.* aspect; air

ai•re•a•do *adj.* aired out, open

ai•re•ar(se) *v.* to air; to cool

ai•re•o *m.* ventilation

ais·la·do, a *adj.* alone, isolated
ais·lar *v.* to seclude; to isolate
a·ja·do, a *adj.* withered
a·jar *v.* to mar; to spoil
a·je·dre·cis·ta *f., m.* chess player
a·je·drez *m.* chess
a·jen·jo *m.* bitterness
a·je·no, a *adj.* alien; strange; foreign
a·je·tre·o *m.* agitation
a·jo *m.* garlic
a·jus·tar *v.* to settle; to adapt; to adjust; to fix; to tighten
a·jus·te *m.* fitting; accommodation
a·jus·ti·cia·mien·to *m.* execution
a·la *f.* wing
a·la·ban·za *f.* praise
a·la·bar *v.* to commend, to praise
a·la·bas·tro *m.* alabaster
a·la·crán *m.* scorpion
a·la·cri·dad *f.* eagerness
a·la·do, a *adj.* winged
a·lam·bre *m.* wire
á·la·mo *m.* poplar
a·lar·de·o *m.* bragging
a·lar·gar *v.* to stretch; to make longer
a·lar·ma *f.* alarm
a·lar·man·te *adj.* alarming
a·lar·mar *v.* to alarm
al·ba *f.* daybreak
al·ba·ri·co·que *m.* apricot
al·ber·gar *v.* to cherish
al·bi·no, na *adj.* albino
al·bo·ro·ta·do, a *adj.* rowdy; excited
al·bo·ro·tar *v.* to excite; to incite
al·bo·ro·zo *m.* joy
al·ca·cho·fa *f.* artichoke
al·cal·de *m.* mayor
al·ca·li·no, a *adj.* alkaline
al·ca·loi·de *m.* alkaloid
al·can·for *m.* camphor
al·can·zar *v.* to attain; to reach; to pass; to grasp
al·car·cil *m.* artichoke
al·cá·zar *m.* castle
al·ce *m.* moose
al·co·ba *f.* bedroom

al·co·hol *m.* alcohol
al·co·hó·li·co *adj.* alcoholic
a·lea·to·rio *adj.* uncertain
a·le·go·rí·a *f.* allegory
a·le·grar *v.* to make happy; to cheer; to rejoice
a·le·gre *adj.* joyous; gay; glad
a·le·gre·men·te *adv.* gaily
a·le·grí·a *f.* gladness; gaiety
a·le·grón *m.* joy
a·le·ja·mien·to *m.* distance; withdrawal
a·le·la·do *adj.* bewildered
a·len·ta·dor, a *adj.* encouraging
a·len·tar *v.* to encourage
a·ler·gia *f.* allergy
a·lér·gi·co, a *adj.* allergic
a·ler·tar *v.* to alert; to warn
a·le·te·o *m.* flapping
al·fa·bé·ti·co *adj.* alphabetical
al·fa·be·to *m.* alphabet
al·fa·re·rí·a *f.* pottery
al·fi·le·rar *v.* to pin
al·fom·bra *f.* carpet
al·fom·brar *v.* to carpet
al·for·za *f.* pleat
ál·ge·bra *f.* algebra
al·go *pron.* anything; something
al·go·dón *m.* cotton
al·guien *pron.* somebody
al·gún *adj.* some
al·gu·no, a *pron.* anybody
al·ha·ja, a *f.* gem
al·hu·ce·ma *f.* lavender
a·lia·do, a *m.* ally
a·lian·za *f.* alliance
a·li·bi *m.* alibi
a·lie·na·ble *adj.* alienable
a·lie·na·ción *f.* alienation
a·lie·nar *v.* to alienate
a·lien·to *m.* courage
a·li·ge·rar(se) *v.* to relieve
a·li·men·tar *v.* to feed
a·li·men·ti·cio *adj.* nutritious
a·li·men·to *m.* food
a·li·nea·ción *m.* alignment
a·li·ñar *v.* to tidy

a·li·ño *m.* tidiness
a·li·sar *v.* to smooth
a·lis·tar *v.* to alleviate
al·ma *f.* spirit
al·má·ci·ga *f.* nursery
al·me·ja *f.* clam
al·men·dro, a *m.* almond tree
al·mi·dón *m.* starch
al·mi·do·nar *v.* to starch
al·miz·cle *m.* musk
al·mo·ha·da *f.* pillow
al·mor·zar *v.* to lunch
al·muer·zo *m.* lunch
a·lo·ca·do, a *adj.* crazy
a·lo·cu·ción *f.* allocution
a·lo·jar(se) *v.* to house, to stay
al·pi·no *adj.* alpine
al·qui·lar *v.* to hire; rent
al·qui·mia *f.* alchemy
al·qui·mis·ta *m.* alchemist
al·re·de·dor *adv.* around; *prep.* round
al·ta·men·te *adv.* extremely, highly
al·tar *m.* altar
al·te·ra·ción *f.* alteration
al·ter·ca·ción *adj.* altercation
al·ter·na·do *adj.* alternate
al·ter·nar *v.* to rotate; to alternate
al·ter·na·ti·va *f.* alternative
al·ti·me·trí·a *f.* altimetry
al·ti·tud *f.* altitude
al·to, a *adj.* upper; high
al·truís·ta *adj.* altruistic
al·tu·ra *f.* elevation; height
a·lu·ci·nar *v.* to hallucinate
a·lu·ci·na·to·rio *adj.* hallucinatory
a·lu·dir *v.* to allude
a·lum·bra·do *m.* electric lighting
a·lu·mi·nio *m.* aluminum
a·lum·no, a *m.* student; alumnus
a·lu·sión *f.* allusion
al·za·do *adj.* elevated
al·zar *v.* to hoist up; to lift up; to raise
a·llá *adv.* there
a·lla·nar *v.* to overcome; to flatten
a·lle·ga·do, a *adj.* related; close; near
a·llí *adv.* there

a·ma·bi·li·dad *f.* kindness
a·ma·ble *adj.* lovable; amiable; kindly
a·ma·do *adj.* beloved
a·ma·es·trar *v.* to train
a·ma·ne·cer *m.* daybreak
a·man·sar *v.* to soothe; to tame
a·ma·ña·do *adj.* skillful; fixed
a·ma·ño *m.* skill, scheme
a·ma·po·la *f.* poppy
a·mar *v.* to love
a·mar·gar *v.* to make bitter
a·mar·go *m.* bitterness
a·ma·ri·llo *m.* yellow
a·ma·rrar *v.* to fasten; to tie
a·ma·teur *adj.* amateur
a·ma·tis·ta *f.* amethyst
ám·bar *m.* amber
am·bi·ción *f.* ambition
am·bi·cio·so *adj.* ambitious
am·bien·ta·ción *f.* atmosphere
am·bi·güe·dad *f.* ambiguity
am·bi·guo *adj.* uncertain; ambiguous
am·bu·lan·cia *f.* ambulance
am·bu·lan·te *adj.* ambulatory
am·bu·lar *v.* to wander about
a·me·ba *f.* amoeba
a·me·na·za *f.* threat
a·me·na·zar *v.* to menace
a·me·ni·dad *f.* amenity
a·me·ri·ca·no *adj.* American
a·mi·ga *f.* girl friend
a·mi·gar *v.* to reconcile
a·míg·da·la *f.* tonsil
a·mi·go *m.* boy friend
a·mi·la·na·do *adj.* intimidated
a·mi·la·nar *v.* to discourage;
    to intimidate; to scare; to frighten
a·mis·to·so, a *adj.* friendly
a·mo *m.* master; boss
a·mo·lar *v.* to sharpen
a·mol·dar *v.* to adjust; to mold
a·mon·to·nar(se) *v.* to amass; to hoard;
    to huddle
amor *m.* love
a·mo·ra·li·dad *f.* amorality
a·mo·ro·so, a *adj.* amorous; loving

am•pa•rar *v.* to defend; to protect
am•pliar *v.* to expand; to increase
am•pli•fi•ca•ción *f.* amplification
am•pli•fi•car *v.* to amplify
am•po•lle•ta *f.* hourglass
am•pu•ta•ción *f.* amputation
am•pu•tar *v.* to amputate
a•na•car•do *m.* cashew
á•na•de *m.* duck
a•na•gra•ma *f.* anagram
a•nal•gé•si•co *adj.* analgesic
a•ná•li•sis *m.* analysis
a•na•lis•ta *m.* analyst
a•na•lí•ti•co *adj.* analytical
a•na•li•zar *v.* to analyze
a•na•lo•gí•a *f.* analogy
a•na•ná *m.* pineapple
a•na•quel *m.* shelf
a•na•ran•ja•do, a *adj.* orange
a•nar•quis•ta *m., f.* anarchist
a•na•to•mí•a *f.* anatomy
a•na•tó•mi•co *adj.* anatomic
an•cia•no, a *adj.* aged
an•cla *f.* anchor
an•cho *adj.* broad
an•cho•a *f.* anchovy
an•dar *v.* to go; to ambulate
an•dra•jo•so, a *adj.* ragged
an•droi•de *m.* android
a•néc•do•ta *f.* anecdote
a•nec•do•tis•ta *m.* anecdotist
a•ne•gar *v.* to flood
a•né•mi•co, a *adj.* anemic
a•nes•te•siar *v.* to anesthetize
án•gel *m.* angel
an•gé•li•co, a *adj.* angelical
an•go•ra *adj.* angora
an•gui•la *f.* eel
án•gu•lo *m.* angle
an•gu•lo•so *adj.* angular
an•gu•rria *f.* greed
an•gus•tiar *v.* to anguish
an•he•lar *v.* to long for; to yearn
a•ni•llo *m.* ring
a•ni•ma•ción *f.* animation
a•ni•ma•do, a *adj.* lively; animate

a•ni•mal *m.* animal
a•ni•mar *v.* to become animated; to enliven
a•ni•qui•lar *v.* to destroy; to annihilate
a•ni•ver•sa•rio, a *adj.* anniversary
a•no•che *adv.* last night
a•nó•ni•mo *adj.* anonymous
a•nor•mal *adj.* subnormal; abnormal
a•no•ta•ción *f.* note
a•no•tar *v.* to note
án•sar *m.* goose
an•sia *f.* yearning
an•siar *v.* to long for
an•sie•dad *f.* anxiety
an•te *prep.* before
an•te•bra•zo *m.* forearm
an•te•ce•der *v.* to antecede
an•te•de•cir *v.* to predict
an•te•pa•sa•do *m.* ancestor
an•te•rior *adj.* prior; anterior
an•tes de *adv.* before
an•ti•á•ci•do *adj.* antacid
an•ti•bió•ti•co *m.* antibiotic
an•ti•ci•pa•do *adj.* advanced
an•ti•ci•par *v.* to bring forward; to advance
an•ti•cuer•po *m.* antibody
an•tí•do•to *m.* antidote
an•ti•guo *adj.* ancient; antique
an•tí•lo•pe *m.* antelope
an•ti•na•tu•ral *adj.* unnatural
an•ti•sép•ti•co *m.* antiseptic
an•ti•so•cial *adj.* antisocial
an•ti•tó•xi•co *adj.* antitoxic
an•to•ni•mia *f.* antonymy
an•tro•poi•de *adj.* anthropoid
a•nual *adj.* annual
a•nua•rio *m.* year book
a•nu•lar *v.* to cancel
a•nun•cia•ción *f.* announcement
a•nun•cia•dor *m.* advertiser
a•nun•ciar *v.* to announce
an•zue•lo *m.* fishhook
a•ña•di•do *m.* addition
a•ña•dir *v.* to add
a•ñe•jo, a *adj.* mature
a•ñil *adj., m.* indigo
a•ño *m.* year

a•pa•bu•llar *v.* to squash; to bewilder
a•pa•ci•ble *adj.* gentle
a•pa•ci•guar(se) *v.* to appease
a•pa•dri•nar *v.* to support; to sponsor
a•pa•le•o *m.* thrashing
a•pa•ñar *v.* to mend; to seize; to grasp;
  to repair
a•pa•ra•to *m.* apparatus
a•pa•ra•to•so *adj.* ostentatious
a•par•car *v.* to park
a•pa•re•cer(se) *v.* to haunt; to come
a•pa•re•jar *v.* to prepare
a•pa•ren•te *adj.* seeming
a•pa•ri•ción *f.* appearance
a•par•ta•do *adj.* isolated
a•par•ta•men•to *m.* apartment
a•par•tar(se) *v.* to divide; to remove;
  to move away
a•par•te *adv.* aside; apart
a•pa•sio•nar *v.* to excite
a•pa•tí•a *f.* apathy
a•pá•ti•co, a *adj.* apathetic
a•pe•ar *v.* to chock
a•pe•la•ble *adj.* appealable
a•pe•lar *v.* to appeal
a•pe•lli•dar *v.* to name; to be called
a•pe•lli•do *m.* name
a•pe•nar *v.* to pain; to grieve
a•pen•di•ci•tis *m.* appendicitis
a•pe•ro *m.* gear
a•pes•tar *v.* to annoy; to infect
a•pe•ten•cia *f.* appetite
a•pe•ti•to *m.* appetite
a•pe•ti•to•so, a *adj.* delicious
a•pio *m.* celery
a•pla•car *v.* to placate
a•pla•nar *v.* to flatten; to stun
a•plas•tar(se) *v.* to flatten
a•plau•dir *v.* to clap; to applaud
a•plau•so *m.* applause; praise
a•pli•ca•ble *adj.* applicable
a•pli•ca•ción *f.* application
a•pli•car *v.* to apply
a•po•ca•do, a *adj.* timid
a•po•de•rar(se) *v.* to take possession
a•po•do *m.* nickname

a•po•lí•ti•co *adj.* apolitical
a•po•rre•ar(se) *v.* to beat; to fall
a•por•tar *v.* to bring; to contribute
a•po•sen•to *m.* lodging; room
a•po•si•ción *f.* apposition
a•pós•tol *m.* apostle
a•pós•tro•fo *m.* apostrophe
a•po•te•ca•rio *m.* apothecary
a•po•te•o•sis *f.* apotheosis
a•po•yar(se) *v.* to rest on; to support
a•po•yo *m.* support
a•pre•cia•ción *f.* appreciation
a•pre•ciar *v.* to value; to appreciate
a•pre•cio *m.* attention; appraisal
a•pre•hen•der *v.* to seize
a•pre•hen•sión *f.* comprehension;
  apprehension
a•pren•der *v.* to learn
a•pren•sión *f.* suspicion
a•pre•sar *v.* to seize
a•pre•su•rar *v.* to hurry
a•pre•tar *v.* to crowd; to clutch
a•pro•ba•do, a *adj.* approved
a•pro•bar *v.* to pass
a•pro•pia•do *adj.* appropriate
a•pro•piar(se) *v.* to appropriate
a•pro•vi•sio•nar *v.* to provision
a•pro•xi•mar(se) *v.* to approximate
ap•ti•tud *f.* talent; aptitude
a•pues•ta *f.* wager
a•pun•tar(se) *v.* to aim; to point
a•pun•te *m.* notation; note
a•pu•rar(se) *v.* to worry; to rush
a•que•jar *v.* to distress
a•quel *adj.* that
a•quél *pron.* that one
a•quí *adv.* now; here; then
a•quie•tar *v.* to soothe; to calm down
a•ra *f.* altar
a•ra•ña *f.* spider
ár•bi•trar *v.* to umpire; to arbitrate
ar•bi•tra•rio, a *adj.* arbitrary
ár•bi•tro, a *m.* arbitrator
ár•bol *m.* tree
ar•bo•re•to *m.* arboretum
ar•bus•to *m.* shrub

ar•ca•da *f.* arcade
ar•ca•ís•ta *f.* archaist
ar•cán•gel *m.* archangel
ar•ce *m.* maple tree
ar•co *m.* arch
ar•chi•du•que *m.* archduke
ar•chi•du•que•sa *f.* archduchess
ar•chi•var *v.* to file
ar•chi•vo *m.* archive
ar•der(se) *v.* to burn
ar•dien•te *adj.* ardent; burning
ar•di•lla *f.* squirrel
ar•dor *m.* heat; burning sensation
ar•duo *adj.* arduous
á•rea *f.* area
a•re•no•so *adj.* sandy
a•ren•que *m.* herring
ar•gen•tar *v.* to silver-plate
ar•gen•ta•rio *m.* silversmith
ar•go•lla *f.* ring
ar•güir *v.* to prove; to argue
ar•gu•men•tar *v.* to argue
á•ri•do *adj.* dry
a•ris•co, a *adj.* wild; unfriendly; surly; churlish
a•ris•to•cra•cia *f.* aristocracy
a•ris•tó•cra•ta *m.* aristocrat
a•rit•mé•ti•co *adj.* arithmetic
ar•le•quín *m.* harlequin
ar•ma *f.* weapon
ar•ma•do *adj.* armed
ar•mar *v.* to assemble; to reinforce; to arm; to equip
ar•ma•rio, a *m.* buffet; closet
ar•mi•ño *m.* ermine
ar•mis•ti•cio *m.* armistice
ar•mo•ní•a *f.* accord
ar•mó•ni•co *adj., m.* harmonic
ar•mo•ni•zar *v.* to harmonize
a•ro *m.* hoop; ring
a•ro•ma *m.* fragrance
a•ro•mar *v.* to scent; to perfume
a•ro•má•ti•co *adj.* aromatic
a•ro•ma•ti•zar *v.* to perfume; to scent
a•ro•mo•so *adj.* aromatic
ar•pis•ta *m., f.* harpist

ar•queo•lo•gí•a *f.* archaeology
ar•qui•tec•to *m., f.* architect
ar•qui•tec•tu•ra *f.* architecture
a•rra•ci•ma•do *adj.* bunched
a•rran•car *v.* to seize; to pull up; to obtain; to stem
a•rra•sar *v.* to clear; to level
a•rras•trar(se) *v.* to pull; to crawl; to draw
a•rre•ar *v.* to harness; to herd
a•rre•ba•ta•dor *adj.* exciting
a•rre•ba•to *m.* rage
a•rre•ci•fe *m.* reef
a•rre•gla•do *adj.* neat
a•rre•glar(se) *m.* order; settle
a•rre•glo *m.* understanding; arrangement
a•rre•me•dar *v.* to copy
a•rre•me•ter *v.* to attack
a•rren•dar *v.* to rent
a•rre•o *m.* drove; herd
a•rre•pen•tir•se *v.* to regret
a•rres•ta•do *adj.* arrested
a•rres•to *m.* arrest
a•rri•ba *adv.* above
a•rri•bar *v.* to arrive
a•rri•bis•ta *adj.* social climbing
a•rri•bo *m.* arrival
a•rrien•do *m.* renting
a•rries•ga•do, a *adj.* hazardous; daring
a•rries•gar(se) *v.* to venture; to jeopardize
a•rri•mar *v.* to draw or bring near
a•rri•mo *m.* support
a•rrin•co•na•do *adj.* distant
a•rrin•co•nar *v.* to corner
a•rris•ca•mien•to *m.* boldness; daring
a•rris•car *v.* to fold up; to turn up
a•rrit•mia *f.* lack of rhythm
a•rro•ba•mien•to *m.* rapture; ecstasy
a•rro•bar *v.* to enrapture
a•rro•di•llar(se) *v.* to kneel
a•rro•gan•te *adj.* proud; arrogant
a•rro•jar(se) *v.* to fling; to emit; to throw
a•rro•jo *m.* boldness
a•rro•lla•dor, a *adj.* overwhelming
a•rro•llar *v.* to carry or sweep away
a•rro•par *v.* to tuck in; to wrap with

clothing

a·rro·yo *m.* brook; stream

a·rroz *m.* rice

a·rro·zal *m.* rice paddy or rice field

a·rru·ga *f.* crease; fold; wrinkle line

a·rru·ga·do *adj.* wrinkled

a·rru·gar(se) *v.* to rumple; to wrinkle

a·rrui·nar *v.* to destroy

a·rru·lla·dor *adj.* soothing

a·rru·llar *v.* to lull to sleep; to coo

a·rru·llo *m.* lullaby

a·rru·ma·co *m.* caress

a·rrum·bar *v.* to neglect; to put or cast aside

ar·se·nal *m.* storehouse; shipyard

ar·sé·ni·co *m.* arsenic

ar·te *f.* craft; art

ar·te·fac·to *m.* appliance

ar·te·ria *f.* artery

ar·te·ro *adj.* sly; cunning

ar·te·sa·ní·a *f.* craftsmanship

ar·te·sa·no *m., f.* craftsman or craftswoman

ar·ti·cu·la·ción *f.* joint

ar·ti·cu·lar *v.* to articulate

ar·tis·ta *f., m.* artist

ar·ti·fi·cio *m.* item; article; thing

ar·ti·fi·cial *adj.* artificial

ar·tís·ti·co *adj.* artistic

ar·tri·tis *f.* arthritis

ar·zo·bis·po *m.* archbishop

as *m.* ace

a·sa·do *m.* roasted meat; barbecue

a·sa·dor *m.* grill

a·sa·la·ria·do, a *adj.* salaried worker

a·sa·la·riar *v.* to set a salary for someone

a·sal·ta·dor, a *f., m.* assailant

a·sal·tar *v.* to attack

a·sal·to *m.* attack

a·sam·ble·a *f.* conference; meeting

a·sam·ble·ís·ta *m., f.* assembly member

as·cen·den·te *adj.* ascending

as·cen·der *v.* to promote; to ascend

as·cen·sión *f.* rise; ascension

as·cen·so *m.* ascent; promotion

as·cen·sor *m.* lift; elevator

as·cen·so·ris·ta *m., f.* one who operates an elevator

as·co *m.* disgust

a·se·ar *v.* to clean; to wash

a·se·char *v.* to trap

a·se·diar *v.* to bother; to pester

a·se·dio *m.* siege

a·se·gu·ra·do *adj.* insured

a·se·gu·rar(se) *v.* to fasten; to assure; to secure

a·se·me·jar(se) *v.* to resemble

a·sen·ta·de·ras *f., pl.* buttocks; behind

a·sen·ta·do *adj.* judicious

a·sen·tar *v.* to record

a·sen·ti·mien·to *m.* consent

a·sen·tir *v.* to agree

a·se·o *m.* tidiness; neatness

a·se·qui·ble *adj.* understandable; accessible

a·ser·ción *f.* affirmation

a·se·rra·de·ro *m.* sawmill

a·se·rrar *v.* to saw

a·se·si·nar *v.* to murder

a·se·si·na·to *m.* murder; assassination

a·se·si·no *adj.* murder, assassin

a·se·sor, a *adj.* advisory; advising

a·se·so·rar *v.* to advise

a·ses·tar *v.* to hit; to punch

a·se·ve·rar *v.* to assert

a·se·ve·ra·ti·vo *adj.* affirmative; assertive

a·se·xua·do *adj.* asexual

as·fal·tar *v.* to spread asphalt

as·fal·to *m.* asphalt

as·fi·xia *f.* suffocation

as·fi·xiar *v.* to asphyxiate

a·sí *adv.* so

a·sien·to *m.* seat

a·sig·nar *v.* to allot; assign

a·sig·nar *v.* to appoint; to assign

a·sig·na·ción *f.* course or subject in school

a·si·lar *v.* to give shelter

a·si·lo *m.* asylum

a·si·mi·lar(se) *v.* to assimilate

a·si·mis·mo *adv.* in a like manner

a•sir(se) *v.* to grip; to hold on to
a•sis•ten•cia *f.* attendance
a•sis•ten•cial *adj.* relief; assisting
a•sis•tir *v.* to accompany; to aid; to attend
as•ma *f.* asthma
as•má•ti•co *adj., m., f.* asthmatic
as•na•da *f.* stupidity
a•so•cia•ción *f.* association
a•so•cia•do *adj.* associated
a•so•ciar(se) *v.* to associate with
a•so•la•dor *adj.* ravaging
a•so•lar *v.* to scorch
a•so•le•a•mien•to *m.* sunstroke
a•so•le•ar *v.* to place in the sun
a•so•mar *v.* to show; to appear
a•som•brar(se) *v.* to amaze; to astonish
as•pi•rar *v.* to breathe; to inhale
as•pi•ri•na *f.* aspirin
as•tro•lo•gí•a *f.* astrology
as•tro•no•mí•a *f.* astronomy
as•tu•ta *adj.* artful; sly; canny; cunning
a•sun•to *m.* issue; concern
a•ta•car *v.* to assault; to charge
a•ta•que *m.* attack
a•tar(se) *v.* to rope; to tie; to brace
a•ten•ción *f.* attention
a•ten•der *v.* to heed; to attend
a•tes•ti•guar *v.* to testify
a•tie•sar(se) *v.* to tighten
at•le•ta *f., m.* athlete
at•lé•ti•co, a *adj.* athletic
a•tó•mi•co *adj.* atomic
á•to•mo *m.* atom
a•trac•ción *f.* attraction
a•trac•ti•vo *adj.* engaging
a•traer *v.* to engage; to lure
a•trás *adv.* aback; back
a•tra•sa•do *adj.* backwards
a•tri•buir *v.* to ascribe
a•tro•ci•dad *f.* atrocity
a•tur•dir(se) *v.* to daze; to bewilder
au•di•ción *f.* audition
au•gus•to *adj.* August
au•men•tar(se) *v.* to augment; to enhance
au•men•to *m.* raise; increase

aún *adv.* still
aun•que *conj.* although
au•sen•te *adj.* missing
au•ten•ti•ci•dad *f.* authenticity
au•to•bús *m.* bus
au•tó•gra•fo *m.* autograph
au•to•mó•vil *m.* car
au•to•ri•za•ción *f.* authorization
a•van•zar(se) *v.* to advance
a•ve *f.* bird
a•ve•ni•da *f.* avenue
a•ven•tu•ra *f.* adventure
a•ver•sión *f.* aversion
a•via•ción *f.* aviation
a•vión *m.* plane; airplane
a•yu•da *f.* aid; help
a•yu•dar *v.* to assist; to help
a•zo•rar *v.* to embarrass
a•zo•rra•do *adj.* foxy
a•zo•ta•do *adj.* whipped
a•zo•tar *v.* to beat upon
a•zo•te *m.* spanking; whip
a•zú•car *m.* sugar
a•zu•ca•ra•do *adj.* sweet
a•zu•fre *m.* sulphur
a•zul *m.* blue
a•zu•la•do *adj.* bluish
a•zu•lar *v.* to color or dye blue
a•zu•le•jo *m.* glazed tile

B

ba•lís•ti•co *adj.* ballistic
ba•lon•ces•to *m.* basketball
ba•lon•ma•no *m.* handball
ba•lon•vo•le•a *m.* volleyball
ba•lo•ta *f.* ballot
bal•sa *f.* balsa
bál•sa•mo *m.* balsam
ba•lle•na *f.* whale
ba•lle•na•to *m.* whale calf
ba•lle•ne•ro, a *adj.* whaling
ba•lles•ta *f.* crossbow
ba•lles•te•ar *v.* to shoot with a crossbow

ba·lles·te·rí·a *f.* archery
bam·ba·le·ar *v.* to sway
bam·bo·le·o *m.* wobble
ba·llet *m.* ballet
bam·bú *m.* bamboo
ba·na·na *f.* banana
ban·ca *f.* banking
ban·ca·rro·ta *f.* bankruptcy
ban·co *m.* bank; band; pew; bench
ban·da·da *f.* flock; group
ban·de·ra *f.* ensign; flag
ban·de·ja *f.* tray
ban·de·ro·la *f.* pennant
ban·di·do *m.* bandit
ban·do·le·ro *m.* bandit
ban·que·ta *f.* stool
ban·que·te *m.* feast
ban·que·tear *v.* to feast
ba·ñar(se) *v.* to bathe
ba·ño *m.* bathtub, bathroom
ba·ra·jar *v.* to shuffle
ba·ra·to *adv.* cheaply; *adj.* inexpensive; cheap
bar·ba *f.* beard
bar·ba·coa *f.* barbecue
bar·ba·do *adj.* bearded
bar·ba·ri·dad *f.* outrage
bár·ba·ra, o *f., m.* savage
bar·bear *v.* to shave
bar·be·ro *m.* barber
bar·bi·lla *f.* chin
bar·bo·tar *v.* to mutter; to mumble
bar·bo·te·o *m.* murmuring
bar·bu·do *adj.* heavily bearded
bar·bu·lla *f.* chatter; jabbering
bar·ca *f.* small boat
bar·ca·za *f.* launch
bar·co *m.* ship; boat
ba·rí·to·no *m.* baritone
bar·niz *m.* glaze; varnish; lacquer
bar·ni·zar *v.* to varnish; to lacquer
ba·ró·me·tro *m.* barometer
ba·rón *m.* baron
ba·ro·ne·sa *f.* baroness
ba·rra *f.* bar
ba·rra·ca *f.* booth

ba·rrer *v.* to sweep
ba·rre·ra *f.* barricade
ba·rri·ga *f.* belly
ba·rril *m.* barrel
ba·rrio *m.* neighborhood
ba·sal·to *m.* basalt
ba·sar *v.* to base
ba·se *f.* foundation
bá·si·co *adj.* basic
ba·sí·li·ca *f.* basilica
bas·quet·bol *m.* basketball
bas·tan·te *adj.* sufficient
bas·tar *v.* to suffice
bas·tar·dear *v.* to debase
bas·to *adj.* rough
bas·tón *m.* baton; stick
ba·su·ra *f.* rubbish
ba·ta *f.* negligee
ba·ta·lla *f.* battle
ba·ta·llar *v.* to battle
ba·ta·llón *m.* battalion
ba·te·rí·a *f.* battery
ba·ti·do *m.* batter
ba·tir(se) *v.* to churn
ba·tu·ta *f.* baton
baúl *m.* trunk
bau·tis·mo *m.* christening
bau·ti·zar *v.* to baptize
ba·ya *f.* berry
ba·yo *adj.* bay
ba·zar *m.* bazaar
ba·zu·ca *f.* bazooka
bea·ti·fi·car *v.* to beatify
bea·tí·fi·co *adj.* beatific
bea·ti·tud *f.* beatitude
be·bé *m.* baby
be·ber *v.* to drink
be·bi·da *f.* beverage
be·ca *f.* scholarship
be·ce·rro *m.* calf
be·far *v.* to taunt
beige *m.* beige
béis·bol *m.* baseball
be·li·co·so, a *adj.* warlike
be·li·ge·ran·te *adj.* belligerent
be·lle·za *f.* beauty

be·llo *adj.* beautiful
be·mol *m.* flat
ben·de·cir *v.* to bless
ben·di·ción *f.* blessing
ben·di·to *adj.* holy
be·ne·fi·ciar(se) *v.* to benefit
be·ne·fi·cio·so *adj.* beneficial
be·né·fi·co *adj.* charitable
be·né·vo·lo *adj.* benevolent
ben·ga·la *f.* flare
be·nig·ni·dad *f.* kindness
be·nig·no *adj.* kind; mild
be·rrin·che *m.* tantrum
be·sar(se) *v.* to smooch; to kiss
be·so *m.* kiss
bes·tia *f.* animal
bes·tial *adj.* bestial
Bi·blia *f.* Bible
bí·bli·co *adj.* Biblical
bi·blio·gra·fí·a *f.* bibliography
bi·blió·gra·fo, a *m.* bibliographer
bi·blio·te·ca *f.* library
bí·ceps *m.* biceps
bi·ci·cle·ta *f.* bicycle
bi·ci·clis·ta *m., f.* bicyclist
bi·cho *m.* bug
bien *m.* good
bien·ve·ni·da *f.* greeting
bi·fur·car·se *v.* to fork
bi·go·te *m.* mustache
bi·la·te·ral *adj.* bilateral
bi·lio·so *adj.* bilious
bi·lis *f.* bile
bi·llar *m.* billiards
bi·lle·te *m.* bill
bi·llón *m.* trillion
bi·na·rio *adj.* binary
bio·gra·fí·a *f.* biography
bio·grá·fi·co *adj.* biographical
bió·gra·fo *m.* biographer
bio·lo·gí·a *f.* biology
bio·ló·gi·co *adj.* biological
bió·lo·go *m.* biologist
biop·sia *f.* biopsy
bi·sa·bue·la, o *f., m.* great-grandmother;
　great-grandfather

bi·se·car *v.* to bisect
bi·sec·ción *f.* bisection
bi·son·te *m.* bison
biz·quear *v.* to squint
blan·co *adj.* blank; white
blan·dir *v.* to brandish
blan·do *adj.* supple; soft
blan·quear *v.* to whiten
blas·fe·mar *v.* to swear
blas·fe·mia *f.* profanity
blin·da·do *adj.* armored
blo·que *m.* block
blo·quear *v.* to block
blu·sa *f.* blouse
bo·bo *m.* fool; ninny
bo·ca *f.* mouth
bo·ca·di·llo *m.* sandwich
bo·ca·do *m.* bite
bo·da *f.* marriage
bo·de·ga *f.* wine cellar
boi·co·teo *m.* boycott
bo·la *f.* fib; ball
bo·le·tín *m.* bulletin
bo·li·che *m.* bowling
bo·li·ta *f.* pellet
bol·sa *f.* bag; pouch
bol·si·llo *m.* pocket
bol·sis·ta *m.* stockbroker
bol·so *m.* handbag
bo·llo *m.* bump
bom·ba *f.* pump; bomb
bom·bar·de·ro *m.* bomber
bom·bear *v.* to pad; pump
bom·bi·lla *f.* bulb
bom·bón *m.* sweet
bon·dad *f.* kindness
bon·da·do·so, a *adj.* good
bo·ni·to, a *adj.* pretty
bo·que·a·da *f.* gasp
bo·qui·lla *f.* nozzle
bor·de *m.* edge
bor·di·llo *m.* curb
bo·rra·cho *m.* drunkard
bo·rra·dor *m.* eraser
bos·que *m.* woods
bos·que·jar *v.* to outline

bo•ta *f.* wine bag
bo•tá•ni•ca *f.* botany
bo•te *m.* jackpot
bo•te•lla *f.* bottle
bo•ti•ca•rio *m.* druggist
bo•tín *m.* loot
bo•tón *m.* stud, button
bo•to•nes *m.* bellhop
bó•ve•da *f.* vault
bo•vi•no, a *adj.* bovine
bo•xea•dor *m.* boxer
bo•xear *v.* to box
bo•ya *f.* buoy
bo•yan•te *adj.* buoyant
bo•zal *m.* muzzle
bra•man•te *m.* twine
bra•mar *v.* to bellow; to roar
bra•mi•do *m.* bellow
bra•vo, a *adj.* brave
bra•za•do *m.* armful
bra•zo *m.* arm
bre•ve *adj.* short
bre•ve•dad *f.* conciseness
bri•bón *adj.* lazy
bri•llan•te *adj.* bright; shiny
bri•llar *v.* to glow; to beam
bri•llo *m.* glow; shine
brin•car *v.* to jump; to gambol
brí•o *m.* jauntiness
bri•sa *f.* breeze
bro•ca•do *m.* brocade
bro•che *m.* brooch
bro•mear(se) *v.* to joke
bro•mis•ta *f.* joker
bron•ce *m.* bronze
bron•cea•do *m.* suntan; bronze
bron•ce•ar *v.* to tan; to bronze
bron•co *adj.* coarse; rough
bron•quial *adj.* bronchial
bron•quio *m.* bronchial tube
bron•qui•tis *f.* bronchitis
bro•quel *m.* small shield
bro•ta•du•ra *f.* budding; sprouting
bro•tar *v.* to bud
bru•je•rí•a *f.* witchcraft
bru•jo *m.* wizard

brú•ju•la *f.* compass
bru•mo•so *adj.* foggy; misty
bru•ñi•du•ra *f.* polishing; burnishing
bru•ñir *v.* to burnish; to polish
brus•co, a *adj.* sudden
bru•to *m.* beast; brute
bu•bón *m.* swelling or very large tumor
bu•ce•ar *v.* to swim under water
bu•cle *m.* curl; ringlet
bu•dín *m.* pudding
bue•na•ven•tu•ra *f.* good luck; good
   fortune
bue•no, a *adj.* sound; good
buey *m.* ox
bú•fa•lo *m.* buffalo
bu•fan•da *f.* muffler; scarf
bu•fón *m.* clown; buffoon
bu•ho•ne•ro *m.* hawker; peddler
bui•tre *m.* vulture
bu•jí•a *f.* candle; sparkplug
bul•bo *m.* bulb
bu•le•var *m.* boulevard
bul•to *m.* mass; heft
bu•lla *f.* uproar; brawl; crowd; mob
bu•lli•cio *m.* riot; racket; hubbub
bu•llir *v.* to boil
bu•me•rang *m.* boomerang
bu•ñue•lo *m.* fried dough
bu•que *m.* vessel; ship
bu•qué *m.* bouquet
bur•bu•ja *f.* bubble
bur•de•os *adj.* deep red in color
bur•do *adj.* rough; coarse
bur•gue•sí•a *f.* middle class
bu•ri•lar *v.* to engrave
bur•la *f.* taunt; joke
bur•lar(se) *v.* to gibe; to joke
bur•les•co *adj.* burlesque
bu•ró•cra•ta *f.* bureaucrat
bu•rra *f.* stupid woman
bu•rro *m.* donkey; burro
bur•sá•til *adj.* stock market
bus•ca *f.* search
bus•ca•pié *m.* feeler
bus•car *v.* to look or search for
bus•ca•vi•das *m., f.* busybody

bús•que•da *f.* search
bus•to *m.* bust; chest
bu•ta•ca *f.* armchair
bu•ta•no *m.* butane
bu•ti•le•no *m.* butylene
bu•zo *m.* deep-sea diver
bu•zón *m.* mailbox

C

ca•bal *adj.* fair; precise
cá•ba•la *f.* cabala
ca•bal•gar *v.* to ride on horseback
ca•bal•ga•ta *f.* cavalcade
ca•ba•lle•rí•a *f.* cavalry
ca•ba•lle•ri•za *f.* stable
ca•ba•lle•ro *m.* gentleman
ca•ba•lle•te *m.* easel; sawhorse
ca•ba•lli•to, a *m.* pony, small horse
ca•ba•llo *m.* horse
ca•ba•llón *f.* ridge
ca•ba•ña *f.* cabin
ca•ba•ret *m.* cabaret; night club
ca•be•ci•lla *m.* ringleader
ca•be•lle•ra *f.* head of chair
ca•be•llo *m.* hair
ca•ber *v.* to fit
ca•bes•tri•llo *m.* sling
ca•bes•tro *m.* halter
ca•be•za *f.* skull; head
ca•be•zón, a *adj.* big-headed
ca•be•zo•ta *m., f.* mule
ca•bil•dear *v.* to lobby
ca•bil•do *m.* town council
ca•ble *m.* cable
ca•ble•gra•fiar *v.* to cable
ca•ble•gra•ma *m.* cablegram
ca•ble•vi•sión *f.* cable television
ca•bo *m.* corporal; cape
ca•bra *f.* goat
ca•brí•o *m.* rafter
ca•bri•to *m.* young goat; kid
ca•bro•na•da *f., coll.* dirty trick
ca•ca•hue•te *m.* peanut

ca•cao *m.* cocoa
ca•ca•re•ar *v.* to crow; to cackle
ca•ca•tú•a *f.* cockatoo
ca•ce•ro•la *f.* casserole
ca•ci•que *m.* Indian chief
ca•ci•que•ar *v., coll.* to order people around
ca•co *m.* burglar
cac•to *m.* cactus
ca•cha•lo•te *m.* sperm whale
ca•char *v.* to split; to chip
ca•cha•za *f.* sluggish
ca•che•ar *v.* to frisk; to search
ca•che•te•ar *v., Amer.* to slap; to hit
ca•che•ti•na *f.* fist fight
ca•che•tu•do *adj.* plump or chubby-cheeks
ca•cho•rro *m.* puppy
ca•da *adj.* every; each
ca•dal•so *m.* platform
ca•dá•ver *m.* body; corpse
ca•da•vé•ri•co *adj.* cadaverous
ca•de•na *f.* chain
ca•den•cia *f.* rhythm; cadence
ca•de•ra *f.* hip, hip joint
ca•de•te *m.* cadet
ca•du•co, a *adj.* lapsed; expired
caer(se) *v.* to fall
ca•fé *m.* coffee; cafe
ca•fe•í•na *f.* caffeine
ca•fe•tal *m.* coffee plantation
ca•fe•te•rí•a *f.* cafeteria; cafe
caí•da *f.* downfall; tumble
cai•mán *m.* alligator
ca•ja *f.* cabinet; chest
ca•je•ro *m.* cashier; teller
ca•jis•ta *m., f.* typesetter
cal *f.* lime
ca•la *f.* cove
ca•la•ba•za *f.* pumpkin; gourd; squash
ca•la•bo•zo *m.* jail; underground prison cell
ca•la•dor *m.* driller
ca•la•fa•te•ar *v.* to calk; to caulk
ca•la•mar *m.* squid
ca•lam•bre *m.* cramp
ca•la•mi•dad *f.* calamity; misfortune

ca·la·mi·to·so *adj.* calamitous

ca·la·ña *f.* character; nature

ca·lar(se) *v.* to swoop; to penetrate

cal·ce·te·rí·a *f.* hosiery

cal·ce·tín *m.* sock

cal·ci·fi·ca·ción *f.* calcification

cal·ci·fi·car(se) *v.* to calcify

cal·cio *m.* calcium

cal·co *m.* tracing

cal·co·ma·ní·a *f.* decal

cal·cu·la·dor, a *m., f.* calculator

cal·cu·lar *v.* to estimate; to calculate

cal·cu·lis·ta *m., f.* planner; calculator

cál·cu·lo *m.* calculation

cal·de·ra *f.* boiler

cal·do *m.* soup; broth; stock

ca·le·fac·ción *f.* heating; heat

ca·le·fac·tor *m.* heater

ca·len·da·rio *m.* calendar; schedule

ca·len·ta·dor *adj.* warming; heating

ca·len·tar(se) *v.* to heat or to warm

ca·lien·te *adj.* warm; hot

ca·li·na *f.* haze

ca·lip·so *m.* calypso

cal·ma *f.* calm

cal·man·te *adj.* sedative *m.* tranquilizer

cal·mar(se) *v.* to soothe; to calm; to settle

ca·lo·frí·o *m.* chill; fever

ca·lor *m.* warmth; heat

ca·lo·rí·a *f.* calorie

ca·ló·ri·co *adj.* caloric

ca·lum·nia *f.* slander; calumny

ca·lum·nia·dor, a *adj.* slanderous

ca·lu·ro·so *adj.* warm; hot

cal·va·rio *m.* Calvary

cal·vi·cie *f.* baldness

cal·vo *adj.* bald

cal·za·da *f.* causeway; drive; highway; road

cal·zo·nes *m., pl.* trousers

ca·llar(se) *v.* to keep quiet; to hush

ca·lle *f.* street

ca·lle·jue·la *f.* alley

ca·llo *m.* callus; corn

ca·ma *f.* bed

ca·ma·da *f.* litter; brood

ca·ma·feo *m.* cameo

cá·ma·ra *f.* room; chamber

ca·ma·ra·da *m., f.* comrade

ca·ma·re·ra *f.* waitress

ca·ma·re·ro *m.* waiter

ca·ma·ro·te *m.* cabin

cam·biar(se) *v.* to change; to alter

cam·bia·ví·a *m.* rail switch

cam·bio *m.* shift; change

cam·bis·ta *m., f.* broker; moneychanger

ca·me·le·ar *v. coll.* to deceive

ca·me·lia *f.* camellia

ca·me·llo *m.* camel

ca·me·ro, a *adj.* double bed

ca·mi·lla *f.* stretcher

ca·mi·nar *v.* to walk; to travel

ca·mi·na·ta *f.* hike; walk

ca·mi·no *m.* route; road

ca·mión *m.* truck

ca·mio·ne·ro, a *m., f.* truck driver

ca·mio·ne·ta *f.* van

ca·mi·sa *f.* shirt

ca·mi·se·ta *f.* shirt; undershirt

ca·mi·so·la *f.* camisole

ca·mi·són *m.* nightgown

ca·mo·rra *f., coll.* squabble

ca·mo·rre·ar *v., coll.* to quarrel; to squabble

cam·pa·men·to *m.* camp

cam·pa·na *f.* bell

cam·pa·ña *f.* campaign

cam·pe·si·no, a *adj.* country; peasant

cam·pes·tre *adj.* rural

cam·pis·ta *m., f.* camper

cam·po *m.* country; field

cam·po·san·to *m.* graveyard; cemetery

ca·mu·fla·je *m.* camouflage

ca·mu·flar *v.* to camouflage

ca·nal *m.* canal; channel

ca·na·le·te *m.* paddle

ca·nas·ta *f.* hamper; basket

can·ce·la·ción *f.* cancellation

can·ce·lar *v.* to cancel

can·ci·ller *m.* chancellor

can·ci·lle·rí·a *f.* chancellery

can·ción *f.* song

can•cio•ne•ro *m.* songbook
can•cro *m.* canker
can•da•do *m.* padlock
can•de•la *f.* candle
can•de•le•ro *m.* candlestick
can•di•da•to *m.* candidate
can•di•da•tu•ra *f.* candidacy
cán•di•do *adj.* unsophisticated
ca•ne•la *f.* cinnamon
ca•ne•lón *m.* roof gutter
ca•ne•lo•nes *m., pl.* canneloni
ca•ne•sú *m.* bodice; yoke
can•gre•jo *m.* crab
can•gu•ro *m.* kangaroo
ca•ní•bal *m.* cannibal
ca•ni•ca *f.* marble
ca•ni•no *adj.* canine
ca•ní•cu•la *f.* midsummer heat; dog days
 of summer
ca•ni•lla *f.* shinbone
ca•ni•lli•ta *m.* newspaper boy
ca•ni•no, a *adj., m.* canine
can•je *m.* trade; exchange
can•je•a•ble *adj.* exchangeable
can•je•ar *v.* to trade; to exchange
ca•no, a *adj.* gray-haired
ca•noa *f.* canoe; rowboat
ca•ñon *m.* canyon, cannon; barrel
can•sa•do *adj.* weary; tired; rundown
can•san•cio *m.* tiredness
can•sar(se) *v.* to weary; to tire
can•ta•lu•po *m.* cantaloupe
can•tan•te *m., f.* singer
can•tar *v.* to sing; to chant *m.* song
can•ti•dad *f.* quantity; amount
can•tim•plo•ra *f.* canteen
can•to *m.* singing; croak
can•tu•rrear *v.* to croon; to hum
ca•ña *f.* cane; reed
ca•os *m.* chaos
ca•pa *f.* cape; coating; layer
ca•pa•ci•dad *f.* capacity; capability
ca•pa•taz *m.* foreman
ca•paz *adj.* roomy; capable
cap•cio•so *adj.* deceitful
ca•pe•llán *m.* chaplain

ca•pe•ru•za *f.* hood
ca•pi•lar *adj. m.* capillary
ca•pi•la•ri•dad *f.* capillarity
ca•pi•lla *f.* chapel
ca•pi•llo *m.* baby bonnet; cap
ca•pi•ro•ta•zo *m.* flip, as with the finger
ca•pi•tal *m.* capital
ca•pi•ta•lis•mo *m.* capitalism
ca•pi•tán *m.* captain
ca•pi•to•lio *m.* capitol
ca•pí•tu•lo *m.* chapter
ca•pó *m.* bonnet; hood
ca•pón *adj.* castrated
ca•pri•cho *m.* whim; fancy; quick
ca•pri•cho•so *adj.* temperamental;
 whimsical
cáp•su•la *f.* capsule
cap•tu•ra *f.* capture; catch
ca•pu•cha *f.* hood
ca•pu•llo *m.* cocoon
ca•qui *m.* khaki
ca•ra *f.* face
ca•ra•col *m.* snail
ca•rác•ter *m.* nature; character
ca•rac•te•rís•ti•co, a *adj.* typical
ca•rac•te•ri•za•do, a *adj.* distinguished
ca•rac•te•ri•za•dor, a *adj.* distinguishing
ca•rac•te•ri•zar *v.* to characterize
ca•ra•cú *m., Amer.* bone marrow
ca•rám•ba•no *m.* icicle
ca•ra•me•li•zar *v.* to cover with caramel
ca•ra•me•lo *m.* caramel
ca•ra•va•na *f.* caravan
car•bo•hi•dra•to *m.* carbohydrate
car•bón *m.* coal
car•bo•na•to *m.* carbonate
car•bo•no *m.* carbon
car•bun•co *m.* carbuncle
car•bu•ra•dor *m.* carburetor
car•bu•ran•te *m.* fuel
cár•cel *f.* prison; jail
car•de•nal *m.* cardinal
car•dí•a•co *adj.* cardiac
ca•re•cer *v.* to lack
ca•ren•cia *f.* need; lack
ca•rey *m.* sea turtle

car•ga *f.* burden; load
car•ga•de•ro *m.* loading platform
car•ga•men•to *m.* cargo
car•gar(se) *v.* to burden; to load
car•go *m.* charge; burden; load
ca•riar•se *v.* to decay
ca•ri•dad *f.* charity
ca•ri•ño, a *m.* affection; love
ca•ri•ta•ti•vo *adj.* charitable
car•nal *adj.* carnal
car•na•val *m.* carnival
car•ne *f.* pulp; flesh; meat
car•ne•ar *v. Amer.* to slaughter
car•ni•ce•rí•a *f.* slaughter; bloodshed
car•ni•ce•ro *m.* butcher
car•pe•ta *f.* folder
car•pin•te•rí•a *f.* carpentry
car•pin•te•ro *m.* carpenter
ca•rre•ra *f.* career; race
ca•rre•ro *m.* carrier
ca•rre•ta•je *m.* cartage
ca•rre•te *m.* reel; spool; coil; bobbin
ca•rre•te•ra *f.* road; highway
ca•rro•za *f.* coach; chariot
ca•rrua•je *m.* carriage
ca•rru•sel *m.* merry-go round
car•ta *f.* card; letter
car•ta•pa•cio *m.* notebook
car•tel *m.* poster
car•te•le•ra *f.* billboard
car•te•ra *f.* billfold; wallet
car•te•ro *m.* postman
car•tí•la•go *m.* gristle; cartilage
car•tón *m.* cardboard
car•tu•cho *m.* cartridge
ca•sa *f.* home; house
ca•sa•ca *f.* dress coat
ca•sa•do, a *adj.* married
ca•sar(se) *v.* to wed; to marry
cas•ca•bel *m.* small bell
cas•ca•be•le•ar *v.* to jingle
cas•ca•do, a *adj.* cracked; decrepit
cas•ca•da *f.* cascade
cas•ca•jo *m.* gravel
cás•ca•ra *f.* hull; shell; skin; rind
ca•se•ta *f.* cottage

ca•se•te *m., f.* tape cartridge; cassette
cas•co•te *m.* rubble
ca•si *adj.* almost
ca•si•mir *m.* cashmere
ca•si•no *m.* casino
ca•so *m.* happening; case
cas•pa *f.* dandruff
cas•ta *f.* breed; caste; cast
cas•ta•ñe•te•ar *v.* to chatter
cas•ti•dad *f.* chastity
cas•ti•gar *v.* to punish
cas•ti•llo *m.* castle
cas•tor *m.* beaver
cas•tra•ción *f.* castration
ca•sual *adj.* accidental; coincidental
ca•sua•li•dad *f.* coincidence; chance
ca•ta•le•jo *m.* small telescope; spyglass
ca•ta•lo•gar *v.* to catalog; to catalogue
ca•tar *v.* to taste; to sample
ca•ta•ra•ta *f.* waterfall; cataract
ca•tás•tro•fe *f.* catastrophe
ca•te•dral *f.* cathedral
ca•te•go•rí•a *f.* category
ca•ter•va *f.* gang
ca•té•ter *m.* catheter
ca•tin•ga *f.* body odor
ca•tor•ce *adj.* fourteen
ca•tre *m.* cot made of canvas
cau•ce *m.* channel; riverbed; ditch
cau•ción *f.* bail; caution
cau•cho *m.* rubber; rubber tree or plant
cau•di•llo *m.* leader
cau•sa *f.* cause
cau•te•la *f.* caution
cau•te•lo•so, a *adj.* cautious
cau•te•ri•zar *v.* to captivate
cau•ti•ve•rio *m.* captivity
cau•ti•vo, a *adj. m., f.* captive
cau•to, a *adj.* cautious
ca•var *v.* to dig
ca•ver•na *f.* cave, cavern
ca•viar *m.* caviar
ca•vi•dad *f.* cavity
ca•vi•la•ción *f.* rumination, pondering
ca•vi•lar *v.* to ruminate; ponder
ca•za *f.* hunt game

ca·za·dor, a *adj.* hunting
ca·zar *v.* to hunt
ca·zo *m.* ladle
ca·zue·la *f.* pan
ce·bar *v.* to fatten
ce·bo·lla *f.* onion
ce·bra *f.* zebra
ce·ce·o *m.* lisp
ce·dro *m.* cedar
cé·du·la *f.* document
cé·fi·ro *m.* zephyr
ce·gar *v.* to blind
ce·gue·ra *f.* blindness
ce·ja *f.* eyebrow
ce·jar *v.* to back up
ce·la·da *f.* ambush
ce·la·dor, a *adj.* vigilant; watchful
ce·lar *v.* to comply with something
cel·da *f.* cell
ce·le·bra·ción *f.* celebration
ce·le·bran·te *adj.* celebrating
ce·le·brar *v.* to celebrate
cé·le·bre *adj.* famous; celebrated
ce·le·bri·dad *f.* celebrity
ce·le·ri·dad *f.* speed
ce·les·te *adj.* sky-blue
ce·les·tial *adj.* heavenly
ce·les·ti·na *f.* madam; procuress
ce·li·ba·to *m.* celibacy
cé·li·be *adj. f.* celibate
ce·lo·fán *m.* cellophane
ce·lo·sí·a *f.* latticework
ce·lo·so, a *adj.* zealous
cé·lu·la *f.* cell
ce·lu·loi·de *m.* celluloid
ce·lu·lo·so *adj.* cellulous
ce·llis·ca *f.* sleet
ce·men·te·rio *m.* cemetery
ce·men·to *m.* cement
ce·na *f.* supper; dinner
ce·na·gal *m.* swamp
ce·nar *v.* to have dinner
cen·ce·rro *m.* cowbell
ce·ni·ce·ro *m.* ashtray
ce·nit *m.* zenith
cen·sor *m.* censor

cen·su·rar *v.* to censor
cen·te·lla *f.* flash
cen·te·lle·an·te *adj.* sparkling
cen·te·na *f.* one hundred
cen·te·nar *m.* one hundred
cen·te·no *m.* rye
cen·té·si·mo *adj.* hundredth
cen·tí·gra·do *adj.* centigrade
cen·tí·me·tro *m.* centimeter
cen·ti·ne·la *m., f.* sentry
cen·to·lla *f.* spider crab
cen·tra·do, a *adj.* centered
cen·tral *adj.* central
cen·tra·li·zar *v.* to centralize
cen·trar *v.* to center
cén·tri·co *adj.* central
cen·tro *m.* core; middle; center
ce·ñir *v.* to encircle; to bind
ce·ño *m.* frown
ce·pa *f.* stump
ce·pi·llo *m.* brush
ce·ra *f.* wax
ce·rá·mi·ca *f.* ceramics
cer·ca *adv.* near; close
cer·ca *f.* fence
cer·ca·ní·a *f.* nearness *pl.* outskirts
cer·ca·no *adj.* near; close
cer·car *v.* to surround; to fence something in
cer·ce·nar *v.* to cut
cer·cio·rar *v.* to assure
cer·co *m.* circle
cer·da *f.* pig; sow
cer·do *m.* pig
cer·do·so *adj.* bristly
ce·real *m.* cereal
ce·re·bral *adj.* cerebral
ce·re·bro *m.* brain
ce·re·mo·nia *f.* ceremony
ce·re·mo·nial *m.* ceremonial
ce·re·za *f.* cherry
ce·ri·lla *f.* match
ce·ro *m.* zero
ce·rra·do *adj.* shut
ce·rra·du·ra *f.* lock
ce·rrar(se) *v.* to close; to seal
ce·rro·jo *m.* bolt

23

cer·ti·fi·ca·do *m.* certificate
cer·ti·fi·car *v.* to certify
cer·va·to *m.* fawn
cer·ve·za *f.* ale; beer
ce·sar *v.* to cease
ce·sión *f.* grant; cession
cés·ped *m.* grass; sod; lawn
ces·ta *f.* basket
cha·le·co *m.* vest
cha·ma·rra *f.* short jacket
cham·pú *m.* shampoo
chan·ta·je *m.* blackmail
cha·pa *f.* metal plate; sheet
cha·que·ta *f.* jacket
char·la *f.* talk; chat
char·lar *v.* to chat; to talk
char·la·tán *adj.* talkative; gossipy
    m. trickster; charlatan
cha·rol *m.* varnish; *Amer.* tray
cha·ro·la *f. Amer.* tray
chas·qui *m. Amer.* messenger; courier
chas·qui·do *m.* click; snap; crack
cha·val *m.* lad; boy; kid
che·que *m.* cheque; check
chi·ca·no *adj.* Mexican-American
chi·cle *m.* chewing-gum
chi·co *adj.* small; little boy; child
chi·llar *v.* to yell; to scream
chi·me·ne·a *f.* chimney
chis·me *m.* piece of gossip
chis·pa *f.* spark
chis·te *m.* joke, funny story
chis·to·so *adj.* funny; amusing
cho·can·te *adj.* startling; shocking
cho·car *v.* to shock; to startle; to collide
cho·co·la·te *adj.* chocolate
chó·fer *m.* driver; chauffeur
cho·que *m.* impact; crash
chu·bas·co *m.* shower; squall; storm
chus·ma *f.* rabble; mob
chu·tar *v.* to shoot (at goal)
cí·cli·co *adj.* cyclic
ci·clis·ta *m., f.* cyclist
ci·clo *m.* circle
ci·clón *m.* cyclone
ci·cu·ta *f.* hemlock

cie·go *adj.* sightless; blind
cie·lo *m.* heaven; sky
cien *adj.* hundred
cié·na·ga *f.* swamp
cien·cia *f.* science
cien·tí·fi·co *m.* scientist
cien·to *m.* hundred
cie·rre *m.* snap
cier·ta·men·te *adv.* certainly
cier· to, a *adj.* certain; sure
cier·vo *m.* stag, deer
ci·fra *f.* figure; cipher
ci·frar *v.* to cipher
ci·ga·rri·llo *m.* cigarette
ci·lin·dro *m.* cylinder
ci·ma *f.* crest; summit; top
cin·co *adj.* five
cin·cuen·ta *adj.* fifty
ci·ne *m.* movies
cin·ta *f.* tape; ribbon
cin·to *m.* girdle
cin·tu·rón *m.* belt
ci·prés *m.* cypress
cir·co *m.* circus
cir·cu·la·ción *f.* circulation
cir·cu·lar *adj.* circular
cír·cu·lo *m.* circle
cir·cun·ci·dar *v.* to circumcise
cir·cun·ci·sión *f.* circumcision
ci·rio *m.* candle; taper
ci·rro *m.* cirrus
ci·rue·la *f.* plum
ci·ru·gí·a *f.* surgery
ci·ru·ja·no *m.* surgeon
cis·ne *m.* swan
ci·ta *f.* meeting; date; appointment
ci·ta·ción *f.* citation; subpoena
ci·tar(se) *v.* to quote; to summon
ciu·dad *f.* town; city
ciu·da·da·no *m.* citizen
cí·vi·co *adj.* civic
ci·vil *adj.* civilian; civil
ci·vi·li·za·ción *f.* civilization
cla·mor *m.* outcry; noise
cla·mo·ro·so *adj.* clamorous
clan *m.* clan

cla·ra·men·te *adv.* clearly
cla·ri·dad *f.* clarity
cla·ri·fi·car *v.* to clarify
cla·rín *m.* bugle
cla·ri·ne·te *m.* clarinet
cla·ro *adj.* clear; light; lucid
cla·se *f.* grade; class; sort
clá·si·co *adj.* classic; classical
cla·si·fi·ca·ción *f.* classification
cla·si·fi·car(se) *v.* to classify
cla·var(se) *v.* to nail; to thrust; to stick
cla·ve *adj.* key
cla·vel *m.* carnation
cla·vi·ja *f.* peg
cla·vo *m.* spike; nail
cle·men·cia *f.* mercy; clemency
cle·men·te *adj.* clement
cle·ri·cal *adj.* clerical
clé·ri·go *m.* priest; parson
cle·ro *m.* ministry; clergy
clien·te *m., f.* client; customer; patron
cli·ma *m.* climate
clí·max *m.* climax
clí·ni·ca *f.* clinic
clo·quear *v.* to cluck
clo·ro *m.* chlorine
coac·ción *f.* compulsion; constraint
coa·gu·la·ción *f.* coagulation
coa·gu·lar(se) *v.* to coagulate; to clot
coa·li·ción *f.* coalition
co·bal·to *m.* cobalt
co·bar·de *m.* coward
co·bra *f.* cobra
co·bra·dor, a *m.* conductor
co·brar(se) *v.* to cash; to receive
co·bre *m.* copper
co·bro *m.* recovery
co·ca·í·na *f.* cocaine
co·cer *v.* to bake; to cook
co·cien·te *m.* quotient
co·ci·na *f.* kitchen; stove
co·ci·nar *v.* to cook
co·co *m.* coconut
co·co·dri·lo *m.* crocodile
coc·tel *m.* cocktail
co·che *m.* automobile

co·di·cia *f.* greed
co·di·ciar *v.* to covet
co·di·cio·so *adj.* greedy
co·di·fi·car *v.* to codify
có·di·go *m.* code
co·do *m.* elbow
co·e·du·ca·ción *f.* coeducation
coe·tá·neo *m.* contemporary
co·fra·dí·a *f.* gang
co·fre *m.* chest
co·ger *v.* to get; to take
co·gi·da *f.* toss; catch
co·he·char *v.* to bribe
co·he·cho *m.* bribery
co·he·ren·te *adj.* coherent
co·he·te *m.* rocket
coin·ci·den·te *adj.* coincidental
coin·ci·dir *v.* to coincide
coi·to *m.* intercourse
co·jear *v.* to hobble
co·je·ra *f.* limp
co·jín *m.* cushion
co·jo *adj.* lame
col *f.* cabbage
co·la *f.* tail
co·la·bo·ra·ción *f.* collaboration
co·la·bo·rar *v.* to collaborate
co·la·dor *m.* strainer
co·lap·so *m.* collapse
col·cha *f.* quilt; spread
col·chón *m.* mattress
co·lec·ción *f.* collection
co·lec·cio·nar *v.* to collect
co·le·ga *m.* colleague
co·le·gio *m.* academy; college; high school
col·ga·du·ra *f.* drape
co·li·brí *m.* hummingbird
có·li·co *f.* colic
co·li·flor *f.* cauliflower
co·li·na *f.* hill
col·me·na *f.* hive; beehive
col·mi·llo *m.* fang; tusk
col·mo *m.* height; climax
co·lo·ca·ción *f.* location; situation
co·lo·car(se) *v.* to place; to locate; to put

colon

co•lon *m.* colon
co•lo•nia *f.* colony
co•lo•nial *adj.* colonial
co•lo•no *m.* settler
co•lor *m.* color
co•lo•re•te *m.* rouge
co•lum•na *f.* pillar
co•lum•nis•ta *m., f.* columnist
co•lum•piar(se) *v.* to swing
co•lu•sión *f.* collusion
co•ma *f.* comma
co•ma•dre *f.* gossip
co•man•dan•te *f.* commander
co•man•dar *v.* to command
co•ma•to•so *adj.* comatose
com•ba *f.* bend
com•bar(se) *v.* to bend; to sag
com•ba•te *m.* fight
com•ba•tir(se) *v.* to combat
com•bi•na•ción *f.* combination
com•bi•nar(se) *v.* to blend; to combine
com•bus•ti•ble *adj.* combustible
com•pe•ler *v.* to compel
com•pen•sa•ción *f.* compensation
com•pe•ten•cia *f.* competence
com•pe•tir *f.* to compete
com•pi•lar *v.* to compile
com•pin•che *m.* chum
com•pla•cer(se) *v.* to please; to humor
com•ple•men•to *m.* complement
com•ple•tar *v.* to complete
com•ple•to *adj.* full; absolute; thorough; complete
com•pli•ca•ción *f.* complication
com•pli•car(se) *v.* to involve, to complicate
cóm•pli•ce *m.* accessory, accomplice
com•po•ner(se) *v.* to make; to compose
com•por•ta•mien•to *m.* behavior
com•por•tar(se) *v.* to behave
com•po•si•ción *f.* composition
com•prar *v.* to purchase; to trade
com•pren•sión *f.* comprehension
com•pren•der *v.* to understand
com•pren•si•vo *adj.* comprehensive
com•pre•sión *f.* compression
com•pri•mir *v.* to compress

com•pro•ba•ción *f.* proof
com•pro•bar *v.* to verify
com•pues•to *m.* compound
com•pul•sión *f.* compulsion
com•pu•ta•dor *m.* computer
com•pu•tar *v.* to compute
co•mún *adj.* common
con *prep.* towards; with; by
con•ca•vi•dad *f.* hollow
con•ce•bir *v.* to conceive
con•ce•der *v.* to allow; to accord
con•ce•jo *m.* council
con•cen•tra•ción *f.* concentration
con•cen•trar(se) *v.* to concentrate
con•cep•ción *f.* conception
con•cep•to *m.* concept; notion
con•ce•sión *f.* allowance; concession
con•cien•cia *f.* conscience
con•cier•to *m.* concert
con•cluir(se) *v.* to end; to conclude
con•cor•dar *v.* to tally; to agree
con•cor•dia *f.* concord
con•cre•to *adj.* concrete
con•cu•bi•na *f.* concubine
con•cu•rrir *v.* to meet; to concur
con•cur•san•te *m., f.* participant
con•cur•so *m.* contest
con•da•do *m.* county
con•de *m.* earl; count
con•de•co•rar *v.* to decorate
con•de•na *f.* sentence
con•de•na•ción *f.* condemnation
con•de•sa *f.* countess
con•di•ción *f.* state; condition
con•di•cio•nal *adj.* conditional
con•di•cio•nar *v.* to condition
con•di•men•to *m.* condiment; seasoning
con•do•len•cia *f.* condolence
con•do•nar *v.* to condone
con•du•cir(se) *v.* to steer; to lead; to conduct; to drive
con•duc•ta *f.* behavior
con•duc•to *m.* duct; conduit
co•nec•tar *v.* to connect
co•ne•ji•to *m.* bunny
co•ne•jo *m.* rabbit

co·ne·xión f. connection
con·fec·ción f. confection
con·fec·cio·nar v. to make up; to concoct
con·fe·de·ra·ción f. confederation; confederacy
con·fe·ren·cia f. lecture; conference
con·fe·rir v. to grant; to bestow
con·fe·sar(se) v. to confess; to admit
con·fe·sión f. confession; avowal
con·fe·sio·na·rio m. confessional
con·fe·sor m. confessor
con·fe·ti m. confetti
con·fia·ble adj. reliable
con·fian·za f. dependence; confidence
con·fiar v. to trust; to rely; to confide
con·fi·den·cial adj. confidential
con·fi·gu·ra·ción f. configuration
con·fín m. confines; bound
con·fir·ma·ción f. corroboration
con·fir·mar v. to ratify; to confirm
con·fis·ca·ción f. confiscation
con·fis·car v. to confiscate
con·fla·gra·ción f. conflagration
con·flic·to m. clash; conflict
con·for·mar(se) v. to adjust; to conform
con·for·me adj. similar; agreeable
con·for·mi·dad f. conformity
con·for·tar v. to comfort
con·fron·ta·ción f. confrontation
con·fron·tar v. to confront
con·fun·dir(se) v. to confound; to perplex; to puzzle; to baffle
con·fu·sión f. mess; jumble; confusion
con·fu·tar v. to disprove; to confute
con·ge·la·ción f. frostbite
con·ge·lar(se) v. to freeze; to congeal
con·gé·ni·to adj. congenital
con·ges·tión f. congestion
con·glo·me·ra·do m. conglomerate
con·gre·gar(se) v. to flock; to assemble
con·gre·so m. convention; congress
con·je·tu·ra f. surmise; guess; conjecture
con·je·tu·rar v. to conjecture
con·ju·gar(se) v. to conjugate
con·jun·ción f. conjunction
con·jun·to m. whole; ensemble

con·ju·rar v. to conjure
con·me·mo·ra·ción f. commemoration
con·me·mo·rar v. to commemorate
con·me·mo·ra·ti·vo adj. memorial
con·mo·ción f. stir; commotion
con·mo·ve·dor adj. stirring
con·mo·ver·(se) v. to shake; to move; to thrill
co·no m. cone
cons·truc·ti·vo adj. constructive
cons·truir v. to build; to construct
con·sue·lo m. consolation
con·sul·tar v. to consult
con·su·mar v. to carry out
con·su·mi·dor m. consumer
con·su·mir(se) v. to waste away; to consume
con·su·mo m. consumption
con·sun·ción f. consumption
con·tac·to m. contact
con·ta·giar(se) v. to catch; to infect
con·ta·gio m. contagion
con·ta·gio·so adj. catching
con·ta·mi·na·ción f. pollution; contamination
con·ta·mi·nar(se) v. to contaminate
con·tar(se) v. to number; to count; to relate; to tell
con·tem·pla·ción f. contemplation
con·tem·plar v. to view; to meditate
con·tem·po·rá·neo adj. contemporary
con·ten·der v. to strive; to content; to contest
con·ten·dien·te m. contestant
con·te·ner(se) v. to hold; to include; to contain
con·te·ni·do m. content
con·ten·to adj. happy; contented
con·tes·ta·ción f. answer
con·tes·tar v. to reply; to answer
con·tien·da f. contest; strife; struggle
con·ti·guo adj. adjacent
con·ti·nen·tal adj. continental
con·ti·nen·te m. mainland; continent; container
con·tin·gen·cia f. contingency

continuación

∙∙

con∙ti∙nua∙ción *f.* continuation
con∙ti∙nuar *v.* to continue
con∙ti∙nuo *adj.* constant; continuous
con∙to∙near(se) *v.* to strut
con∙tor∙no *m.* contour; outline
con∙tra *prep.* versus; against; *adv.* against
con∙tra∙ba∙jo *m.* bass
con∙tra∙ban∙dis∙ta *m., f.* smuggler
con∙tra∙ban∙do *m.* contraband
con∙trac∙ción *f.* contraction
con∙tra∙de∙cir *v.* to contradict
con∙tra∙dic∙ción *f.* contradiction
con∙traer(se) *v.* to contract
con∙tral∙to *m., f.* alto; contralto
con∙tra∙rie∙dad *f.* snag; vexation
con∙tra∙rio *adj.* adverse; contrary
con∙tras∙tar *v.* to contrast
con∙tras∙te *m.* contrast
con∙tra∙tiem∙po *m.* upset; mishap
con∙tra∙to *m.* contract; agreement
con∙tra∙ven∙ta∙na *f.* shutter
con∙tri∙bu∙ción *f.* tax; contribution
con∙tri∙buir *v.* to contribute
con∙trol *m.* control
con∙tro∙lar *v.* to control
con∙tro∙ver∙sia *f.* controversy
con∙tu∙sión *f.* bruise; contusion
con∙va∙le∙cen∙cia *f.* convalescence
con∙va∙le∙cer *v.* to convalesce
con∙va∙le∙cien∙te *m., f.* convalescent
con∙ven∙cer *v.* to satisfy
con∙ven∙ción *f.* convention
con∙ven∙cio∙nal *adj.* conventional
con∙ve∙nien∙cia *f.* expediency
con∙ve∙nien∙te *adj.* handy; fitting; convenient
con∙ve∙nir(se) *v.* to agree; to be fit
con∙ven∙to *m.* abbey
con∙ver∙gir *v.* to converge
con∙ver∙sa∙ción *f.* conversation
con∙ver∙sar *v.* to converse
con∙ver∙tir(se) *v.* to turn into
con∙ve∙xo *adj.* convex
con∙vic∙ción *f.* conviction
con∙vi∙da∙do *m.* guest
con∙vi∙dar(se) *v.* to invite

con∙vi∙te *m.* invitation
con∙vo∙ca∙ción *f.* convocation
con∙vo∙car *v.* to summon
con∙voy *m.* convoy
con∙vul∙sión *f.* convulsion
co∙ñac *m.* brandy
co∙o∙pe∙ra∙ción *f.* teamwork
co∙o∙pe∙rar *v.* to cooperate
co∙or∙di∙na∙ción *f.* coordination
co∙or∙di∙nar *v.* to coordinate
co∙pa *f.* goblet
co∙pe∙te *m.* tuft
co∙pia *f.* imitation; copy
co∙piar *v.* to copy
co∙pio∙so *adj.* copious
co∙que∙ta *f.* coquette
co∙que∙tear *v.* to flirt
co∙ral *adj.* choral
co∙ra∙zón *m.* heart
co∙ra∙zo∙na∙da *f.* hunch
cor∙ba∙ta *f.* tie
cor∙cel *m.* steed
cor∙che∙te *m.* clasp
cor∙cho *m.* cork
cor∙de∙ro *m.* lamb
cor∙dón *m.* cord
co∙reó∙gra∙fo *m.* choreographer
cor∙ne∙ta *f.* bugle
cor∙ni∙sa *f.* cornice
co∙ro *m.* chorus
co∙ro∙la *f.* corolla
co∙ro∙na *f.* crown
co∙ro∙nar *v.* to crown
co∙ro∙na∙ria *f.* coronary
cor∙pi∙ño *m.* bodice
cor∙po∙ral *adj.* corporal
cor∙pó∙reo *adj.* bodily
corps *m., pl.* corps
co∙rral *m.* corral
co∙rrea *f.* strap
co∙rrec∙ción *f.* propriety
co∙rrec∙to, a *adj.* right
co∙rre∙dor *m.* broker
co∙rre∙gir(se) *v.* to correct
co∙rre∙rí∙a *f.* foray
co∙rres∙pon∙der(se) *v.* to concern

co•rrien•te *adj.* current
co•rroer(se) *v.* to erode
co•rrom•per(se) *v.* to rot
co•rro•sión *f.* corrosion
co•rro•si•vo *adj.* corrosive
co•rrup•ción *f.* corruption
cor•sé *m.* corset
cor•ta•do *adj.* abrupt
cor•ta•du•ra *f.* slit
cor•tan•te *adj.* edged
cor•tar(se) *v.* to chop; to cut; to clip
cor•te *m.* court
cor•tés *adj.* civil; polite
cor•te•sí•a *f.* civility
cor•ti•jo *m.* grange
cor•to *adj.* brief
co•sa *f.* thing, affair
co•se•cha *f.* crop
co•ser *v.* to sew
cos•mé•ti•co *adj.* cosmetic
cos•mos *m.* cosmos
cos•qui•llear *v.* to tickle
cos•ta *f.* coast
cos•tar *v.* to cost
cos•te *m.* price
cos•ti•lla *f.* rib
cos•to•so, a *adj.* expensive
cos•tum•bre *f.* custom
cos•tu•ra *f.* joint
co•ti•dia•no *adj.* daily
co•yo•te *m.* coyote
crá•neo *m.* skull
cra•so *adj.* thick
crá•ter *m.* crater
crea•ción *f.* creation
crea•dor *m.* creator
crear *v.* to make; to create
cre•cer(se) *v.* to increase
cre•cien•te *m.* crescent
cre•ci•mien•to *m.* growth
cré•di•to *m.* credit
cre•do *m.* credo
cré•du•lo *adj.* credulous
cre•en•cia *f.* faith
creer(se) *v.* to think
creí•ble *adj.* plausible

cre•ma *f.* cream
cre•sa *f.* maggot
cres•po *adj.* frizzy
cre•ta *f.* chalk
cria•da *f.* maid
criar(se) *v.* to raise; to nurse
cri•men *m.* felony
crip•ta *f.* crypt
cri•sis *f.* breakdown
cri•sol *m.* crucible
cris•tal *m.* crystal; glass
cris•tia•nis•mo *m.* Christianity
Cris•to *m.* Christ
cri•te•rio *m.* criterion
crí•ti•ca *f.* censure; criticism
cri•ti•car *v.* to criticize
crí•ti•co, a *adj.* critical
cro•má•ti•co *adj.* chromatic
cro•mo *m.* chrome
cró•ni•ca *f.* chronicle
cró•ni•co *adj.* chronic
cro•no•me•trar *v.* to tell time
cro•quet *m.* croquet
cro•que•ta *f.* croquette
cru•ce *m.* intersection
cru•ci•fi•car *v.* to crucify
cru•ci•fi•xión *f.* crucifixion
cru•do *adj.* crude; raw
cruel *adj.* heartless; cruel
cru•ji•do *m.* crack
cru•jir *v.* to crunch
cruz *f.* cross
cru•za•da *f.* crusade
cru•za•do, a *m.* crusader
cru•zar(se) *v.* to cross
cua•dra•do *m.* square
cua•dran•te *m.* quadrant
cua•drar(se) *v.* to tally
cua•dri•lon•go *m.* oblong
cua•dro *m.* square; picture
cua•ja•da *f.* curd
cual *adv.* as; *pron.* which
cua•li•dad *f.* quality
cual•quier *adj.* any; either
cuán *adv.* how
cuan•do *prep.* when; *adv.* when; since

cuan·tí·a *f.* amount
cuan·to *adj.* as much as
cuán·to *adj.* how much
cua·ren·ta *adj.* forty
cua·ren·ta·vo *adj.* fortieth
cua·res·ma *f.* Lent
cuar·te·ar *v.* to cut up; to quarter
cuar·tel *m.* barracks
cuar·to *m.* quarter; fourth
cuar·zo *m.* quartz
cua·si *adv.* almost
cua·te *adj.* twin; alike
cua·tre·re·ar *v.* to rustle or steal
cua·tre·ro *adj.* to steal horses
cua·tro *m.* four
cua·tro·cien·tos *adj.* four hundred
cu·be·ta *f.* bucket
cu·bier·to *f.* casing; cover
cu·bil *m.* den
cu·bi·le·te *m.* tumbler
cu·bo *m.* pail
cu·brir(se) *v.* to conceal; to cover
cu·ca·ra·cha *f.* cockroach
cu·cha·ra *f.* spoon
cu·cha·ra·da *f.* spoonful
cu·che·ta *f.* cabin
cu·chi·che·ar *v.* to whisper
cu·chi·che·o *m.* whispering
cu·cha·ri·lla *f.* teaspoon
cu·chi·lla *m.* knife
cue·llo *m.* collar
cuen·ta *f.* count; bill
cuen·ta·go·tas *m.* eyedropper
cuen·te·ro *adj.* gossipy
cuen·tis·ta *m.* storyteller
cuen·to *m.* tale
cuer·da *f.* cord
cuer·do *adj. m., f.* sensible; sane person
cuer·no *m.* horn
cue·ro *m.* hide
cuer·po *m.* body
cuer·vo *m.* crow
cues·ta *f.* hill; slope
cues·tión *f.* question
cues·tio·na·ble *adj.* debatable; questionable

cues·tio·nar *v.* to debate; to discuss
cues·tio·na·rio *m.* questionnaire
cue·va *f.* cave
cui·da·do *m.* heed, care
cui·da·dor *m., f.* caretaker
cui·da·do·so *adj.* careful
cui·dar(se) *v.* to look after
cui·ta *f.* grief
cu·lan·tro *m.* coriander
cu·le·bra *f.* snake
cu·le·bri·lla *f.* ringworm
cu·li·na·rio, a *adj.* culinary
cul·mi·na·ción *f.* culmination
cul·mi·nan·te *adj.* culminating
cul·mi·nar *v.* to culminate
cul·pa *f.* fault
cul·pa·bi·li·dad *f.* guilt
cul·pa·ble *adj.* guilty
cul·par *v.* to criticize; to accuse
cul·ti·va·ción *f.* cultivation
cul·ti·var *v.* farm; to cultivate
cul·ti·vo *m.* cultivation
cul·to *adj.* cultured
cul·tu·ra *f.* culture
cum·bre *f.* peak; top
cum·plea·ños *m.* birthday
cum·pli·do, a *adj.* perfect; complete
cum·pli·dor *adj.* reliable; trustworthy
cum·pli·men·tar *v.* to compliment
cum·pli·mien·to *m.* fulfillment
cum·plir *v.* to accomplish
cun·dir *v.* to expand; to spread
cu·ña·da *f.* sister-in-law
cu·ña·do *m.* brother-in-law
cu·plé *m.* popular song
cu·po *m.* quota
cu·pón *m.* coupon
cu·ra *f.* cure
cu·ra·ble *adj.* curable
cu·ra·ción *f.* treatment; cure
cu·ran·de·ro, a *m., f.* quack
cu·rar(se) *v.* to heal; to recover
cu·ria *f.* court
cu·rio·se·ar *v.* to pry; to snoop
cu·rio·si·dad *adj.* curiosity
cu·rio·so *adj.* curious

cu·rri·cu·lum vi·tae *m.* resume
cur·sar *v.* to study
cur·si *adj.* vulgar
cur·si·vo *adj.* cursive
cur·so *m.* course
cur·ti·do *m.* tanning as in leather
cur·ti·dor *m.* tanner
cur·tim·bre *m.* tannery
cur·tir(se) *v.* to coarsen
cur·va *f.* bend; curve
cur·va·do, a *adj.* bent; curved
cur·var *v.* to curve
cur·va·tu·ra *f.* curvature
cus·to·dia *f.* keeping
cus·to·diar *v.* to protect; to watch over
cus·to·dio *adj. m.* guardian
cu·tí·cu·la *f.* cuticle
cu·tis *m.* complexion; skin

D

da·ble *adj.* feasible; possible
dac·ti·lo·gra·fí·a *f.* typewriting; typing
dac·ti·ló·gra·fo *m., f.* typist
dá·di·va *f.* gift; present
da·di·vo·si·dad *f.* liberality; generosity
da·di·vo·so, a *adj.* lavish; generous
da·do *m.* die
dal·to·nis·mo *m.* color-blindness
da·ma *f.* lady
da·mi·se·la *f.* damsel
dam·ni·fi·car *v.* to harm; to damage
dam·ni·fi·ca·do, a *adj.* harmed; damaged
dan·za *f.* dance
da·ñar(se) *v.* to hurt; to damage
da·ñi·no, a *adj.* harmful; damaging
da·ño *m.* damage
dar(se) *v.* to give; to allow
dar·do *m.* arrow; dart
dár·se·na *f.* dock; inner harbor; port
da·ta *f.* items; date
da·tar *v.* to date
da·to *m.* fact

de *prep.* of; from; with
de·am·bu·lar *v.* to roam or wander around
de·ba·jo *adj.* underneath; below
de·ba·te *m.* discussion; debate
de·ba·tir *v.* to discuss; to debate
de·be *m.* debit
de·ber *v.* to owe; *m.* obligation or duty
de·bi·da·men·te *adv.* duly; properly
de·bi·do *adj.* fitting; due
dé·bil *adj.* feeble; weak; faint
de·bi·li·dad *f.* weakness
de·bi·li·tar *v.* to weaken
de·but *m.* opening; debut
de·bu·tan·te *f.* debutant; *adj.* beginning
de·ca·den·cia *f.* decline; decadence
de·ca·den·te *adj. m., f.* decadent
de·ca·er *v.* to decay
de·cai·mien·to *m.* feebleness; weakness; dejection
de·ca·no *m.* dean
de·can·ta·ción *f.* pouring off
de·can·tar *v.* to pour off; to decant
de·ca·pi·tar *v.* to behead
de·cen·cia *f.* decency
de·ce·nio *m.* decade
de·cen·te *adj.* decent
de·cep·ción *f.* deception; disappointment
de·cep·cio·nar *v.* to disappoint
de·ce·so *m.* death; decease
de·ci·di·do, a *adj.* resolute; determined
de·ci·dir *v.* to resolve
de·ci·mal *adj.* decimal
de·cir *v.* to state; to say
de·ci·sión *f.* decision; verdict; ruling
de·ci·si·vo *adj.* conclusive; decisive
de·cla·mar *v.* to recite
de·cla·ra·ción *f.* declaration; statement; evidence
de·cla·ra·da·men·te *adv.* openly; manifestly
de·cla·rar(se) *v.* to propose; to declare
de·cli·na·ción *f.* decline
de·cli·nar *v.* to decline; to refuse
de·cli·ve *m.* incline; slope
de·co·lo·ra·ción *f.* discoloration

de·co·lo·ran·te *m.* bleaching agent

de·co·lo·rar *v.* to fade; to discolor

de·co·mi·sar *v.* to seize; to confiscate

de·co·ra·do *m.* scenery or set in a theater

de·co·ra·do, ra *adj.* ornamental; decorative

de·co·rar *v.* to decorate

de·co·ra·ti·vo, a *adj.* ornamental; decorative

de·co·ro *m.* honor; respect

de·co·ro·so, a *adj.* decent; honorable

de·cre·cer *v.* to diminish

de·cre·ci·mien·to *m.* decrease

de·cré·pi·to, a *adj.* aged; decrepit

de·cre·tar *v.* to decree; to order

de·dal *m.* thimble

de·di·car(se) *v.* to devote

de·do *m.* finger

de·du·cir *v.* to conclude; to deduce; to subtract

de·fa·mar *v.* to defame

de·fec·ción *f.* defection

de·fec·to *m.* flaw; defect

de·fec·tuo·so, a *adj.* faulty; defective

de·fen·der *v.* to defend

de·fen·sa *f.* defense

de·fen·sor *m.* supporter

de·fi·cien·cia *f.* lacking; deficient

de·fi·ni·ción *f.* definition; determination

de·fi·nir *v.* to define

de·for·mar(se) *v.* to lose shape

de·frau·da·ción *f.* cheating; fraud

de·frau·dar *v.* to cheat

de·fun·ción *f.* death; demise

de·ge·ne·rar *v.* to decline; to degenerate

de·go·lla·de·ro *m.* windpipe; throat

de·go·llar *v.* to cut the throat

de·gra·dar(se) *v.* to demean

de·gus·ta·ción *f.* sampling; tasting

dei·dad *f.* deity

de·ja·do, a *adj.* negligent; careless

de·jar(se) *v.* to quit; to let

de·jo *m.* abandonment

del *contr. of* de and el

de·lan·te *adv.* ahead; before; in front

de·lan·te·ro *adj.* forward; front

de·la·tar *v.* to inform; to denounce; to expose

de·le·ga·ción *f.* delegation

de·le·gar *v.* to delegate

de·lei·ta·ble *adj.* enjoyable; delightful

de·lei·tar(se) *v.* to delight

del·ga·do *adj.* thin; slim

de·li·be·ra·do, a *adj.* intentional; deliberate

de·li·ca·do, a *adj.* sensitive

de·li·cia *f.* pleasure; delight

de·lin·cuen·te *adj.* delinquent

de·li·ne·ar *v.* to outline; to delineate

de·li·ran·te *adj.* delirious

de·li·rar *v.* to rave; to be delirious

de·man·da *f.* challenge; demand

de·man·dar *v.* to demand; to ask for

de·ma·sí·a *f.* surplus; more than what is needed

de·ma·sia·do *adv.* to much

de·mé·ri·to *m.* demerit

de·mo·cra·cia *f.* democracy

de·mo·le·dor, a *adj.* demolishing

de·mo·ler *v.* to demolish; to destroy

de·mo·li·ción *f.* destruction

de·mo·nio *m.* devil; demon

de·mo·ra *f.* wait; delay

de·mo·rar(se) *v.* to delay

de·mos·trar *v.* to display; to demonstrate

de·mos·tra·ti·vo, a *adj.* demonstrative

de·mu·dar *v.* to change

de·ne·gar *v.* to reject; to refuse

de·no·da·do, a *adj.* bold

de·no·mi·na·ción *f.* denomination

de·no·mi·na·dor, a *adj.* denominative

de·nos·tar *v.* to insult; to abuse

de·no·tar *v.* to denote

den·si·dad *f.* density

den·so *adj.* thick; dense

den·ta·du·ra *f.* denture

den·tal *adj.* dental

den·te·lle·ar *v.* to bite; to nibble

den·te·ra *f.* jealousy; envy

den·tí·fri·co *m.* toothpaste

den·tis·ta *m., f.* dentist

den•tro *adv.* within; inside
de•nue•do *m.* courage; bravery
de•nues•to *m.* insult
de•nun•ciar *v.* to denounce
de•pa•rar *v.* to supply
de•par•ta•men•to *m.* office; department
de•par•tir *v.* to converse; to talk
de•pen•den•cia *f.* dependence; kinship; reliance
de•pen•der *v.* to depend
de•plo•rar *v.* to deplore
de•po•ner *v.* to depose; to put aside
de•por•ta•ción *f.* deportation
de•por•tar *v.* to exile; to deport
de•por•te *m.* sport
de•po•si•tar *v.* to bank
de•pó•si•to *m.* deposit
de•pra•va•ción *f.* corruption
de•pra•va•do, a *adj.* corrupted
de•pra•var *v.* to deprave
de•pre•car *v.* to implore
de•pre•ca•to•rio *adj.* imploring
de•pre•ciar *v.* to depreciate
de•pre•dar *v.* to pillage
de•pre•sión *f.* slump; depression
de•pri•mi•do *adj.* depressed
de•pri•mir *v.* to depress
de•re•cho *adj.* right; upright
de•ri•var(se) *v.* to drift
der•ma•to•lo•gí•a *f.* dermatology
der•ma•tó•lo•go *m., f.* dermatologist
de•rra•mar(se) *v.* to overflow; to spill
de•rri•bar *v.* to overthrow; to knock down
de•rro•char *v.* to waste
de•rro•che *m.* squandering
de•rro•tar(se) *v.* to ruin
des•a•co•plar *v.* to disconnect
des•a•fiar *v.* to defy
des•a•fío *m.* challenge
des•a•gra•dar *v.* to displease
des•a•hu•ciar *v.* to evict
des•ai•re *m.* slight
des•a•len•tar *v.* to dishearten
des•a•ni•mar(se) *v.* to dismay
des•á•ni•mo *m.* depression
des•a•pro•bar *v.* to disapprove

des•a•rre•glar(se) *v.* to derange
des•a•rre•glo *m.* disorder
des•a•rro•llar(se) *v.* to unfold
des•a•rro•llo *m.* development
des•a•so•sie•go *m.* unrest
de•sas•tre *m.* disaster
des•a•tar(se) *v.* to undo
des•a•ten•to *adj.* unthinking
de•sa•ti•no *m.* blunder
des•a•yu•nar(se) *v.* to breakfast
des•a•yu•no *m.* breakfast
des•ca•li•fi•car *v.* to disqualify
des•can•sar *v.* to rest
des•can•so *m.* rest
des•ca•ra•do *adj.* brazen
des•car•gar(se) *v.* to unload
des•cen•den•te *adj.* downward
des•cen•der *v.* to descend
des•ci•frar *v.* to decipher
des•co•lo•rar(se) *v.* to fade
des•com•po•ner(se) *v.* to decompose
des•con•cer•tar(se) *v.* to embarrass
des•con•fiar *v.* to distrust
des•co•no•cer *v.* to disavow
des•con•ten•to *m.* discontent
des•con•ti•nuar *v.* to discontinue
des•cor•tés *adj.* impolite
des•co•ser(se) *v.* to come apart
des•cri•bir *v.* to describe
des•crip•ción *f.* description
des•cu•brir *v.* to find
des•cui•da•do *adj.* remiss
des•cui•dar *v.* to neglect
des•de *prep.* since; from
des•de•ñar *v.* to disdain
des•di•cha *f.* unhappiness
de•sea•ble *adj.* eligible
de•sear *v.* to hope; to wish; to desire
des•e•char *v.* to reject
des•em•bo•car *v.* to land
des•em•bol•sar *v.* to disburse
des•en•cor•var *v.* to unbend
des•en•la•ce *m.* ending
de•seo *m.* craving
de•ser•tar *v.* to defect
de•ser•tor *m.* deserter

des·es·pe·rar *v.* to despair
des·fal·car *v.* to embezzle
des·fi·gu·rar *v.* to blemish; to disfigure
des·fi·le *m.* parade
des·ga·rrar(se) *v.* to tear
des·gas·te *m.* waste
des·gra·cia *f.* misfortune
des·gra·cia·do *m.* unfortunate
des·ha·cer(se) *v.* to unwrap
des·he·lar(se) *v.* to thaw
des·hi·dra·ta·ción *f.* dehydration
des·hon·ra *f.* disgrace
des·hon·rar *v.* to disgrace
des·i·gual *adj.* irregular
des·in·flar *v.* to deflate
des·in·te·rés *m.* disinterest
de·sis·tir *v.* to desist
des·leal *adj.* disloyal
des·li·zar(se) *v.* to glide
des·lum·brar *v.* to blind
des·lus·trar(se) *v.* to dull
des·lus·tre *m.* tarnish
des·ma·yo *m.* swoon
des·mi·ga·jar(se) *v.* to crumble
des·mon·tar(se) *v.* to dismantle
des·na·tar *v.* to skim
des·nu·dar(se) *v.* to undress
des·nu·do, a *adj.* nude; bare
des·nu·tri·ción *f.* malnutrition
des·o·be·de·cer *v.* to disobey
des·o·cu·pa·do *adj.* free
des·o·do·ri·zar *v.* to deodorize
de·so·la·ción *f.* desolation
des·or·den *m.* mess
des·or·ga·ni·zar *v.* to disrupt
des·pa·cio *adv.* slowly
des·pa·char *v.* to speed
des·pe·dir(se) *v.* to dismiss; to see off
des·pei·na·do *adj.* unkempt
des·per·di·ciar *v.* to waste
des·per·tar(se) *v.* to awaken; to wake up
des·pier·to *adj.* awake
des·ple·gar(se) *v.* to unfold
des·po·jar(se) *v.* to strip
des·po·sar(se) *v.* to marry
des·pre·cia·ble *adj.* vile; worthless

des·pre·ciar(se) *v.* to scorn
des·pués *adv.* after; later
des·te·rrar *v.* to banish
des·te·tar(se) *v.* to wean
des·ti·lar *v.* to distill
des·tre·za *f.* dexterity; skill
des·truc·ción *f.* destruction
des·truir *v.* to destroy
des·u·nir *v.* to disunite
des·va·ne·cer(se) *v.* to vanish
des·ver·gon·za·do *adj.* unabashed
des·viar(se) *v.* to divert; to wander
de·ta·lla·do *adj.* elaborate
de·ta·llar *v.* to itemize
de·ta·lle *m.* detail
de·tec·ti·ve *m.* sleuth
de·ten·ción *f.* arrest
de·te·ner(se) *v.* to arrest
de·te·rio·rar(se) *v.* to decay
de·ter·mi·nar *v.* to decide
de·tes·tar *v.* to hate
de·trás *adv.* aback; behind
deu·da *f.* debt
de·va·nar *v.* to wind
de·vas·tar *v.* to devastate
de·vo·ción *f.* devotion
de·vol·ver *v.* to refund; to return
de·vo·rar *v.* to devour
día *m.* day
dia·blo *m.* devil
diá·co·no *m.* deacon
dia·frag·ma *m.* diaphragm
diag·nos·ti·car *v.* to diagnose
dia·gra·ma *m.* diagram
dia·lec·to *m.* dialect
dia·man·te *m.* diamond
dia·rio *m.* daily
di·bu·jan·te *m.* cartoonist
di·bu·jar *v.* to sketch
dic·cio·na·rio *m.* dictionary
di·ciem·bre *m.* December
dic·ta·dor *m.* dictator
dic·tar *v.* to dictate
di·cho *m.* remark; saying
die·ci·nue·ve *adj.* nineteen
die·cio·cho *adj.* eighteen

die·ci·séis *adj.* sixteen
die·ci·sie·te *adj.* seventeen
dien·te *m.* tooth
diez *adj.* ten
di·fe·ren·cia *f.* difference
di·fe·ren·te *adj.* different
di·fe·rir *v.* to defer
di·fí·cil *adj.* hard; difficult
di·fun·to *adj.* deceased
di·fu·so *adj.* widespread
di·ge·rir *v.* to digest
di·ges·tión *f.* digestion
dí·gi·to *m.* digit
dig·ni·dad *f.* dignity
di·la·tar(se) *v.* to dilate
di·li·gen·te *adj.* diligent
di·lu·ir *v.* to dilute
di·lu·viar *v.* to pour
di·men·sión *f.* dimension
di·nas·tí·a *f.* dynasty
di·ne·ro *m.* money
dios *m.* god
dio·sa *f.* goddess
di·plo·ma·cia *f.* diplomacy
di·rec·ción *f.* direction
di·rec·ta·men·te *adv.* straight
di·rec·to *adj.* straight
di·ri·gir(se) *v.* to lead; to control
dis·cer·nir *v.* to discern
dis·ci·pli·na *f.* discipline
dis·ci·pli·nar *v.* to discipline
dis·co *m.* record
dis·cre·par *v.* to disagree
dis·cre·to *adj.* discreet
dis·cul·pa *f.* excuse
dis·cul·par *v.* to excuse
dis·cu·sión *f.* discussion
dis·cu·tir *v.* to argue
di·se·mi·nar *v.* to spread
di·se·ñar *v.* to design
dis·fraz *m.* costume
dis·fra·zar *v.* to disguise
dis·gus·tar(se) *v.* to annoy
dis·gus·to *m.* displeasure
dis·lo·ca·ción *f.* dislocation
dis·lo·car(se) *v.* to dislocate

di·sol·ver(se) *v.* to dissolve
dis·per·sar(se) *v.* to dispel
dis·po·ner(se) *v.* to ready
dis·pues·to *adj.* willing
dis·pu·ta *f.* dispute
dis·pu·tar *v.* to fight; to quarrel
dis·tan·te *adj.* distant
dis·tin·guir *v.* to distinguish
dis·traer(se) *v.* to divert; to distract
dis·tri·buir *v.* to distribute
dis·tur·bio *m.* trouble
di·sua·dir *v.* to deter
di·ván *m.* couch
di·ver·gir *v.* to diverge
di·ver·sión *f.* amusement
di·ver·so *adj.* varied; different
di·vi·dir(se) *v.* to split; to divide
di·vi·no *adj.* divine
di·vor·ciar(se) *v.* to divorce
do·blar(se) *v.* to fold; to double
do·ce *adj.* twelve
do·ce·na *f.* dozen
dó·cil *adj.* meek
dó·lar *m.* dollar
do·ler(se) *v.* to pain; to hurt
do·lor *m.* ache; pain
do·mes·ti·car(se) *v.* to domesticate
do·min·go *m.* Sunday
do·nan·te *m.* donor
do·nar *v.* to donate
don·de *adv.* where
dor·mir(se) *v.* to sleep
dos *adj.* two
dra·gón *m.* dragon
dra·má·ti·co *adj.* dramatic
dro·ga *f.* drug
du·cha *f.* shower
du·char·se *v.* to shower
du·dar *v.* to hesitate; doubt
due·ño *m.* owner; master
dul·ce *m.* candy
duo·dé·ci·mo *adj.* twelfth
du·pli·car(se) *v.* to duplicate
du·que·sa *f.* duchess
du·ra·de·ro *adj.* durable
du·ran·te *prep.* during

du•ro *adj.* stiff; hard

E

é•ba•no *m.* ebony
e•brie•dad *f.* inebriation
e•brio *m.* drunk
e•cléc•ti•co *adj.* eclectic
e•cle•siás•ti•co *adj.* ecclesiastic
e•clip•sar *v.* to eclipse
e•clip•se *m.* eclipse
e•co *m.* echo
e•co•lo•gí•a *f.* ecology
e•co•no•mí•a *f.* economy
e•co•no•mis•ta *m.* economist
e•co•no•mi•zar *v.* to economize
e•cua•ción *f.* equation
e•cua•dor *m.* equator
e•cuá•ni•me *adj.* impartial
e•cua•to•rial *adj.* equatorial
ec•ze•ma *m.* eczema
e•cha•da *f.* toss
e•char(se) *v.* to throw; to cast away
e•dad *f.* age
e•di•ción *f.* edition
e•dic•to *m.* edict
e•di•fi•car *v.* to edify
e•di•tar *v.* to edict
e•di•tor *m.* editor
e•di•to•rial *m.* editorial
e•du•ca•ción *f.* education
e•du•car *v.* to instruct; to teach; to train; to educate
e•fe•bo *m.* adolescent
e•fec•ti•vi•dad *f.* effectiveness
e•fec•to *m.* result; impact; effect
e•fec•tuar *v.* to make happen, to effect
e•fi•ca•cia *f.* efficacy
e•fi•cien•cia *f.* efficiency
e•fi•cien•te *adj.* efficient
e•fu•sión *f.* effusion
e•fu•si•vo *adj.* effusive
e•go *m.* ego
e•gre•sar *v.* to graduate

e•je•cu•ción *f.* execution
e•je•cu•tar *v.* to execute
e•je•cu•ti•vo *adj.* executive
e•jem•plar *m.* example
e•jem•pli•fi•car *v.* to exemplify
e•jem•plo *m.* example
e•jer•cer *v.* exercise
e•jer•ci•cio *m.* drill; exercise; practice
e•jér•ci•to *m.* army
e•lec•to *adj.* elect
e•lec•to•ra•do *m.* electorate
e•lec•tri•ci•dad *f.* electricity
e•lec•tri•fi•car *v.* to electrify
e•lec•tro•cu•tar *v.* to electrocute
e•lec•trón *m.* electron
e•le•fan•te *m.* elephant
e•le•gan•cia *f.* grace
e•le•gan•te *adj.* elegant
e•le•gi•do *adj.* chosen
e•le•gir *v.* to choose; to elect
e•le•men•tal *adj.* elementary; essential; elemental
e•le•va•ción *f.* elevation
e•le•va•do *adj.* high
e•le•var(se) *v.* to elevate; to lift
e•li•mi•nar *v.* to eliminate
e•lip•se *f.* ellipse
e•líp•ti•co *adj.* elliptical
e•li•xir *m.* elixir
e•lo•cuen•cia *f.* eloquence
e•lo•cuen•te *adj.* eloquent
e•lo•giar *v.* to eulogize
e•lu•ci•dar *v.* to elucidate
e•lu•dir *v.* to elude
e•lla *pron., f.* she
e•llas *pl.pron., f.* them; they
e•llo *pron.* it
e•llos *pl.pron., m.* them; they
e•ma•nar *v.* to emanate
e•man•ci•par *v.* to emancipate
em•ba•ja•da *f.* embassy
em•ba•ja•dor *m.* ambassador
em•bal•sa•mar *v.* to embalm
em•ba•ra•za•da *adj.* pregnant
em•ba•ra•zo, *m.* embarrassment; pregnancy

em·bar·car(se) v. to embark
em·bar·que m. shipment
em·bas·tar v. to tack; to quilt
em·be·ber v. to wet; to absorb
em·be·lle·cer v. to embellish
em·bes·tir v. to attack
em·blan·que·cer v. to bleach
em·ble·ma m. emblem
em·bo·lia f. embolism
em·bo·rra·char(se) v. to get drunk
em·bos·car v. to ambush
em·bo·ta·do, a adj. dull
em·bo·tar v. to dull
em·bo·te·llar v. to bottle
em·bra·ve·cer v. to infuriate
em·bria·gar(se) v. to intoxicate
em·brión m. embryo
em·bro·llar v. to embroil
e·mer·gen·cia f. emergency
e·mi·gra·do m. emigrant
e·mi·grar v. to emigrate
e·mi·sa·rio m. emissary
e·mi·sión f. issue
e·mi·tir v. to give off; to emit
e·mo·ción f. feeling; emotion
e·mo·cio·nar v. to affect
e·mo·ti·vo, a adj. emotional
em·pal·mar v. to splice; to join
em·pa·par(se) v. to drench; to wet
em·pa·pe·la·do m. lining
em·pa·pe·lar v. to line with paper
em·pa·re·da·do m. recluse; captive;
  prisoner
em·pa·tar v. to tie
em·pa·te m. impediment; draw;
  connection
em·pe·ci·na·do adj. obstinate
em·pe·ci·nar v. to be obstinate
em·pe·llar v. to push
em·pe·ño m. patron; pledge; insistence
em·peo·rar(se) v. to become worse
em·pe·ra·dor m. emperor
em·pe·ra·triz f. empress
em·pe·ro conj. however
em·pe·zar v. to start; to begin
em·pí·ri·co adj. empirical

em·plas·tar v. to hamper; to plaster
em·plas·to m. plaster
em·ple·a·do m. employee
em·ple·a·dor m. employer
em·ple·ar(se) v. to employ
em·pleo m. job; work
em·plu·mar v. to feather
em·po·bre·ci·do adj. impoverished
em·pren·der v. to begin
em·pre·sa f. company; business
em·pre·sa·rio m. director
em·pu·jar v. to thrust; to push
em·pu·je m. push
e·mu·la·ción f. emulation
e·mul·sión f. emulsion
en prep. in
e·na·je·na·ble adj. alienable
e·na·je·na·ción f. alienation
e·na·je·nar v. to alienate
e·na·no m. dwarf
e·nar·de·cer v. to ignite
en·ca·be·za·mien·to m. heading;
  caption
en·ca·be·zar v. to enroll; to head
en·ca·jar v. to force; to insert
en·ca·je m. insertion; lace
en·ca·lle·cer v. to develop a callous
en·can·di·lar v. to excite; to stir
en·can·ta·do adj. happy; delighted
en·can·ta·dor adj. charming; enchanting
en·can·ta·mien·to m. enchantment
en·can·tar v. to charm; to enchant
en·can·to m. enchantment
en·ca·po·ta·do adj. cloudy
en·ca·po·tar v. to become overcast
en·ca·ra·mar v. to elevate; to raise; to
  promote
en·ca·rar v. to confront
en·car·gar v. to advise; to place in
charge;   to request
en·car·go m. assignment; task; job
en·car·na·ción f. incarnation
en·car·nar v. to heal; to mix; to embody
en·car·ni·za·do adj. bloody
en·ca·rri·llar v. to guide
en·ce·fa·li·tis f. encephalitis

en·cen·de·dor *m.* lighter
en·cen·der(se) *v.* to ignite
en·ce·rar *v.* to polish
en·ce·rrar(se) *v.* to confine
en·ci·clo·pe·dia *f.* encyclopedia
en·cie·rro *m.* closing; seclusion; enclosure
en·ci·ma *adv.* above
en·ci·ma de *adv.* upon
en·cin·ta *adj.* pregnant
en·co·co·rar *v.* to annoy
en·co·ger *v.* to shrink; to contract;
    to become smaller
en·co·gi·mien·to *m.* shrinkage;
    contraction
en·co·lar *v.* to glue
en·co·men·dar(se) *v.* to commend
en·co·miar *v.* to extol
en·co·nar *v.* to irritate; to anger
en·con·trar(se) *v.* to find; to encounter
en·cor·var *v.* to curve
en·cru·ci·ja·da *f.* intersection
en·cua·der·nar *v.* to bind
en·cua·drar *v.* to frame
en·cu·brir *v.* to hide
en·cuen·tro *m.* meeting; collision;
    encounter
en·cues·ta *f.* inquiry
en·cum·brar *v.* to honor; to lift; to raise
en·cur·tir *v.* to preserve
en·chi·la·da *f.* enchilada
en·chu·far *v.* to couple; to connect; to
    merge
en·chu·fe *m.* plug; connection; socket
en·de·ble *adj.* weak
en·dé·mi·co *adj.* endemic
en·de·re·zar *v.* to direct; to straighten
en·dia·bla·do *adj.* diabolical
en·di·bia *f.* endive
en·do·sa·ble *adj.* endorsable
en·do·san·te *m.* endorser
en·do·sar *v.* to endorse
en·do·so *m.* endorsement
en·dul·zar *v.* to sweeten
en·du·re·cer(se) *v.* to toughen
e·ne·mi·go *m.* enemy
e·ne·mis·tad *f.* animosity

e·ner·gí·a *f.* energy
e·nér·gi·co *adj.* energetic
e·ne·ro *m.* January
e·ner·va·ción *f.* enervation
e·ner·var *v.* to weaken
en·fa·dar *v.* to annoy; to anger
én·fa·sis *m.* stress; emphasis
en·fer·mar *v.* to become ill
en·fer·me·dad *f.* sickness
en·fer·me·ra *f.* nurse
en·fer·mo *adj.* ill
en·fer·vo·ri·zar *v.* to encourage; to enliven
en·fi·lar *v.* to string; to point; to direct
en·fo·car(se) *v.* to focus
en·fren·te *adv.* in front of
en·friar(se) *v.* to cool
en·fu·re·cer *v.* to infuriate
en·gan·char *v.* to persuade
en·gan·che *m.* hook
en·ga·ña·di·zo *adj.* credulous
en·ga·ñar(se) *v.* to fool; to deceive
en·ga·ño *m.* mistake; trick; error; fraud
en·ga·ño·so *adj.* tricking; deceitful;
    deceiving
en·gar·zar *v.* to curl; to mount; to thread
en·gas·te *m.* mounting
en·gen·drar *v.* to breed
en·gen·dro *m.* fetus
en·go·la·do *adj.* arrogant
en·go·lle·ta·do *adj.* proud
en·go·mar *v.* to glue
en·gor·de *m.* fattening
en·go·rro·so *adj.* troublesome
en·gra·nar *v.* to link; to connect
en·gran·de·cer *v.* to praise; to increase;
    to heighten; to augment; to be promoted;
    to exaggerate
en·gra·pa·do·ra *f.* stapler
en·gra·sa·do *m.* lubricant
en·gra·se *m.* lubricant
en·gre·í·do *adj.* arrogant
en·gro·sar *v.* to swell; to enlarge
en·ha·ci·nar *v.* to heap
en·he·brar *v.* to connect; to string; to link
en·hi·lar *v.* to arrange; to guide; to thread;
e·nig·má·ti·co *adj.* enigmatic

en•jam•brar *v.* to swarm
en•jam•bre *m.* swarm
en•ju•gar *v.* to settle; to dry
en•jui•ciar *v.* to examine; to indict; to judge
en•jun•dia *f.* fat; grease; vitality
en•la•ce *m.* liaison; link; junction; connection
en•lar•dar *v.* to baste
en•la•zar *v.* to connect; to rope; to lace; to lasso
en•lo•que•cer *v.* to make insane; to drive crazy
en•sor•de•cer *v.* to make deaf
en•su•ciar(se) *v.* to soil
en•sue•ño *m.* daydream
en•ta•bla•do *m.* floor
en•ta•llar *v.* to engrave; to carve; to groove
en•ten•de•dor, a *adj.* sharp; expert
en•ten•der(se) *v.* to understand
en•ten•di•mien•to *m.* understanding
en•te•ra•men•te *adv.* totally; entirely
en•te•rar(se) *v.* to learn
en•te•re•za *f.* fortitude; integrity
en•te•ri•zo *adj.* entire
en•te•ro *adj.* whole; entire
en•ti•dad *f.* concern; entity
en•tie•rro *m.* funeral; burial; grave; internment
en•tin•ta•do *m.* inky
en•tin•tar *v.* to ink
en•to•mo•lo•gí•a *f.* entomology
en•to•nar *v.* to modulate; to intone
en•ton•ces *adv.* then
en•tor•no *m.* environment
en•tor•pe•cer *v.* to deaden; to obstruct; to dull
en•tra•da *f.* entrance
en•tram•par *v.* to ensnare; to trick; to entangle
en•tran•te *adj.* coming; next
en•tra•ña•ble *adj.* beloved; close; dear
en•trar *v.* to go into; to enter
en•tre *prep.* among; between
en•tre•ca•no *adj.* graying

en•tre•cor•tar *v.* to interrupt
en•tre•ga *f.* delivery
en•tre•gar(se) *v.* to deliver
en•tre•na•dor *m.* coach
en•tre•na•mien•to *m.* coaching
en•tre•nar *v.* to train
en•tre•ta•llar *v.* to impede; to carve; to engrave
en•tre•te•ner(se) *v.* to entertain
en•tre•te•ni•do *adj.* entertaining
en•tre•ver *v.* to surmise
en•tre•ve•ro *m.* jumble
en•tre•vis•tar *v.* to interview
en•tu•bar *v.* to put a tube into
en•tuer•to *m.* injustice
en•tur•biar *v.* to cloud
en•tu•sias•mar *v.* to enthuse
en•tu•sias•mo *m.* enthusiasm
e•nu•me•ra•ción *f.* enumeration
e•nu•me•rar *v.* to enumerate
e•nun•cia•ción *f.* enunciation
e•nun•ciar *v.* to enunciate
en•va•sar *v.* to package; to bottle
en•va•se *m.* packaging
en•ver•gar *v.* to fasten
en•via•do *m.* envoy
en•viar *v.* to send
en•vi•dia *f.* envy
en•vi•diar *v.* to envy
en•vi•dio•so *adj.* envious
en•ví•o *m.* dispatch; package
en•vol•tu•ra *m.* wrapper
en•vol•ven•te *adj.* enveloping
en•vol•ver(se) *v.* to wrap up
en•ye•sar *v.* to plaster
en•zi•ma *f.* enzyme
e•ón *m.* aeon
e•pi•cen•tro *m.* epicenter
é•pi•co *f.* epic
e•pi•de•mia *f.* epidemic
e•pi•dé•mi•co *adj.* epidemic
e•pi•dér•mi•co *adj.* epidermic
e•pi•glo•tis *f.* epiglottis
e•pi•lep•sia *f.* epilepsy
e•pí•lo•go *m.* epilogue
e•pi•so•dio *m.* episode

e•pi•te•lio *m.* epithelium
é•po•ca *f.* age; time period
e•po•pe•ya *f.* epic
e•qui•dad *f.* equity
e•qui•lá•te•ro *adj.* equilateral
e•qui•li•bra•do *adj.* well-balanced; reasonable
e•qui•li•brar *v.* to balance
e•qui•li•brio *adj.* equilibrium
e•qui•li•bris•ta *f.* acrobat
e•qui•no *adj.* equine
e•qui•pa•je *m.* baggage
e•qui•par *v.* to equip
e•qui•pa•rar *v.* to compare
e•qui•po *m.* team
e•qui•ta•ti•vo *adj.* fair
e•qui•va•len•te *adj.* equivalent
e•qui•vo•ca•do *adj.* being wrong
e•qui•vo•car(se) *v.* to err
e•quí•vo•co *adj.* equivocal
er•bio *m.* erbium
e•rec•to *adj.* erect
er•guir *v.* to lift up
e•ri•gir *v.* to erect
e•ro•sión *f.* erosion
e•ró•ti•co *adj.* erotic
e•rra•di•car *v.* to uproot; to eradicate
e•rra•do *adj.* mistaken
e•rran•te *adj.* errant
e•rrar(se) *v.* to wander; to miss; to roam; to fail
e•rró•ne•o *adj.* erroneous
e•rror *m.* error
e•ruc•to *m.* burp
e•ru•di•ción *f.* erudition
e•rup•ción *f.* eruption
e•sa *adj.* that
es•bel•to *adj.* slender
es•bo•zo *m.* outline
es•ca•bel *m.* footstool; stool
es•ca•bro•so *adj.* rough; rugged
es•ca•la *f.* range; ladder
es•ca•lar *v.* to climb; to scale
es•ca•le•ra *f.* stairs; staircase
es•cal•far *v.* to poach
es•ca•lo•nar *v.* to stagger

es•ca•par(se) *v.* to escape; to get away
es•car•pa•do, a *adj.* short; abrupt
es•ca•so *adj.* scarce
es•ce•na *f.* scene
es•cla•vi•zar *v.* to enslave
es•cla•vo, a *m.* slave
es•co•ba *f.* broom
es•co•ger *v.* to decide; to choose
es•con•der(se) *v.* to hide
es•cor•pión *m.* scorpion
es•cri•bir *v.* to write
es•cu•char *v.* to listen
es•cue•la *f.* school
es•cul•pir *v.* to carve
es•cul•tu•ra *f.* sculpture
e•se *adj.* that; **e•sos** *pl.* those
e•sen•cial *adj.* essential
es•for•zar(se) *v.* to strive for
es•fuer•zo *m.* exertion; attempt
es•mal•te *m.* enamel
es•me•ral•da *f.* emerald
e•so *pron.* that
e•só•fa•go *m.* esophagus
es•pa•ciar(se) *v.* to spread out
es•pa•cio *m.* space
es•pa•da *f.* sword
es•pa•gue•ti *m.* spaghetti
es•pal•da *f.* back
es•pas•mo *m.* spasm
es•pás•ti•co *adj.* spastic
es•pe•cial *adj.* special
es•pe•cia•li•dad *f.* speciality
es•pe•cia•li•zar(se) *v.* to specialize
es•pe•ci•fi•car *v.* to specify
es•pé•ci•men *m.* specimen
es•pec•ta•dor *m.* witness
es•pe•jo *m.* mirror
es•pe•ra *f.* wait
es•pe•rar *v.* to hope; wait
es•piar *v.* to spy
es•pi•na *f.* spine, thorn
es•pi•na•zo *m.* backbone
es•pi•ni•lla *f.* shin
es•pi•ral *adj.* spiral
es•pi•rar *v.* to exhale
es•plén•di•do *adj.* splendid

es·plen·dor *m.* splendor
es·pon·tá·neo *adj.* spontaneous
es·po·sa *f.* wife
es·po·so *m.* husband
es·que·le·to *m.* skeleton
es·quí *m.* ski
es·quiar *v.* to ski
es·qui·na *f.* corner
es·ta *adj., f.* this
és·ta *pron, f.* this
es·ta·ble·cer(se) *v.* to settle; to establish
es·ta·ción *f.* station; season
es·ta·dio *m.* stadium
es·ta·do *m.* state
es·ta·llar *v.* to explode
es·tam·par *v.* to stamp
es·tam·pi·da *f.* stampede
es·tan·car(se) *v.* to stagnate
es·tan·dar·te *m.* standard
es·tar *v.* to lie; to be
es·ta·tua *f.* statue
es·ta·tu·ra *f.* stature
es·te *adj.* east
és·te *pron.* this; *pl.* these
es·te·ri·li·dad *f.* sterility
es·ti·bar *v.* to stow
es·ti·lo *m.* style
es·ti·mar(se) *v.* to estimate
es·ti·mu·lar *v.* to stimulate
es·ti·rar *v.* to stretch
es·tó·ma·go *m.* stomach
es·tor·bar *v.* to block; to impede
es·tor·nu·dar *v.* to sneeze
es·tor·nu·do *m.* sneeze
es·tran·gu·lar *v.* to choke
es·tra·te·gia *f.* strategy
es·tra·ti·fi·car(se) *v.* to stratify
es·tre·char(se) *v.* to narrow
es·tre·lla *f.* star
es·tre·llar(se) *v.* to smash into
es·tre·me·cer(se) *v.* to shake
es·tric·to *adj.* strict
es·tro·pa·jo *m.* mop
es·tro·pear(se) *v.* to ruin
es·truc·tu·ra *f.* form
es·truen·do *m.* thunder

es·tu·dian·te *m., f.* student
es·tu·diar *v.* to study
es·tu·dio *m.* studio
es·tu·fa *f.* stove
es·tu·pen·do *adj.* stupendous
es·tú·pi·do *adj.* stupid
e·ter·no *adj.* eternal
e·ti·que·ta *f.* label
eu·fo·ria *f.* euphoria
e·va·cua·ción *f.* evacuation
e·va·cuar *v.* to evacuate
e·va·dir *v.* to avoid; to dodge
e·va·lua·ción *f.* evaluation
e·va·po·ra·ción *f.* evaporation
e·va·po·rar(se) *v.* to evaporate
e·va·sión *f.* evasion
e·vi·den·cia *f.* evidence
e·vi·den·te *adj.* obvious
e·vi·tar *v.* to shun
e·vo·car *v.* to evoke
e·vo·lu·ción *f.* evolution
ex·ac·ta·men·te *adv.* exactly
ex·a·ge·ra·ción *f.* exaggeration
ex·a·ge·rar *v,* to exaggerate
ex·a·men *m.* test; quiz
ex·a·mi·nar(se) *v.* to examine
ex·ca·va·ción *f.* excavation
ex·ce·der(se) *v.* to surpass
ex·ce·len·cia *f.* excellence
ex·ce·len·te *adj.* excellent
ex·cep·to *prep.* unless
ex·ci·tar(se) *v.* to arouse
ex·cla·ma·ción *f.* exclamation
ex·cla·mar *v.* to exclaim
ex·cluir *v.* to exclude
ex·clu·sión *f.* exclusion
ex·cu·sa *f.* excuse
ex·cu·sar *v.* to excuse
ex·ha·lar *v.* to exhale
ex·i·gir *v.* to require
ex·is·tir *v.* to exist
ex·pan·sión *f.* expansion
ex·pen·der *v.* to expend
ex·pe·rien·cia *f.* experience
ex·pe·ri·men·tar *v.* to experiment
ex·per·to *m.* expert

ex•pli•ca•ción *f.* explanation
ex•pli•car(se) *v.* to explain
ex•plo•ra•ción *f.* exploration
ex•plo•rar *v.* to explore
ex•por•ta•ción *f.* export
ex•por•tar *v.* to export
ex•pre•sar(se) *v.* to tell; to express
ex•pre•sión *f.* expression
ex•pul•sar *v.* to put out; to expel
ex•ten•der(se) *v.* to expand out
ex•te•rior *adj.* exterior
ex•tran•je•ro *m.* alien
ex•tra•ño *adj.* odd; strange
ex•tre•mo *adj.* extreme

F

fá•bri•ca *f.* mill
fa•bri•ca•ción *f.* manufacture
fa•bri•car *v.* to manufacture
fá•bu•la *f.* fiction; fable
fa•bu•lo•sa•men•te *adv.* fabulously
fa•bu•lo•so *adj.* fabulous
fac•ción *f.* feature; faction
fa•ce•ta *f.* facet
fá•cil *adj.* simple
fa•ci•li•dad *f.* chance; facility
fa•ci•li•tar *v.* to expedite; to facilitate
fac•ti•ble *adj.* feasible
fac•tor *m.* factor
fac•to•rí•a *f.* foundry; factory
fac•tu•ra•ción *f.* invoicing
fac•tu•rar *v.* to invoice
fa•cul•tad *f.* power
fa•cul•tar *v.* to empower
fa•cha *f.* appearance
fai•sán *m.* pheasant
fa•ja *f.* sash; band
fa•ja•du•ra *f.* belting
fa•jar *v.* to belt; to wrap
fa•lan•ge *f.* phalanx
fa•laz *adj.* deceptive

fal•da *f.* skirt
fal•dón *m.* tail
fá•li•co *adj.* phallic
fal•se•dad *f.* untruth; lie
fal•si•fi•car *v.* to misrepresent
fal•so *adj.* dishonest
fal•ta *f.* fault; shortage; flaw; want; lack
fal•tar *v.* to fail; to need
fal•to *adj.* wanting; wretched; short
fa•llar *v.* to fail
fa•llo *adj.* judgment; void; decision; ruling
fa•ma *f.* fame
fa•mé•li•co *adj.* famished
fa•mi•lia *f.* family
fa•mi•liar *adj.* familiar; casual; familial
fa•mo•so *adj.* well known
fa•na•ti•zar *v.* to fanaticize
fan•fa•rrón *adj.* showy; bragging
fan•go *m.* mud
fan•go•si•dad *f.* muddiness
fan•ta•se•ar *v.* to dream
fan•ta•sí•a *f.* fantasy
fan•tás•ti•co *adj.* bizarre; fanciful
fa•rán•du•la *f.* business; theater
fa•ra•ón *m.* pharaoh
far•do *m.* bale; pack
fa•rin•ge *f.* pharynx
far•ma•céu•ti•co *m.* pharmacist
far•ma•cia *f.* pharmacy
fa•ro *m.* beacon; light; lighthouse
fa•rol *m.* light; lantern
far•sa *f.* farce
fas•ci•na•ción *f.* fascination
fas•ci•nan•te *adj.* fascinating
fas•ci•nar *v.* to intrigue; to fascinate
fas•cis•ta *m.* fascist
fas•ti•diar(se) *v.* to annoy; to bother
fas•ti•dio *m.* annoyance; repugnance
fas•ti•dio•so *adj.* annoying; tedious; bothersome
fas•to *m.* splendor
fas•tuo•si•dad *f.* splendor
fa•tal *adj.* fatal
fa•ta•li•dad *f.* fatality
fa•tal•men•te *adv.* fatally; unhappily; wretchedly

fa·ti·ga *f.* fatigue
fa·ti·gar(se) *v.* to fatigue; to tire
fa·ti·go·so *adj.* tiring; fatigued; tired
fa·tuo *m.* fool
fau·na *f.* fauna
fa·vor *m.* favor
fa·vo·ra·ble *adj.* favorable
fa·vo·re·cer *v.* to favor; to help another; to support
fa·vo·ri·to *adj.* favorite
fe *f.* trust; faith
fe·bre·ro *m.* February
fe·bril *adj.* hectic
fé·cu·la *f.* starch
fe·cun·di·dad *f.* fertility
fe·cha *f.* date
fe·char *v.* to date
fe·de·ra·ción *f.* federation
fe·de·ral *adj.* federal
fe·de·ra·lis·ta *adj.* federalist
fe·de·rar *v.* to federate
fe·li·ci·dad *f.* bliss; happiness; felicity
fe·li·ci·ta·ción *f.* congratulation
fe·li·ci·tar *v.* to congratulate
fe·li·no *adj.* feline
fe·liz *adj.* happy
fel·po *m.* rug
fel·po·so *adj.* plush
fel·pu·do *m.* rug
fe·me·ni·no *adj.* feminine
fe·mi·nis·ta *adj.* feminist
fé·mur *m.* femur
fe·ne·cer *v.* to pass away; to settle; to finish
fe·no·bar·bi·tal *m.* phenobarbital
fen·ol *m.* phenol
feo *adj.* ugly
fe·ria *f.* fair; market
fe·ria·do *adj.* holiday
fer·men·ta·ción *f.* fermentation
fer·men·tar *v.* to ferment
fe·ro·ci·dad *f.* ferocity
fe·roz *adj.* fierce
fé·rre·o *adj.* iron
fe·rro·ca·rril *m.* railway
fér·til *adj.* rich

fer·ti·li·zan·te *adj.* fertilizing
fer·ti·li·zar *v.* to fertilize
fér·vi·do *adj.* fervid
fer·vor *m.* fervor
fes·te·jar *v.* to celebrate; to entertain; to court
fes·tín *m.* feast
fes·ti·val *m.* festival
fes·ti·vo, a *adj.* merry; festive; witty
fe·tal *adj.* fetal
fe·ti·che *m.* fetish
fe·ti·dez *f.* fetidness
fe·to *m.* fetus
feu·dal *adj.* feudal
feu·da·lis·mo *adj.* feudalism
fia·ble *adj.* dependable
fia·dor *m.* guarantor
fian·za *f.* guarantor; security; deposit
fiar *v.* to entrust; to guaranty
fias·co *m.* fiasco
fi·bro·so *adj.* stringy; fibrous
fic·ción *f.* fiction
fic·ti·cio *adj.* fictitious
fi·cha *f.* chip; token
fi· de·dig·no *adj.* trustworthy
fi·dei·co·mi·so *m.* trust
fi·de·li·dad *f.* accuracy; fidelity
fie·bre *f.* fever
fiel *adj.* true; loyal; honest; faithful; trustworthy
fiel·tro *m.* felt
fie·re·za *f.* ferocity; deformity; fierceness
fies·ta *f.* feast; party
fi·gu·ra *f.* shape; figure; character
fi·gu·ra·ción *f.* figuration
fi·gu·ra·do *adj.* figurative
fi·gu·rar(se) *v.* to figure
fi·gu·ra·ti·vo *adj.* figurative
fi·ja·dor *adj.* fixative
fi·ja·men·te *adv.* firmly
fi·jar(se) *v.* to determine; to set
fi·jo *adj.* permanent; set; steady; fixed
fi·la *f.* row; file; tier
fi·la·men·to *m.* filament
fi·lán·tro·po *m.* philanthropist
fi·la·te·lis·ta *m.* philatelist

fi•li•gra•na *f.* filigree
fil•mar *v.* to film
fíl•mi•co *adj.* movie; film
fi•lo *m.* edge
fi•lo•lo•gí•a *f.* philology
fi•lo•so•fí•a *f.* philosophy
fi•ló•so•fo *m.* philosopher
fil•tra•ción *f.* filtration
fil•trar(se) *v.* to strain; to filter
fil•tro *m.* filter
fin *m.* finish, end
fi•nal *adj.* ending; last; end; final
fi•na•li•dad *f.* finality
fi•na•lis•ta *m.* finalist
fi•na•li•zar *v.* to conclude
fi•nal•men•te *adv.* finally
fin•ca *f.* land; farm
fi•ne•za *f.* politeness; fineness; affection
fin•gir(se) *v.* to pretend; to sham
fi•ni•to *adj.* finite
fi•no *adj.* acute; fine; elegant; delicate
fir•ma *f.* firm
fir•ma•men•to *m.* firmament
fir•mar *v.* to sign
fir•me *adj.* hard; strong; firm
fis•ca•li•zar *v.* to investigate; to oversee;
    to snoop
fí•si•co *adj.* physical
fi•sio•lo•gí•a *f.* physiology
fi•sió•lo•go *m.* physiologist
fi•sión *f.* fission
fís•tu•la *f.* fistula
fi•su•ra *f.* fissure
fla•co *adj.* skinny; gaunt
fla•ge•la•do *adj.* whipped
fla•gran•te *adj.* flagrant
fla•me•ar *v.* to flame
flan•co *m.* side
fla•que•ar *v.* to weaken
fla•que•za *f.* weakness; leanness
flau•ta *f.* flute
flau•tín *m.* piccolo
flau•tis•ta *f.* flutist
fle•bi•tis *f.* phlebitis
fle•cha *f.* arrow
fle•ma *f.* phlegm

fle•te *m.* cargo; freight
fle•xi•bi•li•dad *f.* flexibility
fle•xi•ble *adj.* flexible
fle•xor *adj.* flexor
flo•je•dad *f.* laziness; debility
flo•je•ra *f.* carelessness
flo•jo *adj.* limp; weak
flor *f.* blossom; flower; bloom
flo•re•cer *v.* to bloom; to prosper
flo•reo *m.* flourish
flo•ris•ta *m., f.* florist
flo•tar *v.* to float
fluc•tua•ción *f.* fluctuation
fluc•tuar *v.* to fluctuate
flui•do *adj.* fluid
fluir *v.* to flow
fo•co *m.* focus
fo•lí•cu•lo *m.* follicle
fo•lla•je *m.* foliage
fo•lle•to *m.* brochure
fo•men•tar *v.* to encourage
fon•ta•ne•ro *m.* plumber
for•jar *v.* to forge
for•ma *f.* shape; form
for•ma•ción *f.* formation
for•ma•li•dad *f.* formality
for•mar(se) *v.* to make; to shape
for•ta•le•cer(se) *v.* to fortify
for•ta•le•za *f.* fortress
for•tui•to *adj.* casual
for•tu•na *f.* fortune
for•zar *v.* to strain; to force
fó•sil *m.* fossil
fo•to *f.* picture; photograph
fo•to•gra•fí•a *f.* photography
fra•ca•sar *v.* to fail
frac•ción *f.* fraction
frac•tu•ra *f.* break; fracture
frac•tu•rar(se) *v.* to fracture
frá•gil *adj.* frail
fran•ca•men•te *adv.* frankly
fran•cés *adj.* French
fran•co *adj.* open; candid
fran•que•za *f.* frankness
fra•se *f.* sentence
fra•ter•ni•dad *f.* fraternity

frau•de *m.* deception
fre•cuen•cia *f.* frequency
fre•cuen•te *adj.* frequent
fre•gar *v.* to wash; to scrub
freír(se) *v.* to fry
fre•nar *v.* to brake
fren•te *f.* front; forehand
fres•co *adj.* fresh
fric•ción *f.* friction
frío *adj.* cold; frigid
fron•tal *adj.* frontal
fron•te•ra *f.* border; limit
frun•cir *v.* to gather
frus•tra•ción *f.* frustration
frus•trar(se) *v.* to frustrate
fue•go *m.* fire
fuen•te *f.* spring; fountain
fue•ra *adv.* outside; off
fuer•te *m.* sturdy; strong
fuer•za *f.* power; force
fu•gar•se *v.* to flee
ful•gu•rar *v.* to gleam
fu•mar *v.* to smoke
fun•da•ción *f.* foundation
fun•dar(se) *v.* to establish
fun•dir(se) *v.* to fuse
fu•ria *f.* fury
fu•rio•so *adj.* furious
fu•tu•ro *m.* future

G

ga•bán *m.* topcoat
ga•bar•di•na *f.* gabardine
ga•bi•ne•te *m.* boudoir
ga•ce•la *f.* gazelle
ga•ce•ta *f.* gazette
ga•chí *f.* girl, bird, chick
ga•cho *adj.* floppy; bent
ga•fas *f.* glasses
ga•ga *adj.* foolish
gai•te•ro *adj.* gaudy
ga•jo *m.* section; bunch
ga•lác•ti•co *adj.* galactic

ga•la•na•men•te *adv.* elegantly
ga•la•ní•a *f.* elegance
ga•lan•te *adj.* gallant
ga•lan•te•o *m.* flirting; courting another
ga•len•te•rí•a *f.* generosity; grace
ga•lar•do•nar *v.* to reward
ga•la•xia *f.* galaxy
ga•le•ón *m.* galleon
ga•le•ra *f.* galley
ga•le•rí•a *f.* gallery
ga•li•ma•tí•as *m.* nonsense
ga•lón *m.* gallon
ga•lo•pan•te *adj.* galloping
ga•lo•par *v.* to gallop
ga•lo•pe *m.* gallop
gal•va•ni•zar *v.* to galvanize
ga•llar•dí•a *f.* gallantry; grace; elegance
ga•llar•do *adj.* graceful; brave
ga•lle•ta *f.* cracker
ga•lli•na *f.* chicken; hen
ga•lli•ne•ro *m.* henhouse; coop
ga•llo *m.* cock; rooster
ga•ma *f.* gamut
gam•ba•do *adj.* bowlegged
gam•be•te•ar *v.* to prance
ga•na *f.* longing; appetite
ga•na•de•ro *m.* cattle raiser, rancher
ga•na•do *m.* livestock
ga•nan•cia *f.* profit
ga•nar *v.* to earn; to win
gan•cho *m.* hook
gan•du•le•rí•a *f.* laziness
gan•glio *m.* ganglion
gan•go•so *adj.* nasal
gan•gre•na *f.* gangrene
ga•no•so *adj.* anxious
gan•so *m.* goose
ga•ra•ba•to *m.* grapple
ga•ra•je *m.* garage
ga•ran•tí•a *f.* warrant; guaranty
ga•ran•tir *v.* to defend; to guarantee
ga•ra•tu•sa *f.* compliment
gar•ban•zo *m.* chickpea
gar•be•ar *v.* to steal; to rob
gar•bi•llo *m.* sieve
gar•bo•so *adj.* graceful; generous

gar·fa *f.* claw
gar·ga·je·ar *v.* to spit
gar·gan·ta *f.* neck
gár·ga·ra *f.* gargling
gar·ga·ri·zar *v.* to gargle
gár·go·la *f.* gargoyle
gar·güe·ro *m.* gullet; windpipe
ga·rra *f.* talon
ga·rra·fal *adj.* enormous
ga·rra·pa·ta *f.* tick
ga·rrai·nar *v.* to grab
ga·rrón *m.* claw
ga·ruar *v.* to drizzle
gas *m.* gas
ga·sa *f.* gauze
ga·si·fi·car *v.* to gasify
ga·so·li·na *f.* gas
gas·ta·do, a *adj.* threadbare; exhausted
gas·tar *v.* to exhaust; to spend; to squander; to wear
gas·tri·tis *f.* gastritis
gas·tro·no·mí·a *f.* gastronomy
gas·tro·nó·mi·co *adj.* gastronomic
ga·te·ar *v.* to climb; to swipe
ga·ti·llo *m.* trigger
ga·to *m.* cat
ga·tu·no *adj.* catlike
gau·cho *adj.* gaucho
ga·ve·ta *f.* drawer
ga·vio·ta *f.* gull
ga·za·pi·na *f.* brawl
gaz·na·te *m.* windpipe; throat
géi·ser *m.* geyser
ge·la·ti·na *f.* gelatin
ge·ma *f.* gem
ge·nea·lo·gí·a *f.* genealogy
ge·ne·ra·ción *f.* generation
ge·ne·ral *m.* general
ge·ne·ra·li·dad *f.* generality
ge·ne·ra·li·za·ción *f.* generalization
ge·ne·ra·li·zar *v.* to generalize
ge·ne·ra·ti·vo *adj.* generative
ge·né·ri·ca·men·te *adv.* generically
ge·né·ri·co *adj.* generic
ge·ne·ro·si·dad *f.* generosity
ge·ne·ro·so, a *adj.* fine; generous

ge·nial *adj.* genial; inspired; pleasant
ge·nio *m.* genius; disposition
ge·no·ci·dio *m.* genocide
ge·no·ti·po *m.* genotype
gen·te *f.* nation; people
gen·til *adj.* genteel; excellent; polite
gen·tí·o *m.* mob
ge·nui·no *adj.* real; true; genuine
geo·fí·si·co *adj.* geophysical
geo·gra·fí·a *f.* geography
ge·ó·gra·fo *m., f.* geographer
geo·lo·gí·a *f.* geology
ge·ó·lo·go *m., f.* geologist
geo·me·trí·a *f.* geometry
ge·ra·nio *m.* geranium
ge·ren·te *m., f.* director
ge·riá·tri·co *adj.* geriatric
ger·ma·nio *m.* germanium
ger·men *m.* germ
ger·mi·na·ción *f.* germination
ger·mi·nar *v.* to germinate
ge·ron·to·lo·gí·a *f.* gerontology
ges·ta·ción *f.* gestation
ges·ti·cu·la·ción *f.* gesture; grimace
ges·ti·cu·lar *v.* to gesture
gey·ser *m.* geyser
gi·bar *v.* to annoy
gi·bón *m.* gibbon
gi·gan·tea *f.* sunflower
gi·gan·te *m.* giant
gi·go·lo *m.* gigolo
gim·na·sia *f.* gymnastics
gim·nas·ta *f., m.* gymnast
gi·mo·te·ar *v.* to whine
gi·ne·co·lo·gí·a *f.* gynecology
gin·gi·vi·tis *f.* gingivitis
gi·rar *v.* to rotate; to spin; to gyrate
gi·ra·to·rio *adj.* rotating
gi·ro *m.* rotation; turn
gi·ros·co·pio *m.* gyroscope
gi·ta·nes·co *adj.* gypsy-like
gla·cia·ción *f.* glaciation
gla·cial *adj.* glacial; icy
gla·ciar *m.* glacier
gla·dia·dor *m.* gladiator
glán·du·la *f.* gland

gla•se•ar *v.* to glaze
glau•co•ma *m.* glaucoma
glo•bal *adj.* global
glo•bo *m.* globe
glo•glo *m.* gurgle
glo•ria *f.* glory
glo•ri•fi•ca•ción *f.* glorification
glo•ri•fi•car(se) *v.* to glorify
glo•rio•so *adj.* glorious
glo•sa *f.* gloss
glo•sar *v.* to gloss
glo•sa•rio *m.* glossary
glo•tis *f.* glottis
glu•co•sa *f.* glucose
glu•ti•no•so *adj.* glutinous
go•ber•na•ción *f.* government
go•ber•na•dor *m.* governor
go•ber•nar *v.* to govern
go•bier•no *m.* government
go•la *f.* throat
golf *m.* golf
gol•fo *m.* gulf
go•lo•si•na *f.* craving; delicacy; longing
gol•pe *m.* blow; hit
gol•pear *v.* to slug; to hit; to beat
gol•pe•te•ar *v.* to pummel; hit; to pound; to beat
go•ma *f.* rubber; gum; rubber band
go•mo•so *adj.* gummy
gón•do•la *f.* gondola
gon•do•le•ro *m.* gondolier
go•no•co•co *m.* gonococcus
gor•do *adj.* fat
gor•go•te•o *m.* gurgle
go•ri•la *m.* gorilla
go•te•o *m.* dripping
go•zar *v.* to enjoy; to rejoice
gra•bar *v.* to engrave
gra•cia *f.* kindness; charm; pardon
gra•cio•so *adj.* funny; charming; amusing
gra•do *m.* step; grade
gra•dual *adj.* gradual
gra•fi•to *m.* graphite
gra•má•ti•co *adj.* grammatical
gra•na•te *adj. m.* garnet
gra•ní•ti•co *adj.* granite

gran•je•ro *m., f.* farmer
gra•pa *f.* staple
gra•ti•fi•car *v.* to gratify
gra•ve *adj.* serious; important; grave
gre•ga•rio *adj.* gregarious
gris *adj.* grey; gray
gri•tar *v.* to yell; to cry
gri•to *m.* yell; scream
gro•se•rí•a *f.* roughness; stupidity; vulgarity
gro•se•ro *adj.* vulgar; coarse
gro•tes•co *adj.* grotesque
gru•nón *adj.* grumble; grunt
gru•po *m.* bunch
guan•te *m.* glove
guan•te•ro *m.* glove maker
gua•pe•tón *adj.* bold; flashy
gua•pe•za *f.* daring
gua•po *adj.* flashy; good looking
guar•da *f.* custody; guard
guar•dar(se) *v.* to keep; to guard
guar•dia *f.* guard
guar•dián *m., f.* guardian
guar•ne•cer *v.* to supply
gu•ber•na•men•tal *adj.* governmental
gue•rra *f.* war
gue•rre•ar *v.* to fight
guí•a *m., f.* leader; guide
guiar *v.* to steep; to guide
gui•ta•rra *f.* guitar
gu•sa•no *m.* worm
gus•tar *v.* to like
gus•to *m.* zest; taste

H

ha•ber *v.* to have
há•bil *adj.* skillful
ha•bi•li•dad *f.* ability; skill
ha•bi•ta•ción *f.* habitation; lodging
ha•bi•tar *v.* to dwell
ha•bi•tual *adj.* habitual
ha•bi•tuar *v.* to habituate
ha•bla *f.* speech

ha·bla·do *adj.* spoken
ha·bla·du·rí·a *f.* gossip; chatter
ha·blar *v.* to talk; to speak
ha·ce *adv.* ago
ha·cer(se) *v.* to act; to become; to force; to compose
ha·cia *prep.* about; to
ha·cien·da *f.* ranch
ha·ci·na *f.* pile
ha·ci·nar *v.* to pile up
ha·da *f.* fairy
ha·do *m.* fate
ha·la·güe·ño *adj.* promising; attractive; pleasing
ha·lar *v.* to tow
hal·cón *m.* falcon
hal·co·ne·rí·a *f.* falconry
hal·co·ne·ro *m.* falconer
ha·llar(se) *v.* to locate
ham·bre *f.* hunger
ham·brien·to *adj.* hungry; starved
ham·bur·gue·sa *f.* hamburger
ha·ra·po·so *adj.* tattered
ha·rén *m.* harem
har·tar *v.* to annoy; to stuff
has·ta *prep.* until
has·tiar *v.* to annoy; to sicken
he·bra *f.* filament; thread
he·chi·ce·ro *m., f.* charmer; sorceress; sorcerer
he·chi·zo *m.* charm; spell
he·der *v.* to stink; to smell bad
he·dor *m.* stink
he·la·do *m.* ice cream
he·lar *v.* to freeze
he·li·cóp·te·ro *m.* helicopter
he·lio *m.* helium
he·li·puer·to *m.* heliport
hem·bra *f.* female; woman
he·mo·fi·lia *f.* hemophilia
he·mo·glo·bi·na *f.* hemoglobin
he·mo·rra·gia *f.* hemorrhage
hen·der(se) *v.* to crack
he·nil *m.* hayloft
he·no *m.* hay
he·pa·ti·tis *f.* hepatitis

her·ba·rio *adj.* herbal
he·re·di·ta·rio *adj.* hereditary
he·ren·cia *f.* heritage
he·ri·da *f.* wound
he·rir *v.* to hurt; to injure; to wound
her·ma·na *f.* sister
her·man·dad *f.* sisterhood; brotherhood; league
her·ma·no *m.* brother
her·mo·se·ar *v.* to beautify
her·mo·so, a *adj.* beautiful
her·nia *f.* hernia
he·roi·co *adj.* heroic
he·ro·í·na *f.* heroine
her·pes *m.* herpes
he·rre·ro *m.* blacksmith
he·rrum·brar *v.* to rust
he·rrum·bre *m.* rust
her·vor *m.* boiling
he·si·ta·ción *f.* hesitation
he·si·tar *v.* to hesitate
he·xá·go·no *adj.* hexagonal
hi·ber·na·ción *f.* hibernation
hi·ber·nar *v.* to hibernate
hí·bri·do *m.* hybrid
hi·dra·ta·ción *f.* hydration
hi·dra·tar *v.* to hydrate
hi·dro·car·bu·ro *m.* hydrocarbon
hi·dro·fo·bia *f.* hydrophobia
hi·dró·ge·no *m.* hydrogen
hi·dro·te·ra·pia *f.* hydrotherapy
hi·dró·xi·do *m.* hydroxide
hie·dra *f.* ivy
hie·lo *m.* ice
hier·ba *f.* grass
hi·gie·ne *f.* hygiene
hi·gié·ni·co *adj.* hygienic
hi·ja *f.* daughter
hi·jas·tra *f.* stepdaughter
hi·jas·tro *m.* stepson
hi·jo *m.* son
hi·la·dor *m., f.* spinner
hi·lar *v.* to spin
hi·le·ro *m.* current
hi·lo *m.* filament; thread
hi·men *m.* hymen

him·no *m.* hymn
hin·char *v.* to exaggerate; to swell; to blow up
hi·no·jo *m.* knee
hi·pér·bo·la *f.* hyperbola
hi·per·sen·si·ble *adj.* hypersensitive
hi·per·ter·mia *f.* hyperthermia
hip·no·sis *f.* hypnosis
hip·no·tis·mo *m.* hypnotism
hip·no·ti·zar *v.* to hypnotize
hi·po·con·dria *f.* hypochondria
hi·po·cre·sí·a *f.* hypocrisy
hi·pó·cri·ta *f., m.* hypocrite
hi·po·te·ca *f.* mortgage
hi·po·te·car *v.* to mortgage
hi·po·ter·mia *f.* hypothermia
his·te·ria *f.* hysteria
his·to·ria *f.* story; history
ho·ci·car *v.* to smooch; to nuzzle
hoc·key *m.* hockey
ho·gue·ra *f.* bonfire
ho·ja *f.* petal; leaf; sheet
ho·jo·so *adj.* leafy
hol·gan·za *f.* leisure
ho·lo·caus·to *m.* holocaust
hom·bre *m.* man
hom·bre·ra *f.* shoulder pad
hom·bri·llo *m.* yoke
hom·bro *m.* shoulder
ho·mi·ci·da *adj.* homicidal
ho·mi·ci·dio *m.* homicide
ho·mo·ge·nei·zar *v.* to homogenize
ho·mo·ni·mia *f.* homonymy
hon·do *adj.* intense; deep
hon·do·na·da *f.* gorge
ho·nes·ti·dad *f.* honesty
hon·go *m.* mushroom
ho·nor *m.* honor
ho·no·ra·ble *adj.* honorable
hon·ra·dez *f.* honesty
hon·ra·do *adj.* honest
hon·ro·so *adj.* honorable
ho·ra *f.* time; hour
hor·cón *m.* pitchfork
ho·ri·zon·tal *adj.* horizontal
ho·ri·zon·te *m.* horizon

hor·mi·go·ne·ra *f.* cement plant
hor·mo·na *f.* hormone
hor·ne·ar *v.* to bake
hor·ne·ro *m., f.* baker
hor·ni·llo *m.* stove
hor·no *m.* oven
ho·rós·co·po *m.* horoscope
ho·rren·do *adj.* horrendous
ho·rri·ble *adj.* awful; horrible
hó·rri·do *adj.* horrid
ho·rro·ri·zar *v.* to horrify
ho·rror *m.* terror; horror
hor·tí·co·la *adj.* horticultural
hor·ti·cul·tu·ra *f.* horticulture
hos·pi·tal *m.* hospital
hos·pi·ta·li·zar *v.* to hospitalize
hos·te·rí·a *f.* hostel; inn
hos·ti·gar *v.* to harass; to whip
hos·til *adj.* hostile
hos·ti·li·dad *f.* hostility
ho·tel *m.* hotel
hoy *m.* today
ho·ya *f.* hole
hue·co *adj.* deep; hollow
hue·lla *f.* print; footprint
huer·ta *f.* garden
hue·sa *f.* grave
hue·su·do *adj.* bony
hue·vo *m.* egg
huir(se) *v.* to flee; to escape; to avoid; to run from
hu·ma·nar *v.* to humanize
hu·ma·ni·dad *f.* humanity
hu·ma·ni·zar *v.* to humanize
hu·ma·no *m.* human
hu·me·ar *v.* to steam; to smoke
hu·me·dad *f.* humidity
hú·me·do *adj.* humid
hú·me·ro *m.* humerus
hu·mil·dad *f.* humility
hu·mi·lla·ción *f.* humiliation
hu·mi·llan·te *adj.* humiliating
hu·mi·llo *m.* pride
hu·mo *m.* smoke
hu·mo·ris·mo *m.* wit
hu·mo·so *adj.* smoky

hun•dir *v.* to ruin; to sink; to plunge
hu•ra•cán *m.* hurricane
hur•gón *m.* poker
hu•rón *m.* ferret
hur•tar(se) *v.* to steal; to take
hur•to *m.* robbery
hus•me•ar *v.* to pry
hus•me•o *m.* prying

I

i•bis *f.* ibis
i•ce•berg *m.* iceberg
i•co•no•gra•fí•a *f.* iconography
ic•te•ri•cia *f.* jaundice
ic•tió•lo•go *m.* ichthyologist
i•de•a *f.* notion; thought; image; idea; picture
i•de•al *m.* ideal
i•dea•lis•ta *adj.* idealist
i•dea•li•zar *v.* to idealize
i•dear *v.* to invent; to plan; to design
i•dén•ti•co *adj.* identical
i•den•ti•dad *f.* identify
i•den•ti•fi•ca•ble *adj.* identifiable
i•den•ti•fi•ca•ción *f.* identification
i•den•ti•fi•car *v.* to identify
i•deo•ló•gi•co *adj.* ideological
i•di•lio *m.* idyll
i•dio•má•ti•co *adj.* idiomatic
i•dio•sin•cra•sia *f.* idiosyncrasy
i•dio•ta *m., f.* idiot; *adj.* idiotic; foolish
i•do•la•trar *v.* to idolize
i•do•la•trí•a *f.* idolatry
í•do•lo *m.* idol
i•gle•sia *f.* church
ig•ni•ción *f.* ignition
ig•no•mi•nio•so *adj.* ignominious
ig•no•ran•cia *f.* ignorance
ig•no•ran•te *adj.* ignorant; unaware; uneducated
ig•no•to *adj.* undiscovered
i•gual *adj.* level; even; alike; like
i•gua•la•mien•to *m.* equalization

i•gua•lar *v.* to make equal; to equate; to smooth
i•gual•dad *f.* equality
i•gual•men•te *adv.* too; equally
i•gua•na *m.* iguana
i•la•ción *f.* cohesiveness
i•le•gal *adj.* unlawful; illegal
i•le•ga•li•dad *f.* illegality
i•le•gi•ble *adj.* illegible
i•le•tra•do *adj.* illiterate
i•ló•gi•co *adj.* illogical
i•lu•mi•na•ción *f.* illumination
i•lu•mi•na•dor *adj.* illuminative
i•lu•mi•nar *v.* to light; illuminate
i•lu•sión *f.* illusion
i•lu•so•rio *adj.* illusory
i•lus•tra•ción *f.* illustration
i•lus•tra•dor *adj.* illustrative
i•lus•trar *v.* to illustrate
i•lus•tre *adj.* illustrious
i•ma•gi•na•ble *adj.* imaginable
i•ma•gi•na•ción *f.* imagination
i•ma•gi•nar(se) *v.* to think up; to conceive
i•ma•gi•na•ti•vo *adj.* imaginative
i•ma•nar *v.* to magnetize
im•be•ci•li•dad *f.* imbecility
i•mi•ta•ble *adj.* imitable
i•mi•ta•ción *f.* imitation
i•mi•tar *v.* to imitate
im•pa•cien•cia *f.* impatience
im•pa•cien•te *adj.* impatient
im•par•cial *adj.* impartial
im•par•tir *v.* to concede
im•pa•si•ble *adj.* impassive
im•pe•ca•ble *adj.* impeccable
im•pe•di•men•to *m.* impediment
im•pe•dir *v.* to deter; to hinder
im•pen•sa•ble *adj.* unimaginable; unthinkable
im•pe•rar *v.* to reign
im•per•do•na•ble *adj.* inexcusable
im•per•fec•ción *f.* imperfection
im•pe•rial *adj.* imperial
im•per•me•a•bi•li•dad *f.* impermeability
im•per•me•a•ble *m.* raincoat
im•per•so•nal *adj.* impersonal

im·pé·ti·go *m.* impetigo
ím·pe·tu *m.* energy; impetus
im·pe·tuo·so *adj.* impetuous; violent
im·pla·ca·ble *adj.* implacable
im·plan·tar *v.* to implant
im·pli·ca·ción *f.* implication; consequence
im·pli·car *v.* to mean; to implicate
im·plo·rar *v.* to invoke
im·po·ner *v.* to charge; to inspire;
   to inform
im·po·pu·lar *adj.* unpopular
im·por·ta·ción *f.* importation
im·por·tan·cia *f.* authority; importance
im·por·tan·te *adj.* important
im·por·tu·nar *v.* to importune
im·por·tu·no *adj.* inopportune
im·po·si·bi·li·dad *f.* impossibility
im·po·si·ble *adj.* impossible; difficult
im·pos·tor *m.* imposter
im·po·ten·cia *f.* impotence
im·prac·ti·ca·ble *adj.* unfeasible;
   impracticable
im·pre·ci·so *adj.* imprecise
im·preg·nar *v.* to impregnate
im·pre·sión *f.* impression
im·pre·sio·nan·te *adj.* impressive
im·pre·vis·to *adj.* unexpected; sudden
im·pri·mir *v.* to stamp; to print; to
   imprint
im·pro·ba·ble *adj.* improbable
im·pro·duc·ti·vo *adj.* unproductive
im·pro·vi·sa·ción *f.* improvisation
im·pu·den·cia *f.* impudence
im·pul·sar *v.* to drive; to impel
im·pul·sión *f.* impulse
im·pul·so *m.* impulse
im·pu·ni·dad *f.* impunity
im·pu·re·za *f.* impurity
im·pu·ro *adj.* impure
in·ac·ción *f.* inaction
in·a·cep·ta·ble *adj.* unacceptable
in·ac·ti·vo *adj.* inactive
in·a·de·cua·do *adj.* inadequate
in·ad·ver·ten·cia *f.* carelessness;
   inadvertence
in·al·te·ra·ble *adj.* unalterable

i·na·ne *adj.* vain; useless
i·na·ni·dad *f.* inanity
in·a·pli·ca·ble *adj.* inapplicable
in·a·ten·ción *f.* inattention
in·a·ten·to *adj.* inattentive
in·ca·pa·ci·dad *f.* incapacity
in·ca·pa·ci·tar *v.* to incapacitate
in·ca·paz *adj.* unable; incapable
in·cen·dio *m.* incentive
in·ces·to *m.* incest
in·cien·so *m.* incense
in·cier·to *adj.* vague; uncertain; doubtful
in·ci·ne·rar *v.* to incinerate
in·ci·sión *f.* incision
in·ci·tar *v.* to urge; to incite
in·cle·men·te *adj.* inclement
in·cli·na·ción *f.* slant; inclination; slope
in·cli·nar(se) *v.* to slant; to incline;
   to persuade
in·cluir *v.* to contain; to include
in·clu·sión *f.* inclusion
in·clu·si·vo *adj.* inclusive
in·co·he·ren·te *adj.* incoherent
in·co·mi·ble *adj.* inedible
in·com·pa·ti·ble *adj.* incompatible
in·com·ple·to *adj.* incomplete
in·con·clu·so *adj.* inconclusive
in·cons·tan·te *adj.* fickle
in·cor·po·ral *adj.* incorporeal
in·cor·po·rar *v.* to incorporate
in·co·rrec·to *adj.* incorrect
in·co·rrup·to *adj.* incorrupt
in·cré·du·lo *adj.* incredulous
in·cre·í·ble *adj.* incredible
in·cre·men·tar *v.* to increase
in·cre·men·to *m.* increase
in·cre·par *v.* to reprimand
in·cri·mi·nar *v.* to incriminate
in·crus·tar *v.* to encrust
in·cu·ba·ción *f.* incubation
in·cu·bar *v.* to incubate
in·cul·car *v.* to inculcate
in·cu·ra·ble *adj.* incurable
in·cu·rrir *v.* to incur
in·de·cen·te *adj.* indecent
in·de·ci·sión *f.* indecision

in·de·ci·so *adj.* indecisive
in·de·fen·so *adj.* defenseless
in·de·le·ble *adj.* indelible
in·dem·ne *adj.* unhurt
in·de·pen·di·zar *v.* to liberate
in·de·se·a·ble *adj.* undesirable
in·di·ca·ción *f.* sign; indication; direction
in·di·car *v.* to show; to indicate
in·di·fe·ren·te *adj.* indifferent
in·di·gen·cia *f.* indigence
in·di·gen·te *adj.* indigent
in·di·ges·tión *f.* indigestion
in·dig·nar *v.* to infuriate
in·dig·no *adj.* despicable
ín·di·go *m.* indigo
in·di·rec·to *adj.* hint; indirect
in·dis·cre·ción *f.* indiscretion
in·dis·cu·ti·ble *adj.* indisputable
in·dis·tin·to *adj.* indistinct
in·di·vi·dual *adj.* individual
in·di·vi·duo *m.* individual
in·di·vi·si·ble *adj.* indivisible
in·dó·cil *adj.* indocile
in·do·ci·li·dad *f.* unruliness
in·do·len·cia *f.* indolence
in·do·len·te *adj.* indolent
in·do·ma·ble *adj.* uncontrollable; untamable
in·dó·mi·to *adj.* untamable; indomitable
in·duc·ción *f.* induction
in·du·cir *v.* to induce
in·du·da·ble *adj.* certain
in·dul·gen·te *adj.* indulgent
in·dus·tria *f.* industry
in·dus·trial *adj.* industrial
in·dus·tria·li·zar *v.* to become industrialized
in·dus·trio·so *adj.* industrious
i·ne·fa·ble *adj.* ineffable
in·e·fi·caz *adj.* ineffective
i·nep·ti·tud *f.* ineptitude
i·nep·to *adj.* inept
i·ner·cia *f.* inertia
i·ner·te *adj.* inert
i·nes·pe·ra·do *adj.* unexpected
i·nes·ta·ble *adj.* unstable

i·ne·vi·ta·ble *adj.* inevitable
i·ne·xis·ten·te *adj.* nonexistent; not existing
i·nex·plo·ra·do *adj.* unexplored
in·fa·li·ble *adj.* infallible
in·fa·mar *v.* to slander
in·fa·mia *f.* infamy
in·fan·cia *f.* infancy
in·fan·te *m.* baby; infant
in·fan·til *adj.* childish; baby
in·far·to *m.* infraction
in·fa·tuar *v.* to become conceited
in·fec·ción *f.* infection
in·fec·cio·so *adj.* infectious
in·fec·tar(se) *v.* to infect
in·fe·liz *adj.* wretched
in·fe·ren·cia *f.* inference
in·fe·rior *adj.* under; inferior
in·fe·rio·ri·dad *f.* inferiority
in·fe·rir *v.* to inflict; to infer
in·fes·tar *v.* to infest
in·fiel *adj.* disloyal
in·fier·no *m.* hell
in·fil·trar *v.* to infiltrate
ín·fi·mo *adj.* worst; lowest
in·fi·ni·to *adj. m.* infinite
in·fla·ción *f.* inflation
in·fla·ma·ble *adj.* inflammable
in·fla·mar *v.* to inflame
in·flar *v.* to inflate
in·flex·i·ble *adj.* rigid; unyielding
in·fluen·cia *f.* influence
in·fluen·ciar *v.* to influence
in·flu·jo *m.* influence
in·for·ma·ción *f.* information
in·for·mal *adj.* informal
in·for·mar(se) *v.* to report; to inform; to find out
in·for·me *adj.* formless
in·for·tu·nio *m.* misfortune
in·fra·rro·jo *adj.* infrared
in·fre·cuen·te *adj.* infrequent
in·fruc·tuo·so *adj.* fruitless
in·fun·dir *v.* to infuse
in·fu·sión *f.* infusion
in·ge·nie·rí·a *f.* engineering

in·ge·nie·ro *m.* engineer

in·ge·nio·so *adj.* witty; clever

in·ge·rir *v.* to ingest

in·ges·tión *f.* ingestion

in·glés *m.* English

in·gra·to *adj.* thankless

in·gre·dien·te *m.* ingredient

in·gre·so *m.* entrance

in·ha·bi·li·dad *f.* incompetence

in·ha·lar *v.* to inhale

in·he·ren·te *adj.* inherent

in·hi·bir *v.* to inhibit

in·hu·ma·no *adj.* inhuman

i·ni·cia·ción *f.* initiation

i·ni·cial *adj.* initial

i·ni·ciar *v.* to initiate

i·ni·cio *m.* beginning

i·ni·gua·la·do *adj.* unequaled

i·ni·mi·ta·ble *adj.* inimitable

in·je·rir *v.* to insert

in·jer·to *m.* transplant

in·ju·ria *f.* injury

in·jus·ti·cia *f.* injustice

in·jus·to *adj.* unjust

in·ma·du·ro *adj.* immature

in·me·mo·rial *adj.* immemorial

in·men·so *adj.* immense

in·mer·sión *f.* immersion

in·mi·grar *v.* to immigrate

in·mi·nen·te *adj.* imminent

in·mo·des·to *adj.* immodest

in·mo·lar *v.* to immolate

in·mo·ral *adj.* immoral

in·mor·tal *adj.* immortal

in·mo·vi·ble *adj.* immovable

in·mó·vil *adj.* immobile

in·mun·do *adj.* filthy

in·mu·ni·dad *f.* immunity

in·mu·ni·zar *v.* to immunize

in·mu·ta·ble *adj.* immutable

in·no·ble *adj.* ignoble

in·no·va·ción *f.* innovation

in·no·var *v.* to innovate

i·no·cen·cia *f.* innocence

i·no·cen·te *adj.* innocent

i·no·cu·lar *v.* to inoculate

i·no·cuo *adj.* innocuous

i·no·pe·ra·ble *adj.* inoperable

i·nor·gá·ni·co *adj.* inorganic

in·quie·tar *v.* to alarm

in·quie·tud *f.* uneasiness

in·qui·li·no *m., f.* tenant

in·qui·rir *v.* to probe

in·sa·no *adj.* insane

ins·cri·bir(se) *v.* to record; to engrave

ins·crip·ción *f.* record; inscription

in·sec·to *m.* insect

in·se·gu·ro *adj.* insecure

in·sen·si·ble *adj.* unfeeling; unconscious; insensible

in·ser·ción *f.* insertion

in·ser·tar *v.* to insert

in·sig·nia *f.* emblem

in·sin·ce·ro *adj.* insincere

in·sis·ten·te *adj.* insistent

in·sis·tir *v.* to insist

in·so·len·cia *f.* insolence

ins·pec·ción *f.* inspection

ins·pi·rar *v.* to inspire

ins·truc·ción *f.* instruction

ins·truir(se) *v.* to teach; to learn; to instruct

in·su·li·na *f.* insulin

in·sul·tar *v.* to insult

in·tac·to *adj.* together; intact

in·te·li·gen·cia *f.* intellect; intelligence

in·te·li·gen·te *adj.* smart; intelligent

in·ten·si·fi·car *v.* to intensify

in·te·re·sar(se) *v.* to concern

in·te·rior *m.* inside

in·ter·no *adj.* inside

in·te·rrup·ción *f.* interruption

in·ter·ve·nir *v.* to mediate; to intervene

ín·ti·mo *adj.* intimate

in·tro·duc·ción *f.* introduction

in·va·dir *v.* to invade

in·va·sión *f.* invasion

in·ven·ción *f.* invention

in·ven·tar *v.* to contrive; to think up; to invent

in·ves·tir *v.* to invest

in·vier·no *m.* winter

ir(se)

ir(se) *v.* to depart; to leave
i·rre·gu·lar *adj.* irregular
is·la *f.* island
iz·quier·do, a *adj.* left

J

ja·ba·lí *m.* boar
ja·ba·li·na *f.* javelin
ja·bón *m.* soap
ja·bo·na·do *m.* wash
ja·bo·nar *v.* to lather up
ja·bo·ne·ro *m., f.* soapmaker
ja·ca *f.* nag; pony
ja·ca·re·ro *adj.* lively
ja·co *m.* nag
jac·tan·cia *f.* arrogance; bragging; boast
jac·tan·cio·so *adj.* arrogant
jac·tar·se *v.* to brag
ja·de *m.* jade
ja·de·ar *v.* to gasp for air
ja·diar *v.* to hope
ja·guar *m.* jaguar
ja·lar *v.* to pull on
ja·le·a *f.* jelly
ja·le·ar *v.* to urge on
ja·leo *m.* racket; uproar
ja·lo·nar *v.* to mark
ja·más *adv.* never; ever; never again
jam·ba *f.* jamb
ja·mel·go *m.* nag
ja·món *m.* ham
ja·que *m.* check
ja·que·ar *v.* to check
ja·ra·be *m.* syrup
ja·ra·near *v.* to carouse
jar·ca *f.* acacia
jar·dín *m.* garden
jar·di·ne·ra *f.* gardener
jar·di·ne·ro *m.* gardener
ja·rra *f.* mug; pitcher
ja·rro *m.* jug
ja·rrón *m.* vase
jas·pe *m.* jasper

jau·la *f.* cell; cage
jaz·mín *m.* jasmine
je·fa *f.* master; boss
je·fe *m.* head; boss; master
je·mi·que·ar *v.* to whine
jen·gi·bre *m.* ginger
je·rar·quí·a *f.* hierarchy
je·re·mí·as *m., f.* complainer
jer·ga *f.* jargon; slang
je·ri·gon·za *f.* gibberish
je·rin·gar *v.* to pester
je·rin·ga·zo *m.* injection
je·ro·glí·fi·co *m.* hieroglyph
jer·sey *m.* sweater
ji·fia *f.* swordfish
ji·ne·te *m.* equestrian; horseman
ji·ne·te·ar *v.* to ride a horse
ji·par *v.* to pant
ji·ra *f.* excursion
ji·ra·fa *f.* giraffe
jo·co·si·dad *f.* joke; wit
jo·co·so *adj.* jocular
jo·cun·di·dad *f.* jocundity
jo·fai·na *f.* washbowl; washbasin
jor·na·da *f.* trip
jor·nal *m.* wage
jo·ro·ba *f.* hump
jo·ro·bar *v.* to annoy; to bother
jo·rrar *v.* to haul
jo·ven *m.* youth
jo·vial *adj.* jovial
jo·ya *f.* gem; jewel
jo·ye·ra *f.* box for jewelry
jo·ye·rí·a *f.* jewelry store
jo·ye·ro *m.* jeweler
ju·bi·la·do *m., f.* retired one
ju·bi·lar(se) *v.* to retire
ju·bi·leo *m.* jubilee
jú·bi·lo *m.* joy
ju·bi·lo·so *adj.* joyful
ju·dí·a *f.* bean
jue·go *m.* play; game
jue·ves *m.* Thursday
juez *m.* judge
ju·gar *v.* to game; to play
ju·gue·tear *v.* to play

ju•gue•tón *adj.* playful
jui•cio *m.* verdict; judgement
ju•lio *m.* July
jun•co *m.* junk
ju•nio *j* June
jun•ta *f.* union
jun•ta•men•te *adv.* together
jun•tar(se) *v.* to connect; to join
jun•to *adv.* together
ju•ra•do *m.* jury
ju•rar *v.* to vow; to swear; to curse
ju•ris•ta *f.* jurist
jus•ta•men•te *adv.* fairly
jus•ti•cia *f.* justice
jus•ti•fi•car *v.* to warrant
jus•to *adj.* fair
ju•ve•nil *adj.* youthful, juvenil
ju•ven•tud *f.* youth
juz•gar *v.* to try; to judge

K

ki•lo *m.* kilo
ki•lo•ci•clo *m.* kilocycle
ki•lo•gra•mo *m.* kilogram
ki•lo•mé•tri•co *adj.* kilometric
ki•ló•me•tro *m.* kilometer
ki•lo•va•tio *m.* kilowatt
kirsch *m.* cherry brandy
kum•mel *m.* cumin brandy

L

la *def. art.* the
la•be•rin•to *m.* labyrinth
la•bia *f.* eloquence
la•bio *m.* lip
la•bor *f.* work
la•bo•ra•ble *adj.* working
la•bo•ral *adj.* labor
la•bo•rar *v.* to work
la•bo•ra•to•rio *m.* laboratory

la•bo•re•ar *v.* to work
la•bo•rio•so *adj.* arduous
la•bra•do, a *adj.* plowed; cultivated; wrought
la•bra•dor, a *adj.* farming *m.* farmer; peasant
la•bran•za *f.* farmland; farm
la•brar *v.* to carve; to work; to plow; to cultivate; to tool
la•ca *f.* shellac; lacquer; hair spray
la•ca•yo *m.* valet; attendant
la•ce•ra•ción *f.* laceration
la•ce•rar *v.* to injure; to lacerate
la•ce•ria *f.* want; toil
la•cio *adj.* limp; straight
la•có•ni•co, a *adj.* laconic
la•cra *f.* scar
la•cre *m.* a sealing wax
la•cri•mó•ge•no, a *adj.* tear producing
la•cri•mo•so, a *adj.* tearful; sad; sorrowful
lac•ta•ción *f.* nursing
lac•tan•cia *f.* lactation
lac•tar *v.* to suckle
lác•ti•co, a *adj.* lactic
lac•to•sa *f.* lactose
la•de•ar *v.* to tilt
la•de•o *m.* inclination
la•de•ra *f.* slope
la•di•no, a *adj.* astute
la•do *m.* side; **de** next to; beside; alongside
la•drar *v.* to snarl at something; to growl
la•dri•llo *m.* brick
la•drón *m.* robber
la•dro•ne•rí•a *f.* theft
la•gar•ti•ja *f.* a small lizard
la•gar•to *m.* lizard
la•go *m.* lake
lá•gri•ma *f.* tear
la•gri•me•ar *v.* to tear; to weep; to cry
la•gri•mo•so, a *adj.* tearful; watery
la•gu•na *f.* lagoon
lai•cal *adj.* laical
la•ja *adj. f.* laical
la•ja *f.* slab of stone

la·me·du·ra *f.* licking
la·men·ta·ble *adj.* lamentable
la·men·ta·ción *f.* lamentation
la·men·tar *v.* to be sorry for; to regret something
la·men·to *m.* lament
la·men·to·so, a *adj.* mournful
la·mer *v.* to lap up
la·me·ta·da *f.* lick
la·mi·do, a *adj.* polished
la·mi·na·ción *f.* lamination
la·mi·nar *v.* to laminate
lám·pa·ra *f.* lamp
lam·pa·ri·lla *f.* little or small lamp
lam·pa·rón *m.* stain
lam·pi·ño, a *adj.* hairless
la·na *f.* wool
la·na·do, a *adj.* fleecy
lan·ce *m.* argument; move; occurrence
lan·ce·ar *v.* to lance
lan·ce·ta *f.* lancet
lan·cha *f.* boat
lan·che·ro *m.* boatman
lan·chón *m.* barge
la·ne·ro, a *adj.* woolen
lan·gui·de·cer *v.* to languish
lan·gui·dez *f.* feebleness; lethargy
lán·gui·do, a *adj.* languid
lan·guor *m.* languor
la·no·li·na *f.* lanolin
la·no·so, a *adj.* woolly
lan·za *f.* spear
lan·za·da *f.* wound due to a lance
lan·za·mien·to *m.* throwing
lan·zar *v.* to hurt; to fire; to release; to vomit; to throw; to shoot
lá·pi·da *f.* tombstone
la·pi·da·rio, a *adj.* concise; lapidary
lá·piz *m.* pencil
lap·so, a *m.* interval; lapse
la·que·ar *v.* to varnish
lar·do *m.* fat; land
lar·gar *v.* to let go; to dismiss; to release; to hurt; to throw
lar·go *adj.* lengthy; long; abundant
lar·gor *m.* length

lar·gue·za *f.* length
lar·gui·ru·cho, a *adj.* lanky
la·rin·ge *f.* larynx
la·rin·gi·tis *f.* laryngitis
lar·va *f.* larva
lar·val *adj.* larval
las *pron.* them; *art.* the
la·ser *m.* laser
la·si·tud *f.* lassitude
la·so *adj.* weak; limp
lás·ti·ma *f.* compassion; shame; pity
las·ti·ma·du·ra *f.* wound
las·ti·mar *v.* to hurt; to offend; to injure
las·ti·me·ro, a *adj.* pitiful
la·ta *f.* can; tin; pest
la·te·ar *v.* to bend
la·ten·te *adj.* latent
la·te·ral *adj.* lateral
la·ti·do *m.* beating; throbbing; beat
la·tien·te *adj.* throbbing
la·ti·gue·ar *v.* to whip; to crack the whip
la·tir *v.* to throb
la·ti·tud *f.* breadth; extent; width; scope
la·ti·tu·di·nal *adj.* latitudinal
la·to, a *adj.* wide
la·tón *m.* brass
la·to·ne·ro *m.* brassworker
la·to·so, a *adj.* bothersome
la·tro·ci·nio *m.* theft
lau·da·ble *adj.* laudable
lau·de *f.* tombstone
lau·do *m.* verdict
lau·rel *m.* bay; laurel
láu·re·o *adj.* laurel
la·va *f.* lava
la·va·ble *adj.* washable
la·va·da *f.* washing
la·va·de·ro *m.* laundry
la·va·do *m.* wash
la·va·dor *m.* washer
la·van·da *f.* lavender
la·van·de·ra *f.* laundry woman
la·van·de·ro *m.* laundryman
la·va·pla·tos *m.* dishwasher
la·var *v.* to wash; to clean
la·va·ti·va *f.* enema

la·xar *v.* to slacken
la·xa·ti·vo *adj.* laxative
la·zar *v.* to rope
la·za·ri·no, a *adj.* leprous
la·zo *m.* lasso; knot; trap; snare
le *pron.* him
le·al *adj.* faithful
le·al·tad *f.* loyalty
lec·ción *f.* lesson
lac·tor, a *adj.* reading
lec·tu·ra *f.* reading
le·cha·da *f.* grout; whitewash
le·char *v.* to milk
le·che *f.* milk
le·che·río, a *adj.* dairy; milky
le·cho *m.* layer; bed
le·cho·so *adj.* milky
le·chu·ga *f.* lettuce
le·er *v.* to read
le·ga·ción *f.* legation
le·ga·do *m.* legacy
le·ga·jo *m.* file
le·gal *adj.* legal
le·ga·li·dad *f.* legality
le·ga·lis·ta *f.* legalist
le·ga·li·za·ción *f.* legalization
le·ga·li·zar *v.* to legalize
le·gar *v.* to delegate; to bequeath
le·gi·ble *adj.* legible
le·gión *f.* legion
le·gis·la·ción *f.* legislation
le·gis·la·dor *m.* legislator
le·gis·la·tu·ra *f.* legislative
le·jos *adv.* far away
len·gua *f.* language
le·ón *m.* lion
le·o·na *f.* lioness
le·o·par·do *m.* leopard
les *pron.* for them; for you
le·tal *adj.* lethal
le·tra *f.* letter
le·van·tar *v.* to lift up; to erect
ley *f.* rule; law
li·be·ra·ción *f.* liberation
li·be·ral *adj.* liberal
li·ber·tad *f.* freedom

li·bre *adj.* single; open; free
li·bro *m.* book
li·gar *v.* to commit; to bind
li·mi·ta·ción *f.* limitation
li·mi·ta·do *adj.* limited
li·mi·tar *v.* to restrict; to limit
li·món *m.* lemon
lim·piar *v.* to clear; to clean
lim·pie·za *f.* neatness; cleaning
lim·pio *adj.* pure; clean
lí·nea *f.* outline; line; boundary
lis·ta *f.* list
lis·to *adj.* ready
li·tro *m.* liter
li·via·no, a *adj.* faithless; light
li·vi·dez *f.* lividness
lí·vi·do *adj.* livid
lo *def. art.* the
lo·a *f.* praise
lo·a·ble *adj.* praiseworthy
lo·ar *v.* to praise
lo·ba *f.* the female wolf
lo·bo *m.* the male wolf
ló·bre·go *adj.* somber; dark
ló·bu·lo *m.* lobe
lo·ca·ción *f.* leasing
lo·cal *adj.* local
lo·ca·li·dad *f.* locality
lo·ca·li·zar *v.* to find; to locate
lo·ción *f.* lotion
lo·co *adj.* crazy; extraordinary
lo·grar *v.* to take; to obtain
lo·ro *m.* parrot
los *pron.* them; *art.* the
lú·ci·do *adj.* shining
lu·cir *v.* to illuminate; to light
lue·go *adv.* later; then
lu·na *f.* moon
lu·nar *adj.* lunar
lus·trar *v.* to shine
luz *f.* day; light

M

ma·ca·bro *adj.* macabre

ma·ca·dam *m.* macadam

ma·ca·rrón *m.* macaroon

ma·ce·ra·ción *f.* maceration

ma·ce·rar *v.* to macerate

ma·ce·ta *f.* flowerpot or holder

ma·ci·len·to, a *adj.* lean; thin; emaciated

ma·ci·zo, a *adj.* solid

ma·cro·bió·ti·co *f.* macrobiotics

má·cu·la *f.* spot

ma·cha·ca *f.* pounder

ma·cha·ca·dor, a *adj.* pounding

ma·cha·car *v.* to beat; to pound; to bother

ma·cha·cón, a *adj.* tiresome *m., f.* pest

ma·cha·da *f.* stupidity

ma·cha·do *m.* hatchet

ma·che·te *m.* machete

ma·che·te·ar *v.* to injure or cut with a machete

ma·cho *adj.* manly; male; tough; virile

ma·chu·ca·du·ra *f.* beating; bruising

ma·chu·car *v.* to beat

ma·de·ra *f.* timber; wood; lumber

ma·de·ra·da *f.* raft

ma·de·re·rí·a *f.* lumberyard

ma·de·re·ro, a *adj.* timber

ma·de·ro *m.* log

ma·dras·tra *f.* stepmother

ma·dre *f.* mom; mother

ma·dre·sel·va *f.* honeysuckle

ma·dri·gue·ra *f.* hole; burrow; lair

ma·dri·na *f.* bridesmaid; godmother; patroness

ma·dru·ga·dor, a *m., f.* early riser

ma·dru·gar *v.* to anticipate; to get up early

ma·du·ra·ción *f.* ripening

ma·du·ra·dor, a *adj.* ripening

ma·du·rar *v.* to mature; to ripen; to maturate

ma·du·rez *f.* maturity; ripeness

ma·es·tre *m.* master

ma·es·tro, a *adj.* expert; teacher; master

ma·gan·ce·rí·a *f.* trickery

ma·gia *f.* magic

má·gi·co, a *adj.* magic

ma·gis·tra·do *m.* magistrate

ma·gis·tral *adj.* imposing; masterful; magisterial

mag·na·te *m.* magnate

mag·ne·sia *f.* magnesia

mag·ne·sio *m.* magnesium

mag·né·ti·co, a *adj.* magnetic

mag·ne·tis·mo *m.* magnetism

mag·ne·to·fó·ni·co, a *adj.* magnetic

mag·ni·fi·ca·dor, a *adj.* magnifying

mag·ni·fi·car *v.* to exalt; to magnify; to glorify

mag·ni·fi·cen·cia *f.* magnificence

mag·ni·fi·cen·te *adj.* magnificent

mag·ní·fi·co, a *adj.* excellent; magnificent

mag·ni·tud *f.* size; importance; magnitude

mag·no·lia *f.* magnolia

ma·go, a *adj.* magic

ma·gu·llar *v.* to batter

ma·íz *m.* corn

ma·ja·de·ro, a *adj.* foolish

ma·ja·du·ra *f.* pounding

ma·jar *v.* to pound; to bother; to mash

ma·jes·tad *f.* grandeur; majesty

ma·jo, a *adj.* pretty, nice

mal *adv.* wrongly; badly

ma·la·bar *v.* to juggle

ma·la·ba·ris·ta *m.* juggler

mal·a·cos·tum·bra·do, a *adj.* ill-mannered; having poor or bad habits; spoiled

ma·lan·drín, a *adj.* evil

ma·la·ria *f.* malaria

ma·la·ven·tu·ra *f.* misfortune

ma·la·ven·tu·ran·za *f.* fortune

mal·ba·ra·tar *v.* to squander

mal·co·mer *v.* to eat badly or poorly

mal·co·mi·do *adj.* underfed

mal·con·ten·to, a *adj.* unhappy;
rebellious

mal·cria·do, a *adj.* ill-bred

mal·criar *v.* to spoil

mal·dad *f.* evil

mal·de·cir *v.* to slander; to curse

mal·di·cien·te *adj.* defaming;
slandering *m., f.* curser; slanderer

mal·di·ción *f.* curse

mal·di·to, a *adj.* wicked; bad

ma·le·a·bi·li·dad *f.* malleability

ma·le·a·ble *adj.* malleable

ma·le·an·te *adj.* corrupting; wicked

ma·le·ar *v.* to ruin; to corrupt; to pervert

ma·le·di·cen·cia *f.* slander

ma·le·fi·cen·cia *f.* evil

ma·le·fi·cen·te *adj.* maleficent

ma·les·tar *m.* uneasiness; malaise

ma·le·ta *f.* suitcase; baggage; luggage

ma·le·vo·len·cia *f.* malevolence

mal·for·ma·ción *f.* malformation

mal·gas·tar *v.* to waste

mal·ha·da·do, *adj.* unfortunate

mal·he·rir *v.* to injure

mal·hu·mo·ra·do, a *adj.*
bad-tempered

mal·hu·mo·rar *v.* to irritate; to bother;
to annoy

ma·li·cia *f.* cunning; wickedness; slyness

ma·li·cio·so, a *adj.* malicious; cunning

ma·lig·ni·dad *f.* malignancy

ma·lig·no, a *adj.* malignant

mal·mi·ra·do, a *adj.* disfavored

ma·lo *adj.* harmful; nasty; bad

ma·lo·grar *v.* to fail; to loose; to waste

ma·lo·gro *m.* failure

mal·pa·rar *v.* to harm; to damage

mal·quis·tar *v.* to estrange

mal·quis·to, a *adj.* unpopular

mal·so·nan·te *adj.* harsh

mal·tra·ta·mien·to *m.* mistreatment

mal·tra·tar *v.* to mistreat

mal·va·do, a *adj.* wicked

mal·ver·sa·dor, a *m., f.* embezzler

mal·ver·sar *v.* to embezzle

ma·má *f.* mommy

ma·mar *v.* to nurse; to suck

ma·ma·rio, a *adj.* mammary

ma·me·lón *m.* nipple

ma·na·da *f.* herd; bunch

ma·na·de·ro, a *m., f.* spring

ma·nan·to *adj.* running

ma·nar *v.* to flow

man·car *v.* to disable

man·ci·lla *f.* blemish

man·ci·llar *v.* to blemish

man·ci·par *v.* to enslave

man·co *adj.* one-armed; disabled

man·co·mu·nar *v.* to join together; to
combine

man·co·mu·ni·dad *f.* union; association

man·cha *f.* blot; stain

man·char *v.* to stain; to spot; to soil

man·da *f.* bequest

man·da·do *m.* errand; task; order

man·da·mien·to *m.* command; order

man·dar *v.* to leave; to order

man·da·ri·na *f.* mandarin orange

man·da·to *m.* trust; command; order

man·dí·bu·la *f.* mandible

man·do *m.* leadership; power

man·do·li·na *f.* mandolin

man·dria *adj.* timid; worthless; useless

man·dril *m.* mandrel

ma·ne·ar *v.* to hobble around

ma·ne·ja·ble *adj.* manageable

ma·ne·jar *v.* to handle; to manage

ma·ne·jo *m.* operation; handling;
management

ma·ne·ra *f.* style; way; manner; type

man·ga *f.* strainer; hose

man·ga·ne·so *m.* manganese

man·gar *v.* to swipe; to mooch

man·gos·ta *f.* mongoose

man·gue·ar *v.* to startle

man·gue·ra *f.* garden hose

man·gui·ta *f.* cover

ma·ní *m.* peanut

ma·ní·a *f.* habit; craze

ma·ní·a·co, a *adj.* maniac

ma·ni·fes·ta·ción *f.* manifestation

ma·ni·fes·tar *v.* to reveal; to manifest
ma·ni·fies·to, a *adj.* manifest
ma·ni·lla *f.* bracelet
ma·ni·pu·la·ción *f.* manipulation
ma·ni·pu·la·dor, a *m.* manipulator
ma·ni·pu·lar *v.* to manipulate; to manage
ma·ni·quí *m.* mannequin
ma·no *f.* hand
ma·no·jo *m.* handful; bunch
ma·no·se·ar *v.* to touch
man·so, a *adj.* mild; tame
man·ta *f.* shawl; blanket
man·te·ca *f.* fat; lard
man·tel *m.* tablecloth
man·te·nen·cia *f.* support; maintenance
man·te·ner *v.* to support; to keep; to feed; to maintain
man·te·ni·mien·to *m.* support; sustenance
man·te·que·rí·a *f.* dairy
man·te·que·ro *m.* dairyman
man·te·qui·lla *f.* butter
man·to *m.* mantle; robe; cloak; cover
ma·nual *adj.* manual
ma·nu·fac·tu·rar *v.* to manufacture
ma·nu·ten·ción *f.* maintenance
man·za·na *f.* apple
man·za·nar *m.* apple orchard
man·za·no *m.* apple tree
ma·ña *f.* dexterity; skill
ma·ña·na *f.* morning
ma·ne·jar *v.* to manage
ma·ñe·ro *adj.* shrewd
ma·pa *f.* map
ma·pa·che *m.* raccoon
ma·que·ar *v.* to varnish
má·qui·na *f.* machine
ma·qui·na·ción *f.* machination
ma·qui·na·dor *m., f.* schemer
ma·qui·nar *v.* to scheme
ma·qui·nis·ta *m.* machinist
mar *m.* sea; tide
ma·ra·tón *m.* marathon
ma·ra·vi·lla *f.* marvel; astonishment; wonder
ma·ra·vi·llar *v.* to astonish; to be amazed

ma·ra·vi·llo·so, a *adj.* marvelous
mar·ca *f.* brand; mark; stamp; trademark
mar·ca·do *adj.* notable
mar·ca·dor, a *adj.* marking
mar·car *v.* to stamp; to mark; to note
mar·cial *adj.* military; martial
mar·cha *f.* march; velocity; speed; progress
mar·char *v.* to run; to walk
mar·chi·tar *v.* to weaken; to wilt; to languish
mar·chi·to, a *adj.* wilted
ma·re·ar *v.* to sail; to bother
ma·re·ja·da *f.* turbulence
ma·re·o *m.* nausea
mar·ga·ri·na *f.* margarine
mar·ga·ri·ta *f.* daisy
mar·gen *m.* fringe; margin
mar·gi·nal *adj.* marginal
mar·gi·nar *v.* to marginate
ma·ri·dar *v.* to wed
ma·ri·do *m.* spouse
ma·ri·nar *v.* to marinate
ma·ri·ne·rí·a *f.* sailoring
ma·ri·ne·ro, a *adj.* marine; seaworthy
ma·ri·no *adj.* marine
ma·ri·po·sa *f.* butterfly
ma·ri·qui·ta *f.* ladybug
ma·ris·cal *m.* marshal
ma·ris·co *m.* shellfish; seafood
ma·ri·tal *adj.* marital
ma·rí·ti·mo, a *adj.* maritime
mar·qués *m.* marquis
ma·rra·no *adj.* filthy
ma·rrar *v.* to fail; to miss something
ma·rrón *adj.* brown
ma·rru·lle·ro, a *m., f.* conniver
mar·so·pa *f.* porpoise
mar·su·pial *adj.* marsupial
mar·tes *m.* Tuesday
mar·ti·llar *v.* to hammer
mar·ti·llo *m.* hammer
már·tir *m.* martyr
mar·ti·rio *m.* martyrdom
mar·zo *m.* March
más *adv.* rather; more

ma•sa•crar v. to massacre
ma•sa•cre m. massacre
ma•sa•je m. massage
ma•sa•jis•ta m. masseur
mas•car v. to chew
más•ca•ra f. mask
mas•ca•ra•da f. masquerade
mas•co•ta f. mascot
mas•cu•li•ni•dad f. masculinity
mas•cu•li•no adj. manly; male
ma•si•vo, a adj. massive
mas•ti•car v. to masticate; to ruminate
más•til m. mast
mas•toi•des adj. mastoid
ma•ta f. shrub
ma•ta•dor, a m., f. killer
ma•ta•fue•go m. fire extinguisher
ma•tan•za f. massacre; killing; slaughtering
ma•tar v. to extinguish; to kill; to slaughter
ma•ta•ri•fe m. slaughterer
ma•ta•se•llar v. to cancel
ma•te•má•ti•co, a adj. mathematical
ma•te•ria f. matter
ma•te•rial adj. material
ma•te•ria•li•dad f. materiality
ma•te•ria•lis•ta adj. materialistic
ma•ter•nal adj. maternal
ma•ter•ni•dad f. maternity
ma•ter•no adj. motherly
ma•ti•nal adj. morning
ma•tiz m. tint
ma•ti•zar v. to tint
ma•tre•ro, a adj. shrewd
ma•triar•ca•do m. matriarchy
ma•triar•cal adj. matriarchal
ma•tri•ci•dio m. matricide
ma•trí•cu•la f. list
ma•tri•cu•la•ción f. registration
ma•tri•cu•lar v. to matriculate
ma•tri•mo•nial adj. matrimonial
ma•tri•mo•nio m. matrimony
ma•triz f. uterus
ma•tro•na f. matron
ma•tro•nal adj. matronly
má•xi•ma•men•te adv. chiefly
má•xi•me adv. principally

má•xi•mo adj. maximum
ma•yo m. May
ma•yo•ne•sa f. mayonnaise
ma•yor adj. greatest; larger; older
ma•yo•rí•a f. majority
ma•yo•ri•dad f. majority
ma•yús•cu•lo, a adj. important; capital
maz•mo•rra f. dungeon
ma•zo m. bunch
me pron. me
me•cá•ni•co, a adj. mechanical
me•ca•ni•zar v. to mechanize
me•ce•do•ra f. rocking chair
me•cer v. to sway; to rock
me•cha f. match; wick
me•che•ra f. shoplifter
me•chón m. tuft
me•da•lla f. medal
me•da•llón m. medallion
me•dia f. stocking
me•dia•dor, a m., f. mediator
me•dia•ne•ro, a adj. mediating
me•dia•no•che f. midnight
me•diar v. to intercede
me•di•ca•ción f. medication
me•di•car v. to medicate
me•di•ci•na f. medicine
me•di•ci•nal adj. medicinal
me•di•ci•nar v. to cure; to treat with medicine
mé•di•co, a m., f. doctor
me•di•da f. measurement
me•die•val adj. medieval
me•dio adj. middle; half
me•dio•cre adj. mediocre
me•dio•cri•dad f. mediocrity
me•dio•dí•a m. noon
me•dir v. to weigh; to measure
me•di•ta•ción f. mediation
me•di•tar v. to meditate
me•di•ta•ti•vo, a adj. meditative
mé•dium m. medium
me•drar v. to thrive; to prosper
me•dro•so, a adj. timorous
mé•du•la f. medulla
me•du•sa f. jellyfish

me•gá•fo•no *m.* megaphone
me•ga•tón *m.* megaton
me•ji•lla *f.* cheek
me•jor *adj.* superior; better
me•jo•ra *f.* betterment
me•jo•rar *v.* to make better
me•jo•rí•a *f.* improvement
me•lan•co•lí•a *f.* melancholy
me•la•za *f.* molasses
me•lin•dre•rí•a *f.* affectation
me•lo•co•tón *m.* peach
me•lo•co•to•ne•ro *m.* peach tree
me•lo•dí•a *f.* tune
me•ló•di•co *adj.* tuneful
me•lo•dio•so, a *adj.* melodious
me•lo•dra•ma *m.* melodrama
me•lo•dra•má•ti•co, a *adj.*
  melodramatic
me•lón *m.* melon
me•lo•te *m.* molasses
me•llar *v.* to nick; to chip
mem•bra•na *f.* membrane
me•mo•ra•ble *adj.* memorable
me•mo•rar *v.* to recall
me•mo•ria *f.* remembrance; memory
me•mo•rial *m.* memorial
me•mo•ri•za•ción *f.* memorization
me•mo•ri•zar *v.* to memorize
men•ción *f.* mention
men•cio•nar *v.* to mention
me•ne•ar *v.* to sway
men•gua *f.* poverty
men•gua•do *adj.* decreased; timid
men•guar *v.* to wane; to diminish
me•nin•gi•tis *f.* meningitis
me•no•pau•sia *f.* menopause
me•nor *adj.* lesser; least; less; younger
me•nos *adv.* least; less
me•nos•ca•bar *v.* to impair
me•nos•ca•bo *m.* damage; diminishing
me•nos•pre•cia•ble *adj.* despicable
me•nos•pre•cio *m.* underestimation;
  contempt
men•sa•je *m.* message
men•sa•je•ro, a *adj.* messenger
men•sual *adj.* monthly

men•su•ra *f.* measurement
men•su•ra•ble *adj.* measurable
men•su•rar *v.* to measure
men•ta *f.* mint
men•ta•do, a *adj.* renowned
men•tal *adj.* mental
men•ta•li•dad *f.* mentality
men•tar *v.* to mention
men•te *f.* intellect; mind
men•tir *v.* to lie
men•ti•ra *f.* falsehood
men•ti•ro•so, a *adj.* lying
men•tor *m.* mentor
me•nu•do *adj.* little; insignificant
mer•ca•de•o *m.* marketing
mer•ca•do *adj.* merchant
mer•can•til *adj.* mercantile
mer•car *v.* to buy
mer•ced *f.* gift
mer•ce•na•rio, a *adj.* mercenary
mer•cu•rial *adj.* mercurial
mer•cu•rio *m.* mercury
me•re•ci•mien•to *m.* worth
me•ri•dia•no, a *adj.* meridian
me•rien•da *f.* snack
mé•ri•to *m.* value; worth
me•ri•to•rio, a *adj.* meritorious
mer•mar *v.* to diminish
me•ro, a *adj.* pure
me•ro•de•ar *v.* to plunder
mes *m.* month
me•sa *f.* table
me•són *m.* tavern
me•so•ne•ro, a *m., f.* innkeeper
me•su•ra *f.* moderation
me•su•ra•do, a *adj.* moderate
me•ta•bó•li•co, a *adj.* metabolic
me•ta•bo•lis•mo *m.* metabolism
me•tá•fo•ra *f.* metaphor
me•ta•fó•ri•co, a *adj.* metaphoric
me•tal *m.* metal
me•tá•li•co *adj.* metallic
me•ta•li•zar *v.* to metallize
me•ta•mór•fi•co, a *adj.* metamorphic
me•ta•no *m.* methane
me•te•ó•ri•co, a *adj.* meteoric

me·teo·ri·to *m.* meteorite

me·teo·ro *m.* meteor

me·teo·ro·lo·gí·a *f.* meteorology

me·teo·ro·lo·gis·ta *m., f.* meteorologist

me·ter *v.* to insert into; to cause

me·ti·cu·lo·so, a *adj.* meticulous

me·ti·lo *m.* methyl

me·tó·di·co, a *adj.* methodical

mé·to·do *m.* method

me·to·do·lo·gí·a *f.* methodology

mé·tri·co *adj.* metric

me·tro·po·li·ta·no, a *adj.* metropolitan

mez·cla·dor *adj.* blending

mez·clar *v.* to mingle; to blend

mez·quin·dad *f.* miserliness

mez·qui·no, a *adj.* petty; wretched; miserly

mez·qui·ta *f.* mosque

mí *pron.* me

mi·cro·bio *m.* microbe

mi·cro·bio·lo·gí·a *f.* microbiology

mi·cro·fil·me *m.* microfilm

mi·cró·fo·no *m.* microphone

mi·cros·có·pi·co, a *adj.* microscopic

mi·cros·co·pio *m.* microscope

mie·do *m.* dread

mie·do·so, a *adj.* cowardly

miel *f.* honey

miel·ga *f.* alfalfa

miem·bro *m.* member

mien·tras *adj.* meanwhile; *conj.* while

miér·co·les *m.* Wednesday

mies *f.* grain

mi·ga *f.* substance; scrap

mi·gra·ción *f.* migration

mi·gra·ña *f.* migraine

mil *adj.* thousand

mi·la·gro *m.* miracle

mi·la·gro·so *adj.* miraculous

mi·li·cia *f.* militia

mi·li·cia·no, a *adj.* military

mi·li·gra·mo *m.* milligram

mi·lí·me·tro *m.* millimeter

mi·li·tar *m.* soldier

mi·lla *f.* mile

mi·llón *m.* million

mi·mar *v.* to fondle; to pamper

mí·mi·co, a *adj.* mimic

mi·mo·so *adj.* spoiled

mi·na *f.* mine

mi·na·dor *adj.* mining

mi·nar *v.* to mine

mi·ne·ral *adj.* mineral

mi·ne·ra·lo·gis·ta *m., f.* mineralogist

mi·ni·fal·da *f.* miniskirt

mi·ni·mi·zar *v.* to minimize

mí·ni·mo, a *adj.* least; minimal; minute

mi·nis·te·rial *adj.* ministerial

mi·nis·te·rio *m.* ministry

mi·nis·tro *m.* minister

mi·no·rar *v.* to reduce

mi·no·rí·a *f.* minority

mi·no·ri·ta·rio *adj.* minority

mi·nu·cio·so, a *adj.* minute

mi·nús·cu·lo, a *adj.* tiny; small

mi·nu·ta *f.* record; note

mi·nu·to *m.* minute

mí·o, a *adj.* mine

mio·pí·a *f.* myopia

mi·ra *f.* sight; intention

mi·ra·do, a *adj.* regarded; cautious

mi·rar *v.* to watch; to look at; to observe

mi·ra·sol *m.* sunflower

mi·rí·a·da *f.* myriad

mir·lo *m.* blackbird

mis·ce·lá·neo, a *adj.* miscellaneous

mi·se·ra·ble *adj.* miserable; poor

mi·se·ria *f.* suffering; miserliness; misery

mi·sil *m.* missile

mi·sión *f.* mission

mi·sio·nal *adj.* missionary

mis·mo *adj.* likewise; same thing

mis·te·rio *m.* mystery

mis·te·rio·so *adj.* mysterious

mís·ti·co, a *adj.* mystic

mis·ti·fi·car *v.* to mystify

mis·tu·ra *f.* mixture

mi·tad *f.* half

mi·ti·ga·ción *f.* mitigation

mi·ti·gar *v.* to mitigate

mi·to *m.* myth

mi·tón *m.* mitten; mitt

mi·tra *f.* miter
mix·to, a *adj.* mixed
mix·tu·rar *v.* to mix up
mo·bi·lia·rio, a *adj.* movable
mo·bla·je *m.* furnishing
mo·ce·dad *f.* youth
mo·ción *f.* motion
mo·cho, a *adj.* hornless
mo·da *f.* fashion
mo·de·lo *m.* model
mo·de·ra·ción *f.* moderation
mo·de·ra·do *adj.* moderate
mo·de·rar *v.* to regulate; to restrain
mo·der·ni·za·ción *f.* modernization
mo·der·ni·zar *v.* to modernize
mo·der·no *adj.* modern
mo·des·tia *f.* modesty
mó·di·co, a *adj.* moderate
mo·di·fi·ca·ción *f.* modification
mo·di·fi·ca·dor *adj.* modifying
mo·di·fi·car *v.* to modify
mo·dis·te·rí·a *f.* shop for dresses
mo·do *m.* way
mo·do·so, a *adj.* well-mannered
mo·du·la·ción *f.* modulation
mo·du·la·dor, a *m., f.* modulator
mo·far *v.* to drench; to dip; to wet
mol·de *m.* pattern; mold
mol·de·ar *v.* to shape
mo·le·cu·lar *adj.* molecular
mo·ler *v.* to grind
mo·les·tar *v.* to annoy; to disrupt
mo·les·tia *f.* annoyance; trouble
mo·les·to *adj.* bothered; annoying
mo·men·to *m.* moment
mo·na *f.* a female monkey
mo·nas·te·rio *m.* monastery
mo·ni·tor *m.* monitor
mo·no *m.* male monkey
mo·no·gra·ma *m.* monogram
mons·truo *m.* monster
mons·truo·so *adj.* monstrous
mon·ta·ña *f.* mountain
mon·tar *v.* to mount
mo·nu·men·to *m.* monument
mo·ral *f.* morale

mo·ra·li·dad *f.* morality
mo·ra·li·zar *v.* to moralize
mo·rar *v.* to dwell; to live
mór·bi·do *adj.* morbid
mor·fi·na *f.* morphine
mo·rir *v.* to kill
mor·tal *adj.* fatal; mortal
mor·tuo·rio *m.* mortuary
mos·ca *f.* fly
mos·qui·to *m.* mosquito
mos·ta·za *f.* mustard
mos·trar *v.* to exhibit; to appear; to show
mo·tor *m.* engine
mo·ver *v.* to move
mo·vi·mien·to *m.* movement
mu·cha·cha *f.* girl
mu·cha·cho *m.* boy
mu·cho *adj.* many; a lot
muer·te *f.* death
muer·to *adj.* dead
mu·jer *f.* female; woman
múl·ti·ple *adj.* multiple
mul·ti·pli·car *v.* to multiply
mun·do *m.* world
mu·ni·ci·pal *adj.* municipal
mu·ñe·ca *f.* wrist; doll
mús·cu·lo *m.* muscle
mú·si·ca *f.* music
mu·si·cal *adj.* musical
mus·lo *m.* thigh
muy *adv.* much; greatly

N

na·bo *m.* turnip; mast
na·ca·ri·no *adj.* nacreous; pearly
na·cer *v.* to be born; to be conceived
na·ci·do, a *adj.* born
na·cien·te *adj.* recent; growing; initial; nascent
na·ci·mien·to *m.* hatching; origin; birth; spring
na·ción *f.* nation
na·cio·nal *adj.* domestic; national

na·cio·na·li·dad *f.* nationality

na·cio·na·lis·ta *m., f.* nationalist

na·cio·na·li·za·ción *f.* nationalization

na·da *pron.* no; not anything; none; nothing

na·da·dor *m., f.* swimmer

na·dar *v.* to swim

na·die *pron.* no one; nobody

nai·pe *m.* playing card

nal·ga *f.* behind; buttocks

ña·me *m.* yam

ña·pa *f.* tip; bonus

ña·que *m.* junk

na·ran·ja *f.* orange

na·ran·jal *m.* orange grove

na·ran·je·ro *adj.* orange

na·ran·jo *m.* orange tree

nar·có·ti·co, o *adj.* narcotic

nar·co·ti·zar *v.* to narcotize

na·riz *f.* nostril; nose

na·rra·ción *f.* narration; narrative

na·rra·dor, a *adj.* narrating

na·rrar *v.* to narrate

na·rra·ti·vo, a *adj.* narrative

na·ta·ción *f.* swimming

na·tal *adj.* natal

na·ta·li·dad *f.* natality

na·ti·vi·dad *f.* Christmas

na·ti·vo *adj.* native

na·to, a *adj.* born

na·tu·ra *f.* nature

na·tu·ral *adj.* native; innate; natural

na·tu·ra·le·za *f.* nature

na·tu·ra·li·dad *f.* naturalness

na·tu·ra·li·za·ción *f.* naturalization

nau·fra·gar *v.* to shipwreck

náu·sea *f.* nausea

nau·se·ar *v.* to feel nauseous

náu·ti·co, a *adj.* nautical

na·val *adj.* naval

na·ve·ga·ble *adj.* navigable

na·ve·ga·ción *f.* navigation

na·ve·gar *v.* to sail

na·vi·dad *f.* Christmas

na·ví·o *m.* vessel; boat

ne·bli·na *f.* fog

ne·bli·no·so, a *adj.* foggy

ne·bu·lo·si·dad *f.* haziness

ne·ce·dad *f.* nonsense

ne·ce·sa·rio *adj.* necessary

ne·ce·si·dad *f.* need; poverty; necessity

ne·ce·si·tar *v.* to want; to require; to need

ne·cio, a *adj.* foolish; stubborn

ne·cro·lo·gí·a *f.* necrology

nec·tar *m.* nectar

nec·ta·ri·na *f.* nectarine

ne·fri·tis *f.* nephritis

ne·ga·ble *adj.* refutable

ne·ga·ción *f.* denial; refusal; negation

ne·gar *v.* to refuse; to deny; to forbid

ne·ga·ti·vi·dad *f.* negativity

ne·gli·gen·cia *f.* disregard; negligence

ne·go·cia·ble *adj.* negotiable

ne·go·cia·ción negotiation; transaction

ne·go·ciar *v.* to deal; to negotiate

ne·go·cio *m.* job; work; business; transaction

ne·gro, a *adj.* black

ne·gru·ra *f.* darkness

ne·gruz·co, a *adj.* dark

ne·ne, a *m., f.* neophyte

ne·ón *m.* neon

ne·o·na·to *m.* neonate

ner·vio *m.* nerve

ner·vio·si·dad *f.* nervousness

ne·to, a *adj.* simple; pure

neu·má·ti·co, a *adj.* pneumatic

neu·ro·ci·ru·gí·a *f.* neurosurgery

neu·ró·lo·go *m.* neurologist

neu·ró·ti·co, a *adj.* neurotic

neu·to·nio *m.* newton

neu·tral *adj.* neutral

neu·tra·li·dad *f.* neutrality

neu·tra·li·zar *v.* to neutralize

neu·tro, a *adj.* neutral

neu·trón *m.* neutron

ne·va·do, a *adj.* snow-covered

ne·var *v.* to snow

ne·ve·ra *f.* refrigerator

ne·xo *m.* link

ni *conj.* neither; nor

ni·co·ti·na *f.* nicotine

ni·cho *m.* vault; recess
ni·dal *m.* nest
ni·do *m.* nest; liar; den
nie·bla *f.* mist
nie·ta *f.* granddaughter
nie·to *m.* grandson
nie·ve *f.* snow
ni·hi·lis·ta *adj.* nihilistic
ni·lón *m.* nylon
nim·bo *m.* halo
ni·mio, a *adj.* insignificant
nin·fa *f.* nymph
nin·fo *m.* dandy
nin·fo·ma·ní·a *f.* nymphomania
nin·gu·no, a *adj.* no; none
ni·ñe·rí·a *f.* childish
ni·ñez *f.* infancy; childhood
ni·ño, a *m., f.* child
ní·quel *m.* nickel
ni·que·lar *v.* to nickel
ní·ti·do, a *adj.* clear
ni·tra·to *m.* nitrite
ni·tri·to *m.* nitrite
ni·tró·ge·no *m.* nitrogen
ni·tro·gli·ce·ri·na *f.* nitroglycerin
ni·vel *m.* height; standard
ni·ve·lar *v.* to make level
no *adv.* no
no·ble *adj.* honorable; noble
no·ble·za *f.* nobleness; nobility
no·ción *f.* notion
no·ci·vi·dad *f.* harmfulness
noc·tur·nal *adj.* nocturnal
noc·tur·no, a *adj.* sad; nocturnal
no·che *f.* night
nó·du·lo *m.* nodule
no·gal *m.* walnut
nó·ma·da *adj.* nomadic
nom·bra·mien·to *m.* nomination; naming
nom·brar *v.* to name; to nominate
no·men·cla·tu·ra *f.* nomenclature
nó·mi·na *f.* roll
no·mi·na·ción *f.* nomination
no·mi·nal *adj.* nominal
no·mi·nar *v.* to nominate

non *adj.* uneven
no·na·da *f.* trifle
ño·ñe·rí·a *f.* timidity
ño·ñez *f.* bashfulness
ño·ño, a *m., f. adj.* timid; bashful
no·no, a *adj.* ninth
nor·ma *f.* rule
nor·mal *adj.* normal
nor·ma·li·dad *f.* normality
nor·ma·li·za·ción *f.* normalization
nor·ma·li·zar *v.* to normalize
no·ro·es·te *m.* northwest
nor·te *m.* north
nos *pron.* us
no·ta·ble *adj.* outstanding; notable
no·tar *v.* to observe; to note
no·ti·fi·car *v.* to notify
no·ve·no *adj.* ninth
no·ven·ta *adj.* ninety
no·via *f.* girlfriend
no·vio *m.* boyfriend
nu·bo·si·dad *f.* cloudiness
nu·ca *f.* nape
nu·do *m.* knot
nues·tro *adj.* our
nue·ve *adj.* nine
nue·vo *adj.* new
nú·me·ro *m.* number
nun·ca *adv.* not ever
nu·trir *v.* to feed

O

o *conj.* or
o·a·sis *m.* oasis
ob·ce·ca·mien·to *adv.* blindly
ob·ce·car *v.* to blind
o·be·de·cer *v.* to obey
o·be·dien·cia *f.* obedience
o·be·dien·te *adj.* obedient
o·ber·tu·ra *f.* overture
o·be·si·dad *f.* obesity
ó·bi·ce *m.* obstacle
o·bis·po *m.* bishop

ob·je·ción f. objection
ob·je·ta·ble adj. objectionable
ob·je·tar v. to object
ob·je·ti·var v. to objectify
ob·je·ti·vi·dad f. objectivity
ob·je·to m. theme; object
o·bli·cuo, a adj. oblique
o·bli·ga·ción f. responsibility; obligation
o·bli·gar v. to force; to oblige; to favor
o·bli·ga·to·rio, a adj. obligatory
o·blon·go, a adj. oblong
o·bo·e m. oboe
o·bra v. to act; to work
o·bre·ro, a adj. working
obs·ce·ni·dad f. obscenity
obs·ce·no, a adj. obscene
ob·se·quio m. present; kindness; gift
ob·se·quio·so, a adj. obsequious; attentive
ob·ser·va·ción f. observation
ob·ser·var v. to watch; to observe
ob·se·sión f. obsession
ob·se·sio·nan·te adj. obsessive
ob·se·sio·nar v. to obsess about something
obs·ti·na·ción f. obstinacy
obs·ti·na·do, a adj. obstinate
obs·truc·ción f. obstruction
obs·truir v. to obstruct
ob·ten·ción f. obtaining
ob·te·ner v. to get; to have; to obtain
ob·tu·so, a adj. obtuse
ob·viar v. to prevent
ob·vio, a adj. obvious
o·ca·sión f. cause; occasion; circumstance
o·ca·sio·nar v. to cause; to provoke; to occasion
oc·ci·den·tal adj. occidental
oc·ci·pi·tal adj. occipital
o·cé·a·no m. ocean
o·ce·a·no·gra·fí·a f. oceanography
o·ce·a·no·grá·fi·co, a adj. oceanographic
o·cio m. leisure; idleness
oc·ta·vo adj. eighth
oc·te·to m. octet

oc·to·gé·si·mo adj. eightieth
oc·tó·go·no, a adj. octagonal
oc·tu·bre m. October
o·cul·tar v. to conceal; to silence; to hide
o·cul·tis·mo m. occultism
o·cul·to, a adj. concealed; occult
o·cu·pa·ción f. trade; occupation; job
o·cu·pa·do adj. occupied
o·cu·pan·te adj. occupying
o·cu·par v. to fill; to occupy; to employ; to pay attention to something
o·cu·rren·cia f. occurrence
o·cu·rrir v. to happen; to take place
o·chen·ta adj. eighty
o·chen·ta·vo, a adj. eightieth
o·cho adj. eight
o·cho·cien·tos adj. eight hundred
o·da f. ode
o·da·lis·ca f. odalisque
o·diar v. to loathe
o·dio m. loathing
o·dio·so, a adj. odious
o·di·se·a f. odyssey
o·don·tó·lo·go, a m., f. odontologist
o·es·te m. west
o·fen·der v. to hurt; to offend
o·fen·sa f. offense
o·fen·si·vo, a adj. offensive
o·fen·sor adj. offending
o·fer·tar v. to tender
o·fi·cial m. officer
o·fi·cia·li·dad f. officers
o·fi·cian·te m. officiant
o·fi·ci·na f. office
o·fi·ci·nis·ta m., f. office clerk
o·fi·cio m. work; office
o·fi·cio·so adj. obliging; diligent
o·fre·ci·mien·to m. offering
o·fren·da f. gift
o·fren·dar v. to give an offering for
of·tal·mo·lo·gí·a f. ophthalmology
of·tal·mó·lo·go m. ophthalmologist
o·fus·ca·ción f. confusion; dazzling
o·fus·car v . to bewilder; to blind
o·í·do m. ear
o·ír v. to listen; to hear; to attend

o•jal *m.* buttonhole
o•je•a•da *f.* glimpse
o•je•ri•za *f.* grudge
o•jo *m.* eye
o•jo•ta *f.* sandal
o•le•a•da *f.* wave
o•le•a•je *m.* waves
o•ler *v.* to smell
ol•fa•to *m.* instinct
ol•fa•to•rio, a *adj.* olfactory
o•li•va *f.* olive
o•li•var *f.* olive grove
o•li•vo *m.* olive tree
ol•mo *m.* elm tree
o•lor *m.* smell
o•lo•ro•so, a *adj.* fragrant
ol•vi•da, •da *adj.* forgetful; ungrateful
ol•vi•dar *v.* to omit; to forget; to leave out
ol•vi•do *m.* forgetfulness
o•lla *f.* kettle
om•bli•go *m.* navel
o•mi•sión *f.* omission
o•mi•tir *v.* to omit
óm•ni•bus *m.* omnibus
om•ni•po•ten•cia *f.* omnipotence
om•ni•po•ten•te *adj.* omnipotent
o•na•nis•mo *m.* onanism
on•ce *adj.* eleven
on•ce•no *adj.* eleventh
on•co•lon•gí•a *f.* oncology
on•dear *v.* to flutter; to ripple
on•du•la•ción *f.* undulation
on•du•lar *v.* to undulate
o•ne•ro•so, a *adj.* onerous
ó•nix *f.* onyx
o•no•ma•to•pe•ya *f.* onomatopoeia
on•za *f.* ounce
on•za•vo *adj.* eleventh
o•pa *adj.* foolish
o•pa•ci•dad *f.* opacity
o•pa•co, a *adj.* opaque
ó•pa•lo *m.* opal
op•ción *f.* option
op•cio•nal *adj.* optional
ó•pe•ra *f.* opera
o•pe•ra•ción *f.* operation

o•pe•ran•te *adj.* operating
o•pe•rar *v.* to operate
o•pe•ra•ti•vo, a *adj.* operative
o•pi•nión *f.* opinion
o•pio *m.* opium
o•po•ner *v.* to oppose
o•por•tu•na•men•te *adv.* opportunely
o•por•tu•ni•dad *f.* chance
o•por•tu•nis•ta *adj.* opportunist
o•por•tu•no, a *adj.* opportune; fitting
o•po•si•ción *f.* opposition
o•po•si•tor, a *m.*, *f.* opponent
o•pre•sión *f.* oppression
o•pre•si•vo, a *adj.* oppressive
o•pre•so, a *adj.* oppressed
o•pri•mi•do, a *adj.* oppressed
o•pri•mir *v.* to press; to oppress
o•pro•bio *m.* disgrace
o•pro•bio•so, a *adj.* disgraceful
op•tar *v.* to select
óp•ti•co, a *adj.* optical
op•ti•mis•ta *adj.* optimistic
óp•ti•mo, a *adj.* optimal
op•tó•me•tra *m.*, *f.* optometrist
op•to•me•trí•a *f.* optometry
o•pues•to *adj.* contrary; opposite
o•pu•len•cia *f.* opulence
o•ra *conj.* now
o•ra•ción *f.* oration; speech; sentence
o•rá•cu•lo *m.* oracle
o•ral *adj.* oral
o•ran•gu•tán *m.* orangutan
o•rar *v.* to speak; to pray
o•ra•to•rio, a *adj.* oratorical
or•be *m.* orb
or•den *m.* order
or•de•na•ción *f.* ordination; ordering
or•de•na•da *f.* ordinate
or•de•nar *v.* to command; to put into order
or•de•ñar *v.* to milk
or•di•nal *adj.* ordinal
or•di•na•riez *f.* ordinary; uncouth; coarse
o•re•ar *v.* to ventilate
or•fa•na•to *m.* orphanage
or•fe•li•na•to *m.* orphanage
or•gá•ni•co *adj.* organic

or·ga·nis·mo *m.* organism
or·ga·nis·ta *m.,f.* organist
or·ga·ni·za·dor, a *m., f.* organizer
or·ga·ni·zar *v.* to organize
ór·ga·no *m.* organ
or·gu·llo *m.* conceit
o·rien·ta·ción *f.* orientation
o·rien·tal *adj.* oriental
o·rien·tar *v.* to orient
o·ri·fi·cio *m.* opening
o·ri·gen *m.* source
o·ri·gi·nal *adj.* authentic; original; new
o·ri·gi·na·li·dad *f.* originality
o·ri·gi·nar *v.* to originate
o·ri·gi·na·ria·men·te *adv.* originally
o·ri·lla *f.* edge
o·ri·llar *v.* to edge
o·rín *m.* rust
o·ri·nal *m.* urinal
o·ri·nar *v.* to urinate
or·lar *v.* to edge
or·na·men·tal *adj.* ornamental
or·na·men·tar *v.* to ornament; to decorate
or·na·men·to *m.* ornament
or·nar *v.* to embellish
or·ni·tó·lo·go *m., f.* ornithologist
o·ro *m.* gold
or·ques·ta *f.* orchestra
or·ques·ta·ción *f.* orchestration
or·ques·tal *adj.* orchestral
or·ques·tar *v.* to orchestrate
or·quí·de·a *f.* orchid
or·ti·ga *f.* nettle
or·to·do·xo, a *adj.* orthodox
or·to·gra·fí·a *f.* orthographic
or·to·pe·dis·ta *m., f.* orthopedist
o·ru·ga *f.* caterpillar
o·ru·jo *m.* residue
os *pron.* you
o·sa·dí·a *f.* audacity
o·sa·do, a *adj.* daring
o·sa·men·ta *f.* bones
o·sar *v.* to dare
os·ci·la·ción *f.* wavering; swinging
os·ci·lar *v.* to oscillate; to swing

ós·cu·lo *m.* kiss
os·cu·re·cer *v.* to dim; to obscure; to shade
os·cu·re·ci·mien·to *m.* darkening
os·cu·ri·dad *f.* haziness; obscurity
os·cu·ro, a *adj.* unclear; dark, obscure
o·si·fi·car·se *v.* to ossify
ós·mo·sis *f.* osmosis
o·so *m.* bear
os·ten·si·ble *adj.* ostensible
os·ten·ta·ción *f.* ostentation
os·ten·tar *v.* to flaunt; to show
os·te·ó·lo·go, a *m., f.*
os·tra *f.* oyster
os·tra·cis·mo *m.* ostracism
o·te·ar *v.* to survey
o·to·ñal *adj.* autumnal
o·to·ño *m.* autumn
o·tor·gar *v.* to give; to grant
o·tro *adj.* other
o·va·ción *f.* ovation
o·va·cio·nar *v.* to give an ovation
o·val *adj.* oval
ó·va·lo *m.* oval
o·va·rio *m.* ovary
o·ve·ja *f.* the female sheep
o·ver·tu·ra *f.* overture
o·vi·llo *m.* snarl; ball
o·vi·no *m.* ovine
o·vu·la·ción *f.* ovulation
o·vu·lar *adj.* ovular
o·xi·da·ción *f.* oxidation
o·xi·dar *v.* to oxidize
ó·xi·do *m.* oxide
o·xi·ge·na·do, a *adj.* oxygenated
o·xi·ge·nar *v.* to give oxygen; to oxygenate
o·xí·ge·no *m.* oxygen
o·yen·te *adj.* listening *m., f.* listener
o·zo·no *m.* ozone

P

pa·be·llón *m.* banner; pavilion
pa·bi·lo *m.* candle wick

pá•bu•lo *m.* pabulum; support
pa•cer *v.* to graze
pa•cien•cia *f.* patience
pa•cien•te *adj.* patient
pa•ci•fi•ca•ción *f.* pacification
pa•ci•fi•ca•dor, a *m., f.* pacifier
pa•ci•fi•car *v.* to pacify
pa•cí•fi•co *adj.* pacific
pa•ci•fis•ta *adj.* pacifist
pa•cho•rra *f.* sluggishness
pa•de•cer *v.* to bear; to suffer; to endure
pa•dras•tro *m.* stepfather
pa•dre *m.* dad; father
pa•dri•llo *m.* stallion
pa•dri•no *m.* godfather
pa•ga *f.* payment
pa•ga•de•ro, a *adj.* payable
pa•ga•no, a *adj.* pagan
pa•gar *v.* to repay; to pay
pá•gi•na *f.* page
pa•gi•nar *v.* to paginate
pa•go *adj.* paid
país *m.* land
pai•sa•je *m.* landscape
pa•ja *f.* straw
pa•jar *m.* barn
pa•ja•re•ra *f.* cage for birds
pa•ja•re•rí•a *f.* bird store
pá•ja•ro *m.* bird
pa•la• *f.* blade; spade; shovelful
pa•la•bra *f.* word
pa•la•bre•o *m.* chatter
pa•la•cie•go, a *adj.* magnificent
pa•la•cio *m.* palace
pa•la•da *f.* shovelful
pa•la•de•ar *v.* to relish
pa•la•dio *m.* palladium
pa•la•fre•ne•ro *m.* groom
pa•lan•ca *f.* shaft; lever
pa•lan•ga•na *f.* washbasin
pa•le•ar *v.* to shovel
pa•le•on•to•lo•gí•a *f.* paleontology
pa•le•ta *f.* trowel; palette
pa•lia•ti•vo, a *adj.* palliative
pa•li•dez *f.* pallor
pá•li•do, a *adj.* pallid

pa•li•to *m.* small stick
pa•li•za *f.* thrashing
pal•ma *f.* palm
pal•ma•do, a *adj.* palm-shaped
pal•mar *m.* palm grove
pal•me•a•do, a *adj.* palm-shaped
pal•me•ar *v.* to applaud
pal•me•ra *f.* palm tree
pal•mo *m.* palm
pal•mo•te•ar *v.* to applaud
pa•lo *m.* pole; handle
pa•lo•ma *f.* pigeon
pa•lo•mi•ta *f.* popcorn
pa•lo•te *m.* drumstick
pal•pa•ble *adj.* palpable
pal•par *v.* to feel
pal•pi•ta•ción *f.* palpitation
pal•pi•tan•te *adj.* palpitating
pal•pi•tar *v.* to palpitate; to beat
pal•ta *f.* avocado
pa•lu•dis•mo *m.* malaria
pa•lur•do, a *m., f.* boor
pam•pa *f.* pampa
pan *m.* bread
pa•na *f.* corduroy
pa•na•de•rí•a *f.* bakery
pa•na•de•ro, a *m., f.* baker
pa•nal *m.* honeycomb
pán•cre•as *m.* pancreas
pan•cre•á•ti•co, a *adj.* pancreatic
pan•cho, a *adj.* unruffled
pan•da *f.* panda
pan•de•mo•nio *m.* pandemonium
pan•de•ro *m.* tambourine
pan•di•lla *f.* gang
pan•fle•to *m.* pamphlet
pa•no•ra•ma *f.* panorama
pa•no•rá•mi•co, a *adj.* panoramic
pan•ta•lo•nes *m.* slacks; pants
pan•ta•lla *f.* movie screen; lamp shade
pan•ta•no *m.* difficulty
pan•te•ón *m.* pantheon
pan•te•ra *f.* panther
pan•to•mi•ma *f.* pantomime
pan•to•rri•lla *f.* calf
pa•ño *m.* cloth

pa·ño·le·ta *f.* scarf
pa·ño·lón *m.* shawl
pa·ñue·lo *m.* handkerchief
pa·pá *f.* potato
pa·pa·ga·yo *m.* parrot
pa·pal *adj.* papal
pa·par *v.* to gape
pa·pa·ya *f.* papaya
pa·pel *m.* paper
pa·pe·le·ro, a *adj.* paper
pa·pe·le·ta *f.* card
pa·pe·ra *f.* goiter
pa·pi·la *f.* papilla
pa·pi·ro *m.* papyrus
pa·que·te *m.* packet; pack; package
pa·que·te·rí·a *f.* elegance
pa·qui·der·mo *m.* pachyderm
par *adj.* paired; equal
pa·ra *prep.* for; to; towards
pa·rá·bo·la *f.* parable
pa·ra·bri·sas *m.* windshield
pa·ra·di·sí·a·co, a *adj.* heavenly
pa·ra·do, a *adj.* stopped; stationary; idle
pa·ra·do·ja *f.* paradox
pa·ra·dó·ji·co, a *adj.* paradoxical
pa·ra·fi·na *f.* paraffin
pa·ra·guas *m.* umbrella
pa·ra·í·so *m.* paradise
pa·ra·je *m.* area
pa·ra·le·lo *m.* parallel
pa·ra·le·lo·gra·mo *m.* parallelogram
pa·rá·li·sis *f.* paralysis
pa·ra·lí·ti·co, a *adj.* paralytic
pa·ra·li·za·ción *f.* paralyzation
pa·ra·li·zar *v.* to paralyze
pa·ra·mé·di·co, a *adj.* paramedical
pa·rá·me·tro *m.* parameter
pa·ra·no·ia *f.* paranoia
pa·ra·noi·co, a *adj.* paranoid
pa·ra·plé·ji·co, a *adj.* paraplegic
pa·rar *v.* to halt; to check; to stop
pa·ra·sí·ti·co, a *adj.* parasitic
pa·rá·si·to, a *adj.* parasitic
pa·ra·sol *m.* parasol
par·ce·la *f.* parcel
par·cial *adj.* partial

par·cia·li·dad *f.* partiality
par·do *adj.* brown
pa·re·ar *v.* to pair
pa·re·cer *m.* view; appearance
pa·re·ci·do *adj.* similar
pa·red *f.* wall
pa·re·jo, a *adj.* equal; smooth; alike
pa·ren·te·la *f.* relatives
pa·ren·tes·co *m.* kinship
pa·rén·te·sis *m.* parenthesis
pa·ri·dad *f.* parity
pa·ri·ta·rio, a *adj.* joint
par·la·men·ta·rio *adj.* parliamentary
par·la·men·to *m.* parliament
par·lar *v.* to chatter
par·lo·te·o *m.* chatter
pa·ro *m.* unemployment
pa·ro·dia *f.* parody
pa·ro·dis·ta *m., f.* parodist
pa·ro·xis·mo *m.* paroxysm
par·pa·de·ar *v.* to twinkle
pár·pa·do *m.* eyelid
par·que *m.* park
par·que·o *m.* parking
par·que·dad *f.* moderation
pa·rra *f.* grapevine
pá·rra·fo *m.* paragraph
pa·rri·ci·dio *m.* parricide
pa·rro·quial *adj.* parochial
par·si·mo·nio·so, a *adj.* parsimonious
par·te *f.* share; part
par·te·ra *f.* midwife
par·ti·ción *f.* partition
par·ti·ci·pa·ción *f.* participation
par·ti·ci·par *adj.* to inform
par·tí·ci·pe *adj.* participating
par·tí·cu·la *f.* particle
par·ti·cu·lar *adj.* particular
par·ti·cu·la·ri·dad *f.* peculiarity
par·ti·cu·lar·men·te *adv.* particularly
par·ti·dis·ta *adj.* party
par·ti·da *adj.* group; leaving; departure
par·ti·do *m.* party
par·tir *v.* to depart; to leave
par·ti·ti·vo, a *adj.* partitive
par·ti·tu·ra *f.* score

pa·sa·di·zo *m.* passage
pa·sa·do *m.* past
pa·sa·dor *adj.* passing
pa·sa·je *m.* passage
pa·sa·por·te *m.* passport
pa·sar *v.* to elapse; to occur; to happen
pa·sa·tiem·po *m.* pastime
pa·se *m.* pass
pa·se·o *m.* stroll; outing
pa·sión *f.* passion
pa·so *m.* footstep; pace
pas·ta *f.* paste
pas·tel *m.* cake
pas·teu·ri·zar *v.* to pasteurize
pas·teu·ri·za·ción *f.* pasteurization
pas·to *m.* pasture; grass
pa·ta *f.* foot; leg; paw; female duck
pa·ta·da *f.* kick
pa·ta·ta *f.* potato
pa·te·ar *v.* to kick
pa·ten·tar *v.* to register
pa·ten·te *adj.* patent; evident; obvious
pa·ter·nal *adj.* paternal
pa·ter·ni·dad *f.* paternity
pa·ti·llas *f.* sideburns
pa·tín *m.* skate
pa·ti·nar *v.* to skate
pa·tio *m.* patio
pa·to *m.* duck
pa·tó·lo·go, a *m., f.* pathologist
pa·triar·ca *m.* patriarch
pa·trio·ta *m., f.* patriot
pa·trió·ti·co, a *adj.* patriotic
pa·tro·ci·nar *v.* to patronize
pa·trón *m.* host
pa·tro·nal *adj.* management
pa·tro·na·to *m.* patronage
pa·tru·llar *v.* to patrol
pau·la·ti·no, a *adj.* gradual
pau·sa *f.* interruption
pau·ta *f.* rule
pa·va·da *f.* foolishness
pa·vi·men·ta·ción *f.* paving
pa·vi·men·to *m.* pavement
pa·vo *m.* turkey
pa·vor *m.* terror

pa·ya·so *m.* clown
paz *f.* peace
paz·gua·to, a *adj.* foolish
pe·car *v.* to sin
pe·ce·ra *f.* aquarium
pec·ti·na *f.* pectin
pec·to·ral *adj.* pectoral
pe·cu·liar *adj.* peculiar
pe·cu·lia·ri·dad *f.* peculiarity
pe·cu·lio *m.* savings
pe·cu·nia *f.* money
pe·char *v.* to pay
pe·cho *m.* breast; chest
pe·dal *m.* pedal
pe·da·le·o *m.* pedaling
pe·dan·te·rí·a *f.* pedantry
pe·da·zo *m.* bit; piece
pe·der·nal *m.* flint
pe·des·tal *m.* pedestal
pe·des·tre *adj.* pedestrian
pe·dia·trí·a *f.* pediatrics
pe·di·gre·e *m.* pedigree
pe·dir *v.* to order; to beg; to charge
pe·dre·go·so, a *adj.* rocky
pe·dris·ca *f.* hail
pe·ga·di·zo, a *adj.* catching
pe·ga·jo·so, a *adj.* catching; adhesive
pe·gar *v.* to glue; to attach; to cleave
pei·na·do *m.* hairdresser
pei·ne *m.* comb
pe·la·do, a *adj.* bare; bald
pe·la·du·ra *f.* peeling
pe·la·gra *f.* pellagra
pe·lar *v.* to peel; to cut
pe·le·a·dor *adj.* fighting
pe·lí·ca·no *m.* pelican
pe·lí·cu·la *f.* film; movie
pe·li·gro *m.* danger
pe·li·gro·so *adj.* dangerous
pe·lo *m.* fur; hair
pe·lo·ta *f.* ball
pel·tre *m.* pewter
pe·lu·ca *f.* wig
pe·lu·do, a *adj.* shaggy
pel·vis *f.* pelvis
pe·lliz·car *v.* to nibble

pe·llón *m.* sheepskin
pe·na *f.* anxiety; penalty; distress
pe·na·cho *m.* crest
pe·na·do, a *adj.* grieved
pe·na·li·zar *v.* to penalize
pe·nar *v.* to punish
pen·den·ciar *v.* to quarrel; to argue
pen·der *v.* to hover
pen·dien·te *adj.* hanging
pe·ne·tra·ble *adj.* penetrable
pe·ne·tra·ción *f.* penetration
pe·ne·tran·te *adj.* piercing; penetrating
pe·ne·trar *v.* to pierce; to penetrate
pe·ni·ci·li·na *f.* penicillin
pe·nín·su·la *f.* peninsula
pe·ni·que *m.* penny
pe·ni·ten·cia *f.* penitence
pe·ni·ten·te *adj.* penitent
pe·no·so *adj.* grievous; wearing
pen·sa·mien·to *m.* thought
pen·san·te *adj.* thinking
pen·sar *v.* to think about
pen·sa·ti·vo *adj.* thoughtful; pensive
pen·sio·nar *v.* to pension
pe·ña *f.* circle
pe·ñas·co·so, a *adj.* rocky
pe·or *adj.* worse
pe·pi·no *m.* cucumber
pép·ti·co, a *adj.* peptic
pe·que·ño *adj.* tiny; small
pe·ra *f.* pear
pe·ral *m.* pear tree
per·cep·ción *f.* perception
per·cep·ti·vo, a *adj.* perceptive
per·ci·bir *v.* to sense; to perceive
per·cu·dir *v.* to dull
per·cu·sión *f.* percussion
per·cu·tir *v.* to percuss
per·cha *f.* hanger; prop
per·der *v.* to waste; to lose
pér·di·da *f.* waste
per·di·do *adj.* missing
per·diz *f.* partridge
per·dón *m.* pardon
per·do·nar *v.* to remit; to excuse; to pardon

per·du·rar
pe·re·cer *v.* to
pe·re·gri·na·ción
pe·re·jil *m.* parsley
pe·ren·ne *adj.* perennial
pe·re·za *f.* laziness
pe·re·zo·so, a *adj.* lazy
per·fec·ción *f.* perfection
per·fec·cio·nar *v.* to make something perfect
per·fec·cio·nis·ta *adj.* perfectionist
per·fec·to *adj.* perfect
pér·fi·do, a *adj.* unfaithful
per·fi·lar *v.* to profile
per·fo·ra·ción *f.* perforation
per·fi·lar *v.* to profile
per·fo·ra·ción *f.* perforation
per·fo·ra·dor *adj.* perforating
per·fo·rar *v.* to perforating
per·fo·rar *v.* to perforate
per·fu·mar *v.* to perfume
per·fu·me *m.* perfume
per·fu·me·rí·a *f.* perfumery
pe·ri·car·dio *m.* pericardium
pe·ri·cia *f.* skill
pe·ri·co *m.* parakeet
pe·rí·me·tro *m.* perimeter
pe·rió·di·ca·men·te *adv.* periodically
pe·rió·di·co *m.* periodical
pe·rio·dis·mo *m.* journalism
pe·rio·dis·ta *m., f.* journalist
pe·río·do *m.* period
pe·ri·qui·to *m.* parakeet
pe·ris·co·pio *m.* periscope
pe·rís·to·le *f.* peristalsis
pe·ri·to·ne·o *m.* peritoneum
per·ju·di·car *v.* to harm
per·ju·di·cial *adj.* harmful
per·ju·rio *m.* perjury
per·la *f.* pearl
per·ma·ne·cer *v.* to remain
per·ma·nen·te *adj.* permanent
per·mi·si·ble *adj.* permissible
per·mi·si·vo *adj.* permissive
per·mi·so *m.* consent
per·mi·tir *v.* to allow; to give; to permit

permutar

mu·tar *v.* to exchange
per·ni·cio·so, a *adj.* pernicious
per·no *m.* pin
pe·ro *conj.* but
pe·ro·né *m.* fibula
pe·ró·xi·do *m.* peroxide
per·pe·tra·ción *f.* perpetration
per·ple·ji·dad *f.* perplexity
per·ple·jo, a *adj.* perplexed
pe·rro *m.* dog
per·se·cu·ción *f.* persecution
per·se·guir *v.* to follow; to hound; to pursue
per·se·ve·ran·cia *f.* perseverance
per·se·ve·ran·te *adj.* persevering
per·sia·na *f.* blind
per·sig·nar *v.* to cross
per·sis·ten·cia *f.* persistence
per·sis·tir *v.* to cross
per·sis·ten·cia *f.* persistence
per·sis·tir *v.* to persist
per·so·na *f.* person
per·so·na·li·dad *f.* personality
per·so·na·li·zar *v.* to personalize
per·so·ni·fi·ca·ción *f.* personification
pers·pec·ti·va *f.* perspective
per·sua·dir *v.* to persuade
per·sua·sión *f.* persuasion
per·sua·si·vo, a *adj.* persuasive
per·te·ne·cer *v.* to belong
per·te·ne·cien·te *adj.* pertaining
per·ti·nen·cia *f.* relevancy; relevance
per·ti·nen·te *adj.* relevant
per·tre·char *v.* to equip
per·tur·ba·ción *f.* disturbance
per·tur·bar *v.* to upset
per·ver·si·dad *f.* perversity
per·ver·sión *f.* perversion
per·ver·ti·do, a *adj.* perverted
pe·sa·di·lla *f.* nightmare
pe·sa·do *adj.* dull; heavy; boring
pe·sar *v.* to grieve
pes·ca *f.* fishing
pes·ca·de·rí·a *f.* fish market
pes·ca·di·lla *f.* whiting
pes·ca·do *m.* fish

pes·ca·dor *m.* fisherman
pes·car *v.* to fish
pe·se·bre *f.* manger
pe·si·mis·ta *adj.* pessimistic
pe·so *m.* weight
pes·que·ro, a *adj.* fishing
pes·ta·ña *f.* eyelash
pes·ta·ñe·ar *v.* to wink
pes·ta·ñe·o *m.* winking
pes·te *f.* plague
pé·ta·lo *m.* petal
pe·ti·ción *f.* petition
pé·tre·o, a *adj.* rocky
pe·tri·fi·car *v.* to petrify
pe·tró·le·o *m.* petroleum
pe·tu·lan·cia *f.* arrogance
pe·tu·lan·te *adj.* arrogant
pe·tu·nia *f.* petunia
pez *m.* fish
pia·nis·ta *m., f.* pianist
pia·no *m.* piano
piar *v.* to chirp
pi·can·te *adj.* spicy
pi·car *v.* to sting; to chip; to bite
pi·ca·res·co, a *adj.* mischievous
pí·ca·ro, a *adj.* wicked; sly
pi·ca·zón *f.* itching
pi·co *m.* spout; beak
pi·cor *m.* itching
pi·co·te·ar *v.* to pick; to peck
pic·tó·ri·co, a *adj.* pictorial
pie *m.* foot
pie·dra *f.* stone
piel *f.* fur; skin
pie·za *f.* piece
pi·fiar *v.* to miscue
pig·men·tar *v.* to pigment
pig·me·o *adj.* pygmy
pi·ja·ma *m.* pajamas
pi·lar *m.* pillar
pi·le·ta *f.* sink
pi·lo·tar *v.* to pilot
pi·lo·to *m.* pilot
pi·llar *v.* to plunder
pi·llue·lo, a *adj.* mischievous
pi·men·tón *m.* paprika**

pi•mien•ta *f.* pepper

pim•pan•te *adj.* spruce; graceful

pi•ná•cu•lo *m.* pinnacle

pi•nar *m.* pine grove

pin•cel *m.* brush

pin•cha•du•ra *f.* puncture

pin•char *v.* to puncture

pin•gui•no *m.* penguin

pi•no *m.* pine

pin•tar *v.* to paint

pin•to, a *adj.* speckled

pin•tor, a *m., f.* painter

pin•to•res•co, a *adj.* picturesque

pin•tu•ra *f.* painting

pi•ña *f.* pine cone

pio•jo *m.* louse

pio•la *f.* cord

pi•pa *f.* barrel

pi•pe•ta *f.* pipette

pi•que•ta *f.* pick

pi•que•te *m.* picket

pi•ra•mi•dal *adj.* pyramidal

pi•rá•mi•de *f.* pyramid

pi•ra•ta *m.* pirate

pi•ri•ta *f.* pyrites

pi•rue•ta *f.* pirouette

pi•sa•da *f.* footprint

pi•sar *v.* to walk upon

pis•ci•na *f.* swimming pool

pi•so *m.* story; flat

pi•són *m.* tamper

pi•so•te•ar *v.* to trample

pis•ta *f.* runway; trial

pis•ta•cho *m.* pistachio

pis•to•la *f.* pistol

pis•tón *m.* piston

pi•ti•do *m.* whistle

pi•ti•llo *m.* cigarette

pi•to *m.* whistle

pi•tón *m.* python

pi•to•ni•sa *f.* fortune-teller

pi•tui•ta•rio, a *adj.* pituitary

pi•vo•te *m.* pivot

pla•ca *f.* plaque

pla•ce•bo *m.* placebo

pla•cen•te•ro, a *adj.* pleasant; agreeable

pla•cer *m.* gratification; pleasure

plá•ci•do *adj.* placid

pla•gar *v.* to plague

plan *m.* scheme; plan

plan•cha *f.* sheet

plan•cha•do, a *adj.* ironing

plan•char *v.* to iron

pla•ne•ar *v.* to plan

pla•ne•ta *f.* planet

pla•ne•ta•rio, a *adj.* planetary

pla•ni•cie *f.* plain

pla•ni•fi•ca•ción *f.* planning

pla•ni•fi•car *v.* to plan

pla•no *adj.* plane

plan•ear *v.* to start; to expound; to plan

pla•ña•do *m.* lament

plan•tar *v.* to plant

plas•ma *f.* plasma

plas•mar *v.* to mold

plás•ti•co, a *adj.* plastic

plas•ti•fi•car *v.* to shellac

pla•ta *f.* silver

pla•ta•for•ma *f.* platform

plá•ta•no *m.* banana

pla•te•ar *v.* to silver-plate

pla•te•ro *m.* silversmith

pla•ti•car *v.* to talk

pla•ti•no *m.* platinum

pla•to *m.* dish; plate

pla•tó•ni•co, a *adj.* platonic

plau•si•ble *adj.* plausible

pla•ya *f.* beach

ple•ga•ble *adj.* collapsible

ple•ga•do *m.* folding

ple•gar *v.* to fold; to bend; to pleat

pleu•re•sí•a *f.* pleurisy

pli•sa•do *m.* pleat

plo•me•ro *m.* plumber

plo•mo, a *adj.* lead

plu•ma *f.* pen; feather

plu•ral *adj.* plural

plu•ra•li•dad *f.* plurality

plu•ra•li•zar *v.* to pluralize

plu•to•nio *m.* plutonium

po•bla•ción *f.* population, town

po•bla•do *m.* village

po•blar *v.* to populate
po•bre *adj.* poor
po•bre•za *f.* poverty
po•ción *f.* potion
po•co *adv.* little
po•dar *v.* to prune
po•der *v.* to be able; can
po•de•rí•o *m.* power
po•di•a•tra *m.* podiatrist
poe•ma *m.* poem
po•e•sí•a *f.* poetry
po•e•ta *m.* poet
poé•ti•co *adj.* poetical
po•e•ti•sa *f.* poetess
pó•ker *m.* poker
po•lar *m.* polar
po•la•ri•za•ción *f.* polarization
po•la•ri•zar *v.* to polarize
po•len *m.* pollen
po•li•cí•a *f.* constable; police
po•li•cial *adj.* police
po•li•fo•ní•a *f.* polyphony
po•lí•go•no *m.* polygon
po•li•lla *f.* moth
po•li•ni•za•ción *f.* pollination
po•li•no•mio *m.* polynomial
pó•li•po *m* polyp
po•lí•ti•ca *f.* policy
po•lí•ti•co *adj.* political
po•li•ti•zar *v.* to politicize
po•lo *m.* pole
pol•trón, a *adj.* lazy
po•lu•ción *f.* pollution
pol•vo *m.* powder
po•llo *m.* chicken
po•ma•da *f.* pomade
pom•pa *f.* pomp
pom•po•si•dad *f.* pomposity
pom•po•so, a *adj.* pompous
pon•che *m.* punch
pon•cho *m.* poncho
pon•de•ra•ble *adj.* ponderable
pon•de•rar *v.* to consider
po•ner *v.* to place; to don
pon•ti•fi•car *v.* to pontificate
pon•zo•ño•so, a *adj.* poisonous

po•pu•la•cho *m.* masses
po•pu•lar *adj.* popular
po•pu•la•ri•dad *f.* popularity
po•pu•la•ri•zar *v.* to popularize
po•pu•rrí *m.* potpourri
po•quer *m.* poker
por *prep.* from; via; for
por•cen•ta•je *m.* percentage
por•cen•tual *adj.* percentage
por•ción *f.* part; portion
por•che *m.* porch
por•fia•do, a *adj.* stubborn
po•ro•si•dad *f.* porosity
po•ro•so, a *adj.* porous
por•que *conj.* because
por•qué *m.* why
por•tal *m.* porch
por•tá•til *adj.* portable
por•ten•to•so, a *adj.* marvelous
por•ve•nir *m.* future
po•sar *v.* to rest; to lodge
pos•da•ta *f.* postscripts
po•se•er *v.* to have
po•se•í•do, a *adj.* possessed
po•se•si•vo, a *adj.* possessive
po•se•so, a *adj.* possessed
pos•fe•cha *f.* postdate
po•si•bi•li•tar *v.* to make something
   possible
po•si•ble *adj.* possible
po•si•ción *f.* place; status
pos•po•ner *v.* to postpone
pos•ta *f.* slice
pos•tal *adj.* postal
pos•te *m.* post
pos•te•ga•ción *f.* postponement
pos•te•gar *v.* to postpone
pos•te•rior *adj.* posterior
pos•te•rio•ri•dad *f.* posteriority
pos•ti•zo, a *adj.* artificial
post•o•pe•ra•to•rio, a *adj.* postoperative
pos•tor *m.* bidder
pos•trar *v.* to debilitate; to humiliate
pos•tre *m.* dessert
pos•tre•ro, a *adj.* final
pos•tu•ra *f.* posture

po·ta·ble *adj.* potable
po·ta·sio *m.* potassium
po·te *m.* pot
po·ten·cia *f.* potency
po·ten·cial *adj.* potential
po·ten·ta·do *m.* potentate
po·ten·te *adj.* potent; powerful
po·tre·ar *v.* to frolic
po·tre·ro *m.* pasture
po·tri·llo *m.* colt
po·tro *m.* colt
prác·ti·ca *f.* custom; practice
prac·ti·car *v.* to practice
prác·ti·co *adj.* practical
pra·de·ra *f.* meadow
pre·ám·bu·lo *m.* preamble
pre·ca·rio, a *adj.* precarious
pre·cau·ción *f.* precaution
pre·ca·vi·do, a *adj.* cautious
pre·ce·den·te *adj.* preceding
pre·ce·der *v.* to forgo
pre·cep·to *m.* precept
pre·cep·tor, a *m., f.* tutor
pre·cin·ta·do, a *adj.* sealed
pre·cin·tar *v.* to stamp
pre·cio *m.* fare; cost; price
pre·cio·si·dad *f.* beauty
pre·cio·so *adj.* precious
pre·ci·pi·ta·ción *f.* precipitation
pre·ci·pi·tar *v.* to hasten
pre·ci·sa·men·te *adj.* precisely
pre·ci·sar *v.* to set; to explain
pre·ci·sión *f.* precision
pre·co·ci·dad *f.* precocity
pre·cog·ni·ción *f.* precognition
pre·con·ce·bir *v.* to preconceive
pre·co·ni·zar *v.* to recommend something
pre·coz *adj.* precocious
pre·de·ce·sor, a *m., f.* predecessor
pre·de·cir *v.* to foretell
pre·des·ti·na·ción *f.* predestination
pre·de·ter·mi·nar *v.* to predetermine
pré·di·ca *f.* sermon
pre·di·ca·do *m.* predicate
pre·di·car *v.* to preach
pre·dic·ción *f.* prediction

pre·di·lec·to, a *adj.* favorite
pre·dio *m.* property
pre·dis·po·ner *v.* to predispose
pre·dis·po·si·ción *f.* predisposition
pre·do·mi·nan·te *adj.* predominant
pre·do·mi·nar *v.* to prevail
pre·do·mi·nio *m.* predominate
pre·fa·bri·ca·do, a *adj.* prefabricated
pre·fa·bri·car *v.* to prefabricate
pre·fa·cio *m.* preface
pre·fec·tu·ra *f.* prefecture
pre·fe·ren·te *adj.* preferable
pre·fe·ren·te·men·te *adv.* preferably
pre·fe·ri·do *adj.* preferred
pre·fe·rir *v.* to prefer
pre·go·nar *v.* to divulge; to proclaim
pre·gun·ta *f.* question
pre·gun·tar *v.* to ask; to question
pre·his·to·ria *f.* prehistory
pre·his·tó·ri·co, a *adj.* prehistoric
pre·juz·gar *v.* to prejudge
pre·lu·dio *m.* prelude
pre·ma·tu·ro, a *adj.* premature
pre·me·di·ta·ción *f.* premeditation
pre·me·di·ta·da·men·te *adv.*
    deliberately
pre·me·di·tar *v.* to premeditate
pre·miar *v.* to reward
pre·mio *m.* prize
pre·mi·sa *f.* premise
pre·mo·ni·ción *f.* premonition
pre·mu·ra *f.* urgency
pre·na·tal *adj.* prenatal
pren·da *f.* token; guaranty
pren·der *v.* to catch
pren·sa *f.* press
pren·sar *v.* to press
pre·nup·cial *adj.* prenuptial
pre·ñez *f.* pregnancy
pre·o·cu·pa·ción *f.* concern
pre·o·cu·par *v.* to mind; to occupy
pre·pa·rar *v.* to ready; to fix
pre·pon·de·ran·te *adj.* preponderant
pre·po·si·ción *f.* preposition
pre·po·ten·cia *f.* power; dominance
pre·po·ten·te *adj.* powerful; dominant

prepucio

pre·pu·cio *m.* prepuce
pre·sa *f.* victim; capture
pres·cin·den·cia *f.* omission
pres·cin·di·ble *adj.* nonessential
pres·cin·dir *v.* to ignore
pres·cri·bir *v.* to prescribe
pre·sen·cia *f.* presence
pre·sen·ciar *v.* to witness
pre·sen·ta·ción *f.* presentation
pre·sen·tar *v.* to introduce; to feature
pre·sen·te *adj.* current
pre·ser·va·ción *f.* preserve
pre·ser·va·ti·vo, a *adj.* preservative
pre·si·den·cia *f.* presidency
pre·si·den·cial *adj.* presidential
pre·si·den·ta *f.* president
pre·si·den·te *m.* president
pre·si·dia·rio *m.* convict
pre·si·dio *m.* prison
pre·si·dir *v.* to preside
pre·sión *f.* pressure
pres·ta·ción *f.* services
pres·ta·dor, a *adj.* lending
pres·ta·men·te *adj.* quickly
prés·ta·mo *m.* loan
pres·tar *v.* to loan
pres·te·za *f.* promptness
pres·ti·gio *m.* prestige
pres·ti·gio·so, a *adj.* prestigious
pres·to, a *adj.* prompt
pre·su·mi·ble *adj.* presumable
pre·su·mir *v.* to presume
pre·sun·ción *f.* presumption
pre·sun·tuo·so, a *adj.* presumptuous
pre·su·po·ner *v.* to presuppose
pre·su·po·si·ción *f.* presupposition
pre·su·pues·ta·rio, a *adj.* budgetary
pre·su·ri·zar *v.* to pressurize
pre·ten·cio·so, a *adj.* pretentious
pre·ten·der *v.* to attempt; to pretend
pre·ten·dien·te *adj.* pretending to
pre·ten·sión *f.* desire
pre·ten·sio·so, a *adj.* pretentious
pre·va·le·cer *v.* to prevail
pre·ven·ción *f.* prevention
pre·ve·nir *v.* to prepare; to prevent

pre·ven·ti·vo, a *adj.* preventive
prez *m.* glory
pri·ma, o *f., m.* cousin
pri·ma·rio, a *adj.* primary
pri·ma·te *m.* primate
pri·ma·ve·ra *f.* spring
pri·mo *adj.* prime; first
pri·mi·ti·vo *adj.* primitive
pri·mo·ro·so *adj.* delicate; exquisite
prin·ce·sa *f.* princess
prin·ci·pa·do *m.* principality
prin·ci·pal *adj.* leading; master; principal
prin·ci·pal·men·te *adv.* principally
prín·ci·pe *m.* prince
prin·ci·pes·co, a *adj.* princely
prin·ci·piar *v.* to begin
prin·ci·pio *m.* beginning
prin·go·so, a *adj.* greasy
prio·ri·dad *f.* priority
pri·sa *f.* haste
pri·sión *f.* prison
pri·sio·ne·ro, a *m., f.* prisoner
pris·ma *m.* prism
prís·ti·no, a *adj.* pristine
pri·va·do *adj.* private
pri·va·ti·zar *v.* to privatize
pri·vi·le·gio *m.* privilege
pro·ba·bi·li·dad *f.* probability
pro·ba·ble *adj.* probable
pro·bar *v.* to prove; to try
pro·bi·dad *f.* probity
pro·ble·ma *m.* problem
pro·ble·má·ti·co, a *adj.* problematic
pro·bo, a *adj.* upright
pro·ce·di·mien·to *m.* procedure
pro·ce·sar *v.* to prosecute
pro·ce·sión *m.* action
pro·cla·ma·ción *f.* proclamation
pro·cla·mar *v.* to announce; to proclaim
pro·cre·a·ción *f.* procreation
pro·cre·ar *v.* to produce; to procreate
pro·di·gar *v.* to waste
pró·di·go *adj.* lavish; spendthrift
pro·di·gio·so, a *adj.* marvelous
pro·duc·ción *f.* turnout; production
pro·du·cir *v.* to yield; to produce

pro·duc·ti·vi·dad *f.* productivity
pro·duc·ti·vo, a *adj.* productive
pro·duc·to, a *m.* product
pro·fa·nar *v.* to disgrace
pro·fe·sar *v.* to teach; to practice
pro·fe·sión *f.* vocation; job; profession
pro·fe·sio·nal *adj.* professional
pro·fe·sor, a *m., f.* professor; teacher
pro·fi·la·xis *f.* prophylaxis
pro·fun·di·dad *f.* profundity
pro·fun·do, a *adj.* profound; deep
pro·fu·sión *f.* profusion
pro·fu·so, a *adj.* profuse
pro·gra·ma *m.* program
pro·gra·ma·ción *f.* programming
pro·gra·mar *v.* to program
pro·gre·sar *v.* to progress
pro·gre·sión *f.* progress
pro·gre·sis·ta *adj.* progressive
pro·gre·so *m.* progress
pro·hi·bi·ción *f.* prohibition
pro·hi·bi·do, a *adj.* forbidden
pro·hi·bir *v.* to prohibit something
pro·hi·bi·ti·vo, a *adj.* prohibitive
pro·li·fe·ra·ción *f.* proliferation
pro·li·fe·rar *v.* to proliferate
pro·lí·fi·co, a *adj.* prolific
pró·lo·go *m.* prologue
pro·lon·ga·do, a *adj.* prolonged
pro·lon·gar *v.* to lengthen
pro·me·dio *m.* average
pro·me·sa *f.* vow; promise
pro·me·te·dor, a *adj.* promising
pro·me·ter *v.* to promise
pro·mi·nen·te *adj.* prominent
pro·mi·so·rio, a *adj.* promising
pro·mo·ción *f.* promotion
pro·mo·cio·nar *v.* to promote
pro·mo·ve·dor, a *adj.* promoting
pro·mo·ver *v.* to promote
pro·no, ·na *adj.* prone
pro·no·mi·nal *adj.* pronominal
pro·nos·ti·car *v.* to predict
pron·ti·tud *f.* promptness
pron·to *adj.* prompt
pro·nun·cia·ción *f.* pronunciation

pro·nun·ciar *v.* to pronounce
pro·pa·ga·ción *f.* propagation
pro·pa·lar *v.* to divulge
pro·pen·so, a *adj.* prone
pro·pie·dad *f.* estate
pro·pi·na *f.* gratuity
pro·pio *adj.* proper
pro·po·ne·dor, a *adj.* proposing
pro·po·ner *v.* to intend
pro·por·ción *f.* proportion
pro·por·cio·nal *adj.* proportional
pro·po·si·ción *f.* motion; proposition
pro·pó·si·to *m.* purpose; intention
pro·pues·ta *f.* proposal
pro·pug·nar *v.* to push
pro·pul·sión *f.* propulsion
pro·rra·te·ar *v.* to extend
pro·sa *f.* prose
pro·sai·co, a *adj.* prosaic
pros·cri·bir *v.* to proscribe
pros·crip·ción *f.* proscription
pros·pec·to *m.* prospectus
pros·pe·rar *v.* to thrive; to prosper
pros·pe·ri·dad *f.* prosperity
prós·pe·ro, a *adj.* prosperous
prós·ta·ta *f.* prostate
pros·ti·tu·ción *f.* prostitution
pro·tec·ción *f.* protection
pro·tec·tor, a *adj.* supporting; protective
pro·te·ger *v.* to defend; to protect
pro·te·í·na *f.* protein
pro·tes·ta *f.* protest
pro·tes·tar *v.* to protest
pro·tes·to *m.* protest
pro·tón *m.* proton
pro·to·ti·po *m.* prototype
pro·ve·cho *m.* profit; benefit
pro·ve·cho·so *adj.* profitable
pro·veer *v.* to cater; to fill; to provide
pro·vi·den·cial *adj.* providential
pro·vi·sión *f.* provision
pro·vo·ca·ción *f.* provocation
pro·vo·car *v.* to antagonize
próx·i·mo *adj.* near
pru·den·cia *f.* prudence
psi·co·lo·gí·a *f.* psychology

pu·bli·ca·ción *f.* publication
pu·bli·car *v.* to publish
pú·bli·co *m.* public
pue·blo *m.* nation; town
puer·ta *f.* entrance
pues *conj.* then; for
pul·gar *m.* thumb
pu·lir *v.* to shine; to polish
pul·món *m.* lung
pun·ta *m.* dot; point
pu·ro *adj.* pure
púr·pu·ra *f.* purple

Q

quan·tum *m.* quantum
que *pron.* that; whom
qué *adj.* what; which
que·bra·da *f.* gap; ravine
que·bra·di·zo, a *adj.* fragile
que·bra·do *adj.* rough; broken; bankrupt
que·bra·du·ra *f.* rupture; fracture; crack
que·bra·jar *v.* to crack
que·bran·ta·dor, a *adj.* crushing; breaking
que·bran·to *m.* sorrow; loss
que·brar *v.* to break
que·da·men·te *adv.* calmly
que·dar *v.* to stay; to be; to remain
que·jar·se *v.* to complain; to whine
que·ji·do *m.* groan
que·jo·so *adj.* complaining
que·ma *f.* burning
que·ma·de·ro *m.* incinerator
que·ma·do, a *adj.* burnt; burned out
que·ma·zón *f.* burning
que·re·lla *f.* lament; quarrel
que·re·llan·te *adj.* complaining
que·rer *v.* to desire; to want; to love
que·ri·do, a *adj.* beloved
que·so *m.* cheese
quie·bra *f.* crack
quien *pron.* who
quie·to, a *adj.* quiet

quí·mi·ca *f.* chemistry
quí·mi·co *adj.* chemical
quin·ce *adj.* fifteen
quin·to *adj.* fifth
qui·tar *v.* to remove; to take away

R

rá·ba·no *m.* radish
ra·bí *m.* rabbi
ra·bia *f.* rabies
ra·biar *v.* to have rabies; to rage
ra·bi·no *m.* rabbi
ra·bio·so *adj.* furious
ra·bo *m.* stern; tail
ra·cial *adj.* racial
ra·ci·mo *m.* bunch; cluster
ra·ción *f.* allowance; ration
ra·cio·nal *adj.* rational
ra·cio·na·li·dad *f.* rationality
ra·cio·na·lis·mo *m.* rationalism
ra·cio·na·lis·ta *adj.* rationalist
ra·cio·na·li·zar *v.* to rationalize about
ra·cio·nar *v.* to ration
ra·cha *f.* gust
ra·da *f.* bay
ra·dar *m.* radar
ra·dia·ción *f.* radiation
ra·diac·ti·vi·dad *f.* radioactivity
ra·diac·ti·vo, a *adj.* radioactive
ra·dia·dor *m.* radiator
ra·dial *adj.* radial
ra·dian·te *adj.* radiant
ra·diar *v.* to radiate
ra·di·cal *adj.* radical
ra·dio *m.* radio; radius
ra·dio·di·fun·dir *v.* to broadcast
ra·dio·gra·fí·a *f.* radiography; x-ray
ra·dio·gra·ma *f.* radiogram
ra·dio·lo·gí·a *f.* radiology
ra·dió·lo·go, ·ga *m., f.* radiologist
ra·dios·co·pia *f.* radioscopy
ra·er *v.* to scrape
ra·í·do, a *adj.* worn

ra•ja *f.* split; crack
ra•ja•du•ra *f.* crack
ra•jar *v.* to sliver; to crack
ra•lo, a *adj.* thin
ra•llar *v.* to grate
ra•ma *f.* branch
ra•ma•da *f.* grove
ra•mal *m.* flight; strand
ram•bla *f.* boulevard
ra•mi•fi•ca•ción *f.* ramification
ra•mi•fi•car•se *v.* to branch
ra•mi•lle•te *m.* cluster
ra•mo *m.* bouquet
ra•mo•ne•ar *v.* to graze
ram•pa *f.* ramp
ra•na *f.* frog
ran•ci•dez *f.* rancidity
ra•par *v.* to crop; to shave
rá•pi•da•men•te *adv.* rapidly
rá•pi•do *adj.* fast; express; rapid
rap•so•dia *f.* rhapsody
rap•to *m.* rapture
ra•que•ta *f.* racket
ra•qui•tis•mo *m.* rickets
ra•ra•men•te *adv.* rarely
ra•re•za *f.* rarity
ra•ro *adj.* rare; bizarre; odd
ra•sar *v.* to brush
ras•ca•cie•los *m.* skyscraper
ras•ca•du•ra *f.* scratch
ras•car *v.* to scrape
ras•ca•zón *f.* itch
ras•ga•du•ra *f.* tear
ras•gar *v.* to tear
ras•gu•ñar *v.* to scratch
ras•gu•ño *m.* scratch
ra•so, a *adj.* level; flat
ras•pa•dor *m.* scraper
ras•pa•du•ra *f.* rasping
ras•pan•te *adj.* abrasive
ras•par *v.* to erase; to scrape
ras•tra *f.* trail
ras•tre•ar *v.* to trail
ras•tri•llo *m.* rake
ra•su•ra *f.* shaving
ra•su•rar *v.* to shave

ra•ta *f.* rat
ra•te•ro, a *m., f.* thief
ra•ti•fi•ca•to•rio, a *adj.* ratifying
ra•to *m.* while
ra•tón *m.* mouse
ra•ya *f.* stripe; line
ra•yar *v.* to rule; to streak
ra•yo *m.* beam; ray
ra•yón *m.* rayon
ra•za *f.* race
ra•zón *f.* cause
ra•zo•na•ble *adj.* rational; reasonable
ra•zo•na•do, a *adj.* reasoned
ra•zo•nar *v.* to reason
re•ac•ción *f.* reaction
re•ac•cio•nar *v.* to react
re•ac•ti•va•ción *f.* reactivation
re•ac•ti•var *v.* to reactivate
re•a•dap•ta•ción *f.* readaptation
re•a•dap•tar *v.* to readapt
re•a•fir•mar *v.* to reaffirm
re•a•jus•tar *v.* to readjust
real *adj.* true; real; royal
re•a•le•za *f.* royalty
rea•li•dad *f.* reality
rea•lis•ta *adj.* realistic
re•a•li•za•dor, a *adj.* fulfilling
rea•li•zar *v.* to accomplish; to realize
re•al•zar *v.* to enhance
re•a•ni•mar *v.* to reanimate
re•a•nu•da•ción *f.* resumption
re•a•nu•dar *v.* to resume
re•a•pa•re•cer *v.* to reappear
rea•ta *f.* rope
re•a•vi•var *v.* to revive
re•ba•ja *f.* reduction
re•ba•jar *v.* to reduce
re•ba•na•da *f.* slice
re•ba•nar *v.* to slice
re•ba•ño *m.* flock
re•be•lar•se *v.* to rebel; to revolt
re•bel•de *adj.* rebel
re•be•lión *f.* revolt
re•bor•de *m.* border
re•bo•tar *v.* to bounce
re•buz•no *m.* braying

re·ca·bar *v.* to request
re·ca·do *m.* message
re·ca·er *v.* to relapse
re·cal·car *v.* to squeeze
re·ca·len·ta·mien·to *m.* reheating
re·ca·len·tar *v.* to reheat
re·ca·pa·ci·tar *v.* to reconsider
re·ca·pi·tu·la·ción *m.* recapitulation
re·ca·pi·tu·lar *v.* to recapitulate
re·car·gar *v.* to overload; to reload
re·cau·dar *v.* to collect
re·cau·do *m.* collection
re·ce·lar *v.* to suspect
re·ce·lo *m.* jealousy; mistrust; suspicion
re·ce·lo·so, a *adj.* suspicious
re·cep·ción *f.* reception
re·cep·cio·nis·ta *m., f.* receptionist
re·cep·ti·vo *adj.* receptive
re·ce·tar *v.* to prescribe
re·ci·bi·dor, a *adj.* receiving
re·ci·bi·mien·to *m.* reception
re·ci·bir *v.* to accept; to receive
re·ci·bo *m.* receipt
re·ci·clar *v.* to recycle
re·cien·te *adj.* recent
re·cien·te·men·te *adv.* recently
re·cio, a *adj.* severe; strong
re·ci·pro·car *v.* to reciprocate
re·ci·pro·ci·dad *f.* reciprocity
re·ci·ta·ción *f.* complaint
re·cla·ma·dor *adj.* claiming
re·cla·mar *v.* to reclaim
re·cli·nar *v.* to rest on
re·cluir *v.* to imprison
re·clu·sión *f.* imprisonment
re·clu·so *m.* recluse
re·clu·ta *f.* recruitment
re·clu·ta·mien·to *m.* recruitment
re·clu·tar *v.* to recruit
re·co·brar *v.* to regain; to recover
re·co·bro *m.* recovery
re·co·do *m.* bend
re·co·ge·dor, a *adj.* collecting
re·co·ger *v.* to collect; to gather; to shorten
re·co·gi·mien·to *m.* retirement
re·co·lec·ción *f.* collection

re·co·lec·tar *v.* to gather
re·co·men·da·ble *adj.* advisable
re·co·men·da·ción *f.* recommendation
re·co·men·dar *v.* to recommend
re·com·pen·sa *f.* reward
re·com·pen·sar *v.* to compensate
re·con·ci·lia·ble *adj.* reconcilable
re·con·ci·lia·ción *f.* reconciliation
re·con·ci·liar *v.* to reconcile
re·con·for·tar *v.* to comfort
re·co·no·ci·do, a *adj.* gratitude; recognition
re·con·quis·tar *v.* to recover
re·con·si·de·rar *v.* to reconsider
re·cons·truc·ción *f.* reconstruction
re·cons·ti·tuir *v.* to reconstruct
re·con·tar *v.* to recount
re·co·pi·la·ción *f.* compilation
re·co·pi·la·dor *m.* compiler
re·co·pi·lar *v.* to compile
re·cor·da·ción *f.* memory
re·cor·dar *v.* to remember
re·co·rrer *v.* to travel
re·cor·tar *v.* to reduce
re·cre·a·ción *f.* recreation
re·cre·ar *v.* to re-create
re·crea·ti·vo *adj.* recreational
re·creo *m.* recreation
re·cri·mi·na·ción *f.* recrimination
re·cru·de·ci·mien·to *m.* worsening
rec·tal *adj.* rectal
rec·ta·men·te *adv.* justly
rec·tan·gu·lar *adj.* rectangle
rec·tán·gu·lo *adj.* rectangular
rec·ti·fi·ca·ción *f.* rectification
rec·ti·fi·car *v.* to rectify
rec·ti·tud *f.* honesty
rec·to *adj.* right; upright
re·cu·brir *v.* to cover
re·cuen·to *m.* recount
re·cuer·do *m.* memory; remembrance
re·cu·la·da *f.* backing up
re·cu·pe·ra·ble *adj.* recoverable
re·cu·pe·ra·ción *f.* recovery
re·cu·pe·rar *v.* to recover
re·cu·rren·te *adj.* recurrent

re•cu•rrir *v.* to return
re•cur•so *m.* remedy; resource
re•cu•sa•ción *f.* rejection
re•cu•sar *v.* to refuse
re•cha•za•mien•to *m.* rejection
re•cha•zar *v.* to reject; rebuff
re•cha•zo *m.* rejection
re•chi•fla *f.* hissing
re•chi•flar *v.* to hiss
re•dac•ción *f.* writing
re•dac•tar *v.* to edit
re•da•da *f.* roundup
re•de•ci•lla *f.* mesh
re•den•ción *f.* redemption
re•dil *m.* fold
re•di•mir *v.* to redeem
ré•di•to *m.* rent
re•di•tuar *v.* to yield
re•do•blar *v.* to fold
re•don•dez *f.* roundness
re•don•do, a *adj.* round
re•duc•ción *f.* reduction
re•du•ci•do *adj.* reduced
re•du•cir *v.* to shorten; to reduce
re•duc•tor, a *adj.* reducing
re•dun•dan•cia *f.* redundancy
re•dun•dan•te *adj.* redundant
re•dun•dar *v.* to overflow
re•e•le•gir *v.* to reelect
re•em•bol•sa•ble *adj.* reimbursable
re•em•bol•so *m.* reimbursement
re•em•pla•zar *v.* to replace
re•em•pla•zo *m.* substitution
re•en•car•na•ción *f.* reincarnation
re•es•truc•tu•ra•ción restructuring
re•es•truc•tu•rar *v.* to restructure
re•fec•to•rio *m.* refectory
re•fe•ren•cia *f.* reference
re•fe•ren•te *adj.* referring
re•fe•rir *v.* to refer; to tell
re•fi•na•do, a *adj.* refined
re•fi•na•mien•to *m.* refinement
re•fi•nar *v.* to refine
re•fi•ne•rí•a *f.* refinery
re•fle•jar *v.* to speculate; to reflect
re•fle•xión *f.* reflection

re•fle•xi•vo, a *adj.* reflective
re•for•ma *f.* reform
re•for•ma•ción *f.* reformation
re•for•ma•to•rio, a *adj.* reformatory
re•for•mis•ta *adj.* reformist
re•for•za•do, a *adj.* reinforced
re•for•zar *v.* to reinforce
re•frac•ción *f.* refraction
re•frac•tar *v.* to refract
re•fre•nar *v.* to restrain
re•fres•can•te *adj.* refreshing
re•fres•car *v.* to refresh
re•fres•co *m.* refreshment
re•fri•ge•ra•ción *f.* refrigeration
re•fri•ge•ra•dor *m.* refrigerator
re•fri•ge•rar *v.* to refrigerate
re•fri•to, a *adj.* refried
re•fuer•zo *m.* reinforcement
re•fu•gia•do, a *adj.* refugee
re•fu•gio *m.* shelter; refuge
re•ful•gen•te *adj.* refulgent
re•fun•fu•ñar *v.* to grumble
re•fun•fu•ño *m.* grumble
re•fu•ta•ción *f.* rebuttal
re•fu•tar *v.* to rebut
re•ga•la•do, a *adj.* easy; dainty
re•ga•lar *v.* to give away
re•ga•liz *m.* licorice
re•ga•lo *m.* present
re•ga•ñar *v.* to argue
re•gar *v.* to bathe; to water
re•ga•zo *m.* lap
re•ge•ne•ra•ción *f.* regeneration
re•ge•ne•ra•dor, a *m., f.* regenerator
re•ge•ne•rar *v.* to regenerate
re•gen•tar *v.* to direct
ré•gi•men *m.* regimen
re•gi•men•tar *v.* to regiment
re•gio, a *adj.* regal
re•gión *f.* area; region
re•gio•nal *adj.* regional
re•gio•na•lis•mo *m.* regionalism
re•gir *v.* to govern
re•gis•tra•dor, a *m., f.* register; *adj.*
  registering
re•gis•trar *v.* to record; to register

regla

re·gla *f.* rule
re·gla·men·ta·ción *f.* regulation
re·gla·men·tar *v.* to regulate
re·glar *v.* to regulate
re·go·ci·jo *m.* joy
re·go·de·o *m.* pleasure
re·gre·sar *v.* to return
re·gre·sión *f.* regression
re·gre·si·vo *adj.* regressive
re·gre·so *m.* return
re·gue·ro *m.* trail; stream
re·gu·la·ción *f.* regulation
re·gu·la·dor *m.* regulator
re·gu·lar *adj.* regular
re·gu·la·ri·zar *v.* to regularize
re·gu·lar·men·te *adv.* regularly
re·gur·gi·ta·ción *f.* regurgitation
re·gur·gi·tar *v.* to regurgitate
re·ha·bi·li·ta·ción *f.* rehabilitation
re·ha·bi·li·tar *v.* to rehabilitate
re·ha·cer *v.* to remake
re·ho·gar *v.* to brown
re·huir *v.* to avoid
re·hu·sar *v.* to refuse
re·im·pri·mir *v.* to reprint
rei·na *f.* queen
rei·na·do *m.* reign
rei·nan·te *adj.* ruling
rei·nar *v.* to reign
re·in·ci·den·te *adj.* relapsing
re·in·ci·dir *v.* to relapse
re·in·cor·po·ra·ción *f.* reincorporation
re·in·gre·sar *v.* to re-enter
rei·no *m.* kingdom
re·ins·ta·la·ción *f.* reinstallation
re·ins·ta·lar *v.* to reinstall
re·in·te·gra·ción *f.* reintegration
re·in·te·grar *v.* to reintegrate
re·in·te·gro *m.* reintegration
re·ír(se) *v.* to laugh
rei·te·ra·ción *f.* reiteration
rei·te·rar *v.* to reiterate
rei·te·ra·ti·vo, a *adj.* reiterative
rei·vin·di·car *v.* to recover
re·jun·tar *v.* to gather
re·ju·ve·ne·cer *v.* to rejuvenate

re·la·ción *f.* account; relation
re·la·cio·na·do, a *adj.* related
re·la·ja·ción *f.* relaxation
re·la·ja·do, a *adj.* relaxed
re·la·jar *v.* to relax
re·la·mer *v.* to lick
re·lám·pa·go *m.* lightning
re·lám·pa·gue·o *m.* lightning
re·lap·so, ·sa *adj.* relapsed
re·la·tar *v.* to narrate
re·la·ti·vi·dad *f.* relativity
re·la·ti·vo, a *adj.* relative
re·la·to *m.* story; narration
re·le·gar *v.* to relegate
re·le·var *v.* to relieve; to praise
re·li·ca·rio *m.* reliquary
re·lie·ve *m.* relief
re·li·gión *f.* religion
re·li·gio·si·dad *f.* religiosity
re·li·gio·so *adj.* religious
re·loj *m.* watch; clock
re·lo·je·rí·a *f.* clockmaking
re·lo·je·ro, a *m., f.* watchmaker
re·lu·cir *v.* to shine
re·lum·bran·te *adj.* dazzling
re·lum·brar *v.* to dazzle
re·lle·nar *v.* to refill
re·ma·llar *v.* to mend
re·mar *v.* to row
re·ma·tar *v.* to use up
re·ma·te *m.* conclusion
re·me·dar *v.* to mimic
re·me·dia·ble *adj.* remediable
re·me·diar *v.* to cure; to remedy
re·mem·bran·za *f.* remembrance
re·me·mo·ra·ción *f.* remembrance
re·me·mo·rar *v.* to remember something
re·men·dar *v.* to mend; to repair
re·men·dón, a *m., f.* cobbler; mender
re·mi·sión *f.* remission
re·mi·so, a *adj.* remiss
re·mi·ten·te *adj.* remitting
re·mi·tir *v.* to forgive; to remit; to diminish
re·mo·la·cha *f.* beet
re·mol·car *v.* to tow
re·mo·lo·ne·ar *v.* to loaf

república

re·mol·que *m.* tow truck
re·mon·tar *v.* to remount; to surmount
re·mor·di·mien·to *m.* remorse
re·mo·to *adj.* faraway
re·mo·ver *v.* to remove; to move; to dismiss
re·mo·zar *v.* to rejuvenate
re·mu·ne·ra·ción *f.* remuneration
re·mu·ne·ra·ti·vo, a *adj.* remunerative
re·na·ci·mien·to *m.* revival
re·nal *adj.* renal
ren·ci·lla *f.* quarrel
ren·cor *m.* spite; bitterness; rancor
ren·co·ro·so *adj.* bitter; resentful
ren·di·do *adj.* submissiveness; yield
ren·dir *v.* to yield; to surrender; to defeat
ren·gue·ar *v.* to limp
re·no *m.* reindeer
re·nom·bra·do, a *adj.* renowned
re·nom·bre *m.* renown
re·no·va·ción *f.* renovation
re·no·va·do *adj.* renewed
re·no·var *v.* to renovate; to reform
ren·ta *f.* interest; rent; income
ren·ta·ble *adj.* profitable
ren·tar *v.* to rent
re·nuen·cia *f.* reluctance
re·nuen·te *adj.* reluctant
re·nun·cia *f.* renunciation
re·nun·cia·ción *f.* renunciation
re·nun·ciar *v.* to reject; to surrender; to waive; to renounce
re·ñi·dor, a *adj.* quarrelsome
re·ñir *v.* to fight; to quarrel with another
re·or·ga·ni·za·ción *f.* reorganization
re·or·ga·ni·zar *v.* to reorganize
re·pa·ra·ción *f.* repair
re·pa·ra·dor, a *m., f.* repairer
re·pa·rar *v.* to mend; to repair
re·pa·ro *m.* protection; objection
re·par·ti·ción *f.* sharing
re·par·ti·dor, a *m., f.* distributor
re·par·tir *v.* to share; to divide
re·par·to *m.* delivery
re·pa·sar *v.* to review; to revise
re·pa·so *m.* review

re·pa·tria·ción *f.* repatriation
re·pa·triar *v.* to repatriate
re·pe·len·te *adj.* repellent
re·pe·ler *v.* to repel
re·pen·te *m.* start
re·pen·ti·no, a *adj.* repercussion
re·per·cu·sión *f.* repercussion
re·per·cu·tir *v.* to reverberate
re·per·cu·to·rio *m.* repertoire
re·pe·ti·ción *f.* repetition
re·pe·tir *v.* to repeat
re·pe·ti·ti·vo, a *adj.* repetitive
re·pi·que·te·ar *v.* to beat; to ring
re·pi·sa *f.* shelf
re·plan·tar *v.* to replant
re·plan·te·ar *v.* to restate
re·ple·to, a *adj.* full
ré·pli·ca *f.* answer
re·pli·car *v.* to reply; to respond
re·po·bla·ción *f.* repopulation
re·po·blar *v.* to repopulate
re·po·llo *m.* cabbage
re·po·ner *v.* to replace; to revive
re·por·te·ro, a *adj.* reporting
re·po·sa·do *adj.* quiet
re·po·sar *v.* to lie
re·po·si·ción *f.* reposition
re·po·so *m.* repose
re·pren·der *v.* to reprimand
re·pren·sión *f.* reprimand
re·pre·sa·lia *f.* reprisal
re·pre·sen·tan·te *adj.* representing
re·pre·sen·tar *v.* to represent; to appear to be
re·pre·sen·ta·ti·vo, a *adj.* representative
re·pre·sión *f.* repression
re·pre·si·vo, a *adj.* repressive
re·pri·men·da *f.* reprimand
re·pri·mir *v.* to repress
re·pro·char *v.* to reproach
re·pro·che *m.* rebuke; reproach
re·pro·duc·ción *f.* reproduction
re·pro·du·cir *v.* to reproduce
rep·tar *v.* to crawl
rep·til *v.* reptile
re·pú·bli·ca *f.* republic

85

republicano

re·pu·bli·ca·no, a *adj.* republican
re·pu·dia·ción *f.* repudiation
re·pu·diar *v.* to repudiate
re·pug·nan·te *adj.* repugnant
re·pul·gar *v.* to hem
re·pul·sar *v.* to reject
re·pul·sión *f.* repulsion
re·pul·si·vo, a *adj.* repulsive
re·pun·tar *v.* to turn
re·pun·te *adj.* turning
re·que·brar *v.* to break something again
re·que·ri·mien·to *m.* requirement
re·que·rir *v.* to want; to require
ré·quiem *m.* requiem
re·qui·sar *v.* to requisition
re·qui·si·ción *f.* requisition
re·qui·si·to *m.* requirement
re·sa·la·do, a *adj.* charming
re·sar·cir *v.* to indemnify
res·ba·lar *v.* to glide
res·ca·tar *v.* to rescue; to recover
res·ca·te *m.* rescue
res·cin·dir *v.* to rescind
res·ci·sión *f.* rescission
re·sen·ti·do, a *adj.* resentful
re·sen·ti·mien·to *m.* resentment
re·sen·tir·se *v.* to feel hurt
re·se·ña *f.* account; inspection
re·se·ñar *v.* to review; to inspect
re·ser·va *f.* reserve
re·ser·va·ción *f.* reservation
re·ser·va·do, a *adj.* reserved; confidential
re·ser·var *v.* to reserve
res·fria·do *m.* cold
res·friar *v.* to cool
res·guar·do *m.* guard; protection
re·si·den·cia *f.* residence
re·si·den·cial *adj.* residential
re·si·den·te *m., f.* resident
re·si·dir *v.* to live; to reside
re·si·duo *m.* residue
re·sig·na·ción *f.* resignation
re·sis·ten·cia *f.* endurance; resistance
re·sis·ten·te *adj.* resolute
re·sol·ver *v.* to settle; to solve; to resolve
re·so·nan·cia *f.* resonance

re·so·nan·te *adj.* resounding
re·so·nar *v.* to resound
re·so·pli·do *m.* puffing
res·pal·dar *v.* to back something or someone
res·pal·do *m.* back
res·pec·ti·vo *adj.* respective
res·pec·to *m.* respect
res·pe·ta·ble *adj.* respectable
res·pe·tar *v.* to respect
res·pe·to *m.* respect
res·pe·tuo·so, a *adj.* respectful
res·pi·ra·ción *f.* respiration
res·pi·ra·dor *m.* respirator
res·pi·rar *v.* to breath
res·pi·ro *m.* respite
res·plan·dor *m.* glow; brightness
res·pon·der *v.* to reply; to respond
res·pon·sa·ble *adj.* responsible
res·pues·ta *f.* answer; response
res·que·brar *v.* to crack
res·que·mor *m.* remorse
res·ta·ble·cer *v.* to reestablish
res·ta·ble·ci·mien·to *m.* reestablishment
res·ta·llar *v.* to crack
res·tau·ran·te *m.* restaurant
res·tau·rar *v.* to restore
res·ti·tu·ción *f.* restitution
res·to *m.* remainder
res·tric·ción *f.* restriction
res·tric·ti·vo, a *adj.* restrictive
res·trin·gir *v.* to restrict
re·su·ci·tar *v.* to resuscitate
re·sul·ta *f.* result
re·sul·ta·do *m.* issue; result
re·sul·tar *v.* to result
re·su·mir *v.* to summarize
re·sur·gir *v.* to reappear
re·su·rrec·ción *f.* resurrection
re·tar·dar *v.* to delay
re·ten·ción *f.* retention
re·te·ner *v.* to keep; to retain
re·ti·na *f.* retina
re·ti·ni·tis *f.* retinitis
re·ti·ra·da *f.* retreat

re•ti•ra•do, a *adj.* retired
re•ti•rar *v.* to retire; to withdraw; to retract
re•ti•ro *m.* retreat; withdrawal
re•to *m.* challenge
re•to•ñar *v.* to sprout
re•tor•cer *v.* to twist
re•tor•ci•do, a *adj.* twisted
re•tor•ci•mien•to *m.* twisting
re•tó•ri•co, a *adj.* rhetorical
re•tor•nar *v.* to return
re•to•zar *v.* to frolic
re•to•zo *m.* frolic
re•to•zón, a *adj.* frolicsome
re•trac•ción *f.* retraction
re•trac•tar *v.* to recant; to retract
re•trác•til *adj.* retractable
re•tra•er *v.* to dissuade
re•tra•í•do, a *adj.* withdrawn
re•trai•mien•to *m.* seclusion
re•trans•mi•tir *v.* to retransmit
re•tra•sar *v.* to delay
re•tra•to *m.* portrait
re•tre•ta *f.* retreat
re•tri•bu•ción *f.* retribution
re•tri•bu•ir *v.* to reward
re•tro•ac•ti•vo, a *adj.* retroactive
re•tró•gra•do, a *adj.* retrograde
re•tros•pec•ción *f.* retrospection
re•tum•bar *v.* to resound
reu•má•ti•co *adj.* rheumatic
reu•ma•tis•mo *m.* rheumatism
reu•nión *f.* meeting; reunion
reu•nir *v.* to gather; to mass; to meet
re•va•li•da•ción *f.* revalidation
re•va•li•dar *v.* to revalidate
re•va•lo•ri•zar *v.* to revalue
re•van•cha *f.* revenge
re•ve•la•ción *f.* revelation
re•ve•la•dor, a *adj.* revealing
re•ve•lar *v.* to betray; to reveal
re•ven•der *v.* to resell
re•ven•tar *v.* to blow; to burst
re•ven•tón *m.* burst
re•ver *v.* to review
re•ver•be•rar *v.* to reverberate

re•ve•ren•cia *f.* reverence
re•ve•ren•ciar *v.* to revere
re•ve•ren•do, a *adj.* reverend
re•ve•ren•te *adj.* respectful
re•ver•so *m.* reverse
re•ver•tir *v.* to revert
re•ves•tir *v.* to cover
re•vi•sar *v.* to review
re•vi•sión *f.* revision
re•vi•si•ta *f.* revision
re•vi•sor, a *m.*, *f.* inspector
re•vis•ta *f.* magazine
re•vis•te•ro, a *m.*, *f.* reviewer
re•vi•ta•li•zar *v.* to revitalize
re•vi•vi•fi•car *v.* to revive
re•vi•vir *v.* to revive
re•vo•ca•ción *f.* revocation
re•vo•car *v.* to repeal; to revoke
re•vol•cón *m.* fall
re•vo•lo•te•ar *v.* to flutter
re•vo•lu•ción *f.* revolution
re•vo•lu•cio•nar *v.* to revolutionize
re•vo•lu•cio•na•rio *adj.* revolutionary
re•vol•ver *v.* to revolve; to mix; to shake
re•vól•ver *m.* revolver; gun; pistol
re•vo•que *m.* plaster
re•vue•lo *m.* commotion
rey *m.* king
re•zar *v.* to pray; to say something
re•zon•gar *v.* to grumble
ri•be•ra *f.* shore
ri•be•te•a•do *adj.* trimmed
ri•be•te•ar *v.* to hem
ri•ca•men•te *adv.* richly
ri•co *adj.* wealthy; rich
ri•dí•cu•la•men•te *adv.* ridiculously
ri•di•cu•li•zar *v.* to ridicule
ri•dí•cu•lo *adj.* ridiculous
riel *m.* rail
rien•da *f.* rein
ries•go *m.* danger; risk
ri•fa *f.* raffle
ri•far *v.* to raffle off
ri•fle *m.* rifle
rí•gi•do *adj.* stiff; rigid
ri•gor *m.* rigor

ri·gu·ro·so *adj.* severe; rigorous
ri·ma *f.* rhyme
ri·mar *v.* to rhyme
rim·bom·ban·te *adj.* echoing
rin·cón *m.* corner
ri·no·ce·ron·te *m.* rhinoceros
ri·ña *f.* quarrel
ri·ñón *m.* kidney
río *m.* river
ri·que·za *f.* riches
ri·sa *f.* laughter
ri·si·ble *adj.* laughable
ris·tra *f.* string
ri·sue·ño, a *adj.* smiling
rít·mi·co *adj.* rhythmical
ri·to *m.* ceremony
ri·tual *m.* ritual
ri·val *m.* rival
ri·va·li·dad *f.* rivalry
ri·va·li·zar *v.* to rival
ri·zar *v.* to curl up
ro·bar *v.* to steal
ro·ble *m.* oak
ro·bo *m.* robbery
ro·bus·te·cer *v.* to make strong; to strengthen
ro·bus·to *adj.* hardy; strong
ro·ciar *v.* to sprinkle
ro·cín *m.* donkey
ro·cí·o *m.* sprinkle
ro·dar *v.* to tumble; to roll
ro·de·ar *v.* to circle; to ring
ro·de·o *m.* to go around
ro·de·te *m.* bun
ro·di·lla *f.* knee
ro·e·dor, a *adj.* gnawing
ro·er *v.* to gnaw
ro·gar *v.* to request; to pray
ro·jo *adj.* red
ro·llo *m.* roll
ro·ma·no, a *adj.* Roman
ro·mán·ti·co *adj.* romantic
rom·bo *m.* rhombus
ro·me·ro *m.* rosemary
rom·per *v.* to smash; to break
ron *m.* rum

ron·car *v.* to snore
ron·co, a *adj.* hoarse
ron·que·dad *f.* hoarseness
ro·ño·so, a *adj.* filthy
ro·pa *f.* clothing
ro·pe·ro *m.* closet
ro·sa *f.* rose
ro·sa·do, a *adj.* pink
ro·sal *m.* rosebush
ro·sa·le·da *f.* rose garden
ros·bif *m.* roast beef
ros·ca *f.* coil; ring
ros·tro *m.* face
ro·ta·ción *f.* rotation
ro·ta·to·rio, a *adj.* rotating
ro·ton·da *f.* rotunda
ro·tor *m.* rotor
ro·tu·la·do *m.* label
ro·tu·lar *v.* to label
ro·tu·la·dor, a *adj.* labeling
ro·za·mien·to *m.* rubbing
ro·zar *v.* to scrape; to skim
ru·bé·o·la *f.* rubella
ru·bí· *m.* ruby
ru·bi·cun·do, a *adj.* ruddy
ru·bio *adj.* blonde
ru·bor *m.* blush
ru·bo·ri·zar·se *v.* to blush
ru·da *f.* rue
ru·de·za *f.* rudeness
ru·di·men·tal *adj.* rudimentary
ru·di·men·ta·rio, a *adj.* rudimentary
ru·di·men·to *m.* rudiment
ru·do, a *adj.* rude
rue·da *f.* wheel
rue·do *m.* hem; edge
rue·go *m.* request
ru·gi·do *m.* roar
ru·gien·te *adj.* roaring
ru·go·so, a *adj.* winkled
rui·do *m.* sound; rattle; noise
rui·do·so, a *adj.* noisy
ruin *adj.* poor; despicable
rui·na *f.* ruin
rui·nar *v.* to ruin
rum·bo *m.* direction

ru•mor *m.* rumor
rup•tu•ra *f.* rupture
ru•ral *adj.* rural
ru•ti•lar *v.* to shine
ru•ti•na *f.* route

S

sá•ba•do *m.* Saturday
sá•ba•na *f.* sheet for a bed
sa•ber *v.* to inform; to know
sa•bi•do, a *adj.* known
sa•bi•du•rí•a *f.* knowledge
sa•bio, a *adj.* learned
sa•ble *m.* saber
sa•bor *m.* flavor; taste
sa•bo•re•ar *v.* to taste
sa•bo•ta•je *m.* sabotage
sa•bo•te•a•dor, a *adj.* sabotaging
sa•bo•te•ar *v.* to sabotage
sa•bro•so *adj.* delightful
sa•ca•cor•chos *m.* corkscrew
sa•ca•pun•tas *m.* pencil sharpener
sa•car *v.* to pull out; to get out
sa•ca•ri•na *f.* saccharin
sa•cer•do•cio *m.* priesthood
sa•cer•do•te *m.* priest
sa•cer•do•ti•sa *f.* priestess
sa•co *m.* bag
sa•cra•men•to *m.* sacrament
sa•cri•fi•car *v.* to sacrifice
sa•cri•fi•cio *m.* sacrifice
sa•cri•le•gio *m.* sacrilege
sa•cro *adj.* sacred
sa•cu•di•da *f.* tremor; shake
sa•cu•dir *v.* to beat; to tug
sá•di•co, a *adj.* sadistic
sa•ga *f.* saga
sa•ga•ci•dad *f.* sagacity
sa•gaz *adj.* sagacious
sa•gra•do, a *adj.* sacred
sal *f.* salt
sa•la *f.* living room of a house
sa•la•do, a *adj.* salted; salty

sa•la•man•dra *f.* salamander
sa•laz *f.* salacious
sal•chi•chón *m.* sausage
sal•dar *v.* to pay off something
sal•do *m.* payment
sa•le•ro *m.* saltshaker
sa•li•da *f.* exit; solution
sa•lien•te *adj.* salient; projecting
sa•li•no, a *adj.* saline
sa•lir *v.* to get out; to leave
sa•li•va *f.* saliva
sa•li•val *adj.* salivary
sa•li•var *v.* to salivate
sal•mo *m.* psalm
sal•món *m.* salmon
sa•lo•bre *adj.* briny
sal•pi•car *v.* to splash
sal•pi•men•tar *v.* to season
sal•sa *f.* sauce
sal•ta•dor *m.* jumper
sal•ta•mon•tes *m.* grasshopper
sal•tar *v.* to jump; to leap; to bounce
sal•te•ar *v.* to skip
sal•to *m.* jump
sa•lu•bre *adj.* healthful
sa•lud *f.* health
sa•lu•da•ble *adj.* healthy
sa•lu•dar *v.* to salute
sa•lu•ta•ción *f.* greeting
sal•va•ción *f.* salvation
sal•va•guar•dar *v.* to safeguard
sal•va•guar•dia *f.* safeguard
sal•va•ja•da *f.* savagery
sal•va•je *adj.* untamed; wild; uncivilized
sal•var *v.* to avoid; to save; to cover
sal•via *f.* sage
sal•vo *adj.* safe
sa•na•men•te *adv.* sincerely
sa•nar *v.* to heal
san•ción *f.* sanction
san•cio•nar *v.* to sanction
san•da•lia *f.* sandal
sán•da•lo *m.* sandalwood
san•dez *f.* nonsense
san•dí•a *f.* watermelon
sa•ne•a•mien•to *m.* sanitation

sa•ne•ar *v.* to right
san•grar *v.* to bleed
san•gre *f.* blood
san•grí•a *f.* sangria
san•grien•to *adj.* bloody
san•gui•jue•la *f.* leech
san•gui•na•rio, a *adj.* cruel
sa•ni•dad *f.* healthiness
sa•ni•ta•rio, a *adj.* sanitary
sa•no *adj.* unharmed; wholesome
san•ti•dad *f.* sanctify
san•ti•fi•car *v.* to sanctify
san•to *adj.* blessed
san•tua•rio *m.* sanctuary
sa•pien•cia *f.* wisdom
sa•pien•te *adj.* wise
sa•po *m.* toad
sa•que•ar *v.* to plunder
sa•que•o *m.* plundering
sa•ram•pión *m.* measles
sar•cas•mo *m.* sarcasm
sar•cás•ti•co *adj.* sarcastic
sar•di•na *f.* sardine
sar•dó•ni•co, a *adj.* sardonic
sar•gen•to *m.* sergeant
sar•no•so, a *adj.* scabby
sa•rro *m.* crust
sar•ta *f.* string
sa•sa•frás *m.* sassafras
sa•té•li•te *m.* satellite
sa•tén *m.* satin
sa•ti•na•do, a *adj.* satiny
sá•ti•ra *f.* satire
sa•tí•ri•co, a *adj.* satirical
sa•ti•ri•zar *v.* to satirize
sá•ti•ro *m.* satyr
sa•tis•fac•ción *f.* satisfaction
sa•tis•fa•cer *v.* to satisfy
sa•tis•fac•to•rio, a *adj.* satisfactory
sa•tu•ra•ción *f.* saturation
sa•tu•ra•do, a *adj.* saturated
sa•tu•rar *v.* to saturate
sa•xo•fón *m.* saxophone
sa•yo *m.* tunic
sa•zón *f.* season
sa•zo•na•do *adj.* flavorful

sa•zo•nar *v.* to season
se *pron.* herself; oneself; yourself; himself
se•bá•ce•o, a *adj.* sebaceous
se•bo *m.* fat
se•bo•rre•a *f.* seborrhea
se•ca•do *m.* drying
se•ca•do•ra *f.* clothes dryer
se•can•te *adj.* drying
se•car *v.* to dry
sec•ción *f.* section
sec•cio•nar *v.* to section
se•ce•sión *f.* secession
se•ce•sio•nis•ta *adj.* secessionist
se•co *adj.* dried
se•cre•sión *f.* secretion
se•cre•ta•men•te *adv.* secretly
se•cre•ta•ria *f.* secretary
se•cre•te•ar *v.* to whisper
se•cre•te•o *m.* whispering
se•cre•to *m.* secret
sec•ta•rio, a *adj.* sectarian
sec•tor *m.* sector
sec•to•rial *adj.* sectorial
se•cue•la *f.* consequence
se•cuen•cia *f.* sequence
se•cues•trar *v.* to kidnap
se•cues•tro *m.* kidnapping
se•cu•lar *adj.* secular
se•cu•la•ri•zar *v.* to secularize
se•cun•dar *v.* to second
se•cun•da•rio, a *adj.* secondary
sed *f.* thirst
se•da *f.* silk
se•dan•te *adj.* sedative
se•dar *v.* to soothe
se•dar *v.* to sedate
se•da•ti•vo *adj.* sedative
se•den•ta•rio, a *adj.* sedentary
se•di•ción *f.* sedition
se•dien•to, a *adj.* thirsty
se•di•men•to *m.* sediment
se•do•so *adj.* silky
se•duc•ción *f.* seduction
se•du•cir *v.* to seduce
se•duc•ti•vo, a *adj.* seductive
se•ga•dor, a *adj.* seductive

se•gar *v.* to mow; to harvest
se•glar *adj.* secular
seg•men•ta•ción *f.* segmentation
seg•men•to *m.* segment
se•gre•ga•ción *f.* segregation
se•gre•ga•cio•nis•ta *adj.* segregationist
se•gre•gar *v.* to segregate
se•gui•da•men•te *adv.* continuously
se•gui•do *adj.* consecutive
se•gui•dor, a *m., f.* follower
se•guir *v.* to chase; to follow; to watch
se•gún *prep.* according to
se•gun•do *adj.* second
se•gur *m.* sickle
se•gu•ra•men•te *adv.* probably
se•gu•ri•dad *f.* safety
se•gu•ro *adj.* sure; certain
seis *adj.* six
seis•cien•tos, as *adj.* six hundred
se•lec•ción *f.* selection
se•lec•cio•nar *v.* to select
se•lec•ti•vo, a *adj.* selective
se•lec•to, a *adj.* select
sel•va *f.* forest; jungle
se•llar *v.* to stamp
se•llo *m.* stamp
se•ma•na *f.* week
se•ma•nal *adj.* weekly
se•ma•nal•men•te *adv.* weekly
se•ma•na•rio, a *adj.* weekly
se•mán•ti•co, a *adj.* semantic
sem•bra•dor, a *adj.* sowing
sem•brar *v.* to sow
se•me•jan•te *adj.* similar
se•me•jan•za *f.* similarity
se•men•tar *v.* to seed
se•mes•tral *adj.* semiannual
se•mes•tre *m.* semester
se•mi•au•to•má•ti•co, a *adj.* semiautomatic
se•mi•cír•cu•lo *m.* semicircle
se•mi•fi•na•lis•ta *adj.* semifinalist
se•mi•lla *f.* seed
se•mi•lle•ro *m.* nursery for plants
se•mi•nal *adj.* seminal
se•mi•na•rio *m.* seminary

se•mi•na•ris•ta *m.* seminarian
sé•mo•la *f.* semolina
sem•pi•ter•no, a *adj.* everlasting
se•na•do *m.* senate
se•na•dor *m.* senator
sen•ci•lla•men•te *adv.* simply
sen•ci•llez *f.* simplicity
sen•ci•llo, a *adj.* simple; easy
sen•da *f.* path; trail
se•nil *adj.* senile
se•no *m.* cavity; hollow
sen•sa•ción *f.* sensation
sen•sa•cio•nal *adj.* sensational
sen•sa•to *adj.* sensible
sen•si•bi•li•dad *f.* sensibility; sensitiveness
sen•si•bi•li•zar *v.* to sensitize
sen•si•ble *adj.* sentimental; sensitive
sen•so•rio, a *adj.* sensorial
sen•sual *adj.* sensual
sen•sua•li•dad *f.* sensuality
sen•ta•do, a *adj.* settled; seated
sen•tar *v.* to sit
sen•ten•cia *f.* sentence
sen•ten•ciar *v.* to sentence
sen•ten•cio•so, a *adj.* sententious
sen•ti•do, a *adj.* heartfelt
sen•ti•men•tal *adj.* sentimental
sen•ti•mien•to *m.* sentiment
sen•tir *v.* to feel; to sense; to experience
se•ña *f.* signal; sign
se•ñal *f.* sign
se•ña•lar *v.* to point; to determine
se•ña•li•zar *v.* to put up signs
se•ñe•ro *adj.* solitary
se•ñor *adj.* Mr.; Mister
se•ño•rí•o *m.* domain; solemnity
se•ño•ri•ta *f.* lady; girl
se•ño•ri•to *m.* boy; young man
se•ñue•lo *m.* trap; bait
se•pa•ra•ción *f.* separation
se•pa•ra•da•men•te *adv.* separately
se•pa•ra•do *adj.* separated
se•pa•rar *v.* to divide
se•pa•ra•tis•ta *adj.* separatist
se•pe•lio *m.* burial

sép•ti•co, a *adj.* septic
sep•tiem•bre *m.* September
sép•ti•mo *adj.* seventh
sep•tua•ge•na•rio, a *adj.* septuagenarian
sep•tua•qé•si•mo *adj.* seventieth
se•pul•tar *v.* to bury
se•pul•to, a *adj.* buried
se•pul•tu•ra *f.* burial
se•que•dad *f.* dryness
se•quí•a *f.* drought
ser *v.* to be; to come from
se•ra•fín *m.* angel
se•re•nar *v.* to calm
se•re•na•ta *f.* serenade
se•re•ni•dad *f.* serenity
se•ria•men•te *adv.* seriously
se•rie *f.* series
se•rie•dad *f.* seriousness
se•rio *adj.* serious
ser•món *m.* sermon
ser•mo•ne•ar *v.* to lecture
ser•pien•te *f.* snake
se•rra•do, a *adj.* sawed
se•rra•ní•a *f.* mountains
se•rrar *v.* to saw
se•rre•rí•a *f.* sawmill
se•rru•cho *m.* saw
ser•vi•cio *m.* help; service
ser•vi•dor, a *m., f.* servant
ser•vil *adj.* servile
ser•vi•lle•ta *f.* napkin
ser•vir *v.* to serve
sé•sa•mo *m.* sesame
se•sen•ta *adj.* sixty
se•sen•ta•vo, a *adj.* sixtieth
ses•go *m.* slant
se•sión *f.* session
se•so *m.* brain
se•su•do, a *adj.* wise
se•te•cien•tos, as *adj.* seven hundred
se•ten•ta *adj.* seventy
se•ten•ta•vo, a *adj.* seventieth
se•tiem•bre *m.* September
seu•dó•ni•mo, a *m.* pseudonym
se•ve•ra•men•te *adv.* relentlessly; severely

se•ve•ro, a *adj.* unyielding; severe
se•xa•gé•si•mo, a *adj.* sixtieth
sex•te•to *m.* sextet
sex•to *adj.* sixth
se•xual *adj.* sexual
se•xua•li•dad *f.* sexuality
si *conj.* if; *adv.* yes
si•bi•lan•te *adj.* sibilant
si•co•mo•ro *m.* sycamore
sie•ga *f.* harvesting
siem•bra *f.* sowing
siem•pre *adv.* forever; always
sien *f.* temple
sie•rra *f.* saw
sier•vo *m.* servant; serf
sies•ta *f.* nap in the afternoon
sie•te *adj.* seven
sí•fi•lis *f.* syphilis
si•fi•lí•ti•co, a *adj.* syphilitic
si•gi•lo *m.* secrecy
si•gla *f.* acronym
si•glo *m.* century
sig•ni•fi•ca•ción *f.* significance
sig•ni•fi•ca•do, a *adj.* significant
sig•ni•fi•can•te *adj.* significant
sig•ni•fi•car *v.* to signify; to indicate
sig•ni•fi•ca•ti•vo, a *adj.* significant
sig•no *m.* sign
si•guien•te *adj.* next
sí•la•ba *f.* syllable
si•la•be•ar *v.* to syllable
si•la•be•o *m.* syllabication
sil•ba•to *m.* whistle
sil•bi•do *m.* whistle
si•len•cia•dor *m.* silencer
si•len•ciar *v.* to silence
si•len•cio *m.* silence
si•len•cio•so *adj.* silent
si•li•co•na *f.* silicone
si•lo *m.* silo
si•lo•gís•ti•co, a *adj.* stylogistic
si•lue•ta *f.* outline
sil•ves•tre *adj.* wild
sil•vi•cul•tor *m.* forester
si•lla *f.* chair
si•llín *m* seat; saddle

si·llón *m.* armchair
sim·bio·sis *f.* symbiosis
sim·bió·ti·co, a *adj.* symbiotic
sim·bo·li·zar *v.* to symbolize
sím·bo·lo *m.* symbol
si·me·trí·a *f.* symmetry
si·mé·tri·co, a *adj.* symmetric
si·mien·te *f.* seed
sí·mil *adj.* similar
si·mi·li·tud *f.* similarity
sim·pa·tí·a *f.* congeniality; affection
sim·pá·ti·co, a *adj.* pleasant
sim·pa·ti·zan·te *adj.* sympathizing
sim·ple *adj.* simple
sim·ple·za *f.* simplicity
sim·pli·ci·dad *f.* simplicity
sim·pli·fi·ca·ción *f.* simplification
sim·pli·fi·car *v.* to simplify
sim·po·sio *m.* symposium
si·mu·la·ción *f.* pretense
si·mu·la·dor, a *m., f.* simulator
si·mul·tá·ne·o, a *adj.* simultaneous
sin *prep.* without
si·na·go·ga *f.* synagogue
sin·ce·ri·dad *f.* sincerity
sin·ce·ro, a *adj.* sincere
sín·co·pa *f.* syncope
sin·co·pa·do, a *adj.* syncopated
sín·co·pe *m.* syncope
sin·cro·ní·a *f.* synchrony
sin·cro·ni·za·ción *f.* synchronization
sin·cro·ni·zar *v.* to synchronize
sin·di·ca·li·za·ción *f.* unionization
sin·di·ca·li·zar *v.* to unionize
sín·dro·me *m.* syndrome
si·ner·gia *f.* synergy
sin·fo·ní·a *f.* symphony
sin·fó·ni·co, a *adj.* symphonic
sin·gu·lar *adj.* single
sin·gu·la·ri·zar *v.* to distinguish
sin·nú·me·ro *m.* countless
si·no *conj.* but; fate
si·nó·ni·mia *f.* synonymy
si·nó·ni·mo, a *adj.* synonymous
si·nóp·sis *f.* synopsis
si·nóp·ti·co, a *adj.* synoptic

sin·ta·xis *m.* syntax
sín·te·sis *f.* synthesis
sin·té·ti·co, a *adj.* synthetic
sin·te·ti·za·dor *m.* synthesizer
sin·te·ti·zar *v.* to synthesize
sín·to·ma *m.* symptom
sin·to·má·ti·co, a *adj.* symptomatic
sin·to·ni·zar *v.* to tune
si·nuo·si·dad *f.* sinuosity
si·nuo·so, a *adj.* sinuous
si·quia·tra *m., f.* psychiatrist
si·quia·trí·a *f.* psychiatry
sí·qui·co *adj.* psychic
si·quie·ra *adv.* at least
sir·vien·ta *f.* maid
sir·vien·te *m.* servant
sís·mi·co, a *adj.* seismic
sis·mo *m.* earthquake
sis·mó·gra·fo *m.* seismograph
sis·te·ma *m.* system
sis·te·ma·ti·za·ción *f.* systematization
sis·te·ma·ti·zar *v.* to systematize
sís·to·le *f.* systole
si·tio *m.* place
si·to *m.* site
si·tua·ción *f.* situation
si·tuar *v.* to place
so·ba·co *m.* armpit
so·bar *v.* to thrash; to knead
so·be·o *m.* strap
so·be·ra·no, a *adj.* sovereign
so·ber·bio, a *adj.* superb
so·bor·nar *v.* to bribe another
so·bor·no *m.* bribery
so·bra *f.* excess
so·bra·do, a *adj.* plenty
so·bran·te *adj.* surplus
so·brar *v.* to surpass
so·bre *prep.* over; on; above
so·bre·a·bun·dan·cia *f.* superabundance
so·bre·car·ga *f.* overload
so·bre·car·gar *v.* to overload
so·bre·ce·jo *m.* frown
so·bre·co·ger *v.* to scare
so·bre·en·ten·di·do, a *adj.* understood
so·bre·ex·ci·tar *v.* to overexcite**

93

sobrellenar

so·bre·lle·nar *v.* to overfill
so·bre·lle·var *v.* to bear
so·bre·na·tu·ral *adj.* supernatural
so·bre·nom·bre *m.* nickname
so·bren·ten·der *v.* to understand
so·bre·pa·sar *v.* to surpass
so·bre·pe·so *m.* overload
so·bre·pre·cio *m.* surcharge
so·bre·sa·lien·te *adj.* outstanding
so·bre·sa·lir *v.* to project
so·bre·sal·tar *v.* to startle
so·bre·sal·to *m.* fright
so·bres·cri·to *m.* address
so·bres·ti·mar *v.* to overestimate
so·bre·to·do *m.* coat; overcoat
so·bre·vi·vien·te *adj.* surviving
so·bre·vi·vir *v.* to survive
so·bri·na *f.* niece
so·bri·no *m.* nephew
so·ca·rrón, a *m., f.* one who is sarcastic
so·ca·rro·ne·rí·a *f.* sarcasm
so·ca·var *v.* to excavate
so·cia·bi·li·dad *f.* friendliness
so·cia·ble *adj.* sociable
so·cie·dad *f.* society
so·cio, a *m., f.* member
so·cio·e·co·nó·mi·co, a *adj.*
  socioeconomic
so·cio·lo·gí·a *f.* sociology
so·cio·ló·gi·co, a *adj.* sociological
so·ció·lo·go, a *m., f.* sociologist
so·co·rrer *v.* to aid
so·co·rro *m.* aid
so·dio *m.* sodium
so·fá *f.* sofa
so·fis·ma *m.* sophism
so·fis·ta *adj.* sophistic
so·fis·ti·ca·ción *f.* sophistication
so·fis·ti·ca·do, a *adj.* sophistication
so·fo·ca·ción *f.* suffocation
so·fo·ca·dor, a *adj.* suffocating
so·fo·car *v.* to suffocate; to suppress
so·ga *f.* rope
so·ja *f.* soybean
so·juz·gar *v.* to subjugate
sol *m.* sun

so·la·men·te *adv.* only
so·la·no *m.* the east wind
so·lar *adj.* solar
so·la·rium *m.* solarium
so·laz *m.* relaxation
sol·da·do *m.* soldier
sol·da·dor *m.* welder
sol·da·du·ra *f.* welding
sol·dar *v.* to join; to weld
so·le·a·do *adj.* sunny
so·le·cis·mo *m.* solecism
so·le·dad *f.* loneliness
so·lem·ne *adj.* solemn
so·lem·ni·dad *f.* solemnity
so·le·van·tar *v.* to lift
so·li·ci·ta·ción *f.* request
so·li·ci·tan·te *m., f.* petitioner
so·li·ci·tar *v.* to ask for; to request
so·lí·ci·to, a *adj.* solicitous
so·li·ci·tud *f.* request; solicitude
so·li·da·ri·dad *f.* solidarity
so·li·dez *f.* solidity
so·li·di·fi·ca·ción *f.* solidification
so·li·di·fi·car *v.* to solidify
só·li·do *adj.* solid
so·li·lo·quio *m.* soliloquy
so·lis·ta *f.* soloist
so·li·vian·tar *v.* to irritate
so·li·viar *v.* to lift something
so·lo *adj.* alone
sol·sti·cio *m.* solstice
sol·tar *v.* to let go; to loosen
sol·te·ro *adj.* single
sol·tu·ra *f.* confidence; looseness
so·lu·ble *adj.* soluble
so·lu·ción *f.* solution
so·lu·cio·nar *v.* to solve
sol·ven·cia *f.* solvency
sol·ven·tar *v.* to resolve
sol·ven·te *adj.* solvent
so·má·ti·co, a *adj.* somatic
so·ma·ti·za·ción *f.* somatization
som·bra *f.* shade
som·brar *v.* to shade
som·bre·ro *m.* hat
som·brí·o, a *adj.* sullen

so•me•ter *v.* to subordinate
so•me•ti•mien•to *m.* submission
som•no•len•cia *f.* somnolence
so•na•do, a *adj.* crazy
so•nar *v.* to sound
son•da *f.* sounding
son•de•ar *v.* to sound
son•de•o *m.* survey
so•ne•to *m.* sonnet
so•ni•do *m.* sound
so•no•ri•dad *f.* sonority
so•no•ro, a *adj.* sonority
so•no•ro, a *adj.* sound
son•re•ír *v.* to smile
son•rien•te *adj.* smiling
son•ri•sa *f.* smile
son•ro•jo *m.* blush
son•ro•sar *v.* to turn pink
son•sa•car *v.* to wheedle
so•ña•do, a *adj.* dream
so•ña•dor, a *m., f.* dreamer
so•ñar *v.* to dream
so•ño•len•cia *f.* somnolence
so•ño•lien•to, a *adj.* sleepy
so•pa *f.* soup
so•pa•pe•ar *v.* to slap
so•pa•po *m.* slap
so•pe•sar *v.* to weigh
so•pla•dor, a *adj.* blowing
so•plar *v.* to blow
so•por *m.* sleepiness
so•por•ta•ble *adj.* bearable
so•por•tar *v.* to support
so•por•te *m.* support
so•pra•no *m.* soprano
sor•ber *v.* to absorb
sor•be•te *m.* sherbet
sor•bo *m.* sip
sor•de•ra *f.* deafness
sor•di•dez *f.* squalor
sór•di•do, a *adj.* squalid
sor•do, a *adj.* deaf
sor•na *f.* sarcasm
sor•pren•den•te *adj.* surprising
sor•pren•der *v.* to surprise
sor•pre•si•vo, a *adj.* unexpected

sor•ti•ja *f.* ring
so•se•ga•do, a *adj.* peaceful
so•se•gar *v.* to calm down
so•sie•go *m.* quiet
sos•la•yo, a *adj.* slanted
so•so, a *adj.* dull
sos•pe•cha *f.* suspicion
sos•pe•cho•so, a *adj.* suspicious
sos•tén *m.* support; sustenance
sos•te•ne•dor *m.* supporter
sos•te•ner *v.* to uphold; to support
sos•te•ni•do, a *adj.* sustained
sos•te•ni•mien•to *m.* sustenance; support
so•ta•na *f.* soutane
só•ta•no *m.* basement
Sr. abbr. Señor, *m.* Mr.
Sra. abbr. Señora, *f.* Mrs.
su, sus *adj.* her; his; its; your
sua•ve *adj.* sweet, soft
sua•vi•dad *f.* smoothness; sweetness
sua•vi•za•dor, a *adj.* softening
sua•vi•zar *v.* to smooth; to soften
su•bal•ter•no, a *adj.* subordinate
su•ba•rren•dar *v.* to sublet
su•ba•rrien•do *m.* sublease
su•bas•ta *f.* auction
su•bas•tar *v.* to auction
sub•co•mi•sión *f.* subcommittee
sub•cons•cien•te *adj.* subconscious
sub•cu•tá•ne•o, a *adj.* subcutaneous
sub•di•vi•sión *f.* subdivision
su•bes•ti•mar *v.* to underestimate
su•be y ba•ja *m.* seesaw
su•bi•do, a *adj.* deep
su•bir *v.* to raise; to go up; to come
sú•bi•ta•men•te *adv.* suddenly
sú•bi•to *adj.* hasty
sub•je•ti•vi•dad *f.* subjectivity
sub•je•ti•vo, a *adj.* subjective
su•ble•var *v.* to rebel
su•bli•ma•ción *f.* sublimation
su•bli•mar *v.* to sublimate
sub•ma•ri•no *adj.* submarine
su•bor•di•na•ción *f.* subordination
su•bor•di•na•do, a *adj.* subordinate

subordinar

su·bor·di·nar *v.* to subordinate
sub·sa·nar *v.* to correct
subs·cri·bir *v.* to subscribe to; to sign
subs·crip·ción *f.* subscription
subs·crip·tor, a *m., f.* subscriber
sub·se·cuen·te *adj.* subsequent
sub·si·diar *v.* to subsidize
sub·si·dio *m.* subsidy
sub·sis·ten·cia *f.* subsistence
sub·sis·tir *v.* to subsist
subs·tan·cia *f.* substance
subs·tan·cial *adj.* substantial
subs·tan·ciar *v.* to substantiate
subs·tan·cio·so, a *adj.* substantial
subs·ti·tu·ción *f.* substitution
subs·ti·tuir *v.* to substitute
subs·ti·tu·ti·vo, a *adj.* substitute
subs·trac·ción *f.* subtraction
subs·tra·er *v.* to subtract; to deduce
sub·sue·lo *m.* basement
sub·te·rrá·ne·o, a *adj.* underground
sub·tí·tu·lo *m.* subtitle
su·bur·ba·no, a *adj.* suburban
sub·ven·ción *f.* subsidy
sub·ven·cio·nar *v.* to subsidize
sub·yu·gar *v.* to subjugate
suc·ción *f.* suction
su·ce·dá·ne·o, a *adj.* substitute
su·ce·der *v.* to succeed
su·ce·sión *f.* succession
su·ce·si·va·men·te *adv.* successively
su·ce·si·vo, a *adj.* consecutive
su·ce·so *m.* event
su·ce·sor, a *adj.* succeeding
su·cie·dad *f.* filthiness
su·cio, a *f.* dirty
su·cu·len·to, a *adj.* succulent
su·cum·bir *v.* to succumb
sud *m.* south
su·dar *v.* to sweat
su·des·te *m.* southeast
su·do·es·te *m.* southwest
su·dor *m.* sweat
su·do·rí·fe·ro, a *adj.* sudoriferous;
  secreting sweat
su·do·ro·so, a *adj.* sweaty

sue·gra *f.* mother-in-law
sue·gro *m.* father-in-law
sue·lo *m.* floor; soil; ground
suel·to, a *adj.* nimble; loose
sue·ño *m.* dream; sleep
sue·ro *m.* serum
suer·te *f.* luck
su·fi·cien·te *adj.* sufficient
su·fi·jo *m.* suffix
su·fra·gio *m.* suffrage
su·fra·gis·ta *f., m.* suffragist
su·fri·do, a *adj.* patient
su·frir *v.* to suffer; to endure something
su·ge·ren·cia *f.* suggestion
su·ge·rir *v.* to suggest
su·ges·tión *f.* suggestion
su·ges·ti·vo, a *adj.* suggestive
sui·ci·da *adj.* suicidal
sui·ci·dio *m.* suicide
su·je·ción *f.* subjection
su·je·tar *v.* to subject; to fasten
su·je·to, a *adj.* subject
sul·fu·ro *m.* sulphide
su·ma·men·te *adv.* extremely
su·mar *v.* to add up
su·ma·ria·men·te *adv.* summarily
su·ma·rio, a *adj.* brief
su·mer·gir *v.* to submerge
su·mi·de·ro *m.* drain
su·mi·nis·trar *v.* to supply
su·mi·nis·tro *m.* supply
su·mir *v.* to submerge
su·mi·sión *f.* submission
su·mi·so, a *adj.* submissive
sun·tuo·si·dad *f.* sumptuousness
sun·tuo·so, a *adj.* sumptuous
su·pe·di·tar *v.* to subordinate
su·per·a·bun·dar *v.* to superabound
su·pe·rar *v.* to surpass; to beat
su·per·es·truc·tu·ra *f.* superstructure
su·per·fi·cial *adj.* superficial
su·per·fi·cie *f.* surface
su·per·fi·no, a *adj.* very fine
su·per·fluo, a *adj.* superfluous
su·pe·rin·ten·den·te *m., f.*
  superintendent

su·pe·rior *adj.* superior; better
su·pe·rio·ri·dad *f.* superiority
su·per·mer·ca·do *m.* supermarket
su·per·po·bla·ción *f.* overpopulation
su·per·só·ni·co, a *adj.* supersonic
su·pers·ti·ción *f.* superstition
su·pers·ti·cio·so, a *adj.* superstitious
su·per·vi·sar *v.* to supervise
su·per·vi·sión *f.* supervision
su·per·vi·ven·cia *f.* survival
su·pi·no, a *adj.* supine
su·plan·tar *v.* to supplant
su·ple·men·tal *adj.* supplemental
su·plen·te *adj.* substitute
su·pli·car *v.* to implore
su·po·ner *v.* to imagine; to suppose
su·po·si·ción *f.* supposition
su·po·si·to ·rio *m.* suppository
su·pre·mo, a *adj.* supreme
su·pri·mir *v.* to eliminate
su·pues·to, a *adj.* supposed; assumed
su·pu·rar *v.* to suppurate
sur *m.* south
sur·car *v.* to plow
sur·gir *v.* to arise
su·rre·a·lis·ta *adj.* surrealistic
sur·ti·dor, a *m.* supplier
sur·tir *v.* to supply something
sus·cep·ti·bi·li·dad *f.* susceptibility
sus·cep·ti·ble *adj.* susceptible
sus·pen·der *v.* to interrupt
sus·pen·sión *f.* suspension
sus·pen·si·vo, a *adj.* suspensive
sus·pen·so·rio, a *adj.* suspensory
sus·pi·ca·cia *f.* distrust
sus·pi·caz *adj.* being distrustful
sus·pi·rar *v.* to sigh
sus·pi·ro *m.* sigh
sus·ten·ta·mien·to *m.* sustenance
sus·ten·tar *v.* to uphold; to sustain
sus·to *m.* scare
su·su·rran·te *adj.* rustling
su·su·rrar *v.* to murmur; to whisper
su·su·rro *m.* whisper
su·til *adj.* subtle
su·ti·le·za *f.* subtlety

su·tu·ra *f.* suture
su·tu·rar *v.* to suture a wound
su·yo, a *adj.* their; her; his; your

T

ta·ba *f.* bone of the ankle
ta·ba·cal *m.* field for tobacco
ta·ba·ca·le·ro, a *m., f.* tobacco dealer
ta·ba·co *m.* tobacco
tá·ba·no *m.* gadfly
ta·ba·que·rí·a *f.* tobacco shop
ta·ber·na *f.* tavern
ta·ber·ná·cu·lo *m.* tabernacle
ta·ber·ne·ro, a *m., f.* bartender
ta·bi·que *m.* partition
ta·bla *f.* table
ta·ble·a·do, a *m.* pleats
ta·ble·ro *m.* board
ta·ble·ta *f.* tablet
ta·bu·la·dor *m., f.* tabulator
ta·bu·re·te *m.* stool
ta·co *m.* pad; wedge
ta·cón *m.* heel
tác·ti·co, a *adj.* tactical
tác·til *adj.* tactile
tac·to *m.* touch; tact
ta·cha *f.* flaw
ta·char *v.* to cross something out
ta·cho *m.* can
ta·chue·la *f.* tack
ta·fe·tán *m.* taffeta
ta·hur *m.* cardsharp
tai·ma·do, a *adj.* crafty
ta·ja·da *f.* profit
ta·jan·te *adj.* sharp
ta·jar *v.* to slice
ta·jo *m.* cut
tal *adj.* such
ta·la *f.* ruin
ta·la·dor, a *adj.* cutting
ta·la·drar *v.* to drill
ta·la·dro *m.* drill
ta·lar *v.* to cut something down

tal·co *m.* talc
ta·le·ga *f.* wealth
ta·len·to *m.* talent
ta·len·to·so, a *adj.* talented
ta·lis·mán *m.* talisman
ta·lón *m.* talon; heel
ta·lo·na·rio *m.* checkbook
ta·lla *f.* size; height
ta·lla·do, a *adj.* engraved; carved
ta·lla·dor *m.* engraver
ta·llar *v.* to carve
ta·lle *m.* figure; shape
ta·ller *m.* shop
ta·llo *m.* stern
ta·ma·ño, a *adj.* very big
ta·ma·ño *m.* size
tam·ba·le·an·te *adj.* staggering
tam·ba·le·ar *v.* to stagger
tam·bién *adv.* too; also
tam·bor *m.* drum
tam·bo·ra *f.* drum
tam·bo·ri·le·ar *v.* to beat
tam·bo·ri·le·o *m.* beating
ta·miz *m.* sieve
ta·mi·zar *v.* to filter
tam·po·co *adv.* nor; neither
tan *adv.* as; so
tan·da *f.* shift; turn
tan·gen·te *adj.* tangent
tan·gi·ble *adj.* tangible
tan·go *m.* tango
tan·gue·ar *v.* to tango
tan·que *m.* tanker
tan·te·ar *v.* to consider; to test
tan·to, a *adj.* so many
ta·ñer *v.* to play
ta·pa *f.* cover; lid
ta·pa·do *m.* coat
ta·par *v.* to block something
ta·pe·te *m.* carpet
ta·piar *v.* to wall something in
ta·pi·ce·ro, a *m., f.* upholsterer
ta·pio·ca *f.* tapioca
ta·piz *m.* tapestry
ta·pi·zar *v.* to upholster; to hang
tapestries

ta·pón *m.* cork
ta·qui·gra·fí·a *f.* stenography
ta·qui·gra·fiar *v.* to write using
shorthand
ta·quí·gra·fo, a *m., f.* stenographer
ta·ra *f.* defect
ta·rán·tu·la *f.* tarantula
ta·ras·car *v.* to bite
tar·dan·za *f.* delay
tar·dar *v.* to delay
tar·de *f.* afternoon
tar·dí·o, a *adj.* late
ta·re·a *f.* homework
ta·ri·fa *f.* tariff
ta·ri·far *v.* to give or apply a tariff to
something
tar·je·ta *f.* card
ta·rro *m.* jar
tar·ta *f.* pie
tar·ta·mu·de·o *m.* stammering
tar·tán *m.* tartan
tár·ta·ro, a *adj.* tartar
ta·sa *f.* rate
ta·sa·ción *f.* appraisal
ta·sa·dor, a *adj.* appraising
ta·sa·je·ar *v.* to jerk something
ta·sa·jo *m.* jerky
tas·ca *f.* joint
ta·ta·ra·bue·la *f.* great-great-grandmother
ta·ta·ra·bue·lo *m.* great-great-grandfather
ta·ta·ra·nie·ta *f.* great-great-granddaughter
ta·ta·ra·nie·to *m.* great-great-grandson
ta·tua·je *m.* tattoo
ta·tuar *v.* to tattoo
tau·ro·ma·quia *f.* bullfighting
ta·xi *m.* taxi
ta·xi·der·mia *f.* taxidermy
ta·xis·ta *m., f.* one who drives a taxi
ta·xo·no·mí·a *f.* taxonomy
ta·za *f.* bowl; cup
te *pron.* you
te·a *f.* torch
te·a·tral *adj.* theatrical
te·a·tra·li·dad *f.* theatricality
te·a·tro *m.* theater
te·cla *f.* key

te·cla·do *m.* keyboard
téc·ni·co, a *adj.* technical
tec·no·cra·cia *f.* technocracy
tec·no·lo·gí·a *f.* technology
tec·no·ló·gi·co, a *adj.* technological
te·char *v.* to roof a building
te·cho *m.* ceiling; roof
te·dio *m.* tedium
te·dio·so, a *adj.* tedious
te·ja *f.* tile
te·jar *v.* to tile
te·jer *v.* to knit
te·ji·do *m.* weave
te·jón *m.* badger
te·la *f.* fabric; film
te·la·ra·ña *f.* spider's web
te·le·co·mu·ni·ca·ción *f.* telecommunication
te·le·di·fun·dir *v.* to telecast
te·le·di·fu·sión *f.* to telecast
te·le·fo·na·zo *m.* telephone call
te·le·fo·ne·ar *v.* to phone someone
te·le·fó·ni·ca·men·te *adv.* by a phone
te·le·fo·nis·ta *m., f.* telephone operator
te·lé·fo·no *m.* telephone
te·le·fo·to *m.* telephoto
te·le·gra·fí·a *f.* telegraphy
te·le·gra·fiar *v.* to telegraph
te·le·grá·fi·co, a *adj.* telegraphic
te·le·gra·fis·ta *m., f.* telegrapher
te·lé·gra·fo *m.* telegraph
te·le·gra·ma *f.* telegram
te·le·man·do *m.* remote control
te·le·me·trí·a *f.* telemetry
te·le·pa·tí·a *f.* telepathy
te·le·pá·ti·co, a *adj.* telepathic
te·les·có·pi·co, a *adj.* telescopic
te·les·co·pio *m.* telescope
te·le·ti·po *m.* teletype
te·le·vi·sar *v.* to televise
te·le·vi·sión *f.* television
te·le·vi·sor *m.* television
te·lón *m.* curtain
te·lu·rio *m.* tellurium
te·ma *f.* subject; obsession
te·má·ti·co, a *adj.* thematic

tem·blar *v.* to tremble
tem·ble·que·ar *v.* to tremble
tem·blor *m.* earthquake; tremor
te·mer *v.* to be afraid of
te·me·ro·so, a *adj.* frightening
te·mor *m.* fear
tem·pe·ra·men·tal *adj.* temperamental
tem·pe·ra·men·to *m.* weather
tem·pe·ran·cia *f.* temperance
tem·pe·rar *v.* to calm
tem·pe·ra·tu·ra *f.* temperature
tem·pes·tad *f.* storm
tem·pes·tuo·so, a *adj.* stormy
tem·pla·do, a *adj.* mild
tem·plan·za *f.* moderation
tem·plar *v.* to temper; to tune; to appease
tem·ple *m.* mood; temper
tem·plo *m.* temple
tem·po·ra·da *f.* season
tem·po·ral *adj.* temporal
tem·po·rá·ne·o, a *adj.* temporary
tem·pra·ne·ro, a *adj.* early
tem·pra·no, a *adj.* early
te·na·ci·dad *f.* tenacity
te·naz *f.* tenacious
ten·den·cia *f.* tendency
ten·der *v.* to stretch something out
ten·di·do, a *adj.* spread out
ten·dón *m.* tendon
te·ne·bro·so, a *adj.* obscure; dark
te·ne·dor *m.* one who owns
te·nen·cia *f.* possession
te·ner *v.* to contain; to have; to keep
te·nia *f.* tapeworm
te·nien·te *m.* lieutenant
te·nis *m.* tennis
te·nis·ta *m., f.* one who plays tennis
ten·sar *v.* to stretch
ten·sión *f.* tension
ten·so, a *adj.* tense
ten·ta·ción *f.* temptation
ten·tá·cu·lo *m.* tentacle
ten·ta·dor, a *adj.* tempting
ten·ta·ti·vo, a *adj.* tentative
te·ñir *v.* to make dark
te·o·cra·cia *f.* theocracy

te·ó·lo·go, a *m., f.* theologian
te·o·re·ma *m.* theorem
te·o·rí·a *f.* theory
te·ó·ri·co *adj.* theoretical
te·o·ri·zar *v.* to theorize
te·ó·so·fo, a *m., f.* theosophist
te·qui·la *f.* tequila
te·ra·peu·ta *m., f.* therapist
te·ra·péu·ti·co, a *adj.* therapeutic
te·ra·pia *f.* therapy
ter·ce·ro, a *adj.* third
ter·cio, a *adj.* third
ter·cio·pe·lo *m.* velvet
ter·co, a *adj.* stubborn
ter·gi·ver·sar *v.* to distort
ter·mal *adj.* thermal
ter·mi·na·ción *f.* ending; termination
ter·mi·nal *adj.* terminal
ter·mi·nar *v.* to complete; to end
something
tér·mi·no *m.* ending
ter·mi·no·lo·gí·a terminology
ter·mi·ta *m.* termite
ter·mo·di·ná·mi·ca *f.* thermodynamics
ter·mo·e·léc·tri·co, a *adj.* thermoelectric
ter·mó·me·tro *m.* thermometer
ter·mos·ta·to *m.* thermostat
ter·no *m.* a set of three things
ter·nu·ra *f.* tenderness
te·rra·plén *m.* embankment
te·rrá·que·o, a *adj.* terrestrial
te·rra·za *f.* terrace
te·rre·mo·to *m.* earthquake
te·rre·nal *adj.* earthly
te·rre·no *adj.* earthly
te·rres·tre *adj.* terrestrial
te·rri·ble *adj.* terrible
te·rri·to·rial *adj.* territorial
te·rri·to·rio *m.* territory
te·rror *m.* terror
te·rro·rí·fi·co, a *adj.* terrifying
te·rro·ris·ta *m., f.* terrorist
ter·so, a *adj.* smooth
te·sis *f.* thesis
te·són *m.* tenacity
te·so·ne·ro, a *adj.* tenacious

te·so·re·rí·a *f.* treasury
te·so·re·ro, a *m., f.* treasurer
te·so·ro *m.* treasure
tes·tí·cu·lo *m.* testicle
tes·ti·fi·car *v.* to testify
tes·ti·mo·nio *m.* testimony
te·ta *f.* udder
té·ta·no *m.* tetanus
te·ti·lla *f.* teat
tex·til *adj.* textile
tex·to *m.* textbook
tex·tu·ra *f.* texture
tez *f.* complexion
ti *pron.* yourself
tí·a *f.* aunt
tia·ra *f.* tiara
ti·bia *f.* tibia
ti·bu·rón *m.* shark
tiem·po *m.* weather; time
tien·da *f.* store; shop
tien·to *m.* caution; touch
tier·no, a *adj.* tender
tie·rra *f.* land; country
tie·so, a *adj.* arrogant
ties·to *m.* flowerpot
ti·foi·de·o, a *adj.* typhoid
ti·fón *m.* typhoon
ti·fus *m.* typhus
ti·gre *m.* tiger
ti·gre·sa *f.* tigress
ti·je·re·te·ar *v.* to snip
ti·je·re·te·o *m.* snipping
ti·ma·dor, a *m., f.* cheat
ti·mar *v.* to cheat
tim·bra·do, a *adj.* stamped
tim·brar *v.* to stamp
tim·bre *m.* ring
ti·mi·dez *f.* timidity
tí·mi·do, a *adj.* timid
ti·mo *m.* thymus
ti·mo·ra·to, a *adj.* shy
tin·gla·do *m.* platform
ti·no *m.* good judgement
tin·ta *f.* dye
tin·te *m.* dye
tin·te·ro *m.* inkwell

tin•ti•nar *v.* to clink something
tin•tu•ra *f.* tincture
ti•ña *f.* ringworm
tí•o *m.* uncle
tí•pi•co, a *adj.* typical
ti•pi•fi•car *v.* to typify
ti•po *m.* type; kind
ti•po•gra•fí•a *f.* typography
ti•ra•da *f.* distance
ti•ra•ní•a *f.* tyranny
ti•ra•ni•zar *v.* to tyrannize
ti•ra•no, a *adj.* tyrannical
ti•ran•te *adj.* tight
ti•ran•tez *f.* tightness
ti•rar *v.* to throw
ti•ri•tar *v.* to shiver
ti•ro *m.* shot; throw
ti•ro•te•o *m.* shooting
ti•sis *f.* tuberculosis
tí•te•re *m.* puppet
ti•ti•lar *v.* to quiver
ti•ti•le•o *m.* quivering
ti•ti•ri•tar *v.* to tremble
ti•tu•be•o *m.* staggering
ti•tu•la•do, a *adj.* titled
tí•tu•lo *m.* title
ti•za *f.* chalk
tiz•nar *v.* to smudge
to•a•lla *f.* towel
to•bi•llo *m.* ankle
to•bo•gán *m.* sled
to•ca•dor *m.* dressing room
to•car *v.* to ring; to handle; to touch
to•da•ví•a *adv.* still
to•do, a *adj.* all; every
to•le•ran•cia *f.* tolerance
to•le•ran•te *adj.* tolerant
to•le•rar *v.* to tolerate
to•lon•drón, a *m., f.* scatterbrain
to•ma *f.* intake; taking
to•ma•dor, a *adj.* drinking
to•mar *v.* to have; to take
to•ma•te *m.* tomato
to•na•da *f.* tune
to•na•li•dad *f.* tonality
to•nel *m.* barrel

to•ne•la•da *f.* ton
to•ne•la•je *m.* tonnage
to•ni•fi•car *v.* to tone
to•ni•na *f.* tuna
to•no *m.* tone
ton•te•rí•a *f.* foolishness
ton•to *m.* fool
tó•pi•co *m.* topic
to•po *m.* mole
to•po•gra•fí•a *f.* topography
to•pó•gra•fo *m.* topographer
to•que *m.* beat; touch
to•que•te•ar *v.* to handle
to•que•te•o *m.* handling
to•rá•ci•co, a *adj.* thoracic
tor•ce•du•ra *f.* twist
tor•cer *v.* to sprain; to bend
to•re•a•dor *m.* bullfighter
to•re•ar *v.* to bullfight
to•re•o *m.* bullfighting
tor•men•to *m.* torment
tor•men•to•so, a *adj.* stormy
tor•na•do *m.* tornado
tor•na•sol *m.* sunflower
tor•na•so•la•do, a *adj.* iridescent
tor•ne•ar *v.* to turn on the lathe
tor•ne•o *m.* tournament
tor•ni•llo *m.* screw
tor•ni•que•te *m.* tourniquet
to•ro *m.* bull
to•ron•ja *f.* grapefruit
tor•pe•de•ar *v.* to torpedo
tor•pe•za *f.* stupidity
tor•por *m.* torpor
to•rrar *v.* to roast
to•rre *f.* castle
to•rren•cial *adj.* torrential
to•rren•te *m.* torrent
tó•rri•do, a *adj.* torrid
tor•sión *f.* torsion
tor•so *m.* torso
tor•ta *f.* cake
tór•to•la *f.* turtledove
tor•tu•ga *f.* turtle
tor•tuo•so, a *adj.* tortuous
tor•tu•ra *f.* torture

tor·tu·rar *v.* to torture
tos *f.* coughing
to·ser *v.* to cough
tos·que·dad *f.* coarseness
tos·ta·do, a *adj.* roasted
tos·ta·dor, a *m., f.* toaster
tos·tar *v.* to roast; to toast
to·tal *adj.* total
to·ta·li·dad *f.* totality
to·ta·li·ta·rio, a *adj.* totalitarian
to·ta·li·zar *v.* to total
to·xe·mia *f.* toxemia
to·xi·ci·dad *f.* toxicity
tó·xi·co, a *adj.* poison
to·xi·có·lo·go, a *m., f.* toxicologist
to·xi·na *f.* toxin
to·zu·do, a *adj.* stubborn
tra·ba *f.* obstacle; bolt
tra·ba·ja·dor *m.* worker
tra·ba·jar *v.* to work
tra·ba·jo *m.* job; work
tra·ba·jo·so, a *adj.* demanding
tra·bar *v.* to fasten; to bolt
tra·bu·car *v.* to mix up
trac·ción *f.* traction
trac·tor *m.* tractor
tra·di·ción *f.* tradition
tra·di·cio·nal *f.* traditional
tra·duc·ción *f.* translation
tra·du·cir *v.* to express
tra·duc·tor, a *m.* translator
tra·fi·car *v.* to deal
trá·fi·co *m.* traffic
tra·ga·luz *m.* skylight
tra·gar *v.* to devour; to swallow
tra·ge·dia *f.* tragedy
trá·gi·co, a *adj.* tragic
tra·gi·co·me·dia *f.* tragicomedy
tra·go *m.* gulp
trai·ción *f.* treason
trai·cio·nar *v.* to betray another
tra·je *m.* dress
tra·je·a·do, a *adj.* dressed
tra·je·ar *v.* to dress
tra·ji·nar *v.* to carry
tra·ma *f.* plot

tra·ma·dor, a *m., f.* weaver
tra·mar *v.* to scheme
tra·mi·ta·ción *f.* transaction
tra·mi·tar *v.* to negotiate
tra·mo *m.* flight
tram·pa *f.* trap
tram·pe·ar *v.* to cheat
tram·po·lín *m.* trampoline
tram·po·so, a *adj.* tranquilizing
tran·qui·lo, a *adj.* tranquil
tran·sac·ción *f.* transaction
tran·sat·lán·ti·co, a *adj.* transatlantic
trans·cen·den·cia *f.* transcendence
trans·cen·der *v.* to transcend
trans·con·ti·nen·tal *adj.*
transcontinental
trans·fe·ren·cia *f.* transfer
trans·fe·rir *v.* to transfer
trans·fi·gu·ra·ción *f.* transfiguration
trans·for·ma·ción *f.* transformation
trans·for·ma·dor, a *adj.* transforming
trans·for·mar *v.* to convert; to transform
trans·fun·dir *v.* to transfuse
trans·fu·sión *f.* transfusion
trans·gre·dir *v.* to transgress
trans·gre·sión *f.* transgression
tran·si·ción *f.* transition
tran·sis·tor *m.* transistor
tran·si·tar *v.* to travel
tran·si·ti·vo, a *adj.* transitive
trán·si·to *m.* traffic
tran·si·to·rio, a *adj.* temporary
trans·la·ción *f.* translation
trans·lú·ci·do, a *adj.* translucent
trans·mi·gra·ción *f.* transmigration
trans·mi·grar *v.* to transmigrate
trans·mi·tir *v.* to transmit
trans·mu·tar *v.* to transmute
trans·pa·ren·te *adj.* transparent
trans·pi·ra·ción *f.* perspiration
trans·pi·rar *v.* to perspire
trans·plan·tar *v.* to transplant
trans·po·ner *v.* to transplant; to move
trans·por·ta·ción *f.* transportation
trans·por·tar *v.* to transport
trans·po·si·ción *f.* transposition

trans•ver•so, a *adj.* transverse
tran•ví•a *m.* streetcar
tra•pe•cio *m.* trapezoid
tra•pe•zoi•de *m.* trapezoid
trá•que•a *f.* trachea
tras *prep.* behind; after
tras•at•lán•ti•co, a *adj.* transatlantic
tras•cen•den•te *adj.* transcendent
tras•cen•der *v.* to extend
tra•se•gar *v.* to decant
tras•fon•do *m.* background
tra•sie•go *m.* decanting
tras•la•ción *f.* translation
tras•la•dar *v.* to transcribe; to move
tras•la•do *m.* transfer
tras•no•cha•do, a *adj.* trite
tras•pa•pe•lar *v.* to misplace something
tras•pa•pe•la•do, a *adj.* misplaced
tras•pa•sar *v.* to break
tras•pa•so *m.* transfer
trans•plan•tar *v.* to transplant
tras•qui•lar *v.* to shear
tras•to•car *v.* to twist
tras•tor•nar *v.* to disrupt
tras•tro•car *v.* to twist
tra•sun•tar *v.* to summarize
tra•ta•mien•to *m.* treatment; process
tra•tar *v.* to process; to handle
tra•to *m.* treatment
trau•ma *m.* trauma
trau•má•ti•co, a *adj.* traumatic
trau•ma•ti•zar *v.* to traumatize
tra•ve•sí•a *f.* crosswind; crossroad
tra•ve•su•ra *f.* mischief
tra•vie•so, a *adj.* mischievous
tra•yec•to *m.* way
tra•yec•to•ria *f.* trajectory
tra•za *f.* plan
tra•zar *v.* to outline something
tra•zo *m.* line
tré•bol *m.* clover
tre•ce *adj.* thirteen
tre•cho *m.* in parts; stretch
tre•gua *f.* rest
trein•ta *adj.* thirty
trein•ta•vo *f.* thirtieth

trein•te•na *f.* thirty
tre•men•do, a *adj.* terrible; horrible
tre•men•ti•na *f.* turpentine
tre•mo•lar *v.* to wave
tre•mo•li•na *f.* rustling
tre•mor *m.* tremor
tren *m.* train
tren•ci•lla *f.* braid
tren•za *f.* braid
tre•pi•dar *v.* to vibrate
tres *adj.* three
tres•cien•tos *adj.* three hundred
tre•za•vo, a *adj.* thirteenth
trí•a•da *f.* triad
trian•gu•lar *adj.* triangular
trián•gu•lo *m.* triangular
tri•bal *adj.* tribal
tri•bu *f.* tribe
tri•bu•la•ción *f.* tribulation
tri•bu•no *m.* tribune
tri•bu•ta•rio, a *adj.* tributary
tri•bu•to *m.* tribute
tri•cen•te•na•rio *m.* tricentennial
tri•ci•clo *m.* tricycle
tri•co•lor *adj.* tricolor
tri•cús•pi•de *adj.* tricuspid
tri•gal *m.* field of wheat
tri•gé•si•mo, a *adj.* thirtieth
tri•go *m.* wheat
tri•go•no•me•trí•a *f.* trigonometry
tri•lin•güe *adj.* trilingual
tri•lo•gí•a *f.* trilogy
tri•lla•dor, a *adj.* threshing
tri•lli•zo *m.* triplet
tri•mes•tral *adj.* quarterly
trin•cha•dor, a *adj.* carving
trin•char *v.* to carve
tri•no•mio *m.* trinomial
trí•o *m.* trio
tri•ple *adj.* triple
tri•pli•ca•ción *f.* triplication
tri•pli•ca•do *m.* triplicate
tri•pli•car *v.* to triplicate
tri•plo, a *adj.* triple
trí•po•de *m., f.* tripod
tri•qui•no•sis *f.* trichinosis

tris•ca *f.* crack
tris•car *v.* to stamp
tris•te *adj.* miserable; sad
tris•te•za *f.* sorrow
tri•tu•rar *v.* to chew; to triturate
triun•fa•dor, a *adj.* triumphant
triun•fan•te *adj.* triumphant
triun•fo *m.* triumph
tri•vial *adj.* trivial
tri•via•li•dad *f.* triviality
tri•za *f.* piece
tro•car *v.* to barter
tro•fe•o *m.* trophy
tro•glo•di•ta *adj.* barbarous
tro•le *m.* trolley
trom•bón *m.* trombone
trom•bo•sis *f.* thrombosis
trom•pa *f.* horn
trom•pe•ar *v.* to punch
trom•pe•ta *f.* trumpet
trom•pe•tis•ta *m., f.* trumpeter
trom•pi•car *v.* to trip
trom•po *m.* top
tro•na•da *f.* thunderstorm
tro•na•dor, a *adj.* thundering
tro•nan•te *adj.* thundering
tro•nar *v.* to thunder
tron•co *m.* trunk
tron•cha *f.* slice
tro•pel *m.* confusion
tro•pe•lí•a *f.* violence
tro•pe•zar *v.* to trip
tro•pi•cal *adj.* tropical
tró•pi•co *m.* tropic
tro•pie•zo *m.* stumble
tro•po *m.* trope
tro•que•lar *v.* to mint
tro•ta•da *f.* trot
tro•ta•dor, a *adj.* trotting
tro•va *f.* ballad
tro•zo *m.* chunk; part; piece
tru•co *m.* trick
true•no *m.* thunder
tru•far *v.* to lie
tú *pron.* you
tu•ba *f.* tuba

tu•ber•cu•li•na *f.* tuberculin
tu•ber•cu•lo•sis *f.* tuberculosis
tu•be•ro•so, a *adj.* tuberous
tu•bo *m.* tube
tu•bu•la•do, a *adj.* tubular
tu•bu•lar *adj.* tubular
tu•cán *m.* toucan
tues•te *m.* toasting
tu•fo *m.* fume
tu•li•pán *m.* tulip
tu•llir *v.* to cripple
tum•ba *f.* tomb
tum•bar *v.* to knock out
tum•bo *m.* jolt
tu•mor *m.* tumor
tú•mu•lo *m.* tomb
tu•mul•to *m.* tumult
tu•mul•tuo•so, a *adj.* tumultuous
tu•nan•ta *adj.* cunning
tun•da *f.* beating
tun•de•ar *v.* to beat
tun•di•dor, a *m., f.* one who shears
tun•di•du•ra *f.* shearing
tun•dir *v.* to shear
tun•dra *f.* tundra
tú•nel *m.* tunnel
tungs•te•no *m.* tungsten
tú•ni•ca *f.* tunic
tu•pé *m.* toupee
tu•pi•do, a *adj.* dense; thick
tu•pir *v.* to weave close together
tur•ba *f.* mob
tur•ba•ción *f.* confusion
tur•ba•dor, a *adj.* disturbing
tur•ban•te *m.* turban
tur•bar *v.* to embarrass; to upset another
tur•bie•dad *f.* opaqueness
tur•bi•na *f.* turbine
tur•bio, a *adj.* turbulent; muddy
tur•bión *m.* shower
tur•bu•len•cia *f.* turbulence
tur•bu•len•to, a *adj.* turbulent
tu•ris•ta *f.* tourist
tu•rís•ti•co, a *adj.* tourist
tur•nar *v.* taking turns at something
tur•no *m.* turn

tur•que•sa *f.* turquoise
tu•ru•la•to, a *adj.* being stunned
tu•sa *f.* cornhusk
tu•sar *v.* to trim
tu•te•ar *v.* to address another as "tu"
tu•tor, a *m., f.* guardian
tu•yo, a *adj.* yours

U

u•bé•rri•mo, a *adj.* luxuriant
u•bi•ca•ción *f.* placing
u•bi•car *v.* to locate
u•bre *f.* udder
u•fa•nar•se *v.* to boast about something
u•fa•no, a *adj.* please
úl•ti•mo, a *adj.* final; last
ul•tra *adv.* besides
ul•tra•de•re•cha *f.* the far right
ul•tra•jan•te *adj.* outrageous
ul•tra•jar *v.* to insult
ul•tra•je *m.* insult
ul•tra•ma•ri•no, a *adj.* overseas
ul•tra•mo•der•no, a *adj.* ultramodern
ul•tra•só•ni•co, a *adj.* ultrasonic
ul•tra•so•ni•do *m.* ultrasound
ul•tra•vio•le•ta *adj.* ultraviolet
um•bi•li•cal *adj.* umbilical
um•bral *m.* threshold
um•brí•o, a *adj.* shady
um•bro•so, a *adj.* shady
un *indef. art.* an; a
u•na *indef. art.* an; a
u•ná•ni•me *adj.* unanimous
u•na•ni•mi•dad *f.* unanimity
un•cir *v.* to yoke
un•dé•ci•mo, a *adj.* eleventh
un•du•lar *v.* to undulate
un•güen•to *m.* ointment
u•ni•ce•lu•lar *adj.* unicellular
u•ni•ci•dad *f.* uniqueness
ú•ni•co, a *adj.* single; sole
u•ni•cor•nio *m.* unicorn
u•ni•dad *f.* unity; each

u•ni•do, a *adj.* united
u•ni•fi•ca•ción *f.* unification
u•ni•fi•car *v.* to unify
u•ni•for•mar *v.* to make something uniform
u•ni•for•me *adj.* even; uniform
u•ni•for•mi•dad *f.* uniformity
u•ni•la•te•ral *adj.* unilateral
u•nión *f.* joint; unity
u•nir(se) *v.* to unite together
u•ni•se•xo *adj.* unisex
u•ní•so•no, a *adj.* to be in unison with
u•ni•ta•rio, a *adj.* unified
u•ni•ver•sal *adj.* worldwide; universal
u•ni•ver•sa•li•dad *f.* universality
u•ni•ver•sa•li•zar *v.* to universalize
u•ni•ver•si•dad *f.* university
u•ni•ver•si•ta•rio, a *adj.* university
u•ni•ver•so *m.* universe
u•no,a *adj.* one
un•tar *v.* to spread; to grease
un•to *m.* grease
un•tuo•si•dad *f.* greasiness
un•tuo•so, a *adj.* greasy
un•tu•ra *f.* greasing
u•ña *f.* toenail; fingernail
u•ra•nio *m.* uranium
ur•ba•ni•dad *f.* urbanity
ur•bate•o•rí•a *f.* theory
ur•ba•ni•za•ción *f.* urbanization
ur•ba•ni•zar *v.* to develop
ur•ba•no, a *adj.* urban
u•rea *f.* urea
u•re•tra *f.* urethra
ur•gen•cia *f.* urgency
ur•gen•te *adj.* urgent
u•ri•na•rio, a *adj.* urinary
u•san•za *f.* custom
u•sar *v.* to use
u•so *m.* use
us•ted *pron.* you
u•sual *adj.* usual
u•su•ra *f.* usury
u•sur•par *v.* to usurp
u•ten•si•lio *f.* utensil
ú•til *adj.* useful

V

va•ca *f.* cow
va•ca•ción *f.* vacation
va•can•te *adj.* vacant
va•cia•de•ro *m.* dump
va•cia•do *m.* cast
va•ciar *v.* to void; to empty; to drain
va•ci•la•ción *f.* vacillation; hesitation
va•ci•lan•te *adj.* hesitating
va•ci•lar *v.* to falter; to vacillate
va•cío, a *adj.* devoid; empty; void; hollow
va•cui•dad *f.* vacuity
va•cu•na•ción *f.* vaccination
va•cu•nar *v.* to vaccinate
va•cu•no, a *adj.* bovine
va•cuo, a *adj.* vacuous
va•de•ar *v.* to overcome
va•ga•bun•do, a *adj.* vagabond
va•ga•men•te *adv.* vaguely
va•gan•cia *f.* vagrancy
va•gar *v.* to roam; to stray; to wander
va•gi•do *m.* cry
va•go, a *adj.* hazy; wandering; vague
va•gón *m.* van
va•guear *v.* to wander
va•gue•dad *f.* vagueness
va•ho *m.* vapor; steam
vai•ni•lla *f.* vanilla
vai•vén *m.* fluctuation
va•le *m.* voucher
va•le•de•ro, a *adj.* valid
va•len•cia *f.* valence
va•len•tí•a *f.* courage; valor; bravery
va•len•tón, a *adj.* boastful
va•len•to•na *f.* boast
va•ler *v.* to be of value; to have authority over; to be of worth
va•le•ro•so, a *adj.* valorous; courageous
va•lí•a *f.* worth
va•li•da•ción *f.* validation
va•li•dar *v.* to validate
va•li•dez *f.* validity

vá•li•do, a *adj.* good
va•lien•te *adj.* brave; valiant
va•li•ja *f.* suitcase
va•lio•so, a *adj.* valuable
va•lor *m.* valor; worth; importance
va•lo•ra•ción *f.* appraisal
va•lo•ri•zar *v.* to appraise something
vals *m.* waltz
va•luar *v.* to value something
vál•vu•la *f.* valve
va•llar *v.* to put a fence around; to fence in
va•lle *m.* valley
vam•pi•ro *m.* vampire
va•na•glo•ria *f.* pride
va•na•glo•rio•so, a *adj.* boastful
va•na•men•te *adv.* foolishly; vainly
van•da•lis•mo *m.* vandalism
va•ni•dad *f.* vanity
va•ni•do•so, a *adj.* one who is vain
va•no, a *adj.* vain
va•por *m.* steam
va•po•ri•za•dor *m.* vaporizer
va•po•ri•zar *v.* to vaporize
va•po•ro•so, a *adj.* steamy; vaporous
va•que•ta *f.* hide of a cow
va•ra *f.* rod; stalk
va•rar *v.* to beach
va•re•a•dor, a *m., f.* cowhand
va•re•ar *v.* to cudgel
va•ria•ble *adj.* variable
va•ria•ción *f.* change; variation
va•ria•do, a *adj.* varied
va•rien•te *adj.* varying
va•riar *v.* to change
va•rie•dad *f.* variety
va•ri•lla *f.* rod
va•rio, a *adj.* varied
va•rón *m.* man
va•ro•nil *adj.* virile
va•sa•llo, a *adj.* subordinate
vas•cu•lar *adj.* vascular
va•sec•to•mí•a *f.* vasectomy
va•si•ja *f.* container
va•so *m.* vessel; glass
vas•to, a *adj.* vast
va•ti•ci•nar *v.* to predict

verde

va·ti·ci·nio *m.* prediction
va·tio *m.* watt
ve·ci·nal *adj.* local
ve·ci·na·men·te *adv.* next
ve·cin·dad *f.* vicinity
ve·ci·no, a *adj.* near; next
vec·tor *m.* vector
ve·da *f.* prohibition
ve·da·do, a *adj.* prohibited
ve·dar *v.* to suspend; to prohibit
ve·ge·ta·ción *f.* vegetation
ve·ge·tal *adj.* vegetable
ve·ge·tar *v.* to vegetate
ve·ge·ta·ria·no, a *adj.* vegetarian
ve·ge·ta·ti·vo, a *adj.* vegetative
ve·he·men·cia *f.* vehemence
ve·he·men·te *adj.* vehement
ve·hí·cu·lo *m.* vehicle
vein·te *adj.* twenty
ve·ja·ción vexation
ve·ja·men *m.* vexation
ve·jar *v.* to persecute; to vex
ve·jez *f.* old age
ve·ji·ga *f.* bladder
ve·la *f.* sail
ve·la·da *f.* evening
ve·la·do, a *adj.* veiled
ve·lar *v.* to guard
ve·lei·do·so, a *adj.* fickle
ve·lo *m.* veil
ve·lo·ci·dad *f.* velocity
ve·loz *adj.* swift
ve·llo *m.* fuzz
ve·llón *m.* sheepskin
ve·llu·do, a *adj.* hairy
ve·na *f.* vein
ve·na·blo *m.* javelin
ven·ce·dor, a *m., f.* conqueror
ven·cer *v.* to conquer; to beat another
ven·ci·do, a *adj.* conquered; defeated
ven·ci·mien·to *m.* defeat; collapse
ven·da·je *m.* bandage
ven·dar *v.* to bandage
ven·de·dor, a *m., f.* seller
ven·der *v.* to sell
ven·di·mia·dor, a *m., f.* one who picks

grapes
ve·ne·no *m.* poison
ve·ne·no·si·dad *f.* poisonousness
ve·ne·no·so, a *adj.* poisonous
ve·ne·ra·ble *adj.* venerable
ve·ne·ra·ción *f.* veneration
ve·ne·rar *v.* to venerate
ven·gan·za *f.* revenge; vengeance
ven·gar *v.* to avenge
ve·nia *f.* forgiveness
ve·nial *adj.* venial
ve·ni·da *f.* return
ve·ni·de·ro, a *adj.* upcoming
ve·nir *v.* to come
ven·ta *f.* sale
ven·ta·ja *f.* benefit
ven·ta·jo·so, a *adj.* advantageous
ven·ta·na *f.* window
ven·ti·la·ción *f.* ventilation
ven·ti·la·dor *m.* fan
ven·ti·lar *v.* to air
ven·tis·ca *f.* blizzard
ven·tis·que·ro *m.* blizzard
ven·to·si·dad *f.* gas
ven·to·so, a *adj.* windy
ven·tri·cu·lar *adj.* ventricular
ven·trí·cu·lo *m.* ventricle
ven·trí·lo·cuo, a *m., f.* ventriloquist
ven·tu·ra *f.* happiness
ven·tu·ro·so, a *adj.* fortunate
ver *v.* to sight; to see
ve·ra *f.* edge
ve·ra·ci·dad *f.* veracity
ve·ra·ne·o *m.* vacationing
ve·ra·no *m.* summer
ve·ras *f.* earnestness
ve·raz *adj.* truthful
ver·bal *adj.* verbal
ver·bal·men·te *adv.* verbally
ver·bo *m.* verb
ver·bo·rre·a *f.* verbosity
ver·bo·si·dad *f.* verbosity
ver·bo·so, a *adj.* verbose
ver·dad *f.* truth
ver·da·de·ro, a *adj.* truthful
ver·de *adj.* green

ver•dor *m.* verdancy
ver•do•so, a *adj.* greenish
ver•du•ra *f.* greenery
ve•re•dic•to *m.* verdict
ver•gel *m.* orchard
ver•gon•zo•so, a *adj.* shameful
ver•güen•za *f.* shyness
ve•rí•di•co, a *adj.* true
ve•ri•fi•ca•ción *f.* verification
ve•ri•fi•ca•dor, a *m., f.* checker
ver•mi•ci•da *adj.* vermicidal
ver•nal *adj.* vernal
ve•ro•si•mi•li•tud *f.* probability
ver•sa•do, a *adj.* versed
ver•sá•til *adj.* versatile
ver•sa•ti•li•dad *f.* versatility
ver•sí•cu•lo *m.* versicle
ver•si•fi•car *v.* to versify
ver•sión *f.* version
ver•so *m.* version
ver•so *m.* verse
vér•te•bra *f.* vertebra
ver•te•bra•do, a *adj.* vertebrate
ver•te•bral *adj.* vertebral
ver•ter *v.* to shed
ver•ti•cal *adj.* vertical
ver•ti•ca•li•dad *f.* verticality
ver•tien•te *f.* spring
vér•ti•go *m.* vertigo
ve•sí•cu•la *f.* vesicle
ve•si•cu•lar *adj.* vesicular
ves•ti•do *m.* clothing; dress
ves•ti•du•ra *f.* garment
ves•ti•gio *m.* vestige
ves•ti•men•ta *f.* clothes
ves•tir *v.* to attire; to wear; to dress
ve•tar *v.* to veto
ve•te•ar *v.* to streak
ve•te•ra•no, a *m., f. adj.* veteran
ve•te•ri•na•rio, a *m., f.* veterinarian
vez *f.* time
vía *f.* means; way
via•ble *adj.* viable
via•jar *v.* to journey; to travel
via•je *m.* journey; trip
vial *adj.* traffic

vian•da *f.* food
ví•bo•ra *f.* viper
vi•bra•ción *f.* vibration
vi•brar *v.* to shake; to vibrate
vi•ce•pre•si•den•cia *f.* vice presidency
vi•ce•pre•si•den•te *m.* vice president
vi•ciar *v.* to corrupt; to falsify; to pollute
vi•cio *m.* vice
vi•cio•so, a *adj.* depraved
vi•ci•si•tud *f.* vicissitude
víc•ti•ma *f.* victim
vic•to•ria *f.* victory
vic•to•rio•so, a *adj.* victorious
vid *f.* grapevine
vi•da *f.* life
vi•de•o *m.* video
vi•de•o•ca•se•te *m.* videocassette
vi•de•o•cin•ta *f.* videotape
vi•dria•do, a *adj.* glazed
vi•drie•ro, a *m., f.* glazier
vi•drio *m.* glass
vi•drio•so, a *adj.* glassy
vie•jo, a *adj.* aged; old
vien•to *m.* wind
vier•nes *m.* Friday
vi•gen•cia *f.* force
vi•gi•lan•cia *f.* vigilance
vi•gi•lan•te *adj.* heedful; vigilant
vi•gi•lar *v.* to guard
vi•gi•lia *f.* vigil
vi•gor *m.* strength; vigor
vi•go•ro•so, a *adj.* forceful; vigorous
vi•hue•la *f.* guitar
vi•le•za *f.* vileness
vi•lla *f.* village
vi•lla•no, a *adj.* peasant
vi•na•gre *m.* vinegar
vi•na•gre•ta *f.* vinaigrette
vin•cu•lar *v.* to link
vin•di•ca•ción *f.* vindication
vin•di•car *v.* to vindicate
vi•ni•lo *m.* vinyl
vi•no *m.* wine
vi•ñe•do *m.* vineyard
vio•la *f.* viola
vio•lá•ce•o, a *adj.* violet

vio·la·ción *f.* violation
vio·lar *v.* to violate
vio·len·cia *f.* violence; rape
vio·len·tar *v.* to force; to distort; to break into
vio·len·to, a *adj.* violent
vio·le·ta *f., adj.* violet
vio·lín *f.* violin
vio·li·nis·ta *m., f.* violinist
vio·lón *m.* double bass player; double bass
vi·pe·ri·no *adj.* venomous
vi·ra·je *m.* turning point; veering turn
vi·rar *v.* to turn; to tone; to swerve
vir·gen *adj. f.* virgin
vi·ril *adj.* virile
vir·tual *adj.* virtual
vi·ru·len·to, a *adj.* virulent
vi·rus *m.* virus
vi·ru·ta *f.* shavings
vi·sar *v.* to sight; to endorse
vis·co·si·dad *f.* viscosity
vi·se·ra *f.* visor
vi·si·llo *m.* window curtain
vi·sión *f.* vision
vi·si·tar *v.* to visit
vis·ta *f.* sight; view
vis·to·so, a *adj.* colorful
vi·sual *adj.* visual
vi·tal *adj.* vital
vi·ta·mi·na *f.* vitamin
vi·to ·re·ar *v.* to cheer
vi·tral *m.* stained-glassed window
viu·da *f.* widow
viu·do *m.* widower
vi·vaz *adj.* lively
vi·ven·cia *f.* experience
ví·ve·res *m., pl.* provisions
ví·ve·ro *m.* fish hatchery; nursery
vi·ve·za *f.* liveliness; sharpness; quickness
ví·vi·do, a *adj.* vivid
vi·vien·da *f.* dwelling; housing
vi·vien·te *adj.* living
vi·vi·fi·ca·dor, a *adj.* vivifying
vi·vir *v.* to reside; to live
vi·vo, a *adj.* vivid; lively
vo·ca·blo *m.* term

vo·ca·bu·la·rio *m.* vocabulary
vo·ca·ción *f.* job; occupation; vocation
vo·cal *adj.* vocal
vo·ca·li·za·ción *f.* vocalization
vo·ce·ar *v.* to shout
vo·ce·o *m.* shouting
vo·ce·ro, a *m., f.* spokesman; spokeswoman
vo·la·da *f.* short flight
vo·lan·do *adv.* in a flash
vo·lan·te *adj.* flying; *m.* steering wheel
vo·lar *v.* to fly; to blow up; to disappear
vo·la·tín *m.* acrobatic stunt
vo·la·ti·ne·ro, a *m., f.* tightrope walker
vol·cán *m.* volcano
vo·le·ar *v.* to scatter
vo·li·ción *f.* volition
vol·ta·je *m.* voltage
vol·tear *v.* to upset; to turn over
vol·te·re·ta *f.* somersault
vol·tí·me·tro *m.* voltmeter
vol·tio *m.* volt
vo·lu·men *m.* volume
vo·lun·tad *f.* will; wish; intention
vo·lun·ta·rio, a *adj.* voluntary
vo·lun·ta·rio·so, a *adj.* willing; willful
vo·lup·tuo·si·dad *f.* voluptuousness
vol·ver *v.* to turn; to return; to recur; to restore
vo·mi·tar *v.* to spew; to vomit; to spill
vo·mi·ti·vo, a *adj., m.* vomitive
vo·ra·ci·dad *f.* voracity
vo·rá·gi·ne *f.* whirlpool
vo·ra·gi·no·so, a *adj.* turbulent
vo·raz *adj.* voracious
vór·ti·ce *m.* center of cyclone; vortex
vos *pron. m., f.* you
vo·se·ar *v.* to address
vo·se·o *m.* used in addressing someone
vo·so·tras *pron. f.* you
vo·so·tros *pron. m.* you
vo·ta·ción *f.* voting; vote
vo·tan·te *m., f.* voter
vo·tar *v.* to vote
vo·ti·vo *adj.* votive
voz *f.* voice

vozarrón

vo·za·rrón *m.* booming voice
vuel·co *m.* turn; overturning
vue·lo *m.* flight
vuel·to, a *m., f.* revolution
vues·tra *adj.* your
vul·ca·ni·zar *v.* to vulcanize
vul·gar *adj.* vulgar; common
vul·ga·ri·dad *f.* vulgarity
vul·ga·ris·mo *m.* vulgarism
vul·ga·ri·zar *v.* to popularize; to vulgarize
vul·go *m.* masses
vul·ne·ra·bi·li·dad *f.* vulnerability
vul·ne·rar *v.* to violate; to wound
vul·va *f.* vulva

W

wat *m.* watt
wel·ter *m.* welterweight
whis·ky *m.* whiskey

X

xe·no·fo·bia *f.* xenophobia
xi·ló·fo·no *m.* xylophone
xi·lo·gra·fí·a *m.* xylography

Y

ya·ca·ré *m.* alligator
ya·cer *v.* to lie; to be
ya·guar *m.* jaguar
yám·bi·co *adj.* iambic
yan·qui *adj. m., f.* Yankee
yar·da *f.* yard
ya·te *m.* yacht
ye·gua *f.* mare
ye·gua·da *f.* herd of horses
yel·mo *m.* helmet
ye·ma *f.* yolk

yen *m.* yen
yer·ba *f.* grass
yer·bal *m., f.* field of mate
yer·mar *v.* to strip
yer·mo, a *adj.* barren
yer·no *m.* son-in-law
ye·rra *f.* cattle branding
ye·rro *m.* fault; sin
yer·to *adj.* frozen stiff
ye·se·ro *adj.* plaster
ye·so *m.* gypsum
yo *pron.* I; me
yo·da·do, a *adj.* iodized
yo·do *m.* iodine
yo·du·ro *m.* iodide
yo·ga *m.* yoga
yo·g(h)i *m.* yogi
yo·gur(t) *m.* yogurt
yo·yo *m.* yo-yo
yu·ca *f.* yucca
yu·cal *m.* yucca field
yu·do *m.* judo
yu·ga·da *f.* day's plowing; yoke
yu·gu·lar *adj. f.* jugular
yun·que *m.* anvil
yun·ta *f.* yoke
yu·te *m.* jute
yux·ta·po·ner *v.* to juxtapose
yux·ta·po·si·ción *f.* juxtaposition
yu·yal *m.* weed patch
yu·yo *m.* weed
yu·yu·ba *f.* jujube

Z

za·far(se) *v.* to loosen
za·gal *m.* boy; lad
za·ga·la *f.* lass
za·ma·rro *m.* sheepskin
zam·bu·lli·da *f.* dive
zam·bu·llir *v.* to plunge into
za·na·ho·ria *f.* carrot
zan·ja *f.* trench; ditch
za·pa·te·rí·a *f.* shoestore

za•pa•te•ro *m.* shoemaker
za•pa•ti•lla *f.* slipper
za•pa•to *m.* shoe
zar *m.* czar
za•ri•na *f.* czarina
zar•za•mo•ra *f.* blackberry
zo•co *adj.* left-handed
zo•dí•a•co *m.* zodiac
zo•na *f.* zone
zoo•lo•gí•a *f.* zoology
zoo•ló•gi•co *adj.* zoological
zoó•lo•go *m.* zoologist
zo•rra *f.* fox
zo•rro *m.* fox
zo•zo•brar *v.* to overturn
zum•bar *v.* to whiz; to buzz
zu•mo *m.* juice
zu•mo•so *adj.* juicy
zur•cir *v.* to stitch

English—Spanish
Inglés—Español

A

a *indef. art.* una; un
a•back *adv.* atrás
a•ba•cus *n.* ábaco
a•ban•don *v.* abandonar
a•base *v.* humillar; rebajar
a•bate *v.* disminuir; reducir
ab•bey *n.* monasterio
ab•bre•vi•a•tion *n.* abreviación
ab•di•cate *v.* abdicar
ab•do•men *n.* abdomen
ab•duct *v.* secuestrar
ab•er•ra•tion *n.* aberración
a•bet *v.* instigar; ayudar
ab•hor *v.* aborrecer
a•bide *v.* cumplir; soportar
a•bil•i•ty *n.* habilidad
ab•ject *adj.* abyecto
ab•jure *v.* abjurar
a•ble *adj.* capaz; competente
ab•ne•gate *v.* renunciar; negar
ab•nor•mal *adj.* anormal
a•board *adv., prep.* a bordo
a•bode *n.* domicilio
a•bol•ish *v.* abolir
a•bom•i•nate *v.* abominar
ab•o•rig•i•nes *n.* aborígenes
a•bor•tion *n.* aborto
a•bound *v.* abundar
a•bout *prep.* sobre; alrededor de
a•bove *prep.* sobre; encima de
a•bra•sion *n.* abrasión
a•breast *adv.* de frente; al lado

a•bridge *v.* abreviar; resumir
a•broad *adv.* fuera de casa; en el extranjero
ab•ro•gate *v.* abrogar
ab•rupt *adj.* brusco
ab•scess *n.* absceso
ab•scond *v.* fugarse
ab•sent *adj.* ausente
ab•so•lute *adj.* completo; absoluto
ab•solve *v.* absolver
ab•sorb *v.* absorber
ab•stain *v.* abstenerse
ab•ste•mi•ous *adj.* abstemio
ab•stract *v.* abstraer
ab•surd *adj.* absurdo
a•bun•dant *adj.* abundante
a•buse *v.* insultar; maltratar
a•but *v.* limitar; bordear
a•byss *n.* abismo
ac•a•dem•ic *adj.* academico
a•cad•e•my *n.* academia
ac•cede *v.* acceder; consentir; subir
ac•cel•er•ate *v.* acelerar
ac•cent *n.* acento
ac•cept *v.* recibir
ac•cess *n.* acceso
ac•ces•si•ble *adj.* accesible
ac•ces•so•ry *n., pl.* accesorio; cómplice
ac•ci•dent *n.* accidente
ac•claim *v.* aclamar
ac•cli•mate *v.* aclimatar
ac•co•lade *n.* acolada
ac•com•mo•date *v.* acomodar
ac•cord *n.* acuerdo
ac•cor•di•on *n.* acordeón
ac•count *v.* explicar

ac·count·a·ble *adj.* responsable
ac·cum·u·late *v.* acumular
ac·cu·ra·cy *n.* exactitud
ac·cu·rate *adj.* exacto; fiel
ac·cuse *v.* acusar; culpar
ac·cus·tom *v.* acostumbrar
a·ce·tic *adj.* acético
ace·tone *n.* acetona
ache *n.* dolor
a·chieve *v.* acabar
acid *adj.* ácido
ac·knowl·edge *v.* reconocer; confesar; agradecer
ac·me *n.* cima
ac·ne *n.* acné
ac·o·lyte *n.* acólito
a·corn *n.* bellota
a·cous·tics *n.* acústica
ac·quaint *v.* enterar
ac·quaint·ance *n.* conocido
ac·qui·esce *v.* consentir
ac·quire *v.* adquirir
ac·quit *v.* absolver
a·cre *n.* acre
ac·rid *adj.* acre
ac·ri·mo·ny *n.* acrimonia
ac·ro·bat *n.* acróbata
a·cross *prep.* a través de
act *v.* fingir; hacer
ac·tion *n.* acción
ac·ti·vate *v.* activar
ac·tive *adj.* activo
ac·tor *n.* actor
ac·tress *n.* actriz
ac·tu·al *adj.* actual; real
a·cu·i·ty *n.* agudeza
a·cu·men *n.* agudeza
a·cute *adj.* agudo; fino
ad·age *n.* adagio
ad·a·mant *adj.* firme
a·dapt *v.* adaptar
add *v.* sumar; añadir
ad·di·tion *n.* adición
ad·dress *v.* dirigir (se a)
a·dept *n., adj.* experto
ad·e·quate *adj.* adecuado; suficiente

ad·here *v.* adherirse; pegarse; cumplir
ad·he·sive *adj., n.* adhesivo
ad·ja·cent *adj.* adyacente
ad·jec·tive *n.* adjetivo
ad·join *v.* juntar; estar contiguo
ad·journ *v.* suspender
ad·judge *v.* juzgar; sentenciar
ad·just *v.* ajustar; adaptar
ad·ju·tant *n.* ayudante
ad-lib *v.* improvisar
ad·min·is·ter *v.* administrar
ad·min·is·tra·tion *n.* administración
ad·mire *v.* admirar
ad·mis·si·ble *adj.* admisible
ad·mis·sion *n.* entrada; confesión
ad·mit *v.* confesar; admitir
ad·mon·ish *v.* amonestar
a·do·be *n.* adobe
ad·o·les·cence *n.* adolescencia
a·dopt *v.* adoptar; aceptar
a·dore *v.* adorar
a·dorn *v.* adornar
a·dren·a·line *n.* adrenalina
a·droit *adj.* hábil; diestro
ad·u·la·tion *n.* adulación
a·dult *adj.* mayor
a·dul·ter·y *n.* adulterio
ad·vance *v.* avanzar
ad·van·tage *n.* ventaja
ad·ven·ture *n.* aventura
ad·ven·ture·some *adj.* aventurado
ad·verb *n.* adverbio
ad·ver·sar·y *n.* adversario
ad·verse *adj.* adverso; contrario
ad·ver·si·ty *n.* adversidad
ad·ver·tise *v.* publicar
ad·vice *n.* consejo
ad·vise *v.* avisar
ad·vo·cate *v.* abogar
adz, adze *n.* azuela
ae·gis *n.* patrocinio
aer·ate *v.* airear
aer·i·al *adj.* aéreo
aer·o·naut·ics *n., pl.* aeronáutica
aes·thete *n.* esteta
aes·thet·ic *adj.* estético

a•far *adv.* lejos

af•fa•ble *adj.* afable; cortés

af•fair *n.* asunto

af•fect *v.* afectar

af•fec•ta•tion *n.* afectación

af•fec•tion *n.* afección

af•fec•tion•ate *adj.* cariñoso

af•fi•ance *v.* desposarse

af•fi•da•vit *n.* declaración jurada

af•fil•i•ate *v.* afiliar

af•fin•i•ty *n.* afinidad

af•firm *v.* afirmar

af•firm•a•tive *n.* aserción

af•fix *v.* añadir; fijar

af•flic•tion *n.* aflicción

af•flu•ence *n.* afluencia

af•flu•ent *adj.* rico; opulento

af•ford *v.* tener medios para; dar

af•front *v.* afrentar

a•fire *adj., adv.* ardiendo

a•flame *adj., adv.* en llamas

a•float *adj., adv.* a flote

a•foul *adj., adv.* enredado

a•fraid *adj.* atemorizado

a•fresh *adv.* de nuevo; otra vez

aft *adj., adv.* en (a) popa

af•ter *prep.* detrás de

af•ter•birth *n.* secundinas

af•ter•noon *n.* tarde

af•ter•ward *adv.* después

a•gain *adv.* otra vez

a•gainst *prep.* contra

a•gape *adj., adv.* boquiabierto

age *n.* edad

a•ged *adj.* viejo

a•gen•cy *n.* agencia; acción; medio

a•gen•da *n., pl.* orden del día

a•gent *n.* agente; representante

ag•glom•er•ate *v.* aglomerar

ag•gran•dize *v.* engrandecer

ag•gra•vate *v.* agravar

ag•gre•gate *v.* agregar; juntar

ag•gres•sion *n.* agresión

ag•gres•sive *adj.* agresivo

a•ghast *adj.* horrorizado

ag•ile *adj.* ágil

a•gil•i•ty *n.* agilidad

ag•i•tate *v.* agitar; inquietar

a•glow *adj.* ardiente

ag•nos•tic *n.* agnóstico

a•go *adj.* pasado

ag•o•ny *n.* agonía; angustia

a•grar•i•an *adj.* agrario

a•gree *v.* acordar

a•gree•a•ble *adj.* agradable; conforme

a•gree•ment *n.* acuerdo

ag•ri•cul•ture *n.* agricultura

a•gron•o•my *n.* agronomía

a•ground *adv.* encallado

a•head *adv.* al frente

aid *n.* ayuda

ail•ment *n.* enfermedad; dolencia

aim *v.* aspirar

air *n.* aire

air con•di•tion•er *n.* acondicionador de aire

air•plane *n.* avión

air•port *n.* aeropuerto

air-raid *n.* ataque aéreo

air•y *adj.* ligero; alegre

aisle *n.* nave lateral; pasillo

a•jar *adj., adv.* entreabierto

a•kin *adj.* semejante; consanguíneo

al•a•bas•ter *n.* alabastro

a•lac•ri•ty *n.* alacridad

a•larm *n.* alarma

a•larm•ist *n.* alarmista

al•ba•tross *n.* albatros

al•be•it *conj.* aunque

al•bi•no *n.* albino

al•bum *n.* álbum

al•bu•men *n.* albumen

al•bu•min *n.* albúmina

al•che•my *n.* alquimia

al•co•hol *n.* alcohol

ale *n.* cerveza

a•lee *adv.* a sotavento

a•lert *adj.* alerte

al•fal•fa *n.* alfalfa

al•ga *n.* alga

al•ge•bra *n.* álgebra

a•li•as *n.* alias

al·i·bi *n.* coartada; excusa
a·lien *n.* extranjero
a·light *v.* bajar; posarse
a·lign *v.* alinera; aliar
a·like *adj.* semejante
al·i·ment *n.* alimento
al·i·men·ta·ry *adj.* alimenticio
al·i·mo·ny *n.* alimentos
a·live *adj.* activo
all *adj.* todo
al·lay *v.* aliviar; aquietar
al·le·ga·tion *n.* alegación
al·lege *v.* alegar; declarar
al·leged *adj.* supuesto; alegado
al·le·giance *n.* lealtad
al·le·go·ry *n.* alegoría
al·ler·gy *n.* alergia
al·le·vi·ate *v.* calmar
al·le·vi·a·tion *n.* aligeramiento
al·ley *n.* callejuela
al·li·ance *n.* alianza
al·li·ga·tor *n.* caimán
al·lo·cate *v.* asignar
al·lo·ca·tion *n.* reparto; cupo
al·lot *v.* asignar; distribuir; adjudicar
al·low *v.* dar; permitir
al·low·ance *n.* ración; permiso
al·loy *n.* aleación
al·lude *v.* aludir
al·lure *v.* tentar
al·lu·sion *n.* alusión
al·lu·vi·um *n.* derrubio
al·ly *n.* aliado; confederado
al·ma·nac *n.* almanaque
al·might·y *adj.* omnipotente; todopoderoso
al·mond *n.* almendra; almendro
al·most *adv.* casi
alms *n.* limosna
a·loft *adv.* en alto
a·lone *adj.* solo
a·long *adv., conj., prep.* a lo largo
a·loof *adv.* lejos reservado
a·loud *adv.* en voz alta; alto
al·pha·bet *n.* alfabeto
al·read·y *adv.* ya
al·so *adv.* también; además

al·tar *n.* altar
al·ter *v.* cambiar; alterar; modificar
al·ter·a·tion *n.* alteración
al·ter e·go *n.* álter ego
al·ter·nate *v.* alternar
al·ter·na·tive *n.* alternativa
al·though *conj.* aunque
al·tim·e·ter *n.* altímetro
al·ti·tude *n.* altura; altitud
al·to *n.* alto; contralto
al·to·geth·er *adv.* en total
a·lu·mi·num *n.* aluminio
a·lum·na *n.* graduada
a·lum·nus *n.* graduado
al·ways *adv.* siempre
a.m. *abbr. adj.* antemeridiano
a·mal·gam *n.* amalgama
a·mal·gam·ate *v.* amalgamar
a·mass *v.* acumular; amontonar
am·a·teur *n.* aficionada
am·a·to·ry *adj.* amatorio
a·maze *v.* asombrar
a·maze·ment *n.* sorpresa
am·a·zon *n.* amazona
am·bas·sa·dor *n.* embajador
am·ber *n.* ámbar
am·bi·dex·trous *adj.* ambidextro
am·bi·gu·i·ty *n.* ambigüedad; doble
  sentido
am·big·u·ous *adj.* ambiguo
am·bi·tion *n.* ambición
am·bi·tious *adj.* ambicioso
am·biv·a·lence *n.* ambivalencia
am·ble *v.* amblar; andar lentamente
am·bu·late *v.* andar; ambular
am·bu·la·to·ry *adj.* ambulante
am·bus·cade *n.* emboscada
am·bush *n.* emboscada
a·me·ba *n.* amiba
a·mel·io·rate *v.* mejorar; mejoramiento
a·men *int.* amén
a·me·na·ble *adj.* dócil
a·mend *v.* enmendar; corregir
a·mends *n., pl.* compensación
a·men·i·ty *n.* amenidad
A·mer·i·can *adj.* americano

amethyst

am•e•thyst *n.* amatista
a•mi•a•ble *adj.* amable
am•i•ca•ble *adj.* amistoso
a•mid *prep.* en medio de; entre
a•mid•ships *adv.* en medio del navío
a•miss *adv., adj.* impropiamente
am•mo•nia *n.* amoníaco
am•ne•sia *n.* amnesia
am•nes•ty *n.* amnistía
a•moe•ba *n.* amiba
a•mong *prep.* en medio de
a•mor•al *adj.* amoral
am•o•rous *adj.* amoroso
a•mor•phous *adj.* amorfo
am•or•tize *v.* amortizar
a•mount *n.* cantidad; suma
am•pere *n.* amperio
am•phib•i•an *adj., n.* anfibio
am•phib•i•ous *adj.* anfibio
am•phi•the•a•ter *n.* anfiteatro
am•ple *adj.* abundante
am•pli•fy *v.* amplificar
am•pli•tude *n.* amplitud; abundancia
am•pu•tate *v.* amputar
am•pu•ta•tion *n.* amputación
a•muck *adv.* furiosamente
am•u•let *n.* amuleto
a•muse•ment *n.* pasatiempo
an *indef. art.* una; un; uno
a•nach•ro•nism *n.* anacronismo
an•a•con•da *n.* anaconda
a•nae•mi•a *n.* anemia
an•a•gram *n.* anagrama
a•nal *adj.* anal
an•al•ge•sic *adj.* analgésico
a•nal•o•gize *v.* analogizar
a•nal•o•gy *n.* analogía
a•nal•y•sis *n.* análisis
an•a•lyst *n.* analizador
an•a•lyze *v.* analizar
an•ar•chism *n.* anarquismo
an•ar•chist *n.* anarquista
an•ar•chy *n.* anarquía
a•nat•o•my *n.* anatomía
an•ces•tor *n.* antepasado
an•ces•try *n.* linaje; abolengo

an•chor *n.* ancla; áncora
an•cho•vy *n.* anchoa
an•cient *ajd.* antiguo
and *conj.* y
an•ec•dote *n.* anécdota
a•ne•mi•a *n.* anemia
an•e•mom•e•ter *n.* anemómetro
an•es•the•sia *n.* anestesia
an•es•the•tic, *adj.* anestésico
a•new *adv.* de nuevo; otra vez
an•gel *n.* ángel
an•gel•ic *adj.* angélico
an•ger *n.* ira; cólera
an•gle *n.* ángulo
an•gle•worm *n.* lombriz
An•glo-Saxon *v., adj.* anglosajón
an•gor•a *n.* angora
an•gry *adj.* enfadado
an•guish *n.* angustia; ansiedad
an•gu•lar *adj.* angular; anguloso
an•hy•drous *adj.* anhidro
an•i•mad•ver•sion *n.* animadversión
an•i•mad•vert *v.* censurar
an•i•mal *n.* animal
an•i•mal•ize *v.* animalizar
an•i•mate *v.* dar vida
an•i•ma•tion *n.* animación
an•i•mos•i•ty *n.* animosidad
an•ise *n.* anís
an•kle *n.* tobillo
an•nals *n., pl.* anales
an•neal *v.* templar
an•nex *v.* anexar; adjuntar
an•nex•a•tion *n.* anexión
an•ni•hi•late *v.* aniquilar
an•ni•hi•la•tion *n.* aniquilación
an•ni•ver•sa•ry *n.* aniversario
an•no•tate *v.* anotar
an•nounce *v.* proclamar
an•nounce•ment *n.* anuncio
an•noy *v.* molestar
an•noy•ance *n.* fastidio
an•nu•al *adj.* anual
an•nu•i•ty *n.* renta vitalicia
an•nul *v.* anular
an•nul•ment *n.* anulación

an·nun·ci·ate *v.* anunciar
an·nun·ci·a·tion *n.* anunciación
an·ode *n.* ánodo
a·noint *v.* untar; ungir
a·nom·a·lous *adj.* anómalo
a·nom·a·ly *n.* anomalía
a·non·y·mous *adj.* anónimo
an·oth·er *adj., pron.* otro
an·swer *v.* contestar; responder
ant *n.* hormiga
ant·ac·id *n.* antiácido
an·tag·o·nist *n.* antagonista
an·tag·o·nize *v.* contender
ant·arc·tic *adj.* antártico
ant·eat·er *n.* oso hormiguero
an·te·cede *v.* anteceder
an·te·date *v.* antedatar; preceder
an·te·di·lu·ve·an *adj.* antediluviano
an·te·lope *n.* antílope
an·ten·na *n.* antena
an·te·ri·or *adj.* anterior
an·te·room *n.* antecámara
an·them *n.* antífona;
an·ther *n.* antera
an·thol·o·gy *n.* antología
an·thra·cite *n.* antracita
an·thrax *n.* ántrax
an·thro·poid *adj.* antropoide
an·thro·pol·o·gist *n.* antropólogo
an·thro·pol·o·gy *n.* antropología
an·ti *prefix* anti; contra
an·ti·bi·ot·ic *n.* antibiótico
an·ti·bod·y *n.* anticuerpo
an·tic *n.* travesura; cabriola
an·tic·i·pate *v.* anticipar; esperar
an·tic·i·pa·tion *n.* anticipación;
expectativa
an·ti·cli·max *n.* anticlímax
an·ti·dote *n.* antídoto
an·tip·a·thy *n.* antipatía
an·tip·odes *n.* antípoda
an·ti·quate *v.* anticuar
an·ti·quat·ed *adj.* viejo; anticuado
an·tique *adj.* antiguo
an·tiq·ui·ty *n.* antigüedad
an·ti·sem·i·tism *n.* antisemitismo

an·ti·sep·tic *adj., n.* antiséptico
an·ti·so·cial *adj.* antisocial
an·tith·e·sis *n.* antítesis
an·ti·tox·in *n.* antitoxina
ant·ler *n.* cuerno; asta
an·to·nym *n.* antónimo
a·nus *n.* ano
an·vil *n.* yunque
anx·i·e·ty *n.* inquietud; ansia
anx·ious *adj.* impaciente
an·y *adj., pro.* alguno; algún
an·y·bod·y *pron.* alguien
an·y·how *adv.* de cualquier modo; de
todas formas
an·y·one *pron.* alguien; alguno
an·y·thing *pron.* algo
an·y·way *adv.* de cualquier modo; de
todas fromas
an·y·where *adv.* en todas partes;
dondequiera
a·or·ta *n.* aorta
a·part·ment *n.* apartamento
ap·a·thet·ic *adj.* indiferente
ap·a·thy *n.* apatía
ape *n.* mono
ap·er·ture *n.* abertura
a·pex *n.* ápice
aph·o·rism *n.* aforismo
aph·ro·dis·i·ac *n.* afrodisíaco
a·pi·a·rist *n.* colmenero
a·pi·ar·y *n.* colmenar
a·piece *adv.* cada uno; por persona
a·plomb *n.* aplomo
a·poc·a·lypse *n.* apocalipsis
a·pol·o·gize *v.* disculparse
a·pol·o·gy *n.* apología; disculpa
ap·o·plec·tic *adj.* apoplético
ap·o·plex·y *n.* apoplejía
a·port *adv.* a babor
a·pos·tate *n.* apóstata
a·pos·ta·tize *v.* apostatar
a·pos·tle *n.* apóstol
ap·os·tol·ic *adj.* apostólico
a·pos·tro·phe *n.* apóstrofo
a·poth·e·car·y *n.* boticario
ap·pall, ap·pal *v.* aterrar

apparatus

ap·pa·rat·us *n.* aparato
ap·pa·rel *n.* ropa
ap·par·ent *adj.* claro; aparente
ap·pa·ri·tion *n.* fantasma
ap·peal *n.* apelación
ap·pear *v.* parecer
ap·pear·ance *n.* apariencia
ap·pease *v.* apaciguar
ap·pel·lant *n.* apelante
ap·pel·la·tion *n.* nombre
ap·pend *v.* anexar
ap·pen·dage *n.* apéndice
ap·pen·dec·to·my *n.* apendectomía
ap·pen·di·ci·tis *n.* apendicitis
ap·pen·dix *n.* apéndice
ap·per·tain *v.* pertenecer
ap·pe·tite *n.* gana
ap·pe·tiz·ing *adj.* apetitoso; apetitivo
ap·plaud *v.* aplaudir
ap·plause *n.* aplauso
ap·ple *n.* manzana
ap·pli·cant *n.* suplicante
ap·pli·ca·tion *n.* aplicación
ap·ply *v.* aplicar
ap·point *v.* señalar; nombrar
ap·point·ment *n.* cita; nombramiento
ap·por·tion *v.* repartir
ap·po·si·tion *n.* aposición
ap·prais·al *n.* valoración
ap·praise *v.* valorar
ap·pre·ci·ate *v.* apreciar; valorar; agradecer
ap·pre·ci·a·tion *n.* aprecio; aumento en valor
ap·pre·hend *v.* entender
ap·pre·hen·sion *n.* aprehensión
ap·pren·tice *n.* aprendiz; *v.* poner de aprendiz
ap·prise, ap·prize *v.* informar
ap·proach *v.* aproximarse
ap·pro·ba·tion *n.* aprobación
ap·prov·al *n.* aprobación
ap·prove *v.* aprobar
ap·prox·i·mate *v.* aproximar
ap·ri·cot *n.* albaricoque
A·pril *n.* abril

a·pron *n.* delantal; *m.*
ap·ro·pos of *prep.* a propósito de
apt *adj.* apto; listo
ap·ti·tude *n.* aptitud
a·quar·i·um *n.* acuario
a·quat·ic *adj.* acuático
aq·ue·duct *n.* acueducto
a·que·ous *adj.* ácueo
aq·ui·line *adj.* aguileño
Ar·ab *n., adj.* árabe; *m., f.*
Ar·a·bic nu·me·rals *n.* números arábigos
ar·a·ble *adj.* arable; cultivable
ar·bi·ter *n.* árbitro
ar·bi·trar·y *adj.* arbitrario
ar·bi·trate *v.* arbitrar
ar·bi·tra·tion *n.* arbitraje
ar·bo·re·tum *n.* jardín botánico
arc *n.* arco *v.* formar un arco voltaico
ar·cade *n.* arcada; galería
arch *n.* arco *v.* arquear
arch *prefix* principal
ar·chae·ol·o·gy, ar·che·ol·o·gy *n.* arqueología
ar·cha·ic *adj.* arcaico
arch·an·gel *n.* arcángel
arch·bish·op *n.* arzobispo
arch·duch·ess *n.* archiduquesa
arch·duke *n.* archiduque
arch·er *n.* arquero
arch·er·y *n.* ballestería
ar·che·type *n.* arquetipo
ar·chi·pel·a·go *n.* archipiélago
ar·chi·tect *n.* arquitecto
ar·chi·tec·tur·al *adj.* arquitectónico
ar·chi·tec·ture *n.* arquitectura
ar·chive *n.* archivo
arch·priest *n.* arcipreste
arc·tic *adj.* ártico
ar·dent *adj.* ardiente; fervoroso
ar·dor *n.* ardor
ar·du·ous *adj.* arduo; difícil
a·re·na *n.* arena
ar·gon *n.* argo
ar·got *n.* jerga
ar·gue *v.* razonar

ar•gu•ment *n.* disputa
ar•gu•men•ta•tive *adj.* argumentador
ar•id *adj.* árido
a•rid•i•ty *n.* aridez
a•rise *v.* alzarse; surgir
ar•is•toc•ra•cy *n.* aristocracia
a•ris•to•crat *n.* aristócrata
a•ris•to•crat•ic *adj.* aristocrático
a•rith•me•tic *n.* aritmética
a•rith•me•ti•cian *n.* aritmético
ark *n.* arca
arm *n.* brazo
ar•ma•da *n.* armada
ar•ma•dil•lo *n.* armadillo
ar•ma•ment *n.* armamento
arm•ful *n.* brazado
ar•mi•stice *n.* armisticio
ar•moire *n.* armario
ar•mor *n.* armadura
ar•mored *adj.* blindado
ar•mor•y *n.* armería
arm•pit *n.* sobaco
ar•my *n.* ejército
a•ro•ma *n.* aroma
ar•o•mat•ic *adj.* aromático
a•round *adv.* alrededor
a•rouse *v.* despertar; excitar
ar•range *v.* arreglar; prevenir
ar•range•ment *n.* orden
ar•ray *n.* orden; formación; adorno;
   v. colocar; ataviar
ar•rest *v.* detener
ar•ri•val *v.* llegar
ar•ro•gance *n.* arrogancia
ar•ro•gant *adj.* arrogante
ar•row *n.* flecha
ar•row•head *n.* punta de flecha
ar•sen•al *n.* arsenal
ar•sen•ic *n.* arsénico
ar•son *n.* incendio premeditado
art *n.* arte
ar•te•ri•al *adj.* arterial
ar•ter•y *n.* arteria
art•ful *adj.* ingenioso; astuto
ar•thrit•ic *adj.* artrítico
ar•thri•tis *n.* artritis

ar•ti•cle *n.* artículo; objeto
ar•tic•u•late *v.* articular
ar•tic•u•la•tion *n.* articulación
ar•ti•fi•cial *adj.* artificial
ar•til•ler•y *n.* artillería
art•ist *n.* artista
ar•tis•tic *adj.* artístico
as *conj., adv.* como
as•bes•tos, as•bes•tus *n.* asbesto
as•cend *v.* subir; ascender
as•cen•sion *n.* ascensión
as•cent *n.* subida; cuesta
as•cer•tain *v.* averiguar
as•ce•tic *adj.* ascético; *n.* asceta
as•cet•i•cism *n.* ascetismo
as•cribe *v.* atribuir
a•sex•u•al *adj.* asexual
ash *n.* ceniza
a•shamed *adj.* avergonzado
a•side *adv.* a un lado; *n.* aparte
as•i•nine *adj.* asnal
ask *v.* rogar; preguntar
a•skance *adv.* con recelo
a•slant *adv.* a través; *prep.* a través de
a•sleep *adv., adj.* dormido
asp *n.* áspid
as•par•a•gus *n.* espárrago
as•pect *n.* aspecto; aire
as•per•i•ty *n.* aspereza
as•per•sion *n.* calumnia
as•phalt *n.* asfalto
as•phyx•i•ate *v.* asfixiar
as•pi•ra•tion *n.* aspiración; anhelo
as•pire *v.* aspirar
as•pi•rin *n.* aspirina
ass *n.* burro; tonto
as•sail *v.* acometer
as•sail•ant *n.* asaltador
as•sas•sin *n.* asesino
as•sas•si•na•tion *n.* asesinato
as•sault *v.* atacar
as•sem•ble *v.* juntar
as•sem•bly *n.* asamblea
as•sent *n.* asentimiento
as•sert *v.* afirmar
as•sess *v.* fijar; tasar

as•set *n.* haber
as•sev•er•ate *v.* aseverar
as•sid•u•ous *adj.* asiduo
as•sign *v.* asignar
as•sign•ment *n.* asignación
as•sim•i•late *v.* asimilar
as•sist *v.* ayudar
as•sist•ance *n.* ayuda
asth•ma *n.* asma
asth•mat•ic *adj.* asmático
as•ton•ish *v.* asombrar
as•ton•ish•ment *n.* asombro
as•trol•o•gy *n.* astrología
as•tron•o•my *n.* astronomía
at *prep. a;* en
ath•lete *n.* atleta
ath•let•ic *adj.* atlético
at•om *n.* átomo
a•tom•ic *adj.* atómico
a•top *prep.* sobre
at•tach *v.* pegar; sujetar
at•tack *v.* atacar
at•tempt *v.* intentar
at•tend *v.* asistir
at•ten•tion *n.* atención
a•typ•i•cal *adj.* atípico
au•di•ence *n.* público
au•di•tion *n.* audición
au•di•to•ry *adj.* auditivo
Au•gust *n.* agosto
aunt *n.* tía
au•then•tic•i•ty *n.* autenticidad
au•thor *n.* autor
au•thor•i•ty *n.* autoridad
au•thor•ize *v.* autorizar
au•to•bi•og•ra•pher *n.* autobiógrafo
au•to•bi•og•ra•phy *n.* autobiografía
au•to•mat•ic *adj.* automático
au•to•ma•tion *n.* automatización
au•to•mo•bile *n.* automóvil; coche
au•ton•o•mous *adj.* autónomo
a•venge *v.* vengar
av•e•nue *n.* avenida
a•ver *v.* afirmar
av•er•age *adj.* medio
a•vert *v.* apartar

a•wait *v.* esperar
a•wake *v.* despertar(se)
a•way *adv.* lejos
aw•ful *adj.* horrible
awk•ward *adj.* embarazoso
ax•i•om *n.* axioma
ax•i•o•mat•ic *adj.* axiomático
ax•is *n.* axis; eje
ax•le *n.* eje
aye, ay *interj., n.* sí
az•ure *adj., n.* azul celeste

B

bab•ble *v.* murmurar; barbotar; susurrar
ba•boon *n.* mandril
ba•bush•ka *n.* pañuelo
ba•by *n.* niño
ba•by•hood *n.* infancia
ba•by•ish *adj.* infantil
bac•cha•nal *n.* bacanal
bach•e•lor *n.* soltero
bach•e•lor•hood *n.* soltería
ba•cil•lus *n.* bacilo
back *n.* espalda
back•ache *n.* dolor de espalda
back•bit•ing *n.* murmuración
back•bone *n.* espinazo
back•break•ing *adj.* agobiador
back•date *v.* antedatar
back•er *n.* promotor
back•gam•mon *n.* juego de chaquete
back•ground *n.* fondo
back•hand•ed *adj.* revés
back•lash *n.* sacudida
back•pack *n.* mochila
back•side *n.* trasero
back•stairs *adj.* furtivo
back•track *v.* desandar
back•up *n.* suplente; reserva
back•ward *adv.* atrás
back•ward•ness *n.* retraso
ba•con *n.* tocino

bac·te·rial *adj.* bacteriano
bac·te·ri·cide *n.* bactericida
bac·ter·i·um *n.* bacteria
bad *adj.* malo
badge *n.* insignia
bad·ger *n.* tejón
bad·ly *adv.* mal
bad·min·ton *n.* juego de volante
baf·fle *v.* desconcertar; confundir
baf·fle·ment *n.* confusión
baf·fling *adj.* desconcertante
bag *n.* bolso; saco
bag·gage *n.* equipaje
bag·pipe *n.* gaita
bail *v.* afianzar
bail·iff *n.* alguacil
bail·or *n.* fiador
bait *n.* carnada
bake *v.* cocer en horno
bak·er *n.* panadero
bak·er·y *n.* panadería
bak·ing *n.* cocción
bal·ance *n.* equilibrio
bal·anced *adj.* balanceado
bal·co·ny *n.* balcón
bald *adj.* calvo
bald·ness *n.* calvicie
bale *n.* bala
bale·ful *adj.* funesto
balk *v.* oponerse
ball *n.* pelota
bal·lad *n.* balada
bal·le·ri·na *n.* bailarina
bal·let *n.* ballet
bal·lis·tic *adj.* balístico
bal·loon *n.* globo
bal·lot *n.* votación
balm *n.* bálsamo
bal·sa *n.* balsa
bam·boo *n.* bambú
ban *v.* prohibir
ba·nal *adj.* vulgar
ba·nan·a *n.* plátano
band *n.* banda
band·age *v.* vendar
ban·dit *n.* bandido

ban·do·leer *n.* bandolera
bane·ful *adj.* nocivo
bang *v.* golpear
bangs *n.* flequillo
ban·gle *n.* esclava
ban·ish *v.* desterrar
ban·ish·ment *n.* proscripción; exilio
ban·is·ter *n.* baranda
ban·jo *n.* banjo
bank *n.* banco
bank·er *n.* banquero
bank·ing *n.* banca
bank·rupt *adj.* arruinado
ban·ner *n.* bandera
ban·quet *n.* banquete
ban·ter *f.* broma
bap·tism *n.* bautismo
bap·tist *n.* bautista
bap·tis·ter·y *n.* baptisterio
bap·tize *v.* bautizar
bar *v.* excluir
bar·bar·i·an *adj.* bárbaro
bar·bar·ic *adj.* bárbaro
bar·bar·i·ty *n.* barbaridad
bar·ba·rous *adj.* bárbaro
bar·ber *n.* peluquero
bar·ber·shop *n.* peluquería
bar·bi·tu·ric *n.* barbitúrico
bare *adj.* desnudo; *v.* desnudar
bare·faced *adj.* descarado
bare·ly *adv.* simplemente; apenas
bar·gain *n.* ganga; convenio
bar·gain·ing *n.* negociación
barge *n.* gabarra
bar·i·tone *n.* barítono
bar·i·um *n.* bario
bark *v.* ladrar; *n.* ladrido
bar·ley *n.* cebada
bar·maid *n.* cantinera
barn *n.* granero
bar·na·cle *n.* percebe
ba·rom·et·er *n.* barómetro
bar·o·met·ric *adj.* barométrico
bar·on *n.* barón
bar·on·ess *n.* baronesa
ba·roque *adj.* barroco

barracks

bar•racks *n.* barraca
bar•rel *n.* barril
bar•ren *adj.* infecundo; infructuoso; yermo
bar•ri•cade *n.* barricada
bar•ri•er *n.* barrera
bar•tend•er *n.* camarero
bar•ter *v.* trocar
ba•sal *adj.* básico
ba•salt *n.* basalto
base *n.* base
base•ball *n.* béisbol
base•board *n.* zócalo
base•less *adj.* infundado
base•ment *n.* sótano
bash *v.* golpear
bash•ful *adj.* tímido
ba•sic *adj.* básico
ba•sic•i•ty *n.* basicidad
bas•il *n.* albahaca
ba•sil•i•ca *n.* basílica
ba•sin *n.* jofaina
ba•sis *n.* base
bask *v.* tomar el sol
bas•ket *n.* cesta
bas•ket•ball *n.* baloncesto
bas•ket•ry *n.* cestería
baste *v.* hilvanar
bat *v.* golpear; *n.* mazo
batch *n.* hornada
bate *v.* disminuir
bath *n.* baño
bathe *v.* bañar(se)
bath•ing•suit *n.* traje de baño
bath•tub *n.* bañera
ba•ton *n.* batuta
bat•tal•ion *n.* batallón
bat•ter *v.* estropear; golpear
bat•ter•y *n.* batería
bat•tle *v.* luchar; *n.* lucha
bat•tle•ground *n.* campo de batalla
bat•tle•ship *n.* acorazado
bau•ble *n.* baratija
baud *n.* baudio
bawl *v.* llorar
bay *n.* bahía
bay•o•net *n.* bayoneta

ba•zaar *n.* bazar
ba•zoo•ka *n.* bazuca
be *v.* estar; ser
beach *n.* playa
bea•con *n.* almenara; faro
bead *n.* abalorio
beak *n.* pico
beam *n.* rayo
bean *n.* fríjol; habichuela
bear *n.* oso; *v.* llevar
bear•a•ble *adj.* soportable
beard *n.* barba
beard•ed *adj.* barbudo
bear•er *n.* portador
bear•ing *n.* porte
beast *n.* bestia
beast•ly *adj.* bestial
beat *v.* vencer; golpear
beat•en *adj.* derrotado
beat•er *n.* batidor
be•a•tif•ic *adj.* beatífico
be•at•i•fy *v.* beatificar
beat•ing *n.* latido; paliza
be•at•i•tude *n.* beatitud
beau•ti•ful *adj.* hermoso
beau•ti•ful•ly *adj.* bellamente
beau•ti•fy *v.* embellecer
beau•ty *n.* belleza
bea•ver *n.* castor
be•cause *conj.* porque
beck•on *v.* llamar
be•come *v.* hacer(se)
be•com•ing *adj.* apropiado
bed *n.* cama
be•daz•zle *v.* deslumbrar
bed•cham•ber *n.* alcoba
bed•lam *n.* alboroto
bed•room. *n.* alcoba
bed•side *adj.* (de) cabecera
bee *n.* abeja
beech *n.* haya
beef•y *adj.* musculoso
bee•hive *n.* colmena
beer *n.* cerveza
bees•wax *n.* cera
beet *n.* remolacha

bee·tle *n.* escarabajo
be·fit *v.* convenir
be·fit·ting *adj.* conveniente
be·fore *prep.* antes de; *adv.* delante
be·fore·hand *adv.* de antemano
be·fud·dle *v.* confundir
beg *v.* pedir
beg·gar *n.* pobre
beg·gar·ly *adj.* miserable
be·gin *v.* comenzar
be·gin·ner *n.* novato
be·gin·ning *n.* comienzo
be·grudge *v.* envidiar
be·guile *v.* seducir
be·have *v.* funcionar; comportarse
be·hav·ior *n.* comportamiento
be·head *v.* descabezar
be·hind *adv.* atrás; detrás; *prep.* detrás de
be·hold *v.* contemplar
be·hold·en *adj.* obligado
be·hoove *v.* convenir
beige *adj.* beige
be·ing *n.* ser
be·la·bor *v.* machacar
be·lat·ed *adj.* tardío
be·lief *n.* fe
be·liev·a·ble *adj.* creíble
be·lieve *v.* creer
be·liev·er *n.* creyente
bell *n.* cascabel
bellflower *n.* campanilla
bel·lig·er·ence *n.* beligerancia
bel·lig·er·ent *adj.* beligerante
be·llow *v.* rugir
bel·ly *n.* estómago
be·long *v.* pertenecer
be·long·ings *n.* pertenencias
be·lov·ed *adj.* querido
be·low *adv.* abajo; *prep.* debajo de
belt *n.* cinturón
be·moan *v.* lamentar
bench *n.* banco
bend *v.* doblar; inclinar
bend·er *n.* juerga
be·neath *prep.* debajo de
ben·e·dic·tion *n.* bendición

ben·e·fac·tor *n.* bienhechor
ben·e·fice *n.* beneficio
be·nef·i·cent *adj.* benéfico
ben·e·fi·cial *adj.* beneficioso
ben·e·fi·ci·ar·y *n.* beneficiario
ben·e·fit *n.* beneficio
be·nev·o·lence *n.* benevolencia
be·nev·o·lent *adj.* benévolo
be·nign *adj.* benigno
bent *adj.* empeñado; torcido
be·numb *v.* entorpecer
be·queath *v.* legar
be·quest *n.* legado
be·rate *v.* reprender
be·reave·ment *n.* duelo
be·reft *adj.* privado
ber·ry *n.* baya
berth *n.* camarote
be·ryl·li·um *n.* berilio
be·seech *v.* implorar
be·set *v.* acosar
be·side *prep.* cerca
be·sides *prep.* además de
be·siege *v.* asediar
be·smirch *v.* manchar
best *adj.* mejor
bes·tial *adj.* bestial
bes·ti·al·i·ty *n.* bestialidad
be·stow *v.* conceder
bet *n.* apuesta
be·to·ken *v.* presagiar
be·tray *v.* revelar
be·tray·al *n.* traición
be·trothed *n.* novio
bet·ter *adv., adj.* mejor
bet·ter·ment *n.* mejoramiento
bet·tor *n.* apostador
be·tween *adv.* en medio; *prep.* entre
bev·eled *adj.* biselado
bev·er·age *n.* bebida
bev·y *n.* grupo
be·wail *v.* lamentar
be·wil·der *v.* aturdir
be·wil·der·ment *n.* aturdimiento
be·witch *v.* hechizar
be·witch·ment *n.* hechizo

be•yond *prep.* después de
bi•an•nu•al *adj.* semestral
bi•as *n.* prejuicio
bib *n.* babero
Bi•ble *n.* Biblia
Bib•li•cal *adj.* bíblico
bib•li•og•ra•pher *n.* bibliógrafo
bib•li•og•ra•phy *n.* bibliografía
bib•li•o•phile *n.* bibliófilo
bi•car•bon•ate *n.* bicarbonato
bi•cen•ten•ni•al *adj.* bicentenario
bi•ceps *n.* bíceps
bi•cy•cle *n.* bicicleta
bi•cy•clist *n.* biciclista
bid *n.* oferta; *v.* mandar
bid•ding *n.* oferta
bi•en•ni•al *adj.* bienal
bi•fo•cal *adj.* bifocal
bi•fur•cate *v.* bifucarse
bi•fur•ca•tion *n.* bifurcación
big *adj.* grande
big•a•mist *n.* bígamo
big•a•my *n.* bigamia
big•ness *n.* grandeza
bike *n.* bicicleta
bik•er *n.* motociclista
bi•lat•er•al *adj.* bilateral
bile *n.* bilis
bi•lin•gual *adj.* bilingüe
bil•ious *adj.* bilioso
bilk *v.* defraudar
bill *n.* pico; cuenta
bill•board *n.* cartelera
bil•let *v.* alojar
bill•fold *n.* cartera
bil•liards *n.* billar
bil•lion *n.* billón
bil•lion•aire *n.* billonario
bil•low *n.* oleada
bil•low•y *adj.* ondulante
bi•month•ly *adj.* bimestral
bin *n.* cajón
bi•na•ry *adj.* binario
bind *v.* encuadernar; atar
bind•er *n.* atadura; encuadernador
bind•ing *n.* ecuadernación

bin•oc•u•lar *n.* gemelos
bi•no•mi•al *adj.* binomio
bi•o•chem•i•cal *adj.* bioquímico
bi•o•chem•ist *n.* bioquímico
bi•o•chem•is•try *n.* bioquímica
bi•og•ra•pher *n.* biógrafo
bi•o•graph•ic *adj.* biográfico
bi•og•ra•phy *n.* biografía
bi•o•log•ic *adj.* biológico
bi•ol•o•gist *n.* biólogo
bi•ol•o•gy *n.* biología
bi•on•ics *n.* biónica
bi•o•phys•ics *n.* biofísica
bi•op•sy *n.* biopsia
bi•par•tite *adj.* bipartito
bi•ped *adj.* bípedo
bi•plane *n.* biplano
birch *n.* abedul
bird *n.* pájaro
bird•cage *n.* jaula
bird•seed *n.* alpiste
birth *n.* nacimiento
birth•day *n.* cumpleaños
bis•cuit *n.* bizcocho
bi•sect *v.* bisecar
bi•sec•tion *n.* bisección
bish•op *n.* obispo
bis•muth *n.* bismuto
bi•son *n.* bisonte
bit *n.* pedazo
bite *v.* picar
bit•ing *adj.* mordaz; cortante
bit•ter *adj.* cortante; implacable; amargo
bit•ter•ness *n.* rencor; encarnizamiento
bit•ter•sweet *adj.* agridulce
bi•tu•mi•nous *adj.* bituminoso
bi•va•lent *adj.* bivalent
bi•valve *adj.* bivalvo
bi•week•ly *adj.* quincenal
bi•zarre *adj.* raro
blab•ber *v.* cotorrear
black *adj.* negro
black-and-blue *adj.* amoratado
black•ber•ry *n.* zarzamora
black•bird *n.* mirlo
black•board *n.* pizarra

black•en *v.* difamar
black•head *n.* espinilla
black•mail *v.* chantajear
black•mail•er *n.* chantajista
black•smith *n.* herrero
black•top *n.* asfalto
blad•der *n.* vejiga
blade *n.* pala; hoja
blame *v.* culpar
bland *adj.* suave
blank *n., adj.* blanco
blan•ket *n.* manta
blare *v.* resonar
blas•pheme *v.* blasfemar
blas•phe•mous *adj.* blasfemo
blas•phe•my *n.* blasfemia
blast *v.* destruir; *n.* explosión
blast•ed *adj.* maldito
bla•tant *adj.* ruidoso
blaze *n.* hoguera; llamarada; *v.* arder
bleach *n.* lejía; *v.* blanquear
bleach•ers *n.* gradas
blear *adj.* nublado
bleat *v.* balar
bleed *v.* sangrar
blem•ish *v.* manchar
blend *n.* mezcla; *v.* mezclar
blend•er *n.* licuadora
bless *v.* bendecir
bless•ed *adj.* santo
bless•ing *n.* bendición
blind *v.* cegar; *adj.* ciego
blind•ers *n.* anteojeras
blind•ing *adj.* cegador
blind•ly *adv.* ciegamente
blind•ness *n.* ceguera
blink *v.* pestañear; ceder
blink•ing *adj.* parpadeante
bliss *n.* felicidad
bliss•ful *adj.* feliz
blis•ter *v.* ampollar(se)
blis•ter•ing *adj.* forzado; abrasador
bliz•zard *n.* ventisca
block *n.* manzana; bloque
block•ade *n.* obstrucción
blond *adj.* rubio

blonde *adj.* rubia
blood *n.* sangre
blood•less *adj.* exangüe
blood•thirst•y *adj.* sanguinario
blood•y *adj.* sangriento
bloom *v.* florecer
blos•som *n.* flor
blot *n.* mancha
blotch *n.* mancha
blouse *n.* blusa
blow *v.* inflar; soplar
blow•gun *n.* cerbatana
blow•torch *n.* soplete
blow•up *n.* explosión
bludg•eon *v.* aporrear
blue *adj.* azul
blue•bell *n.* campanilla
blue•print *n.* cianotipo
blunt *adj.* abrupto
blur•ry *adj.* confuso
blush *n.* sonrojo
blus•ter *v.* bramar
boar *n.* verraco
board *n.* consejo
board•er *n.* pensionista
board•ing•house *n.* pensión
boast *v.* alardear
boast•ful *adj.* jactancioso
boast•ing *n.* jactancia
boat *n.* barco
boat•man *n.* lanchero
bob•ber *n.* flotador
bob•bin *n.* bobina
bod•ice *n.* cuerpo
bod•i•ly *adj.* corporal
bod•y *n.* cuerpo
bod•y•guard *n.* guardaespaldas
bog *n.* ciénaga
bo•gus *adj.* falso
boil *v.* cocer; hervir
boil•er *n.* caldera
boil•ing *adj.* hirviente
bois•ter•ous *adj.* ruidoso; bullicioso
bold *adj.* descarado; intrépido
bol•ster *v.* apoyar
bolt *n.* pestillo; rayo

bomb

bomb *n.* bomba
bom•bard *v.* acosar; bombardear
bom•bard•ment *n.* bombardeo
bomb•er *n.* bombardero
bomb•ing *n.* bombardero
bomb•shell *n.* bomba
bo•nan•za *n.* bonanza
bond *n.* atadura; bono
bone *n.* hueso
bon•fire *n.* hoguera
bon•net *n.* gorra
bo•nus *n.* sobresueldo
bon•y *adj.* huesudo
book *n.* libro
book•bind•ing *n.* encuadernación
book•end *n.* sujetalibros
book•ing *n.* reservación
book•sell•er *n.* librero
book•store *n.* librería
boom *n.* prosperidad
boo•mer•ang *n.* bumerang
boor *n.* patán
boor•ish *adj.* tosco
boost *v.* levantar
boot *n.* bota
booth *n.* puesto; cabina
boot•leg *v.* contrabandear
boo•ty *n.* botín
bor•der *n.* borde; frontera
bor•der•line *n.* frontera
bore *v.* aburrir
bore•dom *n.* aburrimiento
bor•ing *adj.* aburrido
born *adj.* nacido
bor•ough *n.* municipio
bor•row *v.* apropiarse
bor•row•er *n.* prestatario
bos•om *n.* pecho
boss *n.* jefe
bo•tan•ic *adj.* botánico
bot•a•nist *n.* botánico
botch *v.* chapucear
both *adj.* los dos
both•er *v.* molestar(se)
both•er•some *adj.* molesto
bot•tle *n.* botella

bot•tom *n.* base; fondo
bot•tom•less *adj.* sin fondo
bot•u•lism *n.* botulismo
bough *n.* rama
bouil•lon *n.* caldo
boul•e•vard *n.* avenida
bounce *v.* rebotar
bounc•ing *adj.* fuerte
bound *v.* saltar
bound•a•ry *n.* límite
bound•less *adj.* ilimitado
boun•te•ous *adj.* abundante
boun•ti•ful *adj.* generoso
boun•ty *n.* generosidad
bou•quet *n.* ramo
bour•geois *n.* burgués
bout *n.* ataque
bo•vine *n.* bovino
bow *v.* inclinarse; doblegarse
bow•el *n.* intestino
bowl *n.* tazón; fuente
bowl•ing *n.* bolos
box *n.* caja
box•er *n.* boxeador
box•ing *n.* boxeo
boy *n.* chico; niño
boy•cott *v.* boicotear
boy•friend *n.* novio
bra *n.* sostén
brace *n.* puntal
brace•let *n.* brazalete
brac•ing *adj.* fortificante
brack•et *n.* corchete
brack•ish *adj.* salobre
brag *v.* jactarse
brain *n.* cerebro
brain•y *adj.* listo
brake *v.* frenar
bran *n.* salvado
branch *n.* rama
brand *n.* modo; marca
brand•ing *n.* hierra
bran•dish *v.* blandir
bran•dy *n.* coñac
brash *adj.* insolente; impetuoso
brass *n.* latón

bras•siere *n.* sostén
brass•y *adj.* descarado
brave *adj.* valiente
brav•er•y *n.* valor
brawn•y *adj.* musculoso
bra•zen *adj.* descarado
bra•zier *n.* brasero
breach *n.* ruptura; violación
bread *n.* pan
bread•bas•ket *n.* panera
breadth *n.* extensión
break *v.* quebrar; romper
break•a•ble *adj.* rompible
break•age *n.* rotura
break•down *n.* depresión; desglose
break•fast *n.* desayuno
break•through *n.* adelanto
break•up *n.* desintegración; separación
breast *n.* pecho
breast•bone *n.* esternón
breath *n.* respiración
breathe *v.* respirar
breath•ing *n.* respiración
breath•tak•ing *adj.* impresionante
breed *v.* criar; reproducirse
breed•er *n.* criador
breed•ing *v.* crianza
breeze *n.* brisa
breez•y *adj.* ventoso
brev•i•ty *n.* brevedad
brew•er *n.* cervecero
brew•er•y *n.* cervecería
bribe *n.* soborno
brick *n.* ladrillo
brick•lay•er *n.* albañil
bri•dal *n.* boda
bride *n.* novia
bridge *n.* puente
bri•dle *n.* brida
brief *adj.* breve
brief•case *n.* cartera
brief•ing *n.* reunión
bri•gade *n.* brigada
bright *adj.* brillante
bright•en *v.* iluminar(se)
bright•ness *n.* lustre

bril•liance *n.* brillo
bril•liant *adj.* brillante
brim *n.* borde
bring *v.* traer
bri•quet *n.* briqueta
brisk *adj.* vigoroso
bris•tle *n.* cerda
brit•tle *adj.* frágil
broach *n.* broche
broad *adj.* extenso; ancho
broad•cast *v.* transmitir; emitir
broad•cast•ing *n.* trasmisión
broad•en *v.* ensanchar(se)
broad•mind•ed *adj.* comprensivo
bro•cade *n.* brocado
broc•co•li *n.* brécol
bro•chure *n.* folleto
bro•ken *adj.* roto; quebrado
bro•ken•down *adj.* decrépito
bro•ker•age *n.* corretaje
bro•mide *n.* bromuro
bro•mine *n.* bromo
bron•chi•al *adj.* bronquial
bron•chi•tis *n.* bronquitis
bronze *n.* bronce
brook *n.* arroyo
broom *n.* escoba
broth *n.* caldo
broth•el *n.* burdel
broth•er *n.* hermano
broth•er•hood *n.* fraternidad
broth•er-in-law *n.* cuñado
broth•er•ly *adj.* fraterno
brow *n.* ceja
brown *adj.* moreno
brown•out *n.* parcial
browse *v.* pacer; curiosear
bruise *n.* contusión
brunt *n.* impacto
brush *n.* cepillo
bru•tal *adj.* brutal
bru•tal•i•ty *n.* brutalidad
bru•tal•ize *v.* brutalizar
brute *n.* bruto
buc•ca•neer *n.* bucanero
buck•et *n.* balde

buck•le *n.* hebilla
bud *n.* yema
bud•dy *n.* compadre
budge *v.* ceder
budg•et *v.* presupuestar
buf•fa•lo *n.* búfalo
buff•er *n.* intercesor
buf•fet *n.* bofetada
buf•foon *n.* bufón
bug *n.* bicho
bu•gle *n.* clarín
build *v.* construir
build•er *n.* constructor
build•ing *n.* contrucción
bulb *n.* bulbo
bulge *n.* bulto
bulk•y *adj.* pesado
bull *n.* toro
bull•dog *n.* buldog
bull•doz•er *n.* excavadora
bul•let *n.* bala
bul•le•tin *n.* boletín
bull•fight•er *n.* torero
bul•rush *n.* espadaña
bul•wark *n.* baluarte
bum•ble•bee *n.* abejorro
bump *n.* choque
bump•y *adj.* agitado
bun *n.* bollo
bunch *n.* racimo
bun•dle *n.* fajo; bulto
bun•ny *n.* conejito
buoy *n.* boya
buoy•ant *adj.* boyante
bur *n.* erizo
bur•den *n.* carga
bu•reauc•ra•cy *n.* burocracia
bu•reau•crat *n.* burócrata
burg•er *n.* hamburguesa
bur•glar *n.* ladrón
bur•glar•ize *v.* robar
bur•i•al *n.* entierro
bur•lap *n.* arpillera
bur•ly *adj.* robusto
burn *v.* incendiar
burn•er *n.* quemador

burn•ing *adj.* ardiente
burn•out *n.* extinción
burnt *adj.* quemado
burp *n.* eructo
bur•ro *n.* burro
burst *v.* romper
bur•y *v.* enterrar
bus *n.* autobús
bus•boy *n.* ayudante
bush *n.* arbusto
bushed *adj.* agotado
busi•ness *n.* oficio
but *conj.* pero
but•ter *n.* mantequilla
but•ter•fly *n.* mariposa
buy *v.* comprar
buy•er *n.* comprador
by *adv.* cerca; *prep.* cerca de; por

C

cab *n.* taxi
ca•bal *n.* cábala
cab•a•la *n.* cábala
cab•a•ret *n.* cabaret
cab•bage *n.* col
cab•driv•er *n.* taxista
cab•in *n.* cabaña
cab•i•net *n.* gabinete
cab•i•net•mak•er *n.* ebanista
cab•i•net•work *n.* ebanistería
ca•ble *n.* cable
ca•ble•gram *n.* cablegrama
ca•ca•o *n.* cacao
cack•le *n.* cacareo
cac•tus *n.* cacto
ca•dav•er *n.* cadáver
ca•dav•er•ous *adj.* cadavérico
cad•die *n.* caddy
ca•dence *n.* cadencia
ca•det *n.* cadete
cad•mi•um *n.* cadmio
ca•du•ce•us *n.* caduceo

ca•fe *n.* café
caf•e•te•ri•a *n.* cafetería
caf•feine *n.* cafeína
caf•tan *n.* túnica
cage *n.* jaula
ca•jole *v.* engatusar
cake *n.* pastel
cal•a•bash *n.* calabaza
cal•a•mine *n.* calamina
ca•lam•i•ty *n.* calamidad
cal•ci•fi•ca•tion *n.* calcificación
cal•ci•fy *v.* calcificar
cal•ci•um *n.* calcio
cal•cu•late *v.* calcular
cal•cu•lat•ed *adj.* intencional
cal•cu•lat•ing *adj.* calculador
cal•cu•la•tion *n.* cálculo
cal•cu•la•tor *n.* calculadora
cal•dron *n.* caldera
cal•en•dar *n.* calendario
cal•i•ber *n.* calibre
cal•i•brate *v.* calibrar
cal•i•bra•tion *n.* calibración
cal•i•co *n.* calicó
ca•liph *n.* califa
cal•is•then•ics *n.* calistenia
ca•lix *n.* cavidad
call *v.* llamar
cal•lig•ra•pher *n.* calígrafo
cal•lig•ra•phy *n.* caligrafía
call•ing *n.* vocación
cal•lous *v.* encallecerse
cal•low *adj.* inmaduro
cal•lus *n.* callo
calm *v.* calmar(se); *n.* calma
calm•ness *n.* traquilidad
ca•lor•ic *adj.* calórico
cal•o•rie *n.* caloría
ca•lum•ni•ate *v.* calumniar
cal•va•ry *n.* calvario
ca•lyx *n.* cáliz
ca•ma•ra•der•ie *n.* camaradería
cam•bi•um *n.* cambium
cam•el *n.* camello
ca•mel•lia *n.* camelia
cam•e•o *n.* camefeo

cam•er•a *n.* cámara
cam•ou•flage *n.* camuflaje
camp *v.* acampar
cam•paign *n.* capaña
camp•er *n.* campista
cam•phor *n.* alcanfor
can *v.* poder
ca•nar•y *n.* canario
can•cel *v.* cancelar; matar; anular
can•cel•la•tion *n.* cancelación
can•cer *n.* cáncer
can•cer•ous *adj.* canceroso
can•did *adj.* franco
can•di•da•cy *n.* candidatura
can•di•date *n.* candidato
can•died *adj.* escarchado
can•dle *n.* cirio; vela
can•dle•hold•er *n.* candelero
can•dle•stick *n.* candelero
can•dor *n.* franqueza
can•dy *n.* azúcar
cane *n.* caña; bastón
ca•nine *adj.* canino
can•is•ter *n.* lata
canned *adj.* enlatado
can•ni•bal *n.* caníbal
can•ni•bal•ism *n.* canibalismo
can•ni•bal•is•tic *adj.* caníbal
can•non *n.* cañón
ca•noe *n.* canoa
ca•non•i•za•tion *n.* canonización
can•on•ize *v.* canonizar
can•ta•loupe *n.* cantalupo
can•teen *n.* cantina
can•vas *n.* lona
can•yon *n.* cañón
cap *n.* tapa
ca•pa•bil•i•ty *n.* capacidad
ca•pa•ble *adj.* capaz
ca•pa•cious *adj.* espacioso
ca•pac•i•ty *n.* capacidad
ca•per *n.* cabriola
cap•il•lar•y *n.* capilar
cap•i•tal *n., adj.* capital
cap•i•tal•ism *n.* capitalismo
cap•i•tal•ist *n.* capitalista

cap·i·tal·is·tic *adj.* capitalista
cap·i·tal·i·za·tion *n.* capitalización
cap·i·tal·ize *v.* capitalizar
cap·i·tal·ly *adv.* admirablemente
cap·i·tol *n.* capitolio
ca·pi·tu·late *v.* capitular
ca·price *n.* capricho
ca·pri·cious *adj.* caprichoso
cap·sule *n.* cápsula
cap·tain *n.* capitán
cap·tion *n.* subtítulo
cap·tious *adj.* capcioso
cap·ti·vate *v.* cautivar
cap·ti·va·tion *n.* encanto
cap·tive *adj.* cautivo
cap·tiv·i·ty *n.* cautividad
cap·tor *n.* captor
cap·ture *v.* capturar
car *n.* coche
car·a·mel *n.* caramelo
car·at *n.* quilate
car·a·van *n.* caravana
car·bide *n.* carburo
car·bine *n.* carabina
car·bo·hy·drate *n.* carbohidrato
car·bon *n.* carbono
car·bun·cle *n.* carbunclo
car·bu·re·tor *n.* carburador
car·cin·o·gen·ic *adj.* cancerígeno
card *n.* tarjeta
car·di·ac *adj.* cardíaco
car·di·nal *adj.* cardinal
car·di·o·gram *n.* cardiograma
car·di·ol·o·gy *n.* cardiología
care *v.* cuidar
ca·reer *n.* carrera
care·free *adj.* despreocupado
care·ful *adj.* cuidadoso
care·less *adj.* espontáneo; descuidado
ca·ress *n.* caricia
care·tak·er *n.* portero
car·go *n.* carga
car·i·ca·ture *n.* caricatura
car·nage *n.* carnicería
car·nal *adj.* carnal
car·ni·val *n.* carnaval

car·ni·vore *n.* carnívoro
car·niv·o·rous *adj.* carnívoro
ca·rous·al *n.* jarana
car·ou·sel *n.* carrusel
car·pen·try *n.* carpintería
car·pet *n.* alfombra
car·riage *n.* carruaje
car·ri·er *n.* carrero
car·rot *n.* zanahoria
car·ry *v.* logra; llevar
car·sick *adj.* mareado
cart *n.* carro
cart·age *n.* acarreo
car·tel *n.* cartel
car·ti·lage *n.* cartílago
cart·load *n.* carretado
car·toon *n.* tira
car·toon·ist *n.* caricaturista
car·tridge *n.* cartucho
carve *v.* esculpir
carv·ing *n.* escultura
case *n.* caja
cash *n.* efectivo
cash·ew *n.* anacardo
cash·ier *n.* cajero
cash·mere *n.* cachemira
ca·si·no *n.* casino
cask *n.* barril
cas·se·role *n.* cacerola
cas·sette *n.* casete
cast *v.* dar; fundir; echar
cas·ta·nets *n.* castañuelas
caste *n.* casta
cas·ti·gate *v.* castigar
cas·tle *n.* castillo
cas·trate *v.* castrar
cas·tra·tion *n.* castración
ca·su·al *adj.* casual
cas·u·al·ly *adv.* casualmente
ca·su·ist·ry *n.* casuística
cat *n.* gato
ca·tab·o·lism *n.* catabolismo
cat·a·log *n.* catálogo
cat·a·lyst *n.* catalizador
cat·a·lyt·ic *adj.* catálitico
cat·a·lyze *v.* catapulta

cat•a•ract *n.* catarata
ca•tas•tro•phe *n.* catástrofe
cat•a•stroph•ic *adj.* catastrófico
cat•a•ton•ic *adj.* catatónico
catch *v.* prender; coger
catch•er *n.* receptor
catch•ing *adj.* contagioso
catch•y *adj.* capcioso
cat•e•chism *n.* catecismo
cat•e•gor•ic *adj.* categórico
cat•e•gor•i•cal•ly *adv.* categóricamente
cat•e•go•rize *v.* clasificar
cat•e•go•ry *n.* categoría
cat•er•pil•lar *n.* oruga
cat•er•waul *v.* chillar
ca•thar•sis *n.* catarsis
ca•the•dral *n.* catedral
cath•ode *n.* cátodo
cath•o•lic *adj.* católico
ca•thol•i•cism *n.* catolicismo
cat•nip *n.* nébeda
cat•tail *n.* espadaña
cat•tle *n.* ganado
cat•tle•man *n.* ganadero
cau•li•flow•er *n.* coliflor
cau•sa•tion *n.* causalidad
caus•a•tive *adj.* causativo
cause *n.* razón; causa
cause•way *n.* elevada
caus•tic *adj.* cáustico
cau•ter•ize *v.* cauterizar
cau•tion *v.* amonestar
cau•tion•ar•y *adj.* preventivo
cau•tious *adj.* cauteloso
cav•al•ry *n.* cabellería
cave *n.* cueva
cav•ern *n.* caverna
cav•ern•ous *adj.* cavernoso
cav•i•ty *n.* cavidad
ca•vort *v.* cabriolar
cay *n.* cayo
cease *v.* suspender
cease•less *adj.* continuo
ce•dar *n.* cedro
cede *v.* ceder
ceil•ing *n.* techo

cel•e•brant *n.* celebrante
cel•e•brate *v.* celebrar
cel•e•brat•ed *adj.* célebre
cel•e•bra•tion *n.* celebración
ce•leb•ri•ty *n.* celebridad
cel•er•y *n.* apio
ce•les•tial *adj.* celestial
cel•i•ba•cy *n.* celibato
cel•i•bate *adj.* célibe
cell *n.* celda
cel•lar *n.* sótano
cel•lo•phane *n.* celofán
cel•lu•lar *adj.* celular
cel•lu•loid *n.* celuloide
cel•lu•lose *n.* celulosa
ce•ment *n.* cemento
cem•e•ter•y *n.* cementerio
cen•ser *n.* incensario
cen•sor *n.* censor
cen•so•ri•ous *adj.* censurado
cen•sor•ship *n.* censura
cen•sure *v.* censurar
cen•sus *n.* censo
cent *n.* centavo
cen•taur *n.* centauro
cen•ten•ni•al *adj.* centenario
cen•ter *n.* centro
cen•ti•grade *adj.* centígrado
cen•ti•gram *n.* centigramo
cen•ti•li•ter *n.* centilitro
cen•ti•me•ter *n.* centímetro
cen•tral *adj.* central
cen•tral•ize *v.* centralizar(se)
cen•tric *adj.* céntrico
cen•trif•u•gal *adj.* centrífugo
cen•tu•ry *n.* siglo
ce•phal•ic *adj.* cefálico
ce•ram•ic *adj.* cerámico
çe•re•al *n.* cereal
cer•e•bral *adj.* cerebral
cer•e•brum *n.* cerebro
cer•e•mo•ni•al *adj.* ceremonial
cer•e•mo•ni•ous *adj.* ceremonioso
cer•e•mo•ny *n.* ceremonia
cer•tain *adj.* seguro; cierto
cer•tain•ly *adv.* ciertamente

certainty

cer•tain•ty *n.* certeza
cer•ti•fi•a•ble *adj.* certificable
cer•tif•i•cate *n.* certificado
cer•ti•fi•ca•tion *n.* certificación
cer•ti•fied *adj.* certificado
cer•ti•fy *v.* certificar
cer•ti•tude *n.* certidumbre
cer•vix *n.* cerviz
ces•sa•tion *n.* cesación
ces•sion *n.* cesión
chafe *v.* frotar; rozar
cha•grin *v.* desilusionar
chain *n.* cadena
chair *n.* silla
chair•man *n.* presidente
chair•man•ship *n.* presidencia
chair•wo•man *n.* presidenta
cha•let *n.* chalet
chal•ice *n.* cáliz
chalk *n.* tiza
chalk•board *n.* pizarra
chal•lenge *v.* desafiar
chal•leng•er *n.* desafiador
cham•ber•lain *n.* chambelán
cha•me•leon *n.* camaleón
champ *n.* campeón
cham•pi•on•ship *n.* campeonato
chance *n.* oportunidad; casualidad
chan•cel•ler•y *n.* cancillería
chan•cel•lor *n.* canciller
change *v.* transformar; cambiar
change•a•ble *adj.* cambiable
change•o•ver *n.* cambio
chang•er *n.* cambiador
chan•nel *n.* canal
chant *n.* canto
cha•os *n.* caos
cha•ot•ic *adj.* caótico
chap•el *n.* capilla
chap•er•one *n.* carabina
chap•lain *n.* capellán
chap•ter *n.* capítulo
char•ac•ter *n.* carácter
char•ac•ter•is•tic *n.* característica
char•ac•ter•ize *v.* caracterizar
char•coal *n.* carboncillo

charge *v.* pedir; cargar
cha•ris•ma *n.* carisma
char•i•ta•ble *adj.* caritativo
char•i•ty *n.* caridad
charm *n.* encanto
charm•er *n.* encantador
chart *v.* trazar
char•ter *n.* carta
chase *v.* perseguir
chaste *adj.* casto
chas•ten *v.* castigar
chas•ti•ty *n.* castidad
chat *v.* charlar
chau•vin•ist *n.* chauvinista
chau•vin•is•tic *adj.* chauvinista
cheap *adj.* barato
cheap•ness *n.* tacañería
cheat *v.* engañar
cheat•er *n.* tramposo
check *n.* cheque; parada; cuenta
check•book *n.* chequera
check•ered *adj.* a cuadros
cheek *n.* mejilla
cheep *n.* gorjeo
cheer *v.* alegrar; alentar
cheer•ful *adj.* alegre
cheer•i•ly *adv.* alegremente
cheer•less *adj.* triste
cheese *n.* queso
cheese•cake *n.* quesadilla
chef *n.* cocinero
chem•i•cal *n.* químico
chem•ist *n.* químico
chem•is•try *n.* química
che•mo•ther•a•py *n.* quimioterapia
cher•ish *v.* abrigar; querer
cher•ry *n.* cerezo
cher•ub *n.* querubín
che•ru•bic *adj.* querúbico
chess *n.* ajedrez
chest *n.* pecho
chest•nut *n.* castaña
chew *v.* masticar
chew•ing *n.* masticación
chick•en *n.* pollo
chick•pea *n.* garbanzo

chief *n.* jefe
chif•fon *n.* gasa
child *n.* hijo; niño
child•birth *n.* parto
child•ish *adj.* aniñado
child•like *adj.* infantil
chil•i *n.* chile
chill *n.* frío
chill•ing *adj.* frío
chime *n.* campaneo
chim•ney *n.* chimenea
chim•pan•zee *n.* chimpancé
chin *n.* barba
chi•na *n.* china
chip *n.* astilla; *v.* astillar
chip•per *adj.* jovial
chi•ro•prac•tor *n.* quiropráctico
chirp *v.* gorjear
chis•el *n.* cincel
chis•el•er *n.* cincelador
chiv•al•rous *adj.* caballeresco
chiv•al•ry *n.* cabellerosidad
chive *n.* cebollino
chlo•ride *n.* cloruro
choc•o•late *n.* chocolate
choice *adj.* selecto; *n.* preferencia
choir *n.* coro
choke *v.* ahogar; atorar; estrangular
chol•er•a *n.* cólera
chol•er•ic *adj.* colérico
cho•les•ter•ol *n.* colesterol
chomp *v.* ronzar
choose *v.* escoger
choos•ing *n.* selección
chop *v.* cortar
cho•ral *n.* coral
cho•re•og•ra•pher *n.* coreógrafo
cho•re•og•ra•phy *n.* coreografía
cho•sen *adj.* escogido
chow *n.* comida
Christ *n.* Cristo
chris•ten *v.* bautizar
chris•ten•ing *n.* cristiano
Christ•tian *n.* cristiano
Chris•ti•an•i•ty *n.* cristianismo
Christ•mas *n.* Navidad

chro•mat•ic *adj.* cromático
chrome *n.* cromo
chro•mi•um *n.* cromo
chro•mo•some *n.* cromosoma
chron•ic *adj.* crónico
chron•i•cle *n.* crónica
chron•o•log•ic *adj.* cronológico
chro•nol•o•gy *n.* cronología
chrys•a•lis *n.* crisálida
chry•san•the•mum *n.* crisantemo
chum *n.* compañero
chunk *n.* trozo
church *n.* iglesia
church•man *n.* clérigo
churn *n.* mantequera
chute *n.* conducto; rampa
ci•ca•da *n.* cigarra
ci•der *n.* sidra
ci•gar *n.* puro
cig•a•rette *n.* cigarrillo
cinch *n.* cincha
cin•der *n.* carbonilla
cin•e•ma *n.* cine
cin•e•mat•ic *adj.* fílmico
cin•e•ma•tog•ra•phy *n.* cinematografía
cin•na•mon *n.* canela
ci•pher *v.* cifrar
cir•cle *n.* ciclo
cir•cuit *n.* circuito
cir•cu•lar *adj.* circular
cir•cu•lat•ing *adj.* circulante
cir•cu•la•tion *n.* circulación
cir•cum•cise *v.* circuncidar
cir•cum•cised *adj.* circunciso
cir•cum•ci•sion *n.* circuncisión
cir•cum•fer•ence *n.* circunferencia
cir•cum•nav•i•gate *v.* circunnavegar
cir•cum•scribe *v.* circunscribir
cir•cum•spect *adj.* circunspecto
cir•cum•stance *n.* circunstancia
cir•cum•stan•tial *adj.* circunstancial
cir•cus *n.* circo
cir•rho•sis *n.* cirrosis
cir•rus *n.* cirro
cis•tern *n.* cisterna
cit•a•del *n.* ciudadela

ci·ta·tion *n.* citación
cite *v.* citar
cit·i·zen *n.* ciudadano
cit·ric *adj.* cítrico
cit·y *n.* ciudad
civ·et *n.* civeta
civ·ic *adj.* cívico
civ·il *adj.* civil
ci·vil·i·ty *n.* civilidad
civ·i·li·za·tion *n.* civilización
civ·i·lize *v.* civilizar
claim *v.* merecer; reclamar
clair·voy·ance *n.* clarividencia
clair·voy·ant *adj.* clarividente
clam *n.* almeja
clam·or *n.* clamor
clam·or·ous *adj.* clamoroso
clamp *n.* abrazadera
clan *n.* clan
clan·gor *n.* estruendo
clap *v.* aplaudir
clap·per *n.* badajo
clap·ping *n.* aplausos
clar·et *n.* clarete
clar·i·fi·ca·tion *n.* clarificación
clar·i·fy *v.* clarificar
clar·i·net *n.* clarinete
clar·i·on *adj.* sonoro
clar·i·ty *n.* claridad
clash *v.* entrechocarse
class *n.* clase
clas·sic *adj.* clásico
clas·si·cal *adj.* clásico
clas·si·cism *n.* clasicismo
clas·si·cist *n.* clasicista
clas·si·fi·ca·tion *n.* clasificación
clas·si·fied *adj.* clasificado
clas·si·fy *v.* clasificar
class·y *adj.* elegante
clause *n.* cláusula
claus·tro·pho·bi·a *n.* claustrofobia
clav·i·chord *n.* clavicordio
clav·i·cle *n.* clavícula
claw *n.* garra
clay *n.* arcilla
clean *v.* limpiar

clean·cut *adj.* definido
clean·er *n.* limpiador
clean·ing *n.* limpieza
cleanse *v.* limpiar
cleans·er *n.* limpiador
clear *adj.* despejado; transparente
clear·cut *adj.* claro
clear·ing *n.* claro
clear·ly *adv.* claramente
cleav·age *n.* división
cleave *v.* adherir; partir
cleav·er *n.* cuchilla
clem·en·cy *n.* clemencia
cler·gy *n.* clero
cler·gy·man *n.* clérigo
cler·ic *adj.* clérigo
cler·i·cal *adj.* clerical
clerk *n.* oficinista
clev·er *adj.* listo
clev·er·ness *n.* inteligencia
cli·ent *n.* cliente
cli·mac·tic *adj.* culminante
cli·mate *n.* clima
cli·mat·ic *adj.* climático
cli·max *n.* clímax
climb *v.* trepar
climb·er *n.* alpinista
climb·ing *adj.* trepador
clin·ic *n.* clínica
clin·i·cal *adj.* clínico
cli·ni·cian *n.* clínico
clip *v.* cortar
cloak *n.* manto
clock *n.* reloj
clog *n.* atasco
clois·ter *n.* claustro
clone *n.* clón
close *v.* cerrar
closed *adj.* cerrado; vedado
close·down *n.* cierre
close·ly *adv.* atentamente; de cerca
close·ness *n.* proximidad
close·out *n.* liquidación
clos·et *n.* armario
clos·ing *n.* cierre
clot *n.* cóagulo

cloth *n.* tela
clothe *n.* tela
clothe *v.* arropar
clothes *n.* ropa
cloth·ing *n.* ropa
cloud *n.* nube
cloud·burst *n.* aguacero
cloud·y *adj.* nuboso
clout *n.* bofetada
clo·ver *n.* trébol
clown *n.* payaso
club *n.* palo
clue *n.* pista
clump *n.* grupo
clum·sy *adj.* pesado
coach *n.* vagón; coche
coach·man *n.* cochero
co·ag·u·late *v.* coagular(se)
co·ag·u·la·tion *n.* coagulación
coal *n.* carbón
co·a·lesce *v.* unirse
co·a·li·tion *n.* coalición
coarse *adj.* tosco
coars·en *v.* vulgarizar
coarse·ness *n.* vulgaridad
coat *n.* pelo
coat·ed *adj.* bañado
coat·ing *n.* capa; baño
coat·tail *n.* faldón
coax *v.* engatusar
coax·ing *n.* engatusamiento
cob *n.* elote
co·balt *n.* cobalto
cob·bler *n.* zapatero
co·bra *n.* cobra
cob·web *n.* telaraña
co·caine *n.* cocaína
coc·cyx *n.* cóccix
cock *n.* gallo
cock·ade *n.* escarapela
cock·a·too *n.* cacatúa
cock·i·ness *n.* presunción
cock·le *n.* berberecho
cock·pit *n.* cancha
cock·roach *n.* cucaracha
cock·tail *n.* coctel

co·coa *n.* cacao
co·co·nut *n.* coco
co·coon *n.* capullo
code *n.* código
co·de·fend·ant *n.* coacusado
co·deine *n.* codeína
cod·fish *n.* bacalao
cod·i·fy *v.* codificar
co·di·rec·tion *n.* codirección
co·ed *adj.* coeducacional
co·ed·u·ca·tion *n.* coeducación
co·ed·u·ca·tion·al *adj.* coeducacional
co·ef·fi·cient *n.* coeficiente
co·erce *v.* coercer
co·er·cion *n.* coerción
co·ex·ist *v.* coexistir
co·ex·is·tence *n.* coexistencia
co·ex·ten·sive *adj.* coextenso
cof·fee *n.* café
cof·fer *n.* cofre
cof·fin *n.* ataúd
cog *n.* diente
cog·i·tate *v.* meditar
cog·nac *n.* coñac
cog·ni·tion *n.* cognición
cog·ni·zance *n.* conocimiento
cog·ni·zent *adj.* enterado
co·hab·it *v.* cohabitar
co·here *v.* adherirse
co·her·ence *n.* coherencia
co·her·ent *adj.* coherente
co·he·sion *n.* cohesión
co·he·sive *adj.* cohesivo
co·hort *n.* cohorte
coil *n.* rollo
coin *v.* acuñar; *n.* moneda
co·in·cide *v.* coincidir
co·in·ci·dence *n.* coincidencia
co·in·ci·den·tal *adj.* coincidente
co·la *n.* cola
col·an·der *n.* colador
cold *n., adj.* frío
cold·blood·ed *adj.* de sangrefria
cold·heart·ed *adj.* insensible
cold·ness *n.* frialdad
col·ic *n.* cólico

col•i•se•um *n.* coliseo
co•li•tis *n.* colitis
col•lab•o•rate *v.* colaborar
col•lab•o•ra•tion *n.* colaboración
col•lab•o•ra•tion•ist *n.* colaboracionista
col•lab•o•ra•tive *adj.* cooperativo
col•lab•o•ra•tor *n.* colaborador
col•lage *n.* collage
col•lapse *v.* desplomarse; caerse
col•laps•i•ble *adj.* plegable
col•lar *n.* cuello
col•lar•bone *n.* clavícula
col•late *v.* colacionar
col•lat•er•al *adj.* colateral
col•league *n.* colega
col•lect *v.* recoger; reunir; coleccionar
col•lect•ed *adj.* sosegado
col•lec•tion *n.* colección
col•lec•tive *adj.* colectivo
col•lec•tiv•ist *n.* colectivista
col•lec•tiv•ize *v.* colectivizar
col•lec•tor *n.* colector
col•lege *n.* colegio
col•le•gian *n.* estudiante
col•le•giate *adj.* universitario
col•lide *v.* chocar
col•li•sion *n.* choque
col•loid *n.* coloide
col•lo•qui•al *adj.* familiar
col•lo•qui•um *n.* coloquio
col•lude *v.* confabularse
col•lu•sion *n.* cofabulación
co•logne *n.* colonia
colo•nel *n.* coronel
co•lo•ni•al *adj.* colonial
co•lo•ni•al•ist *n.* colonialista
col•o•nist *n.* colonizador
col•o•ni•za•tion *n.* colonización
col•o•nize *v.* colonizar
col•o•niz•er *n.* colonizador
col•on•nade *n.* columnata
col•o•ny *n.* colonia
col•or *v.* colerear; *n.* color
col•or•a•tion *n.* coloración
col•ored *adj.* coloreado
col•or•ful *adj.* pintoresco

col•or•ing *n.* coloración
col•or•less *adj.* incoloro
co•los•sal *adj.* coloso
co•los•to•my *n.* colostomía
col•umn *n.* columna
col•umn•ist *n.* columnista
co•ma *n.* coma
co•ma•tose *adj.* comatoso
comb *v.* peinar; *n.* peine
com•bat *v.* combatir
com•bat•ant *n.* combatiente
com•bi•na•tion *n.* combinación
com•bine *v.* combinar
com•bo *n.* conjunto
com•bus•ti•ble *adj.* combustible
com•bus•tion *n.* combustión
come *v.* llegar; venir
come•back *n.* reaparición
co•me•di•an *n.* comediante
co•me•di•enne *n.* comedianta
com•e•dy *n.* comedia
come-on *n.* incentivo
com•et *n.* cometa
com•fort *v.* confortar
com•fort•a•ble *adj.* confortable
com•fort•er *n.* consolador
com•ic *adj.* cómico
com•i•cal *adj.* cómico
com•ing *adj.* venidero
com•ma *n.* coma
com•mand *n.* mando; *v.* mandar
com•man•dant *n.* comandante
com•mand•er *n.* comandante
com•mand•ing *adj.* imponente
com•man•do *n.* comando
com•mem•o•rate *v.* conmemorar
com•mem•o•ra•tion *n.* conmemoración
com•mence *v.* comenzar
com•mence•ment *n.* comienzo
com•mend *v.* encomendar
com•men•da•tion *n.* recomendación
com•men•su•rate *adj.* proporcionado
com•ment *n.* observación
com•men•tar•y *n.* comentario
com•men•tate *v.* comentar
com•merce *n.* comercio

com•mer•cial *adj.* comercial
com•mer•cial•ism *n.* comercialismo
com•mer•cial•ize *v.* comercializar
com•mis•er•ate *v.* compadecerse
com•mis•sar *n.* comisario
com•mis•sar•y *n.* economato
com•mis•sion *v.* encargar; *n.* comisión
com•mis•sion•er *n.* comisario
com•mit *v.* entregar
com•mit•ment *n.* compromiso
com•mit•tal *n.* obligación
com•mit•ee *n.* comité
com•mode *n.* cómoda
com•mo•dore *n.* comodoro
com•mon *adj.* común
com•mon•place *adj.* ordinario
com•mon•wealth *n.* comunidad
com•mo•tion *n.* tumulto
com•mu•nal *adj.* comunal
com•mune *v.* comulgar
com•mu•ni•ca•ble *adj.* comunicable
com•mu•ni•cate *v.* comunicar(se)
com•mu•ni•ca•tion *n.* comunicación
com•mu•ni•ca•tive *adj.* comunicativo
com•mu•ni•ca•tor *n.* comunicante
com•mun•ion *n.* comunión
com•mu•nism *n.* comunismo
com•mun•ist *n.* comunista
com•mu•nis•tic *adj.* comunista
com•mu•ni•ty *n.* comunidad
com•mu•ta•tive *adj.* conmutativo
com•mute *v.* conmutar
com•pact *adj.* compacto
com•pan•ion *n.* compañero
com•pan•ion•ship *n.* compañerismo
com•pa•ny *n.* compañía
com•pa•ra•ble *adj.* comparable
com•par•a•tive *adj.* comparativo
com•pare *v.* comparar
com•par•i•son *n.* comparación
com•part•ment *n.* compartimiento
com•pass *n.* compás
com•pas•sion *n.* compasión
com•pas•sion•ate *adj.* compasivo
com•pat•i•ble *adj.* compatible
com•pa•tri•ot *n.* compatriota

com•pel *v.* obligar; imponer
com•pel•ling *adj.* incontestable
com•pen•sate *v.* compensar
com•pen•sa•tion *n.* compensación
com•pete *v.* competir
com•pe•tence *n.* competencia
com•pe•tent *adj.* competente
com•pe•ti•tion *n.* competencia
com•pe•ti•tive *adj.* competitivo
com•pe•ti•tor *n.* competidor
com•pi•la•tion *n.* compilación
com•pile *v.* compilar
com•plain *v.* quejarse
com•plain•ant *n.* demandante
com•plaint *n.* queja
com•plai•sant *adj.* complaciente
com•ple•ment *n.* complemento
com•ple•men•ta•ry *adj.* complementario
com•plete *adj.* completo
com•ple•tion *n.* terminación
com•plex *adj.* complejo
com•plex•ion *n.* carácter
com•plex•i•ty *n.* complejidad
com•pli•ance *n.* conformidad
com•pli•ant *adj.* obediente
com•pli•cate *v.* complicar
com•pli•cat•ed *adj.* complicado
com•pli•ca•tion *n.* complicación
com•plic•i•ty *n.* complicidad
com•pli•ment *n.* honor; elogio
com•pli•men•tar•y *adj.* elogioso
com•ply *v.* obedecer
com•po•nent *n.* componente
com•port•ment *n.* comportamiento
com•pose *v.* redactar
com•posed *adj.* tranquilo
com•pos•er *n.* compositor
com•pos•ite *adj.* compuesto
com•po•si•tion *n.* composición
com•po•sure *n.* serenidad
com•pound *adj.* compuesto
com•pre•hend *v.* comprender
com•pre•hen•si•ble *adj.* comprensible
com•pre•hen•sive *adj.* comprensivo; general
com•press *n.* compresa

compressed

com•pressed *adj.* comprimido
com•pres•sion *n.* compresión
com•prise *v.* constar de; comprender
com•pro•mise *n.* compromiso;
  v. componer
com•pro•mis•ing *adj.* comprometedor
com•pul•sion *n.* compulsión
com•pul•so•ry *adj.* compulsorio
com•pu•ta•tion *n.* cálculo
com•pute *v.* computar
com•pu•ter *n.* computador
com•put•er•ize *v.* computarizar
com•rade *n.* camarada
con *adv.* contra
con•cave *adj.* cóncavo
con•ceal *v.* ocultar
con•ceal•ment *n.* encubrimiento
con•cede *v.* conceder
con•ceit•ed *adj.* vanidoso
con•ceiv•a•ble *adj.* concebible
con•ceive *v.* concebir
con•cen•trate *v.* concentrar(se)
con•cen•tra•tion *n.* concentración
con•cen•tric *adj.* concéntrico
con•cept *n.* concepto
con•cep•tion *n.* concepción
con•cep•tu•al *adj.* conceptual
con•cern *v.* concernir
con•cerned *adj.* preocupado
con•cern•ing *prep.* acerca de
con•cert *n.* concierto
con•cert•ed *adj.* conjunto
con•ces•sion *n.* concesión
con•cil•i•ate *v.* conciliar
con•cil•i•a•tion *n.* conciliación
con•cise *adj.* conciso
con•clude *v.* concluir
con•clu•sion *n.* conclusión
con•clu•sive *adj.* concluyente
con•coc•tion *n.* confección
con•cord *n.* concordia
con•crete *adj.* concreto
con•cur *v.* concurrir
con•cur•rence *n.* concurrencia
con•cur•rent *adj.* concurrente
con•cus•sion *n.* concusión

con•dem•na•ble *adj.* condenable
con•den•sa•tion *n.* condensación
con•dense *v.* condensar(se)
con•dens•er *n.* condensador
con•de•scend•ing *adj.* condescendiente
con•di•ment *n.* condimento
con•di•tion *v.* condicionar
con•done *v.* condonar
con•duc•tor *n.* cobrador
con•fed•er•a•cy *n.* confederación
con•fer *v.* conferenciar
con•fess *v.* confesar
con•fide *v.* confiar
con•fi•dence *n.* confianza
con•fi•den•tial *adj.* confidencial
con•firm *v.* confirmar
con•flict *v.* chocar
con•form•i•ty *n.* conformidad
con•fron•ta•tion *n.* confrontación
con•fuse *v.* confundir
con•fu•sion *n.* confusión
con•gest *v.* acumular
con•ges•tion *n.* congestión
con•glom•er•a•tion *n.* conglomeración
con•grat•u•la•tion *n.* felicitación
con•gre•gate *v.* congregar(se)
con•junc•tion *n.* conjución
con•jure *v.* conjurar
con•nect *v.* conectar
con•no•ta•tion *n.* connotación
con•note *v.* connotar
con•sec•u•tive *adj.* consecutivo
con•serv•a•to•ry *n.* conservatorio
con•serve *v.* conservar
con•sid•er *v.* considerar
con•sid•er•a•tion *n.* consideración
con•sist *v.* consistir
con•sol•i•date *v.* consolidar
con•sol•i•da•tion *n.* consolidación
con•sist *v.* consistir
con•stan•cy *n.* constancia
con•stant *adj.* continuo
con•sti•tu•tion *n.* constitución
con•struc•tion *n.* construcción
con•sult *v.* consultar
con•sume *v.* consumir

con·sump·tion *n.* consumo
con·tain *v.* contener
con·tam·i·na·tion *n.* contaminación
con·tem·plate *v.* proyectar
con·tem·po·rar·y *n.* contemporáneo
con·tend *v.* afirmar; contender
con·ti·nen·tal *adj.* continental
con·tin·gen·cy *n.* contingencia
con·tin·ue *v.* seguir; continuar
con·trac·tion *n.* contracción
con·tra·dict *v.* contradecir
con·trast *v.* contrastar
con·tri·bu·tion *n.* contribución
con·trol *v.* dirigir; controlar
con·va·lesce *v.* convalecer
con·verge *v.* convergir
con·ver·sa·tion *n.* conversación
con·verse *v.* conversar
con·ver·sion *n.* conversión
con·vey *v.* llevar
con·vic·tion *n.* convicción
con·vince *v.* convencer
con·vul·sion *n.* convulsión
cook *n.* cocinero; *v.* cocinar
cook·ie *n.* galleta
cool *adj.* fresco
co·or·di·nate *v.* coordinar
co·or·di·na·tion *n.* coordinación
cop·per *n.* cobre
cop·y *v.* copiar
cor·dial·i·ty *n.* cordialidad
corn *n.* maíz
cor·po·ral *adj.* corporal
cor·po·ra·tion *n.* corporación
cor·pu·lent *adj.* gordo
cor·pus·cu·lar *adj.* corpuscular
cor·ral *v.* acorralar
cor·rect *v.* corregir
cor·rec·tion *n.* corrección
cor·re·spond *v.* escribir
cor·re·spond·ence *n.* correspondencia
cor·rode *v.* corroer
cor·ro·sion *n.* corrosión
cor·rup·tion *n.* corrupción
cos·met·ic *n.* cosmético
cos·mic *adj.* cósmico

cost *v.* costar; *n.* precio
couch *n.* sofá
count *n.* cuenta; *v.* contar
coun·try *n.* campo; país
cou·ple *n.* pareja
cou·ra·geous *adj.* valiente
course *n.* plato; dirección
cous·in *n.* prima; primo
cov·er *n.* cubierta; *v.* cubrir
cow *n.* vaca
cow·boy *n.* vaquero
coy·o·te *n.* coyote
crab *n.* cangrejo
crack·er *n.* galleta
cra·dle *v.* mecer
crash *n.* choque; estallido
crate *n.* cajón
cra·ter *n.* cráter
crave *v.* ansiar
crav·ing *n.* anhelo
crawl *v.* gatear; arrastrarse
cray·on *n.* lápiz de color
craze *v.* enloquecer
crazed *adj.* loco
cra·zy *adj.* loco
cream *n.* crema
cream·y *adj.* cremoso
crease *v.* doblar
cre·ate *v.* producir; crear
cre·a·tion *n.* creación
cre·a·tive *adj.* creador
cre·a·tiv·i·ty *n.* originalidad
cre·a·tor *n.* creador
crea·ture *n.* criatura
cre·dence *n.* crédito
cre·den·tial *n.* credencial
cred·i·ble *adj.* creíble
cred·it *n.* crédito; reconocimiento
cred·it·a·ble *adj.* loable
cred·u·lous *adj.* crédulo
creed *n.* credo
creep·y *adj.* espeluznante
cre·mate *v.* incinerar
cre·ma·tion *n.* incineración
crepe *n.* crespón
cres·cent *n.* medialuna

crest *n.* cresta
cre•tin *n.* cretino
crew *n.* equipo
crib *n.* pesebre
crick•et *n.* grillo
crime *n.* crimen
crim•i•nal *n., adj.* criminal
crin•kle *v.* arrugar(se)
crip•ple *v.* mutilar
cri•sis *n.* crisis
crisp *adj.* crespo
crisp•y *adj.* crujiente
crit•ic *n.* crítico
crit•i•cism *n.* crítica
crit•i•cize *v.* criticar
cri•tique *n.* crítica
croc•o•dile *n.* cocodrilo
cro•cus *n.* azafrán
crook *n.* curba, ladrón
crook•ed *adj.* corvo
cross *v.* cruzar; *n.* cruz
cross•beam *n.* traviesa
cross•bow *n.* ballesta
cross•cur•rent *n.* contracorriente
cross•ex•am•ine *v.* interrogar
cross•ing *n.* cruce
cross•word puz•zle *n.* crucigrama
crouch *v.* acuclillarse
crow *v.* cacarear
crowd *n.* gentío; multitud
crowd•ed *adj.* concurrido
crown *n.* corona
crown•ing *n.* coronación
cru•ci•ble *n.* crisol
cru•ci•fix *n.* crucifijo
cru•ci•fix•ion *n.* crucifixión
cru•ci•fy *v.* crucificar
crude *adj.* tosco; ordinario; crudo
crude•ness *n.* tosquedad
cru•el *adj.* cruel
cru•el•ty *n.* crueldad
cruise *v.* navegar
crumb *n.* migaja
crum•ble *v.* desmigajar(se)
crum•ple *v.* estrujar(se)
crunch•y *adj.* crujiente

cru•sade *n.* cruzada
cru•sad•er *n.* cruzado
crush *v.* aplastar
crust *n.* costra; corteza
crus•ta•cean *n.* crustáceo
crust•y *adj.* costroso
cry *v.* llorar
crypt *n.* cripta
crys•tal *n.* cristal
crys•tal•line *adj.* cristalino
crys•tal•lize *v.* cristalizar(se)
crys•tal•log•ra•phy *n.* cristalografía
cube *n.* cubo
cu•bic *adj.* cúbico
cu•bi•cle *adj.* cubículo
cu•bi•cle *n.* compartimiento
cub•ist *n.* cubista
cu•cum•ber *n.* pepino
cud•dle *v.* abrazar(se)
cue *n.* taco
cu•li•nar•y *adj.* culinario
cul•mi•nate *v.* culminar
cul•pa•ble *adj.* culpable
cul•prit *n.* culpable
cult *n.* culto
cul•ti•vate *v.* cultivar
cul•ti•va•tion *n.* cultivo
cul•ti•va•tor *n.* cultivador
cul•tur•al *adj.* cultural
cul•ture *n.* cultura
cul•tured *adj.* culto
cum•ber *v.* embarazar
cum•ber•some *adj.* embarazoso
cu•mu•late *v.* acumular
cu•mu•la•tive *adj.* acumulativo
cun•ning *adj.* hábil; astuto
cup *n.* taza
cup•ful *n.* taza
cur•a•ble *adj.* curable
curb *n.* bordillo
curd *n.* cuajada
cure *n.* cura
cu•ri•os•i•ty *n.* curiosidad
cu•ri•ous *adj.* curioso
curl *v.* enrollar(se); rizar(se)
cur•ren•cy *n.* moneda

cur•rent *n., adj.* corriente
cur•rent•ly *adj.* actualmente
curse *n.* desgracia; maldición
curs•ed *adj.* maldito
cur•sor *n.* cursor
cur•tain *n.* telón
cur•va•ture *n.* curvatura
curve *n.* curva
curved *n.* curva
curved *adj.* curvo
cus•to•di•an *n.* custodio
cus•to•dy *n.* custodia
cus•tom *n.* costumbre
cus•tom•ar•i•ly *adv.* acostumbrada mente
cut *adj.* cortado; *n.,* cortadura; *v.* cortar
cu•ta•ne•ous *adj.* cutáneo
cute *adj.* mono
cu•ti•cle *n.* cutícula
cut•ler•y *n.* cubiertos
cy•a•nide *n.* cianuro
cy•cle *n.* ciclo
cy•clic *adj.* cíclico
cy•clist *n.* ciclista
cy•clone *n.* ciclón
cyl•in•der *n.* cilindro
cy•lin•dri•cal *adj.* cilíndrico
cym•bal *n.* címbalo
cyn•i•cal *adj.* cínico
cyn•i•cism *n.* cinismo
cy•press *n.* ciprés
cyst *n.* quiste
cys•tic *adj.* cístico
cys•ti•tis *n.* cistitis
cy•to•plasm *n.* citoplasma
czar *n.* zar
cza•ri•na *n.* zarina

D

dab *v.* tocar ligeramente
dab•ble *v.* salpicar
dad *n.* papá
daft *adj.* loco

dag•ger *n.* puñal
dai•ly *adj.* diario
dain•ti•ness *n.* delicadeza
dain•ty *adj.* delicado
dair•y *n.* lechería; quesería
dair•y•man *n.* lechero
da•is *n.* estrado
dale *n.* valle
dal•li•ance *n.* diversión
dal•ly *v.* perder tiempo; entretenerse
dam *v.* represar; *n.* presa
dam•age *v.* dañar; perjudicar
damn *v.* condenar
dam•na•ble *adj.* detestable
damned *adj.* condenado
damp *adj.* húmedo
damp•en *v.* mojar
dance *n.* baile; *v.* bailar
dan•cer *n.* bailador
dan•druff *n.* caspa
dan•ger *n.* peligro
dan•ger•ous *adj.* peligroso
dan•gle *v.* colgar
dank *adj.* húmedo
dap•pled *adj.* rodado
dare *v.* arriesgarse
dar•ing *n.* atrevimiento
dark *n.* oscuridad; *adj.* oscuro
dark•en *v.* oscurecer
dark•ness *n.* oscuridad
darl•ing *n.* querido
darn *v.* zurcir
dash *v.* precipitarse; romper
dash•board *n.* tablero de instrumentos
date *n.* cita; fecha
daub *v.* pintarrajear
daugh•ter *n.* hija
daugh•ter-in-law *n.* nuera
daunt•less *adj.* impávido
daw•dle *v.* perder el tiempo
dawn *v.* amanecer
day *n.* día
day•break *n.* amanecer
day•dream *n.* ensueño
day•light *n.* luz del día
day•time *n.* día

daze v. aturdir

daz·zle v. deslumbrar

dea·con n. diácono

dea·con·ry n. diaconía

dead adj. muerto

dead·en v. amortiguar

dead·end n. calle sin salida

dead·ly adj. mortal

deaf adj. sordo

deaf·en v. ensordecer

deal n. cantidad; trato; reparto

deal·er n. tratante

dean n. decano; deán

dear adj. querido; caro

dear·ness n. carestía

death n. muerte

death·less adj. inmortal

death·ly adj. mortal

de·ba·cle n. fracaso

de·bar v. prohibir

de·bate v. debatir

de·bauch v. corromper

de·bauch·er·y n. libertinaje

de·bil·i·tate v. debilitar

de·bil·i·ta·tion n. debilitación

de·bil·it·y n. debilidad

deb·it n. debe

deb·o·nair adj. cortés; elegante

de·bris n. escombros

debt n. deuda

debt·or n. deudor

de·but, de·but n. presentación; estreno

deb·u·tant, deb·u·tante n. debutante

de·cade n. decenio

dec·a·dence n. decadencia

dec·a·dent adj. decadente

de·can·ter n. garrafa

de·cay v. decaer; cariarse; deteriorar

de·cease v. morir

de·ceased adj. muerto

de·ceit·ful adj. engañoso

de·ceive v. engañar

De·cem·ber n. diciembre

de·cen·cy n. decencia

de·cent adj. decente

de·cep·tion n. fraude

de·cide v. decidir

de·cid·ed·ly adv. decididamente

dec·i·mal n. decimal

de·ci·pher v. descifrar

de·ci·sion n. decisión; firmeza

de·ci·sive adj. decisivo

de·ci·sive·ly adv. con resolución

deck v. adornar

dec·la·ra·tion n. declaración

de·clare v. declarer

de·cline v. rehusar

de·com·pose v. descomponer(se)

de·com·po·si·tion n. descomposición

de·cor·ate v. adornar; condecorar

dec·o·ra·tion n. decoración; ornato

dec·o·ra·tor n. decorador

de·coy n. señuelo

de·crease v. disminuir(se)

de·creas·ing·ly adv. en disminución

de·cree n. decreto

de·crep·it adj. decrépito

de·cry v. rebajar

de·duce v. deducir

de·duct v. restar

de·duc·tion n. descuento

deed n. hecho

deem v. juzgar

deep adj. profundo

deep·en v. intensificar

de·face v. desfigurar

def·a·ma·tion n. difamación

de·fame v. difamar

de·fault n. a falta de

de·feat n. derrota; v. vencer; frustrar

de·fect n. defecto

de·fec·tion n. defección

de·fec·tive adj. defectuoso

de·fend v. defender

de·fend·ant n. demandado

de·fense, de·fence n. defensa

de·fen·sive adj. defensivo

de·fer v. diferir; aplazar

def·er·ence n. deferencia

de·fer·ment n. aplazamiento

de·fi·ance n. desafío

de·fi·ant adj. provocativo

de·fi·cien·cy *n.* deficiencia
de·fi·cient *adj.* insuficiente
def·i·cit *n.* déficit
de·file *v.* manchar
de·fine *v.* definir
def·i·nite *adj.* concreto; definido
de·fi·ni·tion *n.* definición
de·fin·i·tive *adj.* definitivo
de·flate *v.* desinflar
de·fla·tion *n.* desinflación
de·flect *v.* desviar
de·form·i·ty *n.* deformidad
de·fraud *v.* defraudar; estafar
de·fray *v.* pagar
deft *adj.* diestro
deft·ness *n.* habilidad
de·funct *adj.* difunto
de·fy *v.* desafiar; contravenir
de·gen·er·ate *v.* degenerar
deg·ra·da·tion *n.* degradación
de·grade *v.* degradar
de·gree *n.* rango
de·hy·drate *v.* deshidratar
de·hy·dra·tion *n.* deshidratación
de·i·fy *v.* deificar
deign *v.* dignarse
de·i·ty *n.* deidad
de·ject·ed *adj.* abatido
de·jec·tion *n.* melancolía; abatimiento
de·lay *v.* aplazar; demorar
de·lec·ta·ble *adj.* deleitable
de·le·gate *v.* delegar
de·le·ga·tion *n.* diputación
de·lete *v.* tachar
de·le·tion *n.* supresión; borradura
de·lib·er·ate *v.* deliberar
del·i·ca·cy *n.* delicadeza
del·i·cate *adj.* delicado; fino
de·li·cious *adj.* delicioso
de·light *v.* deleitar
de·light·ful *adj.* encantador
de·lin·e·ate *v.* delinear
de·lin·e·a·tion *n.* bosquejo
de·lin·quen·cy *n.* delincuencia
de·lin·quent *adj.* delincuente
de·lir·i·ous *adj.* delirante

de·lir·i·um *n.* delirio
de·liv·er *v.* entregar
de·liv·er·y *n.* entrega
del·ta *n.* delta
de·lude *v.* engañar
del·uge *n.* diluvio
de·lu·sion *n.* engaño; ilusión
de·luxe *adj.* de lujo
delve *v.* cavar
de·mand *v.* demandar; exigir
de·moc·ra·cy *n.* democracia
dem·o·crat *n.* demócrata
dem·o·crat·ic *adj.* democrático
dem·on·strate *v.* demostrar
dem·on·stra·tion *n.* demostración
de·mor·al·ize *v.* desmoralizar
den *n.* estudio
de·nom·i·na·tion *n.* denominación
de·nom·i·na·tor *n.* denominador
de·note *v.* denotar
de·nounce *n.* denunciar
dense *adj.* denso
den·si·ty *n.* densidad
den·tist *n.* dentista
de·nun·ci·ate *v.* denunciar
de·nun·ci·a·tion *n.* denuncia
de·par·ture *n.* salida
de·pend·en·cy *n.* dependencia
de·port *v.* deportar
de·por·ta·tion *n.* deportación
de·prave *v.* depravar
de·praved *adj.* depravado
de·pres·sion *n.* desaliento
depth *n.* fondo
de·ride *v.* mofar
de·ri·sion *n.* irrisión
der·i·va·tion *n.* derivación
de·rive *v.* derivar(se)
der·rick *n.* grúa
de·scend *v.* bajar; descender
de·scend·ant *n.* descendiente
de·scribe *v.* describir
de·scrip·tion *n.* descripción
de·scrip·tive *adj.* descriptivo
des·ert *n.* desierto
de·sert·er *n.* desertor

deserve

de•serve v. merecer
de•sign v. idear; diseñar
des•ig•nate v. señalar; nombrar
des•ig•na•tion n. nombramiento
de•sign•er n. diseñador; dibujante
de•sire v. desear
de•sist v. desistir
desk n. pupitre
des•o•la•tion n. desolación
de•spair v. desesperar
des•per•ate adj. desesperado; arriesgado
des•per•a•tion n. desesperación
des•pi•ca•ble adj. despreciable
de•spise v. despreciar
de•spite prep. a pesar de
des•sert n. postre
de•stroy v. destruir
de•struct•i•ble adj. destructible
de•struc•tion n. destrucción
de•tain v. retener
de•ter v. disuadir
de•ter•mi•na•tion n. determinación
de•test•a•ble adj. detestable
de•val•u•a•tion n. devaluación
dev•as•tate v. devastar
dev•as•ta•tion n. devastación
de•vel•op v. desenvolver
de•vice n. ingenio; estratagema
dev•il n. diablo
de•vi•ous adj. tortuoso
de•vise v. inventar
de•void adj. desprovisto
de•vote v. dedicar
dev•o•tee n. devoto
dev•o•tion n. devoción; lealtad
de•vour v. devorar
di•a•be•tes n. diabetes
di•a•bet•ic adj. diabético
di•ag•nose v. diagnosticar
di•a•bol•ic adj. diabólico
di•a•dem n. diadema
di•ag•nose v. diagnosticar
di•ag•no•sis n. diagnóstico
di•ag•o•nal adj., n. diagonal
di•a•gram n. diagrama
di•a•lect n. dialecto

di•am•e•ter n. diámetro
di•a•met•ric adj. diametral
dia•mond n. diamante
dia•per n. pañal
di•a•phragm n. diafragma
di•ar•rhe•a n. diarrea
di•a•ry n. diario
dice n. dados
dick•er v. regatear
dic•tate v. mandar; dictar
dic•ta•tion n. dictado
dic•ta•tor n. dictador
dic•tion•ar•y n. diccionario
die v. morir
dif•fer•ence n. diferencia
dif•fer•ent adj. diferente
dif•fi•cult adj. difícil
dif•fi•cul•ty n. dificultad
dig n. excavación; v. extraer
di•ges•tion n. digestión
dig•it n. dedo
dig•ni•fy v. dignificar
di•lem•ma n. dilema
dil•i•gence n. diligencia
dil•i•gent adj. diligente
di•lute v. diluir
di•lu•tion n. dilución
dim adj. oscuro
di•min•ish v. disminuir(se)
dine v. cenar
din•ner n. cena
di•plo•ma•cy n. diplomacia
dip•lo•mat n. diplomático
dip•lo•mat•ic adj. diplomático
di•rect v. dirigir; adj. directo
di•rec•tion n. dirección
di•rec•tor n. director
dis•a•ble v. inutilizar
dis•ap•pear v. desaparecer
dis•ap•pear•ance n. desaparición
dis•as•trous adj. desastroso
dis•a•vow v. desconocer
dis•charge v. despedir
dis•ci•pli•nar•y adj. disciplinario
dis•ci•pline v. disciplinar; n. castigo
dis•con•nect v. desconectar

drama

dis•con•tin•u•ous *adj.* discontinuo
dis•cov•er *v.* descubrir
dis•crep•an•cy *n.* discrepancia
dis•cus•sion *n.* discusión
dis•ease *n.* enfermedad
dis•guise *n.* disfraz; *v.* disfrazar
dish *n.* plato
dis•hon•or *v.* deshonrar
dis•hon•or•a•ble *adj.* deshonroso
dis•in•fect•ant *n.* desinfectante
dis•in•ter•est *n.* desinterés
disk *n.* disco
dis•lo•cate *v.* dislocar
dis•lo•ca•tion *n.* dislocación
dis•o•bey *v.* desobedecer
dis•or•der *n.* desorden
dis•pense *v.* dispensar
dis•play *n.* demostrar
dis•pute *n.* disputa; *v.* disputar
dis•qual•i•fy *v.* descalificar
dis•solve *v.* disolver(se)
dis•suade *v.* disuadir
dis•sua•sion *n.* disuasión
dis•tance *n.* distancia
dis•tant *adj.* distante
distill *v.* destilar
dis•till•er•y *n.* destilería
dis•tinc•tion *n.* distinción
dis•tin•guish *v.* distinguir
dis•tract *v.* distraer
dis•trac•tion *n.* distracción
dis•tri•bu•tion *n.* distribución
dis•turb *v.* perturbar
dis•turb•ance *n.* disturbio
di•verge *v.* divergir
di•ver•gence *n.* divergencia
di•ver•sion *n.* diversión
di•vert *v.* divertir
di•ver•si•ty *n.* diversidad
di•vide *v.* dividir(se)
di•vin•i•ty *n.* divinidad
di•vide *v.* dividir(se)
diz•zy *adj.* mareado
do *v.* cumplir; hacer
doc•tor *n.* médico
doc•u•ment *n.* document; *v.* documentar

dog *n.* perro
dog•mat•ic *adj.* dogmático
doll *n.* muñeca
dol•lar *n.* dólar
do•mes•tic *adj.* doméstico
do•mes•ti•cate *v.* domesticar
dom•i•nant *v.* dominar
dom•i•na•tion *n.* dominación
dom•i•neer *v.* tiranizar
dom•i•neer•ing *adj.* dominante
do•min•ion *n.* dominio
don *v.* ponerse
do•nate *v.* donar
done *adj.* hecho
do•nor *n.* donante
doom *n.* juicio; suerte
door *n.* puerta
dope *n.* narcótico
dor•mi•to•ry *n.* dormitorio
dor•sal *adj.* dorsal
dos•age *n.* dosificación
dose *n.* dosis
dot *n.* punto
dot•age *n.* chochez
dou•ble *v.* doblar(se)
doubt *n.* duda; *v.* dudar
dough *n.* maza
dough•nut *n.* buñuelo
dour *adj.* austero
douse *v.* mojar; zambullir
dow•a•ger *n.* viuda de un titulado
dow•dy *adj.* desaliñado; poco elegante
down *prep., adv.* abajo
down•cast *adj.* abatido
down•fall *n.* caída
down•heart•ed *adj.* desanimado
down•ward *adv.* hacia abajo
doze *v.* dormitar
doz•en *n.* docena
drab *adj.* monótono
draft *n.* giro; *mil.* destacamento
drag *v.* arrastar
drag•on *n.* dragón
drain *v.* agotar; desaguar
drain•age *n.* desagüe; drenaje
dra•ma *n.* drama

145

dra•mat•ic *adj.* dramático
dram•a•tist *n.* dramaturgo
dram•a•tize *v.* dramatizar
drape *v.* poner colgaduras
dra•per•y *n.* colgadura
dras•tic *adj.* drástico; enérgico
draw *v.* sacar; dibujar; arrastrar
draw•back *n.* desventaja
draw•bridge *n.* puente levadizo
draw•er *n.* cajón
dread *v.* temer
dread•ful *adj.* terrible
dream *v.* soñar; *n.* sueño
dream•er *n.* soñador
dredge *v.* dragar
dreg *n.* heces
drench *v.* empapar
dress *n.* vestido; *v.* vestir(se)
dress•er *n.* aparador
drib•ble *v.* caer gota a gota
drift *n.* impulso de la corriente; montón
drift•wood *n.* madera llevada por el agua
drill *v.* taladrar
drink *n.* bebida; *v.* beber
drip *v.* gotear
drive *v.* manejar; empujar; conducir
driz•zle *v.* lloviznar
droll *adj.* gracioso
drone *n.* zángano
drool *v.* babear
droop *v.* inclinar
drop *n.* gota; declive
drop•sy *n.* hidropesía
dross *n.* escoria
drought *n.* sequía
drown *v.* ahogar; anegar
drowse *v.* adormecer(se)
drow•sy *adj.* soñoliento
drudg•er•y *n.* faena penosa
drug *n.* droga
drug•gist *n.* farmacéutico; boticario
drum *n.* tambor
drum•stick *n.* baqueta
drunk *adj.* borracho
drunk•ard *n.* borracho
drunk•en *adj.* borracho

du•al•i•ty *n.* dualidad
dub *v.* armar; apodar
du•bi•ous *adj.* dudoso
duch•ess *n.* duquesa
duck *n.* pato
duct *n.* conducto
dude *n.* petimetre
due *adj.* debido; oportuno
duel *n.* duelo
du•et *n.* dúo
duke *n.* duque
dull *adj.* embotado; torpe
dumb *adj.* mudo
dum•found *v.* pasmar
dum•my *n.* maniquí
dump *v.* descargar
dump•ling *n.* bola de masa
dunce *n.* zopenco
dune *n.* duna
dung *n.* estiércol
dun•geon *n.* mazmorra
du•pli•cate *adj.* duplicado; *v.* duplicar
du•pli•ca•tion *n.* duplicación
du•ra•tion *n.* duración
dur•ing *prep.* durante
dusk *n.* crepúsculo
dusk•y *adj.* oscuro
dust *n.* polvo
du•ti•ful *adj.* obediente
du•ty *n.* derechos
dwell *v.* habitar
dwell•ing *n.* morada
dwin•dle *v.* disminuir
dye *n.* tinte
dy•nam•ic *adj.* dinámico
dy•na•mite *n.* dinamita
dy•na•mo *n.* dinamo
dy•nas•ty *n.* dinastía
dys•en•ter•y *n.* disentería

E

each *adv.* para cada uno
ea•ger *adj.* impaciente

ea·ger·ness *n.* ansia
ea·gle *n.* águila
ear *n.* oído; oreja
ear·drum *n.* tímpano del oído
earl *n.* conde
ear·li·ness *n.* precocidad
ear·ly *adj.* primitivo; *adv., adj.* temprano
earn *v.* merecer
ear·nest *adj.* fervoroso; serio
ear·nest·ly *adv.* con seriedad
earn·ings *n.* sueldo
ear·ring *n.* pendiente
ear·shot *n.* alcance del oído
earth *n.* mundo; tierra
earth·en·ware *n.* loza de barro
earth·ly *adj.* mundano
earth·quake *n.* terremoto
earth·y *adj.* terroso
ease *v.* facilitar; *n.* facilidad
ea·sel *n.* caballete
eas·i·ly *adv.* fácilmente
eas·i·ness *n.* facilidad
east *n.* este
east·ern *adj.* del este
east·ward *adv.* hacia el este
eas·y *adj.* fácil
eas·y·go·ing *adj.* acomodadizo; de manga ancha
eat *v.* gustar; comer
eat·a·ble *adj.* comestible
eaves *n.* alero
eaves·drop *v.* escuchar a escondidas; espiar
ebb *v.* menguar; decaer
eb·on·y *n.* ébano
ec·cen·tric *adj.* excéntrico
ec·cen·tric·i·ty *n.* excentricidad
ec·cle·si·as·tic *adj., n.* eclesiástico
ech·o *n.* eco
e·clipse *v.* eclipsar
e·clip·tic *adj.* eclíptico
ec·o·lo·gic *adj.* ecológico
e·col·o·gist *n.* ecólogo
e·col·o·gy *n.* ecología
e·co·nom·ic *adj.* económico
e·co·nom·ic·al *adj.* económico

e·co·nom·ics *n.* economía
e·con·o·mist *n.* economista
e·con·o·mize *v.* economizar
e·con·o·my *n.* economía
ec·sta·sy *n.* éxtasis
ec·stat·ic *adj.* extático
ec·u·men·i·cal *n.* ecuménico
ec·ze·ma *n.* eczema; eccema
ed·dy *n.* remolino
e·den·tate *adj.* desdentado
edge *n.* filo; agudeza; borde
ed·i·ble *adj.* comestible
e·dict *n.* edicto
ed·i·fi·ca·tion *n.* edificación
ed·i·fice *n.* edificio
ed·i·fy *v.* edificár
ed·it *v.* editar
e·di·tion *n.* edición
ed·i·tor *n.* editor
ed·i·to·ri·al *n.* editorial
ed·i·to·ri·al·ist *n.* editorialista
ed·u·cate *v.* educar
ed·u·ca·tion *n.* educación
eel *n.* anguila
ee·rie *adj.* espantoso; fantástico
ef·face *v.* borrar
ef·fect *v.* efectuar; *n.* resultado
ef·fec·tive *adj.* efectivo; eficaz
ef·fec·tu·al *adj.* eficaz
ef·fem·i·nate *adj.* afeminado
ef·fer·vesce *v.* estar en efervescencia
ef·fer·ves·cence *n.* efervescencia
ef·fer·ves·cent *adj.* efervescente
ef·fi·ca·cious *adj.* eficaz
ef·fi·cien·cy *n.* eficiencia
ef·fi·cient *adj.* eficiente
ef·fi·gy *n.* efigie
ef·fort *n.* esfuerzo
ef·fort·less *adj.* sin esfuerzo
ef·fuse *v.* derramar
ef·fu·sion *n.* efusión
ef·fu·sive *adj.* expansivo; efusivo
egg *n.* huevo
e·go *n.* el yo
e·go·tist *n.* egotista
e·gress *n.* salida**

eight *adj.* ocho
eight•een *adj.* dieciocho
eighth *adj.* octavo
eight•y *adj.* ochenta
ei•ther *adv.* tampoco; también; *adj.* cualquier
e•ject *v.* echar; expulsar
e•jec•tion *n.* expulsión
eke *v.* aumentar
e•lab•o•rate *v.* elaborar
e•lab•or•a•tion *n.* elaboración
e•lapse *v.* pasar
e•last•ic *adj.* elástico
e•las•tic•i•ty *n.* elasticidad
e•late *v.* alegrar
e•la•tion *n.* regocijo
el•bow *n.* codo
eld•er *adj.* mayor
el•der•ly *adj.* de edad
eld•est *adj.* el mayor
e•lect *v.* elegir
e•lec•tion *n.* elección
e•lec•tive *adj.* electivo
e•lec•tor *n.* elector
e•lec•tor•ate *n.* electorado
e•lec•tric *adj.* eléctrico; vivo
e•lec•tri•cian *n.* electricista
e•lec•tro•cute *v.* electrocutar
e•lec•trode *n.* electrodo
e•lec•tron *n.* electrón
e•lec•tron•ic *adj.* electrónico
el•e•gance *n.* elegancia
el•e•gant *adj.* elegante
el•e•gy *n.* elegía
el•e•ment *n.* elemento
el•e•men•ta•ry *adj.* elemental
el•e•phant *n.* elefante
el•e•vate *v.* elevar
el•e•va•tion *n.* elevación
el•e•va•tor *n.* ascensor
e•lev•en *adj.* once
e•lev•enth *adj., n.* undécimo
elf•in *a.* elfo
e•lic•it *v.* sacar
el•i•gi•bil•i•ty *n.* elegibilidad
el•i•gi•ble *adj.* elegible; deseable

e•lim•i•nate *v.* eliminar
e•lim•i•na•tion *n.* eliminación
e•lite *n.* lo mejor
e•lix•ir *n.* elixir
elk *n.* alce
el•lipse *n.* elipse
el•lip•ti•cal *adj.* elíptico
elm *n.* olmo
el•o•cu•tion *n.* elocución
e•lon•gate *v.* alargar
e•lope *v.* fugarse con su amante para casarse
e•lope•ment *n.* fuga
el•o•quence *n.* elocuencia
el•o•quent *adj.* elocuente
else *adv.* otro; más
e•lu•ci•date *v.* elucidar
e•lude *v.* eludir; escapar de
e•lu•sive *adj.* esquivo
e•ma•ci•ate *v.* enflaquecer(se)
e•man•ci•pate *v.* emancipar
e•man•ci•pa•tion *n.* emancipación
em•balm *v.* embalsamar
em•bar•go *n.* embargo
em•bark *v.* embarcar(se)
em•bar•rass *v.* desconcertar
em•bas•sy *n.* embajada
em•ber *n.* ascua
em•bez•zle *v.* desfalcar
em•blem *n.* emblema
em•boss *v.* realzar
em•brace *v.* abrazar; aceptar; abarcar
em•broi•der *v.* recamar
em•bry•o *n.* embrión
em•er•ald *n.* esmeralda
e•merge *v.* salir
e•mer•gence *n.* salida
e•mer•gen•cy *n.* crisis
em•er•y *n.* esmeril
em•i•grant *n.* emigrante
em•i•gra•tion *n.* emigración
em•i•nence *n.* eminencia
em•i•nent *adj.* eminente
em•is•sar•y *n.* emisario
e•mis•sion *n.* emisión
e•mit *v.* emitir
e•mo•tion *n.* emoción

em•per•or *n.* emperador
em•pha•sis *n.* énfasis
em•pha•size *v.* acentuar; recalcar
em•phat•ic *adj.* enfático
em•pire *n.* imperio
em•ploy *v.* emplear
em•ploy•ee *n.* empleado
em•ploy•er *n.* amo; patrón
em•ploy•ment *n.* empleo; colocación
em•pow•er *v.* autorizar
em•press *n.* emperatriz
emp•ti•ness *n.* vacuidad; vacío
emp•ty *v.* vaciar; *adj.* desocupado
em•u•late *v.* emular
e•mul•sion *n.* emulsión
e•mul•sive *adj.* emulsivo
en•a•ble *v.* hacer que; permitir
en•act *v.* decretar; hacer el papel de
e•nam•el *n.* esmalte
en•am•or *v.* enamorar
en•case *v.* encerrar; encajar
en•chant *v.* encantar
en•chant•ing *adj.* encantador
en•chant•ment *n.* encanto
en•cir•cle *v.* ceñir
en•close *v.* encerrar; incluir
en•clo•sure *n.* cercamiento; carta adjunta
en•com•pass *v.* cercar; abarcar
en•core *n.* repetición
en•coun•ter *n.* encuentro
en•cour•age *v.* animar; fomentar
en•croach *v.* usurpar; pasar los límites
en•cum•ber *v.* estorbar; gravar
en•cy•clo•pe•dia *n.* enciclopedia
end *n.* final; fin
en•dan•ger *v.* poner en peligro
en•dear *v.* hacer querer
en•deav•or *n.* esfuerzo
end•ing *f.* fin
en•dorse *v.* endosar
en•dorse•ment *n.* endoso
en•dow *v.* dotar
en•dur•ance *n.* resistencia
en•dure *v.* durar
en•e•my *n.* enemigo
en•er•get•ic *adj.* enérgico

en•er•gy *n.* energía
en•force *v.* hacer cumplir; exigir
en•gage *v.* engranar; apalabrar
en•gage•ment *n.* obligación
en•gine *n.* motor; locomotora
en•gi•neer *n.* ingeniero
en•gi•neer•ing *n.* ingeniería
Eng•lish *n.* inglés
en•grave *v.* grabar
en•gross *v.* absorber; monopolizar
en•hance *v.* aumentar
e•nig•ma *n.* enigma
en•join *v.* imponer
en•joy *v.* disfrutar
en•joy•ment *n.* disfrute
en•large *v.* extender(se)
en•large•ment *n.* aumento; ampliación
en•light•en *v.* iluminar; instruir
en•list *v.* alistar(se)
en•liv•en *v.* avivar
en•mi•ty *n.* enemistad
e•nor•mous *adj.* enorme
e•nough *adv.* bastante
en•slave *v.* esclavizar
en•ter•tain•ment *n.* espectáculo
en•thu•si•asm *n.* entusiasmo
en•thu•si•ast *n.* entusiasta
en•tire *adj.* entero
en•tire•ly *adv.* totalmente
en•trance *n.* entrada
en•trust *v.* entregar
en•try *n.* partida; entrada
en•vel•op *v.* envolver
en•zyme *n.* enzima
ep•i•dem•ic *n.* epidemia
ep•i•sode *n.* episodio
ep•och *n.* época
eq•ua•bil•i•ty *n.* uniformidad
eq•ua•ble *adj.* uniforme
e•qual *v.* igualar; *n.* igual
e•qual•i•ty *adj.* igualdad
e•qual•ly *adv.* igualmente
e•qual•ize *v.* igualar
e•qua•nim•i•ty *n.* ecuanimidad
e•quate *v.* comparar
e•qua•tion *n.* ecuación

e•qua•tor *n.* ecuador

e•ques•tri•enne *n.* jineta

e•qui•lib•ri•um *n.* equilibrio

e•quip *v.* proveer; equipar

e•quip•ment *n.* equipo

eq•ui•ta•ble *adj.* equitativo

eq•ui•ty *n.* equidad

e•quiv•a•lent *adj.* equivalente

e•ra *n.* era

e•rad•i•cate *v.* desarraigar

e•rase *v.* borrar

e•ras•er *n.* borrador

ere *conj.* antes de que

e•rect *v.* erigir

e•rec•tion *n.* erección

er•mine *n.* armiño

e•rode *v.* corroer

e•ro•sion *n.* erosión

e•rot•ic *adj.* erótica

e•rot•ic *adj.* erótico

err *v.* vagar; errar

er•rand *n.* recado

er•rant *adj.* errante

er•ror *n.* error

er•u•dite *adj.* erudito

er•u•di•tion *n.* erudición

e•rup•tion *n.* erupción

es•ca•la•tor *n.* escalera móvil

es•ca•pade *n.* aventura

es•cape *v.* escapar; huir

es•chew *v.* evitar

es•cort *v.* acompañar; *n.* acompañante

e•soph•a•gus, oe•soph•a•gus *n.* esófago

es•o•ter•ic *adj.* esotérico

es•pe•cial *adj.* especial

es•pe•cial•ly *adv.* especialmente

es•pi•o•nage *n.* espionaje

es•pouse *v.* adherirse a; casarse

es•py *v.* divisar; percibir

es•say *n.* ensayo

es•sence *n.* esencia; perfume

es•sen•tial *adj.* esencial

es•tab•lish *v.* establecer; probar; fundar

es•tab•lish•ment *n.* establecimiento

es•tate *n.* finca; propiedad

es•teem *v.* estimar

es•thet•ic *adj.* estético

es•ti•mate *v.* calcular; estimar

es•ti•ma•tion *n.* juicio; aprecio

es•trange *v.* apartar

es•tu•ar•y *n.* estuario

et•cet•er•a *n.* etcétera

etch *v.* grabar al agua fuerte

etch•ing *n.* aguafuerte

e•ter•nal *adj.* eterno

e•ter•nal•ly *adv.* eternamente

e•ter•ni•ty *n.* eternidad

e•ther *n.* éter

e•the•re•al *adj.* etéreo

eth•i•cal *adj.* ético

eth•ics *n.* ética

eth•nol•o•gy *n.* etnología

et•i•quette *n.* etiqueta

e•tude *n.* estudio

eu•lo•gize *v.* elogiar

eu•lo•gy *n.* elogio

eu•pho•ri•a *n.* euforia

eu•phor•ic *adj.* eufórico

e•vac•u•ate *v.* evacuar

e•vac•u•a•tion *n.* evacuación

e•vade *v.* evadir

e•val•u•a•tion evaluación

e•van•gel•i•cal *adj.* evangélico

e•van•ge•list *n.* evangelista

e•vap•o•rate *v.* evaporar(se)

e•vap•o•ra•tion *n.* evaporación

e•va•sion *n.* evasión

e•va•sive *adj.* evasivo

eve *n.* víspera

e•ven *adj.* igualar

eve•ning *n.* tarde

e•vent *n.* suceso

e•vent•ful *adj.* memorable

e•ven•tu•al•i•ty *n.* eventualidad

ev•er *adv.* siempre; nunca; jamás

eve•ry *adj.* todo

e•vict *v.* expulsar

e•vic•tion *n.* desahucio

ev•i•dence *n.* evidencia

e•vil *n.* mal

e•vil•do•er *n.* malhechor

e•voke *v.* evocar
ev•o•lu•tion *n.* desarrollo; evolución
e•volve *v.* desarrollar
ewe *n.* oveja
ew•er *n.* aguamanil
ex•act *adj.* exacto
ex•act•ing *adj.* exigente
ex•ag•ger•ate *v.* exagerar
ex•ag•ger•a•tion *n.* exageración
ex•alt *v.* exaltar; honrar
ex•al•ta•tion *n.* exaltación
ex•am•in•a•tion *n.* examen
ex•am•ine *v.* examinar
ex•am•in•er *n.* examinador
ex•am•ple *n.* ejemplo
ex•as•per•ate *v.* exasperar
ex•as•per•a•tion *n.* exasperación
ex•ca•vate *v.* excavar
ex•ca•va•tion *n.* excavación
ex•ceed *v.* superar; exceder
ex•ceed•ing•ly *adv.* sumamente
ex•cel *v.* sobresalir; aventajar
ex•cel•lence *n.* excelencia
ex•cel•lent *adj.* excelente
ex•cept *v.* exceptuar
ex•cep•tion *n.* excepción
ex•cep•tion•al *adj.* excepcional
ex•cerpt *v.* citar un texto
ex•cess *n.* exceso
ex•change *v.* cambiar
ex•cise *n.* impuestos sobre ciertos artículos
ex•cit•a•ble *adj.* excitable
ex•cite *v.* excitar
ex•cite•ment *n.* agitación; emoción
ex•cit•ing *adj.* emocionante
ex•claim *v.* exclamar
ex•cla•ma•tion *n.* exclamación
ex•clude *v.* excluir
ex•clu•sion *n.* exclusión
ex•clu•sive *adj.* exclusivo
ex•com•mu•ni•cate *v.* excomulgar
ex•com•mu•ni•ca•tion *n.* excomunión
ex•cre•ment *n.* excremento
ex•cur•sion *n.* viaje; excursión
ex•cuse *v.* excusar; perdonar
ex•e•cute *v.* ejecutar; llevar a cabo

ex•e•cu•tion *n.* ejecución
ex•ec•u•tive *adj.* ejecutivo
ex•ec•u•tor *n.* albacea
ex•em•pla•ry *adj.* ejemplar
ex•er•cise *n.* ejercicio
ex•hale *v.* exhalar; expirar
ex•haust *v.* agotar
ex•hib•it *v.* mostrar; presentar
ex•hi•bi•tion *n.* exposición
ex•hil•a•rate *v.* vigorizar; alegrar
ex•hort *v.* exhortar
ex•i•gent *adj.* exigente
ex•ile *n.* exilado; destierro
ex•ist *v.* existir
ex•ist•ence *n.* existencia
ex•it *n.* salida
ex•o•dus *n.* éxodo
ex•or•bi•tant *adj.* excesivo
ex•o•tic *adj.* exótico
ex•pand *v.* extender; ensanchar
ex•panse *n.* extensión
ex•pan•sion *n.* expansión
ex•pan•sive *adj.* expansivo
ex•pect *v.* esperar; contar con
ex•pect•an•cy *n.* expectación
ex•pect•ant *adj.* expectante
ex•pec•ta•tion *n.* expectación
ex•pe•di•en•cy *n.* conveniencia
ex•pe•di•ent *adj.* conveniente
ex•pe•dite *v.* facilitar; acelerar
ex•pe•di•tion *n.* expedición
ex•pel *v.* expulsar
ex•pend *v.* expender
ex•pend•i•ture *n.* gasto
ex•pe•ri•ence *v.* experimentar
ex•per•i•ment *n.* experimento
ex•pire *v.* terminar
ex•pla•na•tion *n.* explicación
ex•pli•cit *adj.* explícito
ex•plode *v.* estallar; volar
ex•ploit *n.* hazaña
ex•plo•ra•tion *n.* exploración
ex•plore *v.* explorar; examinar
ex•plor•er *n.* explorador
ex•plo•sion *n.* explosión
ex•po•nent *n.* exponente

export

ex·port *v.* exportar
ex·por·ta·tion *n.* exportación
ex·pose *v.* exponer; desenmascarar
ex·press *v.* expresar
ex·pres·sion *n.* expresión
ex·pres·sive *adj.* expresivo
ex·tend *v.* extender
ex·ten·sion *n.* extensión
ex·te·ri·or *adj.* exterior
ex·tinct *adj.* extinto
ex·tinc·tion *n.* extinción
ex·tra *n.* extra
ex·tra·or·di·nar·y *adj.* extraordinario
ex·treme *adj.* extremo
ex·ul·ta·tion *n.* exultación
eye *n.* ojo
eye·let *n.* ojete
eye·sight *n.* vista
eye·tooth *n.* colmillo
eye·wit·ness *n.* testigo ocular

F

fa·ble *n.* fábula
fab·ric *n.* tela
fab·ri·cate *v.* inventar
fab·u·lous *adj.* fabuloso
fa·cade *n.* fachada
face *n.* cara
fa·cial *adj.* facial
fa·cile *adj.* fácil
fa·cil·i·tate *v.* facilitar
fa·cil·i·ty *n.* facilidad
fac·sim·i·le *n.* facsímile
fact *n.* hecho
fac·tion *n.* facción
fac·tor *n.* factor
fac·to·ry *n.* fábrica
fac·tu·al *adj.* basado en datos
fac·ul·ty *n.* facultad
fad *n.* novedad
fade *v.* descolorar(se)
fag *v.* fatigar

fag·ot *n.* haz de leña
Fahr·en·heit *adj.* de Fahrenheit
fail *v.* acabar; faltar
fail·ure *n.* fracaso
faint *v.* desmayarse
faint·ness *n.* debilidad
fair *adj.* justo; rubio
fair·ly *adv.* justamente
fair·y *n.* hada
faith *n.* fe
faith·ful *adj.* fiel
faith·less *adj.* desleal
fake *n.* impostura
fal·con *n.* halcón
fall *v.* caer(se)
fal·la·cious *adj.* engañoso
fal·la·cy *n.* error; falacia
fal·li·ble *adj.* falible
fal·low *adj.* en barbecho
false *adj.* falso
false·hood *n.* mentira
false·ly *adv.* falsamente
fal·si·fy *v.* falsificar
fal·si·ty *n.* falsedad
fal·ter *v.* vacilar; titubear
fame *n.* fama
fa·mil·iar *adj.* familiar
fa·mil·i·ar·i·ty *n.* familiaridad
fam·i·ly *n.* familia
fam·ine *n.* hambre
fam·ish *v.* morirse de hambre
fa·mous *adj.* famoso
fan *n.* aficionado
fa·nat·ic *n., adj.* fanático
fa·nat·i·cism *n.* fanatismo
fan·ci·er *n.* aficionado
fan·ci·ful *adj.* fantástico
fan·cy *n.* fantasía
fan·fare *n.* toque de trompetas
fang *n.* colmillo
fan·tas·tic *adj.* fantástico
fan·ta·sy *n.* fantasía
far *adv.* lejos
far·a·way *adj.* remoto
farce *n.* farsa
far·ci·cal *adj.* ridículo

fare v. pasarlo
fare•well v. adiós
far•fetched adj. improbable
farm n. granja
farm•house n. alquería
far•off adj. lejano
fas•ci•nate v. fascinar
fas•cism n. fascismo
fas•cist n. fascista
fash•ion n. estilo; moda; uso
fash•ion•a•ble adj. de moda
fast adj. rápidamente; rápido
fas•ten v. abrochar; asegurar
fas•tid•i•ous adj. fino; quisquilloso
fat adj. gordo
fa•tal adj. fatal
fa•tal•ism n. fatalismo
fa•tal•ist n. fatalista
fa•tal•i•ty n. fatalidad
fate n. suerte
fate•ful adj. fatal
fa•ther n. padre
fa•ther•hood n. paternidad
fa•ther-in-law n. suegro
fath•om n. braza; v. penetrar
fa•tigue n. fatiga
fat•ten v. engordar
fau•cet n. grifo
fault n. culpa; falta
fault•y adj. defectuoso
fa•vor n. favor
fa•vor•a•ble adj. favorable
fa•vored adj. favorecido
fa•vor•ite adj. favorito
fa•vor•it•ism n. favoritismo
fawn n. cervato
faze v. perturbar
fear n. miedo
fear•ful adj. temeroso
fear•less adj. intrépido
fear•some adj. temible
fea•si•bil•i•ty n. viabilidad
fea•si•ble adj. factible
feast n. banquete; fiesta
feat n. proeza
feath•er n. pluma

feath•er•y adj. plumoso
fea•ture n. facción; rasgo
Feb•ru•ar•y n. febrero
fe•ces n. excrementos
fe•cund adj. fecundo
fed•er•al adj. federal
fed•er•a•tion n. federación
fee n. honorario
fee•ble adj. débil
fee•bly adv. flojamente
feed v. alimentar
feel v. sentir(se)
feel•er n. antena
feel•ing n. emoción
feign v. fingir
feint n. treta
fe•lic•i•tate v. felicitar
fe•lic•i•tous adj. oportuno; feliz
fe•lic•i•ty n. felicidad
fe•line adj. felino
fell v. talar
fel•low n. compañero
fel•low•ship n. compañerismo
fel•on n. criminal
fel•o•ny n. crimen
felt n. fieltro
fe•male n. hembra
fem•i•nine adj. femenino
fe•mur n. fémur
fence v. esgrimir
fenc•ing n. esgrima
fend v. rechazar
fen•der n. guardafango
fer•ment v. fermentar
fer•men•ta•tion n. fermentación
fern n. helecho
fe•ro•cious adj. feroz
fe•ro•ci•ty n. ferocidad
fer•ret n. hurón
fer•ry n. transbordador
fer•tile adj. fecundo; fértil
fer•til•i•ty n. fecundidad
fer•ti•lize v. fertilizar
fer•ti•liz•er n. abono
fer•vid adj. férvido
fer•vor n. fervor

fester

fes•ter v. enconarse
fes•ti•val n. fiesta
fes•tive adj. festivo
fes•tiv•i•ty n. regocijo; fiesta
fes•toon n. festón
fetch v. ir por
fetch•ing adj. atractivo
fete n. fiesta
fet•id adj. fétido
fet•ish n. fetiche
fet•ter n. grillos
fet•tle n. condición
fe•tus n. feto
feud n. enemistad
feu•dal adj. feudal
feu•dal•ism n. feudalismo
fe•ver n. fiebre
fe•ver•ish adj. febril
few adj. pocos
fi•an•ce n. novio
fi•an•cee n. novia
fi•as•co n. fiasco
fi•at n. fíat
fib v. mentir
fi•ber, fi•bre n. fibra
fi•brous adj. fibroso
fick•le adj. inconstante
fic•tion n. ficción
fic•tion•al adj. novelesco
fic•ti•tious adj. ficticio
fid•dle n. violín
fi•del•i•ty n. fidelidad
fidg•et v. inquietar
fidg•et•y adj. inquieto; azogado
field n. prado; campo
fiend n. demonio
fiend•ish adj. diabólico
fierce adj. feroz
fier•y adj. ardiente; apasionado
fif•teen adj. quince
fif•teenth adj. decimoquinto
fifth adj. quinto
fif•ti•eth adj. quincuagésimo
fif•ty adj. cincuenta
fig n. higo
fight v. pelear; luchar; n. pelea; lucha

fight•er n. guerrero
fig•ment n. invención
fig•ur•a•tive adj. figurativo
fig•ure n. tipo; figura
fig•ure•head n. mascarón de proa
fig•ur•ine n. figurín
fil•a•ment n. filamento
filch v. ratear
file n. lima; archivo; fila
fi•let n. filete also **fil•let**
fil•i•bus•ter n. obstruccionista
fil•i•gree n. filigrana
fil•ings n. limaduras
fill v. llenar
fill•ing n. empaste; relleno
fil•ly n. potra
film n. película
fil•ter n. filtro
filth n. inmundicia
filth•y adj. sucio
fin n. aleta
fi•nal adj. final
fi•na•le n. final
fi•nal•ist n. finalista
fi•nal•i•ty n. finalidad
fi•nal•ly adv. finalmente; por fin
fi•nance n. finanzas
fi•nan•cial adj. financiero
fin•an•cier n. financiero
finch n. pinzón
find v. hallar; encontrar
fine adj. fino; admirable; n. multa; v. multar
fin•er•y n. adornos
fi•nesse n. sutileza; diplomacia
fin•ger n. dedo
fin•ger•nail n. uña
fin•ger•print n. huella dactilar
fin•ish v. terminar; acabar
fi•nite adj. finito
fir n. abeto
fire n. fuego
fire•arm n. arma de fuego
fire•crack•er n. petardo
fire•en•gine n. bomba de incendios
fire•fly n. luciérnaga

flour

fire•man *n.* bombero

fire•place *n.* hogar

firm *adj.* firme

fir•ma•ment *n.* firmamento

firm•ly *adj.* firmemente

firm•ness *n.* firmeza

first *adj.* primero

first-class *adj.* de primera clase

first-hand *adj.* de primera mano

first-rate *adj.* de primera clase

fis•cal *adj.* fiscal

fish *n.* pez

fish•er•man *n.* pescador

fish•ery *n.* pesquera

fish•y *adj.* sospechoso

fis•sion *n.* fisión

fis•sure *n.* grieta

fist *n.* puño

fist•i•cuffs *n.* puñetazo

fit *v.* probar; acomodar; *adj.* adecuado

fit•ful *adj.* espasmódico

fit•ting *n.* ajuste; *adj.* propio; conveniente

five *adj.* cinco

fix *v.* arreglar

fix•a•tion *n.* fijación

fix•ed *adj.* fijo

fix•ture *n.* cosa o instalación fija

fla•bby *adj.* flojo; débil

flag *n.* bandera

flag•on *n.* jarro; frasco

fla•grant *adj.* notorio

flag•stone *n.* losa

flail *n.* mayal

flair *n.* instinto

flake *n.* escama; *v.* formar hojuelas

flak•y *adj.* escamoso

flam•boy•ant *adj.* llamativo

flame *n.* llama; *v.* flamear

flam•ma•ble *adj.* inflamable

flank *n.* ijada; lado; *v.* lindar; flanquear

flap *v.* ondear

flare *v.* brillar; fulgurar; *n.* bengala

flash *n.* relámpago; ráfaga; *v.* lanzar

flash•light *n.* linterna eléctrica

flash•y *adj.* charro

flask *n.* frasco

flat *adj.* plano; llano

flat•ter•y *n.* adulación

flaunt *v.* lucir

fla•vor *n.* sabor

fla•vor•ing *n.* condimento

flaw *n.* imperfección

flax *n.* lino

flay *v.* desollar

flea *n.* pulga

fleck *n.* mancha

flee *v.* fugarse; huir

fleece *n.* vellón

fleec•y *adj.* lanudo

fleet *adj.* veloz

fleet•ing *adj.* fugaz

flesh *n.* carne

flex *v.* doblar

flex•i•ble *adj.* flexible

flick *n.* golpecito

fli•er *n.* aviador

flight *n.* vuelo

flim•sy *adj.* endeble

flinch *v.* acobardarse

fling *v.* arrojar

flint *n.* pedernal

flip *n.* capirote

flip *v.* mover de un tirón

flip•pant *adj.* ligero

flirt *v.* flirtear; coquetear

flit *v.* revolotear

float *v.* flotar; hacer flotar

flock *n.* rebaño

floe *n.* témpano

flog *v.* azotar

flood *n.* diluvio

floor *n.* suelo; piso

flop *v.* caer pesadamente; fracasar

flo•ra *n.* flora

flo•ral *adj.* floral

flor•id *adj.* florido

flo•rist *n.* florista

floss *n.* seda floja

flo•til•la *n.* flotilla

flounce *v.* moverse airadamente

floun•der *v.* tropezar

flour *n.* harina

155

flour•ish v. florecer; blandir
flout v. mofarse
flow v. fluir
flow•er n. flor
flu n. gripe
fluc•tu•ate v. fluctuar
flue n. cañón de chimenea
flu•en•cy n. fluidez
flu•ent adj. facundo
fluff•y adj. plumosa
flu•id adj. fluido
fluke n. chiripa
flunk v. no aprobar
flu•o•res•cent adj. fluorescente
flur•ry n. ráfaga; agitación
flush adj. nivelado
flus•ter v. aturdir
flute n. flauta
flut•ter n. aleteo; v. revolotear
flux n. mudanza; flujo
fly v. volar, n. mosca
fly•er n. aviador
fly•wheel n. rueda volante
foal n. potro
foam n. espuma
fo•cus v. enfocar
fod•der n. forraje
foe n. enemigo
fog n. niebla
fo•gey n. persona de ideas anticuadas
foi•ble n. flaco
foil n. hoja; florete
foist v. encajar
fold v. plegar; doblar
fold•er n. carpeta
fo•li•age n. follaje
folk n. gente
folk•lore n. folklore
fol•li•cle n. folículo
fol•low v. perseguir; seguir
fol•low•er n. seguidor
fol•ly n. locura; tontería
fo•ment v. fomentar
fond adj. cariñoso
fon•dle v. acariciar
fond•ly adv. afectuosamente

food n. alimento
fool n. tonto
fool•har•dy adj. temerario
fool•ish adj. necio
fool•proof adj. infalible
foot n. pata; pie
foot•ball n. fútbol
foot•note n. nota
foot•print n. huella
foot•step n. paso
fop n. petimetre
for conj. pues, prep. para; por
for•age n. forraje
for•ay n. correría
for•bear v. contenerse
for•bid v. prohibir
for•bid•den adj. prohibido
for•ceps n. fórceps
for•ci•ble adj. enérgico; eficaz
ford n. vado
fore adj. anterior
fore•arm n. antebrazo
fore•bode v. presagiar
fore•cast v. pronosticar
fore•fa•ther n. antepasado
fore•fin•ger n. dedo índice
fore•go v. renunciar
fore•gone adj. predeterminado
fore•ground n. primer plano
fore•head n. frente
for•eign adj. extranjero
for•eign•er n. extranjero
fore•man n. capataz
fore•most adj. primero
fore•run•ner n. precursor
fore•see v. prever
fore•sight n. previsión; perspicacia
fore•skin n. prepucio
for•est n. bosque
fore•tell v. predecir
for•ev•er adv. siempre
fore•word n. prefacio
for•feit v. perder
forge n. fragua
for•ger•y n. falsificación
for•get v. olvidar(se)

for·get·ful *adj.* olvidadizo
for·give *v.* perdonar
fork *n.* tenedor
for·lorn *adj.* abandonado
form *n.* forma
for·mal *adj.* ceremonioso
for·mal·i·ty *n.* formalidad
for·mat *n.* formato
for·ma·tion *n.* formación
for·mer *adj.* anterior
for·mer·ly *adv.* antiguamente
for·mi·da·ble *adj.* formidable
for·mu·la *n.* fórmula
for·ni·cate *v.* fornicar
for·ni·ca·tion *n.* fornicación
for·sake *v.* abandonar
fort *n.* fuerte
forth *adv.* en adelante
forth·com·ing *adj.* próximo
forth·right *adj.* directo
for·ti·fi·ca·tion *n.* fortificación
for·tune *n.* fortuna
for·ty *adj.* cuarenta
for·ward *adv.* adelante
fos·sil *n.* fósil
foul *adj.* sucio
foun·da·tion *n.* fundación
foun·tain *n.* fuente
four *adj.* cuatro
four·teen *adj.* catorce
fourth *adj.* cuarto
fox *n.* zorra
fra·cas *n.* riña
frac·tion *n.* fracción
frac·ture *v.* quebrar; *n.* fractura
frag·ile *adj.* frágil
frag·ment *n.* fragmento
fra·grance *n.* fragancia
fra·grant *adj.* oloroso
frail *adj.* débil; frágil
frail·ty *n.* fragilidad
frame *n.* estructura; marco
frame·work *n.* esqueleto
franc *n.* franco
fran·chise *n.* derecho de sufragio
frank *adj.* franco

frank·in·cense *n.* incienso
frank·ly *adv.* francamente
frank·ness *n.* franqueza
fran·tic *adj.* frenético
fra·ter·ni·ty *n.* fraternidad
fraud *n.* fraude
fraught *adj.* lleno de
fray *v.* deshilacharse
freak *n.* monstruosidad; fenómeno
freck·le *n.* peca
free *v.* libertar; *adj.* libre
free·dom *n.* libertad
free·way *n.* autopista
freeze *v.* helar(se); congelar
freight *n.* flete
freight·er *n.* buque de carga
French *n., adj.* francés
fre·net·ic *adj.* frenético
fren·zy *n.* frenesí
fre·quen·cy *n.* frecuencia
fre·quent *adj.* frecuente
fresh *n.* fresco
fresh·en *v.* refrescar
fret *v.* apurarse
fri·ar *n.* fraile
fric·tion *n.* fricción
Friday *n.* viernes
friend *n.* amigo; amiga
friend·ly *adj.* amistoso
frieze *n.* friso
fright *n.* susto
fright·en *v.* asustar
frig·id *adj.* frío
frill *n.* lechuga
fringe *n.* orla; margen
frisk *v.* retozar
fro *adv.* atrás
frock *n.* vestido
frog *n.* rana
from *prep.* desde; de
front *n.* frente
fron·tal *adj.* frontal
frown *n.* ceño
fru·gal *adj.* frugal
fruit *n.* fruta
frus·trate *v.* frustrar

frus•tra•tion *n.* frustración
fry *v.* freír
fu•gi•tive *n., adj.* fugitivo
full *adj.* completo; lleno
ful•ly *adv.* completamente
func•tion *v.* funcionar
func•tion•al *adj.* funcional
fun•da•men•tal *adj.* fundamental
fun•ny *adj.* cómico
fur *n.* piel
fu•ri•ous *adj.* furioso
fur•ni•ture *n.* mueblaje
fur•ther *adj., adv.* mas lejos
fuse *n.* fusible; espoleta
fu•tile *adj.* inútil
fuzz *n.* pelusa

G

gab•ar•dine *n.* garbardina
gad *v.* andorrear
gad•get *n.* aparato
gaff *n.* arpón
gag *v.* amordazar
gai•e•ty *n.* alegría
gai•ly *adv.* alegremente
gain *v.* amordazar
gain•say *v.* contradecir
gait *n.* modo de andar
ga•la *n.* fiesta
gal•ax•y *n.* galaxia
gale *n.* ventarrón
gall *n.* bilis
gal•lant *adj.* valeroso
gal•lant•ry *n.* galantería
gal•ler•y *n.* galería
gal•ley *n.* galera; fogón
gal•lon *n.* galón
gal•lop *n.* galope
gal•lows *n.* horca
gal•va•nize *v.* galvanizar
gam•bit *n.* gambito
gam•ble *v.* jugar
gam•bol *v.* brincar

game *n.* partido; juego
gam•ut *n.* gama
gan•der *n.* ganso
gang *n.* pandilla
gan•grene *n.* gangrena
gang•ster *n.* gángster; pistolero
gang•way *n.* pasillo
gap *n.* hueco
ga•rage *n.* garaje
garb *n.* vestido
gar•bage *n.* basura
gar•ble *v.* mutilar
gar•den *n.* jardín
gar•gan•tu•an *adj.* colosal
gar•gle *v.* gargarizar
gar•ish *v.* llamativo
gar•land *n.* guirnalda
gar•ment *n.* prenda de vestir
gar•ner *n.* granero
gar•net *n.* granate
gar•nish *v.* adornar
gar•ret *n.* guardilla
gar•ri•son *n.* guarnición
gar•ru•lous *adj.* gárrulo
gar•ter *n.* liga
gas *n.* gasolina
gas•e•ous *adj.* gaseoso
gash *n.* cuchillada
gas•o•line *n.* gasolina
gasp *v.* boquear
gas•tric *adj.* gástrico
gas•tron•o•my *n.* gastronomía
gate *n.* puerta
gate•way *n.* paso
gath•er *v.* fruncir; reunir
gauche *adj.* torpe
gaud•y *adj.* chillón
gauge *n.* norma de medida; indicador
gaunt *adj.* flaco
gaunt•let *n.* guantelete
gauze *n.* gasa
gawk•y *adj.* desgarbado
gay *adj.* alegre; vistoso
gaze *v.* mirar
ga•zelle *n.* gacela
ga•zette *n.* gaceta

glamour

gaz·et·teer *n.* diccionario geográfico

gear *v.* engranar

gel·a·tin *n.* gelatina

ge·lat·i·nous *adj.* gelatinoso

geld *v.* castrar

gem *n.* joya; gema

gen·der *n.* género

gene *n.* gen

ge·ne·al·o·gy *n.* genealogía

gen·er·al *adj.* general

gen·er·al·i·ty *n.* generalidad

gen·er·al·ize *v.* generalizar

gen·er·ate *v.* generar

gen·er·a·tion *n.* generador

ge·ner·ic *adj.* genérico

gen·er·os·i·ty *n.* generosidad

gen·er·ous *adj.* generoso

gen·e·sis *n.* génesis

ge·net·ic *adj.* genético

gen·ial *adj.* afable

gen·i·tal *adj.* genital

gen·ius *n.* genio

gen·o·cide *n.* genocidio

gen·teel *adj.* elegante; bien criado

gen·til·i·ty *n.* gentileza

gen·tle *adj.* suave; apacible

gen·tle·man *n.* caballero

gen·tly *adv.* suavemente

gen·u·ine *adj.* genuino; sincero

ge·nus *n.* género

ge·o·gra·pher *n.* geógrafo

ge·o·pra·phic, ge·o·graph·i·cal *adj.*
  geográfico

ge·o·gra·phy *n.* geografía

ge·o·log·ic *adj.* geológico

ge·ol·o·gist *n.* geólogo

ge·ol·o·gy *n.* geología

ge·o·met·ric *adj.* geométrico

ge·om·e·try *n.* geometría

ge·o·phys·i·cal *adj.* geofísico

ge·o·phys·ics *n.* geofísica

ger·i·at·rics *n.* geriatría

germ *n.* germen

ger·mane *adj.* relativo

ger·mi·na·tion *n.* germinación

ger·und *n.* gerundio

ges·tic·u·late *v.* gesticular

ges·ture *n.* gesto

get *v.* lograr; obtener

gey·ser *n.* géiser

ghast·ly *adj.* horrible

gher·kin *n.* pepinillo

ghost *n.* fantasma

ghost·ly *adj.* espectral

ghoul *n.* demonio

GI *n.* soldado

giant *adj.* gigantesco

gib·ber·ish *n.* galimatías; jerga

gib·bon *n.* gibón

gib·let *n.* menudillos

gid·di·ness *n.* vértigo

gid·dy *adj.* mareado; ligero

gift *n.* regalo; don

gi·gan·tic *adj.* gigantesco

gig·gle *n.* risa sofocada

gild *v.* dorar

gill *n.* agalla

gilt *adj.* dorado

gim·mick *n.* truco

gin *n.* desmotadera de algodón; ginebra

gin·ger·ale *n.* cerveza de jengibre

gin·ger·bread *n.* pan de jengibre

gin·ger·ly *adj.* cauteloso

gip·sy *n.* gitano

gi·raffe *n.* jirafa

gird *v.* ceñir

gird·er *n.* viga

gir·dle *n.* cinto; faja

girl *n.* chica; niña

girl·ish *adj.* de niña

girth *n.* cincha

gist *n.* esencial; clave

give *v.* entregar; dar

giv·en *adj.* citado

giz·zard *n.* molleja

gla·cial *n.* glacial

glad *adj.* alegre

glade *n.* claro

glad·ly *adv.* con mucho gusto

glad·ness *n.* alegría

glad·i·o·lus *n.* gladiolo

glam·our, glam·or *n.* encanto

158

159

glamourous

glam•our•ous *adj.* encantador
glance *v.* rebotar; mirar
gland *n.* glándula
glan•du•lar *adj.* glandular
glare *v.* relumbrar
glar•ing *adj.* evidente
glass *n.* vidrio; vaso
glass•y *adj.* vítreo
glau•co•ma *n.* glaucoma
glaze *v.* vidriar
glean *n.* espigar
glee *n.* júbilo
glen *n.* cañada
glide *v.* deslizarse
glim•mer *v.* brillar débilmente
glimpse *n.* vislumbre
glint *v.* destellar
glis•ten *v.* relucir
glit•ter *v.* relucir
gloat *v.* manifestar satisfacción maligna
globe *n.* globo; esfera
glob•ule *n.* glóbulo
gloom *n.* tristeza
gloom•y *adj.* lóbrego; melancólico
glo•ri•fy *v.* glorificar
glo•ri•ous *adj.* glorioso
glo•ry *n.* gloria
gloss *n.* lustre
glos•sa•ry *n.* glosario
gloss•y *adj.* lustroso
glot•tis *n.* glotis
glove *n.* guante
glow *v.* brillar
glow•er *v.* mirar con ceño
glow•worm *n.* luciérnaga
glue *v.* encolar
glum *adj.* abatido
glut *v.* hartar
glut•ton *n.* glotón
glut•ton•y *n.* gula
gnarl *v.* torcer
gnash *v.* rechinar
gnat *n.* jején
gnaw *v.* roer
gnome *n.* gnomo
go *v.* ir

goad *n.* aguijada; incitar
goal *n.* meta; gol
goat *n.* cabra
gob•ble *v.* engullir
gob•let *n.* copa
gob•lin *n.* duende
God *n.* Dios
god•child *n.* ahijado
god•daugh•ter *n.* ahijada
god•dess *n.* diosa
god•fa•ther *n.* padrino
god•ly *adj.* piadoso
god•moth•er *n.* madrina
god•par•ent *n.* padrino; madrina
god•send *n.* buena suerte
god•son *n.* ahijado
gog•gles *n.* anteojos
go•ing *n.* ida; estado del camino
gold *n.* oro
golf *n.* golf
gon•do•la *n.* góndola
gon•do•lier *n.* góndolero
gong *n.* gong
gon•or•rhe•a *n.* gonorrea
good *n.* bien
good•by *int.* adiós
good•heart•ed *adj.* amable
good•look•ing *adj.* guapo
good•ly *adj.* agradable; considerable
good•ness *n.* bondad
good•y *n.* golosina
goose *n.* ganso
goose•ber•ry *n.* uva espina
gore *n.* sangre
gorge *n.* barranco
gor•geous *adj.* magnífico; vistoso
gos•pel *n.* evangelio
gos•sa•mer *n.* gasa
gos•sip *n.* chisme; comadre
gouge *n.* gubia
gourd *n.* calabaza
gour•met *n.* gastrónomo
gout *n.* gota
gov•ern *v.* gobernar
gov•ern•ess *n.* institutriz
gov•ern•ment *n.* gobierno

gov•er•nor *n.* gobernador

gown *n.* vestido

grab *v.* asir; arrebatar

grace *n.* gracia

grace•ful *adj.* gracioso

gra•cious *adj.* agradable

gra•da•tion *n.* gradación

grade *n.* grado; clase

grad•u•al *adj.* gradual

grad•u•al•ly *adv.* poco a poco

grad•u•ate *v.* graduar(se)

grad•u•a•tion *n.* graduación

graft *n.* injerto; soborno

grain *n.* grano; fibra

gram *n.* gramo

gram•mar *n.* gramática

gram•mat•i•cal *adj.* gramatical

gra•na•ry *n.* granero

grand *adj.* magnífico; grandioso

grand•child *n.* nieto

grand•daugh•ter *n.* nieta

grand•fa•ther *n.* abuelo

grand•par•ent *n.* abuelo

grand•son *n.* nieto

grange *n.* cortijo

grant *v.* conferir; otorgar

gran•u•late *v.* granular

gran•ule *n.* gránulo

grape *n.* uva

grape•fruit *n.* toronja; pomelo

graph *n.* gráfica

graph•ic *adj.* gráfico

graph•ite *n.* grafito

grap•nel *n.* arpeo

grap•ple *n.* lucha; garfio

grasp *v.* agarrar; comprender

grasp•ing *adj.* codicioso

grass *n.* hierba

grass•hop•per *n.* saltamontes

grass•y *adj.* herboso

grate *n.* parrilla de hogar

grate•ful *adj.* agradecido

grat•i•fi•ca•tion *n.* gratificación; placer

grat•i•fy *v.* complacer; satisfacer

grat•ing *n.* reja

gra•tis *adj.* gratis

grat•i•tude *n.* reconocimiento

gra•tu•i•tous *adj.* gratuito; injustificado

gra•tu•i•ty *n.* propina

grave *n.* sepultura

grav•el *n.* cascajo

grav•en *adj.* grabado

grave•yard *n.* cementerio

grav•i•tate *v.* gravitar

grav•i•ta•tion *n.* gravitación

grav•i•ty *n.* seriedad; gravedad

gra•vy *n.* salsa

gray, grey *adj.* gris

graze *v.* pacer; rozar

grease *n.* grasa

greas•y *adj.* grasiento

great *adj.* grande; gran

greed *n.* avaricia; codicia

greed•y *adj.* avaro; codicioso; goloso

green *adj., n.* verde

green•er•y *n.* verdura

greet *v.* saludar

greet•ing *n.* saludo

gre•gar•i•ous *adj.* gregario

gre•nade *n.* granada de mano

grid *n.* reja; parrilla

grid•dle *n.* tortera

grid•i•ron *n.* campo de fútbol; parrilla

grief *n.* pesar

griev•ance *n.* agravio

grieve *v.* afligirse

griev•ous *adj.* grave; penoso

grif•fin, grif•fon *n.* grifo

grill *v.* asar a la parrilla

grille, grill *n.* verja

grim *adj.* inflexible; severo

grim•ace *n.* visaje

grime *n.* mugre

grim•y *adj.* mugriento

grin *v.* sonreír

grind *v.* moler; pulverizar

grind•stone *n.* muela

grip *n.* agarro; apretón; saco de mano

grippe *n.* gripe

gris•ly *adj.* horroroso

gris•tle *n.* cartílago

grit *n.* arena; firmeza

gritty

grit•ty *adj.* arenoso
griz•zled, griz•zly *adj.* gris
groan *v.* gemir
gro•cer *n.* abacero
gro•cer•y *n.* abacería
groin *n.* ingle
groom *n.* novio; mozo de caballos
groove *n.* estría
grope *v.* buscar a tientas
gross *adj.* bruto; grosero; grueso
gro•tesque *adj.* grotesco
grot•to *n.* gruta
grouch *v.* refunfuñar
ground *n.* tierra; terreno; razón; poso
ground•work *n.* fundamento
group *n.* grupo
grouse *v.* quejarse
grove *n.* arboleda
grov•el *v.* arrastrarse
gus•to *n.* entusiasmo
gym *n.* gimnasio
gym•nast *n.* gimnasta
gym•nas•tic *adj.* gimnástico
gy•ne•col•o•gy *n.* ginecología
gyp *v.* estafar
gyp•sum *n.* yeso

H

hab•it *n.* costumbre
hab•it•a•ble *adj.* habitable
hab•i•tat *n.* habitación
hab•i•ta•tion *n.* habitación
ha•bit•u•al *adj.* habitual
ha•bit•u•ate *v.* acostumbrarse
hack *v.* acuchillar
hack•neyed *adj.* trillado
had *v. pt.* and *pp.* of have
hag *n.* bruja
hag•gard *adj.* ojeroso
hag•gle *v.* regatear
hail *n.* granizo; *v.* granizar

hail•stone *n.* piedra de granizo
hair *n.* pelo; cabello
hair•breadth *n.* ancho de un pelo
hair•dress•ser *n.* peluquero
hair•pin *n.* horquilla
hale *adj.* robusto
half *n.* mitad
half•way *n.* a medio camino
hall *n.* sala
hal•le•lu•jah *interj.* aleluya
hal•low *v.* consagrar
hal•lu•cin•a•tion *n.* alucinación
hall•way *n.* passillo
hal•o *n.* halo; aureola
halt *v.* parar
hal•ter *n.* cabestro
halve *v.* partir por mitad
ham *n.* jamón
ham•burg•er *n.* hamburguesa
ham•let *n.* aldehuela
ham•mer *v.* martillar; *n.* martillo
ham•mock *n.* hamaca
ham•per *v.* impedir
hand *n.* mano
hand•bag *n.* bolso
hand•book *n.* manual
hand•cuff *n.* esposas
hand•ful *n.* puñado
hand•i•cap *n.* desventaja
hand•ker•chief *n.* pañuelo
han•dle *n.* mango; manubrio
hand•some *adj.* hermoso
hand•y *adj.* conveniente; próximo; hábil
hang *v.* pegar; colgar
hang•er•on *n.* pegote
hank•er *v.* anhelar
hap•haz•zard *adj.* fortuito
hap•pen *v.* pasar
hap•pen•ing *n.* acontecimiento
hap•pi•ly *adv.* alegremente
hap•pi•ness *n.* alegría
hap•py *adj.* feliz
har•bor *n.* puerto
hard *adj.* firme
har•dy *adj.* robusto
harm *v.* dañar

harm·ful *adj.* dañino

har·mo·ni·ous *adj.* armonioso

har·mo·ny *n.* armonía

harsh *adj.* severo

harsh·ness *n.* severidad

har·vest *v.* cosechar

hat *n.* sombrero

hatch *v.* empollar; *n.* portezuela

hatch·et *n.* hacha

hate *n.* odio; *v.* odiar

hate·ful *adj.* odioso

have *v.* tener

hawk *n.* halcón

haz·ard *v.* arriesgar; *n.* azar

he *pron.* él

head *n.* cabeza

head·ache *n.* dolor de cabeza

head·ing *n.* título

head·land *n.* promontorio

head·light *n.* faro

head·quar·ters *n.* cuartel general

head·way *n.* progreso

heal *v.* sanar; curar

health *n.* salud

health·ful *adj.* sano

heap *n.* montón

hear *v.* oír

hear·ing *n.* oído

hearse *n.* coche fúnebre

heart *n.* corazón

heart·ache *n.* angustia

heart·break *n.* angustia

heart·en *v.* alentar

heart·felt *adj.* sincero

hearth *n.* hogar

heat *v.* calentar; *n.* calor

heat·er *n.* calentador

heath *n.* brezal

heave *v.* levantar

heav·en *n.* cielo

heav·y *adj.* fuerte

heck·le *v.* interrumpir

hec·tic *adj.* febril

hedge *n.* seto

heed *v.* escuchar

heel *n.* talón

heft *n.* bulto

heif·er *n.* vaquilla

height *n.* altura

height·en *v.* elevar

hei·nous *adj.* atroz

heir *n.* heredero

heir·ess *n.* heredera

heir·loom *n.* herencia; reliquia de familia

hel·i·cop·ter *n.* helicóptero

he·li·um *n.* helio

he·lix *n.* hélice

hell *n.* infierno

hell·ish *adj.* infernal

hel·lo *interj.* hola

helm *n.* timón

hel·met *n.* casco

help *n.* ayuda; *v.* ayudar

help·ful *adj.* útil

help·ing *n.* ración

help·less *adj.* incapaz

hem *n.* dobladillo

hem·i·sphere *n.* hemisferio

hem·i·spher·ic *adj.* hemisférico

hem·or·rhage *n.* hemorragia

hem·or·rhoid *n.* hemorroides

hemp *n.* cáñamo

hen *n.* gallina

hence *adv.* de aquí; por lo tanto

her *pron. obj. and poss.* she

her·ald *n.* heraldo; precursor

he·ral·dic *adj.* heráldico

herb *n.* hierba

her·ba·ceous *adj.* herbáceo

her·cu·le·an *adj.* hercúleo

herds·man *n.* pastor

here *adv.* aquí

here·af·ter *adv.* en el futuro

he·red·i·tar·y *adj.* hereditario

he·red·i·ty *n.* herencia

here·in *adv.* incluso

her·e·sy *n.* herejía

here·to·fore *adv.* hasta ahora

her·it·age *n.* herencia

her·mit *n.* ermitaño

her·mit·age *n.* ermita

her·ni·a *n.* hernia

hero

he•ro *n.* héroe
he•ro•ic *adj.* heroico
her•o•ine *n.* heroína
her•o•ism *n.* heroísmo
her•on *n.* garza
hers *pron. poss.* she
her•self *pron.* ella misma; sí misma
hes•i•tant *adj.* vacilante
hes•i•tate *v.* vacilar
het•er•o•ge•ne•ous *adj.* heterogéneo
hew *v.* tajar
hex•a•gon *n.* hexágono
hex•ag•o•nal *adj.* hexagonal
hi•ber•nate *v.* invernar
hic•cup *n.* hipo
hide *v.* ocultar(se)
hid•e•ous *adj.* horrible; feo
hi•er•ar•chy *n.* jerarquía
hi•er•o•glyph•ic *adj.* jeroglífico
high *adj.* alto
hike *n.* caminata
hi•lar•i•ous *adj.* alegre
hi•lar•i•ty *n.* alegría
hill *n.* colina
hilt *n.* puño
him *pron. obj.* of he
him•self *pron.* el mismo
hind *adj.* trasero
hin•der *v.* impedir
hind•most *adj.* postrero
hinge *n.* gozne
hint *n.* indirecta
hip *n.* cadera
hip•po•pot•a•mus *n.* hipopótamo
hire *v.* alquilar
hire•ling *n.* mercenario
his *pron.* suyo
hiss *v.* silbar
his•to•ri•an *n.* historiador
his•tor•ic *adj.* histórico
his•to•ry *n.* historia
hit *n.* golpe; *v.* golpear
hitch *v.* atar
hitch•hike *v.* hacer autostop
hith•er *adv.* acá
hive *n.* colmena

hoard *n.* provisión
hoarse *adj.* ronco
hoax *n.* engaño
hob•ble *v.* cojear
hob•by *n.* pasatiempo
ho•bo *n.* vagabundo
hoe *n.* azadón
hog *n.* puerco
hoist *v.* alzar
hold *v.* contener; tener
hold•ing *n.* tenencia
hole *n.* hoyo
hol•i•day *n.* día de fiesta
hol•low *adj.* vacío
hol•ly *n.* acebo
hol•o•caust *n.* holocausto
hol•ster *n.* pistolera
hom•age *n.* homenaje
home *n.* casa
home•ly *adj.* feo
home•sick *adj.* nostálgico
home•ward *adv.* hacia casa
home•y *adj.* cómodo
hom•i•cide *adj.* homicidio
hom•i•ly *n.* homilía
ho•mo•gen•e•ous *adj.* homogéneo
hone *n.* piedra de afilar
hon•est *adj.* honrado
hon•es•ty *n.* honradez
hon•ey *n.* miel
hon•ey•comb *n.* panal
hon•ey•moon *n.* luna de miel
hon•ey•suck•le *n.* madreselva
hon•or *v.* honrar; *n.* honor
hon•or•a•ble *adj.* honorable
hon•or•ar•y *adj.* honorario
hood *n.* capucha
hood•lum *n.* matón
hood•wink *v.* engañar
hoof *n.* casco
hook *n.* gancho; *v.* enganchar; encorvar
hoop *n.* aro
hoot *v.* ulular; *n.* grito
hop *n.* salto; *v.* saltar
hope *v.* desear; *n.* esperanza
hope•less *adj.* desesperado

horde *n.* horda
ho·ri·zon *n.* horizonte
hor·i·zon·tal *adj.* horizontal
hor·mone *n.* hormona
horn *n.* cuerno
hor·o·scope *n.* horóscopo
hor·ri·ble *adj.* horrible
hor·ri·fy *v.* horrorizar
hor·ror *n.* horror
horse *n.* caballo
horse·man *n.* jinete
horse·pow·er *n.* caballo de fuerza
horse·rad·ish *n.* rábano picante
horse·shoe *n.* herradura
hor·ti·cul·ture *n.* horticultura
hose *n.* medias
hose *n.* manga
ho·sier·y *n.* calcetería
hos·pi·ta·ble *adj.* hospitalario
hos·pi·tal *n.* hospital
hos·pi·tal·i·ty *n.* hospitalidad
host *n.* anfitrión; patrón; multitud
hos·tage *n.* rehén
host·ess *n.* anfitriona
hos·tile *adj.* hostil
hos·til·i·ty *n.* hostilidad
hot *adj.* caliente
ho·tel *n.* hotel
hot·house *n.* invernáculo
hound *n.* podenco; *v.* perseguir
hour *n.* hora
house *n.* casa
house·keep·er *n.* ama de llaves
hous·ing *n.* alojamiento
how *adv.* cómo
how·ev·er *adv.* en todo caso; *conj.* sin embargo
howl *v.* aullar
hub *n.* cubo
hud·dle *v.* amontonar(se)
hue *n.* color; matiz
hug *v.* abrazar
huge *adj.* enorme
hull *n.* cáscara; casco
hum *v.* zumbar; canturrear
hu·man *n.* humano

hu·man·i·ty *n.* humanidad
hum·ble *adj.* humilde
hu·mid·i·ty *n.* humedad
hu·mil·i·ate *v.* humillar
hu·mil·i·a·tion *n.* humillación
hum·ming·bird *n.* colibrí
hu·mor *n.* complacer
hump *n.* giba; joroba
hunch *v.* corazonada
hunch·back *n.* jorobado
hun·dred *adj.* ciento
hun·dredth *adj.* centésimo
hun·ger *n.* hambre
hun·gry *adj.* hambriento
hunt *v.* cazar
hunt·er *n.* cazador
hur·dle *n.* valla; zarzo
hurl *v.* lanzar
hur·ri·cane *n.* huracán
hur·ry *v.* apresurar; darse prisa
hurt *v.* hacer daño; doler; dañar
hus·band *n.* esposo
husk *n.* cáscara
husk·y *adj.* ronco
hus·sy *n.* pícara
hus·tle *v.* empujar
hy·brid *n.* híbrido
hy·drant *n.* boca de riego
hy·dro·gen *n.* hidrógeno
hy·e·na *n.* hiena
hy·giene *n.* higiene
hymn *n.* himno
hyp·no·sis *n.* hipnosis
hyp·no·tize *v.* hipnotizar
hyp·o·crite *n.* hipócrita
hy·po·der·mic *adj.* hipodérmico
hy·pot·e·nuse *n.* hipotenusa
hy·poth·e·sis *n.* hipótesis
hy·po·thet·i·cal *adj.* hipotético
hys·te·ri·a *n.* histerismo
hys·ter·ic *adj.* histérico

I *pron.* yo
i•bis *n.* ibis
ice *n.* hielo
ice•berg *n.* iceberg
ice cream *n.* helado
i•ci•cle *n.* carámbano
ic•ing *n.* garapiña
i•con *n.* icono
i•con•o•clast *n.* iconoclasta
i•cy *adj.* helado
i•de•a *n.* idea
i•de•al *adj.* ideal
i•de•al•ize *v.* idealizar
i•den•ti•cal *adj.* idéntico
i•den•ti•fi•ca•tion *n.* identificación
i•den•ti•fy *v.* identificar
i•den•ti•ty *n.* identidad
i•de•ol•o•gy *n.* ideología
id•i•om *n.* idiotismo
id•i•o•mat•ic *adj.* idiomático
id•i•o•syn•cra•sy *n.* idiosincrasia
id•i•ot *n.* idiota
i•dle *adj.* ocioso
i•dol *n.* ídolo
i•dol•a•try *n.* idolatría
i•dol•ize *v.* idolatrar
if *conj.* si
ig•nite *v.* encender(se)
ig•no•ble *adj.* innoble
ig•no•min•y *n.* ignominia
ig•no•rance *n.* ignorancia
ig•no•rant *adj.* ignorante
ig•nore *v.* no hacer caso de
ill *adj.* enfermo
il•le•gal *adj.* ilegal
il•leg•i•ble *adj.* ilegible
il•le•git•i•ma•cy *n.* ilegitimidad
il•le•git•i•mate *adj.* ilegítimo
il•lic•it *adj.* ilícito
il•lit•er•ate *adj., n.* analfabeto
ill•ness *n.* enfermedad
il•lu•mi•nate *v.* iluminar

il•lu•sion *n.* ilusión
il•lus•trate *v.* ilustrar
il•lus•tra•tion *n.* ilustración; ejemplo
im•age *n.* imagen
im•ag•i•nar•y *adj.* imaginario
im•ag•i•na•tion *n.* imaginación
im•ag•ine *v.* imaginar
im•be•cile *n., adj.* imbécil
im•i•tate *v.* imitar
im•i•ta•tion *n.* imitación; copia
im•ma•ture *adj.* inmaduro
im•meas•ur•a•ble *adj.* inmensurable
im•me•di•ate *adj.* inmediato
im•mense *adj.* inmenso
im•mer•sion *n.* inmersión
im•mi•grant *n.* inmigrante
im•mi•grate *v.* inmigrar
im•mi•gra•tion *n.* inmigración
im•mi•nent *adj.* inminente
im•mo•bile *adj.* inmóvil
im•mo•dest *adj.* impúdico
im•mor•al *adj.* inmoral
im•mor•tal *adj.* inmortal
im•mune *adj.* inmune
im•mu•ni•ty *n.* inmunidad
imp *n.* diablillo
im•pact *n.* impacto
im•pair *v.* deteriorar
im•part *v.* comunicar; relatar; dar
im•par•tial *n.* imparcial
im•pa•tient *adj.* impaciente
im•peach *v.* acusar
im•pec•a•ble *adj.* impecable
im•pede *v.* impedir; estorbar
im•ped•i•ment *n.* impedimento; estorbo
im•pel *v.* impulsar
im•pe•ri•al *adj.* imperial
im•pe•ri•ous *adj.* imperioso
im•per•son•al *adj.* impersonal
im•per•ti•nent *adj.* impertinente
im•pe•tus *n.* ímpetu
im•pi•e•ty *n.* impiedad
im•ple•ment *n.* herramienta
im•pli•cate *v.* implicar
im•plore *v.* implorar
im•ply *v.* dar a entender; significar

im•po•lite *adj.* descortés
im•port *v.* importar
im•por•tance *n.* importancia
im•por•tant *adj.* importante
im•pose *v.* imponer
im•pos•si•ble *adj.* imposible
im•pos•tor *n.* impostor
im•po•tence *n.* impotencia
im•pov•er•ish *v.* empobrecer
im•prac•ti•cal *adj.* impracticable
im•press *v.* estampar; imprimir; impresionar
im•pres•sion *n.* impresión
im•print *v.* imprimir
im•prove *v.* mejorar
im•prove•ment *n.* mejora
im•pro•vise *n.* improvisar
im•pulse *n.* impulso
in *adv.* dentro; *prep.* durante, en
in•a•bil•i•ty *n.* inhabilidad
in•ca•pac•i•tate *v.* incapacitar
inch *n.* pulgada
in•ci•den•tal *adj.* incidental
in•cin•er•ate *v.* incinerar
in•ci•sion *n.* incisión
in•cite *v.* incitar
in•cli•na•tion *n.* inclinación
in•clu•sion *n.* inclusión
in•com•pa•ra•ble *adj.* incomparable
in•com•plete *adj.* incompleto
in•cor•rect *adj.* incorrecto
in•crease *v.* crecer; acrecentar
in•crim•i•nate *v.* incriminar
in•de•cen•cy *n.* indecencia
in•de•cent *adj.* indecente
in•deed *adv.* de veras
in•def•i•nite *adj.* indefinido
in•dem•ni•ty *n.* indemnización
in•dent *v.* mellar
in•den•ta•tion *n.* mella
in•de•pend•ence *n.* independencia
in•de•pend•ent *adj.* independiente
in•de•struct•i•ble *adj.* indestructible
in•dex *n.* índice
in•di•cate *v.* indicar
in•di•ca•tion *n.* indicación

in•dict *v.* acusar
in•dif•fer•ent *adj.* indiferente
in•dig•e•nous *adj.* indígena
in•di•gent *adj.* indigente
in•di•ges•tion *n.* indigestión
in•dig•ni•ty *n.* indignidad
in•di•go *n.* añil
in•di•rect *adj.* indirecto
in•dis•creet *adj.* indiscreto
in•dis•cre•tion *n.* indiscreción
in•dis•pen•sa•ble *adj.* imprescindible
in•di•vid•u•al *n.* individuo
in•di•vid•u•al•i•ty *n.* individualidad
in•doc•tri•nate *v.* adoctrinar
in•do•lent *adj.* indolente
in•door *adj.* interior; de puertas adentro
in•doors *adv.* dentro
in•duce *v.* inducir
in•duct *v.* iniciar
in•dulge *v.* satisfacer; consentir
in•dus•tri•al *adj.* industrial
in•er•tia *n.* inercia
in•ev•i•ta•ble *adj.* inevitable
in•fa•my *n.* infamia
in•fan•cy *n.* infancia
in•fect *v.* infectar
in•fec•tion *n.* infección
in•fe•ri•or *adj.* inferior
in•fi•del•i•ty *n.* infidelidad
in•fil•trate *v.* infiltrarse
in•fi•nite *adj.* infinito
in•fin•i•tive *n.* infinitivo
in•fin•i•ty *n.* infinidad
in•fir•ma•ry *n.* enfermería
in•flame *v.* inflamar; provocar
in•flam•ma•ble *adj.* inflamable
in•flate *v.* inflar
in•fla•tion *n.* inflación
in•flec•tion *n.* inflexión
in•flict *v.* infligir; imponer
in•flu•ence *n.* influencia
in•flu•en•za *n.* gripe
in•form *v.* informar
in•for•mal *adj.* sin ceremonia
in•for•ma•tion *n.* información
in•for•ma•tive *adj.* informativo

in·fre·quent *adj.* infrecuente
in·fu·ri·ate *v.* enfurecer
in·fuse *v.* infundir
in·fu·sion *n.* infusión
in·gen·ious *adj.* ingenioso
in·ge·nu·i·ty *n.* ingeniosidad
in·got *n.* lingote
in·gre·di·ent *n.* ingrediente
in·hab·it *v.* habitar
in·hab·i·tant *n.* habitante
in·hale *v.* inhalar; aspirar
in·her·ent *adj.* inmanente; inherente
in·her·it *v.* heredar
in·her·it·ance *n.* herencia
in·hib·it *v.* inhibir
in·hi·bi·tion *n.* inhibición
in·hu·man *adj.* inhumano; cruel
in·iq·ui·ty *n.* iniquidad
in·i·tial *adj.* inicial
in·i·ti·ate *v.* iniciar
in·i·ti·a·tion *n.* iniciación
in·i·ti·a·tive *n.* iniciativa
in·ject *v.* inyectar
in·jec·tion *n.* inyección
in·jure *v.* hacer daño a; ofender
in·ju·ry *n.* daño; injuria
in·jus·tice *n.* injusticia
ink *n.* tinta
ink·ling *n.* sospecha
in·let *n.* entrada; ensenada
in·mate *n.* inquilino
inn *n.* posada
in·nate *adj.* innato
in·ner *adj.* interior
in·no·cence *n.* inocencia
in·no·cent *adj.* inocente
in·no·va·tion *n.* innovación
in·nu·en·do *n.* indirecta
in·nu·mer·a·ble *adj.* innumerable
in·oc·u·late *v.* inocular
in·oc·u·la·tion *n.* inoculación
in·quest *n.* pesquisa judical
in·quire *v.* preguntar
in·quir·y *n.* indagación; pregunta
in·qui·si·tion *n.* inquisición
in·sane *adj.* insensato; loco

in·san·i·ty *n.* locura
in·scribe *v.* inscribir
in·scrip·tion *n.* inscripción
in·sect *n.* insecto
in·se·cure *adj.* inseguro; precario
in·sert *v.* insertar; meter
in·ser·tion *n.* inserción
in·side *n.* interior
in·sight *n.* perspicacia
in·sig·ni·a *n.* insignias
in·sig·nif·i·cance *n.* insignificancia
in·sin·u·ate *v.* insinuar
in·sin·u·a·tion *n.* insinuación; indirecta
in·sip·id *adj.* insípido
in·sist *v.* insistir
in·sist·ent *adj.* insistente; porfiado
in·so·lence *n.* insolencia
in·so·lent *adj.* insolente
in·som·ni·a *n.* insomnio
in·spect *v.* examinar; inspeccionar
in·spec·tion *n.* inspección
in·spi·ra·tion *n.* inspiración
in·spire *v.* inspirar; estimular
in·stall *v.* instalar
in·stall·ment *n.* plazo; entrega
in·stance *n.* ejemplo
in·stant *n.* instante
in·stan·ta·ne·ous *adj.* instantáneo
in·stead *adv.* en lugar; en vez de
in·step *n.* empeine
in·sti·gate *v.* instigar
in·stinct *n.* instinto
in·stinc·tive *adj.* instinctivo
in·sti·tute *v.* instituir; empezar
in·sti·tu·tion *n.* institución
in·struct *v.* instruir; enseñar
in·struc·tion *n.* instrucción
in·stru·ment *n.* instrumento
in·suf·fi·cient *adj.* insuficiente
in·su·late *v.* aislar
in·su·la·tion *n.* aislamiento
in·su·lin *n.* insulina
in·sult *n.* insulto; ultraje
in·sur·ance *n.* seguro
in·sure *v.* asegurar
in·sur·rec·tion *n.* insurrección

in•tact *adj.* intacto
in•te•ger *n.* número entero
in•te•grate *v.* integrar
in•te•gra•tion *n.* integración
in•teg•ri•ty *n.* integridad
in•tel•lect *n.* intelecto
in•tel•li•gence *n.* inteligencia
in•tel•li•gent *adj.* inteligente
in•tend *v.* proponerse; querer decir
in•tense *adj.* intenso
in•ten•si•ty *n.* intensidad
in•tent *adj.* atento; absorto
in•ter *v.* enterrar
in•ter•cede *v.* interceder
in•ter•cept *v.* interceptar
in•ter•ces•sion *n.* intercesión
in•ter•change *v.* intercambiar
in•ter•course *n.* comercio; trato; coito
in•ter•est *n.* interés
in•ter•fere *v.* intervenir; meterse
in•ter•im *n.* ínterin
in•ter•jec•tion *n.* interjección
in•ter•lude *n.* intermedio
in•ter•me•di•ate *adj.* intermedio
in•ter•mis•sion *n.* intermisión
in•tern *n.* interno
in•ter•nal *adj.* interior
in•ter•na•tion•al *adj.* internacional
in•ter•play *n.* interacción
in•ter•pose *v.* interponer
in•ter•pret *v.* explicar; interpretar; entender
in•ter•pre•ta•tion *n.* interpretación
in•ter•ro•gate *v.* interrogar
in•ter•ro•ga•tion *n.* interrogación
in•ter•rupt *v.* interrumpir
in•ter•rup•tion *n.* interrupción
in•ter•twine *n.* entretejer(se)
in•ter•val *n.* intervalo
in•ter•vene *v.* intervenir
in•ter•view *n.* entrevista
in•tes•tine *n.* intestino
in•ti•mate *v.* intimar
in•tim•i•date *v.* intimidar
in•to *prep.* en
in•tol•er•ant *adj.* intolerante

in•to•na•tion *n.* entonación
in•tox•i•cate *v.* embriagar; intoxicar
in•tran•si•tive *adj.* intransitivo
in•tra•ve•nous *adj.* intravenoso
in•trep•id *adj.* intrépido
in•tri•ca•cy *n.* complejidad; enredo
in•tri•cate *adj.* intrincado
in•trigue *v.* intrigar; fascinar
in•trin•sic *adj.* intrínseco
in•tro•duce *v.* introducir
in•tro•duc•tion *n.* introducción
in•trude *v.* entremeterse
in•tu•i•tion *n.* intuición
in•ure *v.* habituar
in•vade *v.* invadir
in•va•lid *adj.* inválido
in•var•i•a•ble *adj.* invariable
in•va•sion *n.* invasión
in•vent *v.* inventar
in•ven•tion *n.* invención
in•ven•to•ry *n.* inventario
in•ver•sion *n.* inversión
in•vert *v.* invertir
in•ver•te•brate *adj., n.* invertebrado
in•vest *v.* investir
in•ves•ti•ga•tion *n.* investigación
in•vig•or•ate *v.* vigorizar
in•vin•ci•ble *adj.* invencible
in•vis•i•ble *adj.* invisible
in•vi•ta•tion *n.* invitación
in•vite *v.* invitar
in•vo•ca•tion *n.* invocación
in•voice *n.* factura
in•voke *v.* invocar; implorar
in•vol•un•tar•y *adj.* involuntario
in•volve *v.* complicar; comprometer; enredar
in•ward *adv.* hacia dentro
i•o•dine *n.* yodo
i•on *n.* ion
i•ron *v.* planchar; *n.* plancha
i•ron•ic *adj.* irónico
i•ro•ny *n.* ironía
ir•ra•di•ate *v.* irradiar
ir•ra•tion•al *adj.* irracional
ir•rec•on•cil•a•ble *adj.* irreconciliable

ir·ref·u·ta·ble *adj.* irrefutable
ir·reg·u·lar *adj.* irregular
ir·rel·e·vant *adj.* inaplicable
ir·re·sist·i·ble *adj.* irresistible
ir·re·spon·si·ble *adj.* irresponsable
ir·ri·gate *v.* regar
ir·ri·tate *v.* irritar; provocar; molestar
is·land *n.* isla
isle *n.* isla
i·so·late *v.* aislar
i·so·ce·les *adj.* isósceles
is·sue *v.* publicar; salir; *n.* resultado; emisión
isth·mus *n., pl.* istmo
it *pron.* le; la; lo; ello; ella; el
i·tal·ic *n.* usu. pl. letra bastardilla
i·tal·i·cize *v.* impirmir en bastardilla
itch *v.* picar
itch·y *adj.* que da picazón; impaciente
i·tem *n.* artículo; partida
i·tem·ize *v.* detallar
it·er·ate *v.* iterar; repetir
i·tin·er·ar·y *n.* itinerario
it *pron.* el, ella, ello
i·vo·ry *n., pl.* marfil
i·vy *n.* hiedra

J

jab *v.* golpear
jab·ber *v.* farfullar
jack *n.* mozo; marinero; gato; sota
jack·al *n.* chacal
jack·ass *n.* burro
jack·et *n.* chaqueta
jack·knife *n.* navaja
jack·pot *n.* bote
jade *n.* jade
jag·uar *n.* jaguar
jail *v.* encarcelar; *n.* cárcel
jam *v.* apiñar; atascar
jamb *n.* jamba
jam·bo·ree *n.* francachela
jangle *n.* sonido discordante

jan·i·tor *n.* portero
Jan·u·ar·y *n.* enero
jar *n.* jarra
jar·gon *n.* jerga
jas·mine *n.* jazmín
jaun·dice *n.* ictericia
jaunt *n.* excursión
jave·lin *n.* jabalina
jaw *n.* quijada
jay *n.* arrendajo
jazz *n.* jazz
jeal·ous *adj.* celoso
Jeep *n.* trademark; jeep
jeer *v.* mofarse; befar
jell *v.* cuajar(se)
jel·ly *n.* jalea
jel·ly·fish *n.* medusa
jeop·ar·dize *v.* arriesgar
jeop·ar·dy *n.* peligro
jer·kin *n.* justillo
jer·sey *n.* jersey
jest *n.* chanza
jet *n.* chorro; surtidor; avión a reacción; azabache
jet·sam *n.* echazón
jet·ti·son *n.* echazón
jet·ty *n.* malecón; muelle
jew·el *n.* joya
jew·el·er *n.* joyero
jew·el·ry *n.* joyas
jif·fy *n.* instante
jib *n.* jiga
jig·saw *n.* sierra de vaivén
jig·saw puzzle *n.* rompecabezas
jilt *v.* dar calabazas
jim·my *n.* palanqueta
jin·gle *v.* tintinear
jinx *n.* gafe
jit·ters *n.* inquietud
job *n.* trabajo
jock·ey *n.* jockey
jo·cose *adj.* jocoso
joc·u·lar *adj.* jocoso
joc·und *adj.* alegre
jog *v.* empujar; correr; despacio
join *v.* unir(se)

joint *n.* juntura; unión

joist *n.* viga

joke *n.* chiste; broma

jok•er *n.* bromista

jol•ly *adj.* alegre

jolt *v.* sacudir

jon•quil *n.* junquillo

jour•nal *n.* periódico

jour•nal•ism *n.* periodismo

jour•nal•ist *n.* periodista

jour•ney *v.* viajar; *n.* viaje

joy•ous *adj.* alegre

judge *n.* juez; *v.* juzgar

ju•di•cial *adj.* judicial

jug•gle *v.* hacer juegos malabares

jug•u•lar *adj.* yuqular

juice *n.* jugo

July *n.* julio

jum•ble *v.* mezclar

jump *n.* salto; *v.* saltar

jump•er *n.* saltador

junc•tion *n.* juntura; empalme

junc•ture *n.* juntura; coyuntura

June *n.* junio

jun•gle *n.* selva

jun•ior *adj.* más joven; menor

ju•ni•per *n.* enebro

junk *n.* trastos viejos; junco

ju•ris•dic•tion *n.* jurisdicción

ju•ris•pru•dence *n.* jurisprudencia

ju•rist *n.* jurista

ju•ror *n.* jurado

ju•ry *n.* jurado

just *adj.* justo; imparcial

jus•ti•fy *v.* justificar

ju•ve•nile *adj.* joven

K

ka•lei•do•scope *n.* caleidoscopio

kan•ga•roo *n.* canguro

kar•at *n.* quilate

keel *n.* quilla

keen *adj.* agudo; perspicaz; entusiasta;
afilado

keep *v.* detener; tener; cumplir

keep•ing *n.* custodia

keg *n.* cuñete

ken *n.* alcance

ken•nel *n.* perrera

ker•chief *n.* pañuelo

ker•nel *n.* almendra; núcleo

ker•o•sene *n.* queroseno

ketch *n.* queche

ketch•up *n.* salsa picante de tomate

ket•tle *n.* tetera

key *n.* llave

key•board *n.* teclado

key•stone *n.* piedra clave

kha•ki *n.* caqui

kick *v.* dar patadas; dar un puntapié

kid *n.* cabrito

kid•nap *v.* secuestrar

kid•ney *n.* riñón

kill *v.* matar

kiln. *n.* honor

kil•o•cy•cle *n.* kilociclo

kil•o•gram *n.* kilogramo

kil•o•me•ter *n.* kilómetro

kil•o•watt *n.* kilovatio

kin *n.* parientes

kind *adj.* bueno; *n.* género

kin•der•gar•ten *n.* jardín de la infancia

kind•heart•ed *adj.* bondadoso

kin•dle *v.* encender

kind•ly *adj.* bondadoso

kind•ness *n.* benevolencia

kin•dred *n.* parientes

king *n.* rey

king•dom *n.* reino

kink *n.* coca; peculiaridad

kin•ship *n.* parentesco

kins•man *n.* pariente

kiss *n.* beso; *v.* besar

kit *n.* equipo; avíos

kitch•en *n.* cocina

kite *n.* cometa

kith *n.* amigos

kit•ten *n.* gatito

knack *n.* maña

knap•sack *n.* mochila
knave *n.* bribón
knav•er•y *n.* bellaquería
knav•ish *adj.* bellaco
knead *v.* amasar
knee *n.* rodilla
knee•cap *n.* rótula
kneel *n.* arrodillar
knee•pad *n.* rodillera
knell *n.* doble
knick•ers *n.* bombachos
knick•knack *n.* chuchería
knife *v.* acuchillar; *n.* cuchillo
knight *n.* caballero
knight•hood *n.* caballerosidad
knit *v.* hacer punto; tejer
knit•ting *n.* tejido
knob *n.* tirador; pomo; puño
knock *v.* golpear
knock•down *adj.* que derriba
knock•er *adj.* golpeador
knock•ing *n.* llamada
knoll *n.* otero
knot *v.* anudar
knot•hole *n.* agujero
knot•ted *adj.* anudado; nudoso
knot•ty *adj.* enredado; nudoso
know *v.* saber; conocer
know•a•ble *adj.* conocible
know•how *n.* pericia
know•ing *adj.* astuto; hábil
know•ing•ly *adv.* a sabiendas
knowl•edge *n.* saber
knowl•edge•a•ble *adj.* erudito
known *adj.* conocido
know•noth•ing *n.* ignorante
knuck•le *n.* nudillo
ko•a•la *n.* koala
kook *n.* excéntrico
Ko•ran *n.* Alcorán; Corán
ko•sher *adj.* legítimo; conforme a las reglas
kow•tow *v.* postrarse

L

lab *n.* laboratorio
la•bel *v.* marcar; *n.* etiqueta; rótulo
la•bi•al *adj.* labial
la•bor *v.* trabajar; *n.* trabajo
lab•o•ra•to•ry *n.* laboratorio
la•borer *n.* peón; trabajador; jornalero
la•bo•ri•ous *adj.* laborioso
lab•y•rinth *n.* laberinto
lac *n.* laca
lace *v.* encordonar; *n.* encaje
lac•er•ate *v.* lacerar
lac•er•ation *n.* laceración
lach•ry•mal *adj.* lagrimal
lack *v.* faltar; hacer falta; *n.* falta
lack•ey *n.* lacayo
lack•ing *adj.* deficiente; *prep.* sin
lack•lus•ter *adj.* deslustrado
la•con•ic *adj.* lacónico
lac•quer *n.* laca
lac•tase *n.* lactasa
lac•tate *v.* lactar
lac•ta•tion *n.* lactancia
lac•tic *adj.* láctico
lac•tose *n.* lactosa
la•cu•na *n.* laguna
lac•y *adj.* de encaje
lad *n.* chico
lad•der *n.* escalera
lad•die *n.* chico
lade *v.* agobiar
lad•en *adj.* agobiado; cargado
la•dle *n.* cucharón
la•dy *n.* dama
la•dy•bug *n.* mariquita
lag *v.* atrasarse; rezagarse
lag•gard *adj.* rezagado
la•goon *n.* laguna
la•ic *adj.* laico
lair *n.* madriguera
la•i•ty *n.* laicos
lake *n.* lago
lamb *n.* cordero
lame *v.* encojar; *adj.* renco; cojo

la•me *n.* lame
la•ment *v.* deplorar; lamentar
la•men•ta•ble *adj.* lamentable
lam•en•ta•tion *n.* lamentación
la•ment•ed *adj.* lamentado
lam•i•na *n.* lámina
lam•i•nate *v.* laminar
lam•i•nat•ed *adj.* laminado
lam•i•na•tion *n.* laminación
lamp *n.* lámpara
lam•poon *v.* satirizar; *n.* sátira
lam•prey *n.* lamprea
lance *n.* lanza
lan•cet *n.* lanceta
land *v.* país; tierra
land•ed *adj.* hacendado
land•fall *n.* recalada
land•hold•er *n.* terrateniente
land•ing *n.* aterrizaje; desembarco
land•lord *n.* arrendador
land•mark *n.* mojón
land•own•er *n.* terrateniente
land•scape *n.* panorama
lane *n.* ruta; vereda; camino
lan•guage *n.* lenguaje
lan•guid *adj.* lánguido
lan•guish *v.* decaer; languidecer
lan•guish•ing *adj.* lánguido
lan•guor *n.* languidez
lan•guor•ous *adj.* lánguido
lan•o•lin *n.* lanolina
lan•tern *n.* linterna
lap *n.* falda; *v.* plegar; doblar
la•pel *n.* solapa
lap•i•dar•y *n.* lapidario
lapse *v.* faltar; caer; decaer; deslizarse
lapsed *adj.* caduco
lar•ce•ny *adj.* robo
lard *n.* lardo
large *adj.* grande
lar•gess *n.* donativo; generosidad
lar•va *n.* larva
lar•val *adj.* larval
lar•yn•gi•tis *n.* laringitis
lar•ynx *n. n.* laringe

la•ser *n.* laser
lash *n.* látigo; azote; latigazo
lash•ing *n.* fustigación; azotaína
lass *n.* muchacha
las•si•tude *n.* lasitud
las•so *n.* lazo
last *adv.* finalmente; *adj.* final
last•ing *adj.* duradero
last•ly *adv.* finalmente
latch *n.* aldabilla
late *adv.* tarde
late•ly últimamente
la•ten•cy *n.* latencia
late•ness *n.* tardanza
la•tent *adj.* latente
la•ter *adj.* posterior
lat•er•al *adj.* lateral
lat•est *adj.* último
la•tex *n.* látex
lath•er *n.* espuma
lat•i•tude *n.* latitud
la•trine *n.* letrina
lat•ter *adj.* último
lat•ter•day *adj.* reciente
lat•tice *n.* celosía; *v.* enrejar
lat•tice•work *n.* enrejado
laud *v.* alabar; elogiar
laud•a•able *adj.* laudable
laud•a•tor•y *adj.* laudatorio
laugh *n.* risa; *v.* reír(se)
laugh•a•ble *adj.* absurdo; cómico
laugh•ing *adj.* risueño
laugh•ter *n.* risa
launch *v.* lanzar; iniciar; botar
launch•er *n.* lanzador
launch•ing *n.* lanzamiento
laun•der *v.* lavar(se)
laun•dered *adj.* lavado
laun•der•er *n.* lavandero
laun•dry *n.* lavandería
lau•rel *n.* laurel
la•va *n.* lava
lav•en•der *n.* lavanda
lav•ish *adj.* espléndido; generoso
law *n.* derecho; ley
law•ful *adj.* legítimo

law•less *adj.* sin leyes
law•mak•er *n.* legislador
lawn *n.* césped
law•yer *n.* abogado
lax *adj.* laxo
lax•a•tive *n.* laxante
lax•i•ty *n.* laxitud
lay *v.* acostar; poner
lay•er *n.* estrato
lay•out *n.* disposición
la•zi•ness *n.* pereza
la•zy *adj.* perezoso
lead *v.* mandar; conducir
lead•en *adj.* plomizo
lead•er *n.* líder
lead•er•ship *n.* mando
lead•ing *n.* emplomado
leaf *n.* hoja
leaf•let *n.* panfleto
leaf•y *adj.* hojoso
league *n.* liga
leak *v.* gotear; salir(se); *n.* gotera; agujero
lean *adj.* magro
lean•ing *n.* inclinación
leap *v.* saltar
learn *v.* aprender
learn•ed *adj.* erudito
learn•er *n.* principiante
learn•ing *n.* aprendizaje
lease•hold *n.* arrendamiento
lease•hold•er *n.* arrendador
leash *n.* traílla
leas•ing *n.* arrendamiento
least *adv.* menos; *adj.* menor
leath•er *n.* cuero
leath•er•y *adj.* curtido
leave *v.* salir; dejar; irse
leav•en *v.* levadura
leav•ing *n.* salida
lech•er•ous *adj.* lujurioso
lech•er•y *n.* lujuria
lec•tor *n.* lector
lec•ture *v.* sermonear; reprender, *n.* reprimenda; conferencia
lec•tur•er *n.* conferenciante
leech *n.* sanguijuela

leek *n.* puerro
left *adj.* izquierdo
left•over *adj.* sobrante
left•y *n.* zurdo
leg *n.* pierna
leg•a•cy *n.* herencia
le•gal *adj.* legal
le•gal•ist *n.* legalista
le•gal•is•tic *adj.* legalista
le•gal•i•ty *n.* legalidad
le•gal•ize *v.* legalizar
leg•ate *n.* legado
le•ga•tion *n.* legación
leg•end *n.* leyenda
leg•end•ar•y *adj.* legendario
leg•gings *n.* polainas
leg•i•bil•i•ty *n.* legibilidad
leg•i•ble *adj.* legible
le•gion *n.* legión
le•gion•ar•y *n.* legionario
le•gion•aire *n.* legionario
leg•is•late *v.* legislar
leg•is•la•tion *n.* legislación
leg•is•la•tor *n.* legislador
le•git•i•ma•cy *n.* legitimidad
le•git•i•mate *adj.* legitimar
lei•sure *n.* ocio
lem•on *n.* limón
lem•on•ade *n.* limonada
lend *v.* impartir; prestar
lend•er *n.* prestador
length *n.* extensión; longitud; tramo; largo
length•en *v.* prolongar(se); alargar(se)
length•y *adj.* prolongado
le•nient *adj.* indulgente
lens *n.* lente
len•til *n.* lenteja
le•o•nine *adj.* leonino
leop•ard *n.* leopardo
lep•er *n.* leproso
lep•ro•sy *n.* lepra
lep•rous *adj.* leproso
le•sion *n.* lesión
less *adv., adj.* menos
less•en *v.* disminuir
less•er *adj.* menor

les•son *n.* lección

let *v.* dejar; permitir

let•down *n.* desilusión

le•thal *adj.* letal

le•thar•gic *adj.* letárgico

leth•ar•gy *n.* letargo

let•ter *n.* carta

let•tered *adj.* letrado

let•ter•ing *n.* rótulo

let•tuce *n.* lechuga

leu•ke•mi•a *n.* leucemia

lev•el *n.* llano; nivel

lev•i•ta•tion *n.* levitación

lev•y *v.* recaudar; exigir

lewd *adj.* lujurioso

lewd•ness *n.* lujuria

lex•i•cog•ra•phy *n.* lexicografía

lex•i•con *n.* léxico

li•a•bil•i•ty *n.* obligación

li•a•ble *adj.* sujeto; responsable

li•ar *n.* mentiroso

li•ba•tion *n.* libación

lib•er•al *adj.* liberal

lib•er•ate *v.* libertar

lib•er•ty *n.* libertad

li•brar•y *n.* biblioteca

lie *v.* mentir; acostarse

life *n.* vida

lift *v.* levantar(se) elevar

light *n.* lámpara; luz

light•ly *adv.* ligeramente

like *n.* gusto; *v.* gustar

like•ness *n.* semejanza

li•lac *n.* lila

lil•y *n.* lirio

lim•bo *n.* limbo

lime *n.* lima

lim•it *v.* limitar

lim•ou•sine *n.* limousina

line *v.* alinear; rayar; *n.* raya; línea

li•on *n.* león

lip *n.* labio

liq•uid *n.* líquido

liq•ui•date *v.* liquidar

liq•uor *n.* licor

list *n.* lista

lit•er•al *adj.* literal

lit•er•ar•y *adj.* literario

lit•er•a•ture *n.* literatura

lit•tle *n., adj., adv.* poco; *adj.* pequeño

live *v.* vivir

liz•ard *n.* lagarto

lob•ster *n.* langosta

lo•cal *adj.* local

lo•cal•i•ty *n.* localidad

lo•cate *v.* encontrar

lone *adj.* solitario

lone•ly *adj.* solo

long *adj.* largo

look *n.* mirada; *v.* buscar; mirar

loose *v.* soltar; *adj.* disoluto; suelto

lost *adj.* perdido

lo•tion *n.* loción

loud *adj.* alto

love *v.* amar; querer; *n.* amor

love•ly *adj.* hermoso

low *adv., adj.* bajo; *adv.* abajo

low•er *v.* bajar

loy•al *adj.* fiel

loy•al•ty *n.* fidelidad

lu•bri•cant *n.* lubricante

lu•bri•cious *adj.* lúbrico

lu•cent *adj.* luciente

lu•cid *adj.* cuerdo; lúcido

lu•cid•i•ty *n.* lucidez

luck *n.* suerte

luck•less *adj.* desafortunado

luck•y *adj.* afortunado

lu•cra•tive *adj.* lucrativo

lu•di•crous *adj.* ridículo

lug *v.* halar

lug•gage *n.* equipaje

luke•warm *adj.* tibio

lull *v.* sosegar; embaucar

lum•bar *adj.* lumbar

lum•ber•ing *adj.* torpe; pesado

lu•mi•nance *n.* luminancia

lu•mi•na•ry *n.* luminar

lum•i•nes•cence *n.* luminescente

lu•mi•nous *adj.* luminoso

lump *n.* masa; terrón

lu•na•cy *n.* locura

lu•nar *adj.* lunar
lunch *v.* almorzar; *n.* almuerzo
lus•ter *n.* lustre
lus•ty *adj.* robusto
lute *n.* laúd
lux•u•ri•ant *adj.* lozano
lux•u•ry *n.* lujo
lye *n.* lejía
lymph *n.* linfa
lynch *n.* linchar
lynx *n.* lince
lyre *n.* lira
lyr•ic *adj.* lírico

M

ma•ca•bre *adj.* macabro
mac•a•ro•ni *n.* macarrones
mac•a•roon *n.* mostachón
ma•caw *n.* guacamayo
mac•er•ate *v.* macerar(se)
ma•chet•e *n.* machete
mach•i•nate *v.* maquinar
mach•i•na•tion *n.* maquinación
ma•chine *n.* máquina
ma•chine-gun *n.* ametralladora
ma•chin•er•y *n.* maquinaria
ma•chin•ist *n.* maquinista
mack•er•el *n.* caballa
mac•ra•me *n.* macramé
mac•ro•bi•ot•ics *n.* macrobiótica
mac•ro•cosm *n.* macrocosmo
mac•ro•scop•ic *adj.* macroscópico
mad *adj.* furioso
mad•cap *adj.* alocado
mad•den *v.* enloquecer
mad•den•ing *adj.* enloquecedor
made-up *adj.* inventado
mad•ness *n.* locura
mag•a•zine *n.* revista
mag•got *n.* gusano
mag•ic *n.* magia
mag•i•cal *adj.* mágico

ma•gi•cian *n.* mago
mag•is•te•ri•al *adj.* magistral
mag•is•trate *n.* magistrado
mag•nate *n.* magnate
mag•ne•si•um *n.* magnesio
mag•net•ic *adj.* magnético
mag•net•ism *n.* magnetismo
mag•net•ize *v.* magnetizar
mag•ni•fi•ca•tion *n.* ampliación
mag•nif•i•cence *n.* magnificencia
mag•nif•i•cent *adj.* magnífico
mag•ni•fi•er *n.* amplificador
mag•ni•fy *v.* aumentar
mag•ni•tude *n.* magnitud
ma•hog•a•ny *n.* caoba
maid *n.* soltera
mail *n.* correo
mail•box *n.* buzón
mail•man *n.* cartero
main•tain *v.* mantener
main•te•nance *n.* mantenimiento
ma•jes•tic *adj.* majestuoso
maj•es•ty *n.* majestad
ma•jor *adj.* mayor
ma•jor•i•ty *n.* mayoría
make *v.* ganar; crear; hacer
mak•er *n.* fabricante
mak•ing *v.* fabricación
mal•a•dy *n.* dolencia
ma•lar•i•a *n.* malaria
mal•con•tent *adj.* malcontento
male *adj.* masculino; macho
mal•e•dic•tion *n.* maldición
ma•lev•o•lent *adj.* malévolo
mal•fun•tion *v.* funcionar mal
mal•ice *n.* malicia
ma•li•cious *adj.* malicioso
ma•lig•nan•cy *n.* malignidad
ma•lig•nant *adj.* maligno
mall *n.* alameda
mal•le•a•ble *adj.* maleable
mal•nour•ished *adj.* desnutrido
mal•nu•tri•tion *n.* desnutrición
malt *n.* malta
mal•treat *v.* maltratar
mal•treat•ment *n.* maltratamiento

mam·mal *n.* mamífero
mam·ma·li·an *adj.* mamífero
mam·ma·ry *adj.* mamario
man *n.* hombre
man·age *v.* manejar
man·age·a·ble *adj.* manejable
man·age·ment *n.* gerencia
man·da·rin *n.* mandarín
man·date *n.* mandato
man·da·to·ry *adj.* mandate
man·do·lin *n.* mandolina
ma·neu·ver *v.* maniobrar
ma·neu·ver·a·ble *adj.* maniobrable
man·ga·nese *n.* manganeso
man·gle *v.* mutilar
man·go *n.* mango
man·hood *n.* madurez
ma·ni·a *n.* manía
ma·ni·ac *adj.* maníaco
ma·ni·a·cal *adj.* maníaco
man·ic *adj.* maníaco
man·i·cure *n.* manicura
man·i·cur·ist *n.* manicuro
man·i·fest *adj.* manifiesto
man·i·fes·ta·tion *n.* manifestación
man·i·fes·to *n.* manifiesto
ma·ni·kin *n.* maniquí
ma·nip·u·late *v.* manipular
ma·nip·u·la·tion *n.* manipulación
ma·nip·u·la·tive *adj.* manipulativo
ma·nip·u·la·tor *n.* manipulador
man·li·ness *n.* hombría
man·ly *adj.* masculino
man·ne·quin *n.* maniquí
man·ner *n.* manera
man·nered *adj.* amanerado
man·ner·ism *n.* amaneramiento
man·nish *adj.* hombruno
man·tel *n.* manto
man·tle *n.* manto
man·u·al *n.* manual
man·u·fac·ture *n.* manufactura
man·u·fac·tured *adj.* manufacturado
man·u·fac·tur·ing *adj.* manufacturero
man·u·script *n.* manuscrito
man·y *adj.* muchos

map *n.* mapa
ma·ple *n.* arce
map·mak·er *n.* cartógrafe
mar *v.* desfigurar
mar·a·thon *n.* maratón
ma·raud·er *n.* merodeador
mar·ble *n.* mármol
mar·bled *adj.* jaspeado
mar·bling *n.* marmoración
march *v.* marchar
March *n.* marzo
mar·ga·rine *n.* margarina
mar·gin *s.* márgen
mar·gin·al *adj.* marginal
mar·i·gold *n.* maravilla
ma·ri·na *n.* marina
mar·i·nate *v.* marinar
ma·rine *n.* marino
mar·i·ner *n.* marinero
mar·i·tal *adj.* marital
mar·i·time *adj.* marítimo
mark *n.* marca
marked *adj.* marcado
mark·er *n.* marcador
mar·ket *v.* vender; *n.* mercado
mar·ket·a·ble *adj.* vendible
mar·ket·er *n.* vendedor
mar·king *n.* marca
mar·ma·lade *n.* mermelada
ma·roon *v.* abandonar
mar·quis *n.* marqués
mar·riage *n.* matrimonio
mar·ried *adj.* casado
mar·row *n.* médula
mar·ry *v.* casar(se)
marsh *n.* pantano
mar·shal *n.* mariscal
marsh·y *adj.* pantanoso
mar·su·pi·al *adj.* marsupial
mart *n.* mercado
mar·tial *adj.* marcial
mar·tyr *n.* mártir
mar·tyr·dom *n.* martirio
mar·vel *s.* maravilla
mar·vel·lous *adj.* maravilloso
mas·cot *n.* mascota

mas•cu•line *adj.* masculino
mas•cu•lin•i•ty *n.* masculinidad
mash *v.* majar
mash•er *n.* majador
mask *n.* máscara
mas•och•ism *n.* masoquismo
mas•och•ist *n.* masoquista
mas•och•is•tic *adj.* masoquista
ma•son•ry *n.* albañilería
mas•quer•ade *n.* mascarada
mass *n.* masa
mas•sa•cre *n.* matanza
mas•sage *v.* masajear
mas•sive *adj.* masivo
mast *n.* mástil
mas•tec•to•my *n.* mastectomía
mas•ter *n.* maestro
mas•ter•ful *adj.* hábil
mas•ter•ly *adj.* magistral
mas•ter•y *n.* maestría
mas•tic *adj.* pegante
mas•ti•cate *v.* masticar
mas•toid *n.* mastoides
mat *n.* estera
mate *n.* hembra; compañero
ma•te•ri•al *adj., n.* material
ma•te•ri•al•ist *n.* materialista
ma•te•ri•al•ist•ic *adj.* materialista
ma•te•ri•al•i•ty *n.* materialidad
math *n.* matemáticas
math•e•mat•i•cal *adj.* matemático
math•e•ma•ti•cian *n.* matemático
math•e•mat•ics *n.* matemáticas
mat•i•nee *n.* funcion de tarde
mat•ri•arch *n.* matriarca
ma•tri•ar•chal *adj.* matriarcal
ma•tri•ar•chy *n.* matriarcado
ma•tric•u•late *v.* matricular(se)
ma•tric•u•la•tion *n.* matrícula
mat•ri•mon•ial *adj.* matrimonial
mat•ri•mo•ny *n.* matrimonio
ma•trix *n.* matriz
ma•tron *n.* matrona
ma•tron•ly *adj.* matronal
mat•ted *adj.* estera
mat•ter *n.* materia

mat•ting *n.* estera
mat•tress *n.* colchón
mat•u•ra•tion *n.* maduración
ma•ture *v.* madurar; *adj.* maduro
ma•tur•i•ty *n.* madurez
maul *v.* maltratar
mauve *n.* malva
max•im *n.* máxima
max•i•mal *adj.* máximo
max•i•mum *adj.* máximo
May *n.* mayo
may *v.* poder
may•be *adv.* tal vez
may•on•naise *n.* mayonesa
may•or *n.* alcade
may•or•al•ty *n.* alcaldía
me *pron.* mí; me
mead•ow *n.* pradera
mea•ger *adj.* pobre; magro
meal *n.* comida
mean *v.* intentar
me•an•der *v.* vagar
mean•ing *n.* significado
mean•ing•ful *adj.* significativo
mean•ing•less *adj.* insignificante
mea•sles *n.* rubéola
meas•ure *v.* medir
meas•ured *adj.* mesurado
meas•ure•ment *n.* medida
meat *n.* carne
meat•y *adj.* carnoso
me•chan•ic *n.* mecánico
me•chan•i•cal *adj.* mecánico
mech•a•nism *n.* mecanismo
mech•a•nize *v.* mecanizar
med•al *n.* medalla
me•dal•lion *n.* medallón
med•dle *v.* entremeterse
med•dler *n.* entremetido
me•di•an *adj.* mediano
me•di•ate *v.* mediar
me•di•a•tion *n.* mediación
me•di•a•tor *n.* mediador
med•ic *n.* médico
med•i•cal *adj.* médico
med•i•cate *v.* medicinar

med·i·ca·tion *n.* medicación
med·i·cine *n.* medicina
me·di·e·val *adj.* medieval
me·di·o·cre *adj.* mediocre
me·di·oc·ri·ty *n.* mediocridad
med·i·tate *v.* meditar
med·i·ta·tion *n.* meditación
meet *v.* reunirse; encontrar(se)
mel·o·dy *n.* melodía
mel·on *n.* melón
mem·ber *n.* miembro
mem·o·ra·ble *adj.* memorable
men·tal *adj.* mental
men·tion *v.* mencionar; *n.* mención
mer·cu·ry *n.* mercurio
mer·it *v.* merecer
mer·ry *adj.* festivo
mes·sage *n.* mensaje; comunicación
mes·sen·ger *n.* mensajero
met·al *n.* metal
me·te·or·ol·o·gy *n.* meteorología
meth·od *n.* método
mi·crobe *n.* microbio
mi·cro·phone *n.* micrófono
mid·dle *n., adj.* medio
mid·night *n.* medianoche
mi·grate *v.* emigrar
mil·i·tar·y *adj.* militar
mi·li·tia *n.* milicia
milk *n.* leche
mil·lion *n.* millón
mil·lion·aire *n.* millonario
mind *v.* obedecer; *n.* mente
min·er·al *n.* mineral
min·is·ter *n.* ministro
mi·nor *adj.* menor
mi·nor·i·ty *n.* minoría
mi·nus *prep.* menos
mir·a·cle *n.* milagro
mir·ror *n.* espejo
mis·chie·vous *adj.* malicioso
miss *v.* perder
mis·sion *n.* misión
mis·sion·ar·y *n.* misionero
mis·take *v.* equivocar(se)
mis·ter *n.* señor

mis·treat *v.* maltratar
mit·i·gate *v.* mitigar
mit·ten *n.* mitón
mix *n.* mezcla; *v.* mezclar(se)
mix·ture *n.* mezcla
mod·el *v.* modelar; *n.* modelo
mod·er·ate *v.* moderar; *adj.* moderno
mod·ern *n.* moderno
mod·est *adj.* modesto
mod·i·fi·ca·tion *n.* modificación
mod·i·fy *v.* modificar
mod·u·late *v.* modular
moist *adj.* húmedo
mois·ten *v.* humedecer(se)
moist·ness *n.* humedad
mois·ture *n.* humedad
mois·tur·iz·er *v.* humedecer
mo·lar *n.* molar
mo·las·ses *n.* melaza
mold *v.* moldear; *n.* molde
mold·er *v.* desmoronar(se)
mold·ing *n.* mohoso
mo·lec·u·lar *adj.* molecular
mol·e·cule *n.* molécula
mole·hill *n.* topera
mol·li·fy *v.* molificar
mol·lusk *n.* molusco
mol·ten *adj.* fundido
mom *n.* mamá
mo·ment *n.* momento
mo·men·tar·i·ly *adv.* momentáneamente
mo·men·tar·y *adj.* momentáneo
mo·men·tum *n.* momento
mon·arch *n.* monarca
mo·nar·chic *adj.* monárquico
mon·ar·chist *n.* monárquico
mon·ar·chy *n.* monarquía
mon·as·ter·y *n.* monasterio
mo·nas·tic *adj.* monástico
Mon·day *n.* lunes
mon·e·tar·y *adj.* monetario
mon·ey *n.* dinero
mon·eyed *adj.* adinerado
mon·goose *n.* mangosta
mo·ni·tion *n.* admonición
mon·i·tor *n.* monitor

mon·i·to·ry *adj.* monitorio
monk *n.* monje
mon·key *n.* mono
monk·hood *n.* monacato
monk·ish *adj.* monacal
mon·o·chro·mat·ic *adj.* monocromático
mo·noc·u·lar *adj.* monóulo
mo·nog·a·my *n.* monogamia
mo·no·gram *n.* monograma
mo·no·graph *n.* monografía
mon·o·lith *n.* monolito
mon·o·lith·ic *adj.* monolítico
mon·o·plane *n.* monoplano
mo·nop·o·lize *v.* monopolizar
mo·nop·o·ly *n.* monopolio
mon·o·rail *n.* monocarril
mo·no·tone *n.* monotonía
mo·not·o·nous *adj.* monótono
mo·not·o·ny *n.* monotonía
mon·ox·ide *n.* monóxido
mon·soon *n.* monzón
mon·ster *n.* monstruo
mon·stros·i·ty *n.* monstruosidad
mon·strous *adj.* monstruoso
mon·tage *n.* montaje
month *n.* mes
month·ly *adj.* mensual
mon·u·ment *n.* monumento
mon·u·ment·al *adj.* monumental
moo *v.* mugir
mood *n.* humor
moon *n.* luna
moor *v.* amarrar
moor·age *n.* amarraje
moor·ing *n.* amarradero
moose *n.* anta
mop *n.* estropajo
mo·ped *n.* ciclomotor
mor·al *adj.* moral
mo·rale *n.* moral
mor·al·ist *n.* moralista
mor·al·is·tic *adj.* moralizador
mo·ral·it·y *n.* moralidad
mor·al·ize *v.* moralizar
mor·bid *adj.* morboso
mor·bid·i·ty *n.* morbosidad

more *n.*, *adv.* más
more·o·ver *adv.* además
morn·ing *n.* mañana
mor·phine *n.* morfina
mor·phol·o·gy *n.* morfología
mor·tal *n.*, *adj.* mortal
mor·tal·i·ty *n.* mortalidad
mor·tu·ar·y *n.* mortuorio
mos·qui·to *n.* mosquito
most *adj.* muy; más
moth *n.* polilla
moth·er *n.* madre
moth·er·hood *n.* maternidad
moth·er-in-law *n.* suegra
mo·tor·cy·cle *n.* motocicleta
moun·tain *n.* montaña
mouse *n.* ratón
mouth *n.* boca
move *v.* mudar; mover
mov·ie *n.* película
Mr. *n.* señor
Mrs. *n.* señora
Ms. *n.* señora
much *adj.* muy; *n.*, *adv.*, *adj.* mucho
mul·ti·ple *adj.* múltiple
mul·ti·pli·ca·tion *n.* multiplicación
mul·ti·ply *v.* multiplicar
mul·ti·pur·pose *adj.* multiuso
mul·ti·tude *n.* multitud
mum·ble *v.* mascullar
mum·my *n.* momia
munch *v.* ronzar
mun·dane *adj.* mundano
mu·nic·i·pal *adj.* municipal
mu·nic·i·pal·i·ty *n.* municipalidad
mu·ni·fi·cence *n.* munificencia
mu·nif·i·cent *adj.* muníficente
mur·der *v.* asesinato
mur·der·er *n.* asesino
mur·der·ous *adj.* asesino
mur·mur *v.* murmurar
mus·cle *n.* músculo
mus·cu·lar *adj.* musculoso
muse *v.* meditar
mu·se·um *n.* museo
mu·sic *n.* música

mu•si•cal *adj.* musical
mu•si•cal•i•ty *n.* musicalidad
mu•si•cian *n.* músico
mus•ing *n.* contemplación
mus•ket *n.* mosquete
mus•ket•eer *n.* mosquetero
mus•lin *n.* muselina
mus•sel *n.* mejillón
must *v.* deber
mus•tache *n.* bigote
mu•ti•late *v.* mutilar
muz•zle *n.* hocico; boca
my *adj.* mi
myr•i•ad *n.* miríada
my•self *pron.* yo mismo
mys•te•ri•ous *adj.* misterioso
mys•ter•y *n.* misterio
mys•tic *adj.* místico
mys•ti•cism *n.* misticismo; mística
myth *n.* mito
myth•ic *adj.* mítico
my•thol•o•gy *n.* mitología

N

nab *v.* prender
na•dir *n.* nadir
nag *n.* jaca
nail *v.* clavar; *n.* clavo
na•ive *adj.* ingenuo
name *v.* apellido; nombre
name•less *adj.* anónimo
name•ly *adv.* a saber
name•sake *n.* tocayo
nap *n.* siesta
nape *n.* nuca
nap•kin *n.* servilleta
nar•cis•sism *n.* narcisismo
nar•cis•sus *n.* narciso
nar•cot•ic *n.* narcótico
nar•rate *v.* narrar
nar•ra•tive *adj.* narrativo

nar•ra•tor *n.* narrador
nar•row *adj.* estrecho; limitado; angosto
nar•row•ing *n.* limitación
na•sal *adj.* nasal
na•sal•i•ty *n.* nasalidad
nas•ty *adj.* antipático; sucio; obsceno
na•tal *adj.* natal
na•tal•i•ty *n.* natalidad
na•tion *n.* nación
na•tion•al *n., adj.* nacional
na•tion•al an•them *n.* himno nacional
na•tion•al•ist *n.* nacionalista
na•tion•al•is•tic *adj.* nacionalista
na•tion•al•i•ty *n.* nacionalidad
na•tion•al•ize *v.* nacionalizar
na•tive *adj.* natal; innato; nativo
na•tiv•i•ty *n.* natividad
nat•u•ral *adj.* natural
nat•ur•al•ist *n.* naturalista
nat•u•ral•is•tic *adj.* naturalista
nat•u•ral•ize *v.* naturalizar(se)
nat•u•ral•ly *adv.* naturalmente
na•ture *n.* género; naturaleza
naught *n.* nada
naugh•ty *adj.* verde; travieso
nau•se•a *n.* náusea
nau•se•ate *v.* dar náuseas a
nau•se•at•ing *adj.* nauseabundo
nau•seous *adj.* nauseabundo
nau•ti•cal *adj.* náutico
na•val *adj.* naval
nav•i•ga•ble *adj.* navegable
nav•i•gate *v.* navegar
nav•i•ga•tion *n.* navegación
nav•i•ga•tor *n.* navegante
nay *adv.* no
near *prep.* cerca de; *adv.* cerca; *adj.* próximo
near•by *adj.* próximo
near•ly *adj.* casi
neat *adj.* claro; limpio; fantástico
neb•u•la *n.* nebulosa
nec•es•sar•y *adj.* necesario
ne•ces•si•tate *v.* necesitar
ne•ces•si•ty *n.* necesidad
neck *n.* cuello

neck·lace *n.* collar
neck·line *n.* escote
ne·crol·o·gy *n.* necrología
ne·cro·sis *n.* necrosis
nec·tar *n.* néctar
nec·tar·ine *n.* nectarino
need *v.* necesitar
need·ful *adj.* necessario
nee·dle *n.* aguja
need·less *adj.* superfluo
need·y *adj.* necesitado
ne·far·i·ous *adj.* nefario
ne·gate *v.* negar
ne·ga·tion *n.* negación
neg·a·tive *n.* negativa
ne·glect *v.* descuidar
ne·glect·ful *adj.* negligente
neg·li·gence *n.* negligencia
neg·li·gent *adj.* negligente
neg·li·gi·ble *adj.* insignificante
ne·go·ti·able *adj.* negociable
ne·go·ti·ate *v.* negociar
ne·go·ti·a·tion *n.* negociación
ne·go·ti·a·tor *n.* negociador
neigh·bor *n.* prójimo; vecino
neigh·bor·hood *n.* barrio
neigh·bor·ing *adj.* vecino
neigh·bor·ly *adj.* amable
nei·ther *pron.* ninguno; *conj.* tampoco; ni
ne·ol·o·gism *n.* neologismo
ne·ol·o·gist *n.* neólogo
ne·on *n.* neón
ne·o·phyte *n.* neófito
neph·ew *n.* sobrino
nep·o·tism *n.* nepotismo
nerve *n.* nervio
nerve·less *adj.* sin nervios
nerv·ous *adj.* nervioso
nerv·ous·ness *n.* nerviosidad
nest *n.* nido
net *n.* red
net·ting *n.* red
net·tle *n.* ortiga
net·work *n.* red
neu·ral·gia *n.* neuralgia
neu·ral·gic *adj.* neurálgico

neu·ri·tis *n.* neuritis
neu·ro·sis *n.* neurosis
neu·rol·o·gist *n.* neurólogo
neu·rol·o·gy *n.* neurología
neu·rot·ic *adj.* neurótico
neu·tral *adj.* neutral
neu·tral·i·ty *n.* neutralidad
neu·tral·ize *v.* neutralizar
neu·tral·iz·er *n.* neutralizador
neu·tron *n.* neutrón
nev·er *adv.* jamás; nunca
nev·er·more *adv.* nunca más
nev·er·the·less *adv.* sin embargo
new *adj.* nuevo
new·found *adj.* nuevo
new·ly *adv.* nuevamente
news *n.* nuevas
news·cast *n.* noticiario
news·cast·er *n.* locutor
news·pa·per *n.* diario
news·y *adj.* informativo
newt *n.* tritón
new·ton *n.* neutonio
next *adj.* próximo
nib·ble *v.* mordiscar
nice *adj.* agradable; amable
ni·cety *n.* delicadeza; precisión
niche *n.* nicho
nick *n.* muesca; mella
nick·el *n.* níquel
nick·name *n.* apodo
nic·o·tine *n.* nicotina
niece *n.* sobrina
nigh *adv.* cerca
night *n.* noche
night·fall *n.* anochecer
night·gown *n.* camisón
night·in·gale *n.* ruiseñor
night·light *n.* lamparilla
night·ly *adj.* nocturno
night·mare *n.* pesadilla
night·time *n.* noche
nine *adj.* nueve
nine·teen *adj.* diecinueve
nine·ty *adj.* noventa
ninth *adj.* noveno

no *n., adv.* no
no•bod•y *n., pron.* nadie
noise *n.* ruido
nois•y *adj.* ruidoso
none *pron.* nadie; nada
noon *n.* mediodía
nor *conj.* ni
nor•mal *adj.* normal
nor•mal•ly *adv.* normalmente
north *n.* norte
north•east *n.* nordeste
north•west *n.* noroeste
nose *n.* nariz
not *adv.* no
no•ta•ble *adj.* notable
no•ta•tion *n.* notación
note *v.* notar; *n.* nota
no•ti•fy *v.* notificar
no•tion *n.* noción
no•to•ri•ous *adj.* notorio
No•vem•ber *n.* noviembre
now *adv.* ahora
nu•cle•ar *adj.* nuclear
nude *n., adj.* desnudo
num•ber *v.* numerar; *n.* número
nu•mer•i•cal *adj.* numérico
num•er•ous *adj.* numeroso
nut *n.* nuez
nu•tri•tion *n.* nutrición
nu•tri•tious *adj.* nutritivo
nu•tri•tive *adj.* nutritivo
nuz•zle *v.* hocicar
ny•lon *n.* nilón

O

oak *n.* roble
oak•en *adj.* de roble
oar *n.* remo
o•a•sis *n.* oasis
oat *n.* avena
oath *n.* juramento
oat•meal *n.* gachas de avena
ob•du•ra•cy *n.* obstinación

ob•du•rate *adj.* obstinado; insensible
o•be•di•ence *n.* obediencia
o•be•di•ent *adj.* obediente
ob•e•lisk *n.* obelisco
o•bese *adj.* obeso
o•be•si•ty *n.* obesidad
o•bey *v.* obedecer
ob•fus•cate *v.* ofuscar
ob•fus•ca•tion *n.* ofuscación
o•bit•u•ar•y *n.* obituario
ob•ject *v.* desaprobar; *n.* objeto
ob•jec•tion *n.* objeción
objec•tion•a•ble *adj.* ofensivo
ob•jec•tive *n., adj.* objetivo
ob•li•gate *v.* obligar
ob•li•ga•tion *n.* obligación
o•blig•a•to•ry *adj.* obligatorio
o•blige *v.* obligar
o•blig•ing *adj.* complaciente
o•blique *adj.* oblicuo
o•blit•er•ate *v.* aniquilar; arrasar
o•bliv•i•on *n.* olvido
o•bliv•i•ous *adj.* olvidadizo
ob•long *adj.* oblongo
ob•nox•ious *adj.* insoportable;
    desagradable
o•boe *n.* oboe
ob•scene *adj.* obsceno
ob•scen•i•ty *n.* obscenidad
ob•scure *adj.* imperceptible; oscuro
ob•scu•ri•ty *n.* oscuridad
ob•se•qui•ous *adj.* servil
ob•ser•vance *n.* observación; cumplimiento
ob•ser•vant *adj.* observador
ob•ser•va•tion *n.* observación
ob•ser•va•to•ry *n.* observatorio
ob•serve *v.* cumplir; observar
ob•serv•er *n.* observador
ob•sess *v.* obsesionar
ob•session *n.* obsesión
ob•ses•sive *adj.* obsesivo
ob•so•lete *adj.* obsoleto
ob•sta•cle *n.* obstáculo
ob•stet•ric *adj.* obstétrico
ob•sti•na•cy *n.* obstinación
ob•sti•nate *adj.* obstinado

ob•struct v. obstruir
ob•struc•tion n. obstrucción
ob•struc•tion•ist n. obstruccionista
ob•tain v. obtener
ob•trude v. introducir
ob•tru•sion n. intrusión
ob•tuse adj. obtuso
ob•vi•ate v. obviar
ob•vi•ous adj. obvio
ob•vi•ous•ly adj. claro
oc•ca•sion n. ocasión
oc•ca•sion•al adj. ocasional
oc•clude v. ocluir
oc•cu•pan•cy n. ocupación
oc•cu•pant n. pasajero; inquilino
oc•cu•pa•tion n. ocupación
oc•cu•pa•tion•al adj. ocupacional
oc•cu•pied adj. ocupado
oc•cu•py v. ocupar
oc•cur v. ocurrir
oc•cur•rence n. presencia; suceso
o•cean n. océano
o•ce•an•ic adj. oceánico
oc•ta•gon n. octágono
oc•tag•o•nal adj. octagonal
oc•tane n. octano
oc•tave n. octavo
Oc•to•ber n. octubre
oc•to•ge•nar•i•an adj. octogenario
oc•to•pus n. pulpo
oc•u•lar adj. ocular
oc•u•list n. oculista
odd adj. raro
odd•i•ty n. rareza
odds n. probabilidades
o•di•ous adj. odioso
o•di•um n. odio
o•dom•e•ter n. odómetro
o•dor n. olor
o•dor•less adj. inodoro
od•ys•sey n. odisea
of prep. de
off adv. fuera
of•fend v. ofender
of•fend•er n. infractor
of•fense n. ofense

of•fen•sive adj. ofensivo
of•fer n. ofrecimiento; v. ofrecer
of•fer•ing n. ofrecimiento
of•fice n. oficina
of•fi•cer n. oficial
of•fi•cial n., adj. oficial
of•fi•ci•ate v. oficiar
of•fi•cious adj. oficioso
off•set v. compensar
of•ten adv. a menudo
oil n. aceite
oil•can n. aceitera
oiled adj. aceitado
oil•y adj. aceitoso
oint•ment n. pomada
o•kra n. okra
old adj. anciano; viejo
old•en adj. pasado
old-fash•ioned adj. anticuado
ol•fac•to•ry adj. olfativo
ol•ive n. oliva
om•in•ous adj. ominoso
o•mis•sion n. omisión
o•mit v. omitir
om•ni•bus n. ómnibus
om•nip•o•tence n. omnipotencia
om•nip•o•tent adj. omnipotente
on prep. sobre
once n., adv. una vez
on•col•o•gy n. oncología
on•com•ing adj. que viene
one adj. uno; un
one-di•men•sion•al adj.
    unidimensional
on•er•ous adj. oneroso
one•self pron. uno
one•sid•ed adj. desigual
on•ion n. cebolla
on•look•er n. espectador
on•ly adj., adv. solo
on•rush n. embestida
on•to prep. sobre; en
on•ward adj. hacia adelante
on•yx n. onix
o•pac•i•ty n. opacidad
o•pal n. ópalo

o·pal·es·cence *n.* opalescencia
o·paque *adj.* opaco
o·pen *v.* abrir; *adj.* abierto
o·pen·er *n.* abridor
o·pen·ing *n.* abertura
o·pen·mind·ed *adj.* receptivo
o·per·a *n.* ópera
op·er·a·ble *adj.* operable
op·er·ate *v.* operar; actuar; manejar
op·er·at·ing *adj.* de mantenimiento
op·er·a·tion *n.* operación
op·er·a·tion·al *adj.* de operación
op·er·a·tive *adj.* operante
oph·thal·mol·ogy *n.* oftalmología
o·pi·ate *n.* opiato
o·pine *v.* opinar
o·pin·ion *n.* opinión
o·pi·um *n.* opio
op·po·nent *n.* adversario
op·por·tune *adj.* oportuno
op·por·tun·ist *n.* oportunista
op·por·tu·ni·ty *n.* oportunidad
op·pose *v.* oponerse
op·po·site *adj.* opuesto
op·po·si·tion *n.* oposición
op·press *v.* oprimir
op·pres·sive *adj.* opresivo
op·pres·sor *n.* opresor
opt *v.* optar
op·tic *adj.* óptico
op·ti·cal *adj.* óptico
op·ti·cian *n.* óptico
op·ti·mal *adj.* óptimo
op·ti·mism *n.* optimismo
op·ti·mist *n.* optimista
op·ti·mis·tic *adj.* optimista
op·tion *n.* opción
op·tion·al *adj.* opcional
op·tom·e·try *n.* optometría
op·u·lent *adj.* opulento
or *conj.* u; o
o·ral *adj.* oral
or·ange *adj.* anaranjado; *n.* naranja
o·ra·tion *n.* oración
or·ches·tra *n.* orquesta
or·der *n.* orden

or·din·ar·y *adj.* ordinario
or·gan·ism *n.* organismo
or·gan·i·za·tion *n.* organización
or·gan·ize *v.* organizar
o·rig·i·nal *adj.* original
o·rig·i·nate *v.* originar
os·ten·ta·tion *n.* ostentación
oth·er *prep.* el otro; *adj.* otro
ounce *n.* onza
our *adj.* nuestro
out *prep.* fuera de; *adv.* fuera
out·er *adj.* externo
out·fit *n.* traje
out·line *v.* bosquejar; *n.* bosquejo
out·side *adv.* fuera; *n.* exterior
out·ward *adj.* exterior
o·va·ry *n.* ovario
o·va·tion *n.* ovación
ov·en *n.* horno
o·ver *adj.* otra vez; *prep.* sobre; encima de
o·ver·lap *v.* solapar
o·ver·night *adj.* de noche
o·ver·sight *n.* olvido
o·vert *adj.* público
o·ver·turn *v.* volcar
o·ver·weight *adj.* gordo
o·vum *n.* óvulo
owe *v.* tener deudas
owl *n.* búho
own *v.* reconocer
ox·ide *n.* óxido
ox·i·dize *v.* oxidar(se)
ox·y·gen *n.* oxígeno
ox·y·gen·ate *v.* oxigenar
oys·ter *n.* ostra
o·zone *n.* ozono

P

pa *n.* papá
pace *n.* paso
pa·cif·ic *adj.* pacífico
pac·i·fism *n.* pacifismo

pac•i•fy *v.* pacificar
pack *n.* fardo
pack•age *n.* paquete
pact *n.* pacto
pad *n.* almohadilla
pad•dle *n.* canalete
pad•lock *n.* candado
pa•gan *n.* pagano
page *n.* página
pag•eant *n.* espectáculo
pa•go•da *n.* pagoda
pail *n.* cubo
pain *v.* doler; *n.* dolor
pain•ful *adj.* doloroso
pains•tak•ing *adj.* laborioso; esmerado
paint *n.* pintura; *v.* pintar
paint•ing *n.* pintura
pair *n.* pareja; par
pa•jam•as *n.* pijama
pal•ace *n.* palacio
pal•ate *n.* paladar
pale *adj.* pálido; claro
pa•le•on•tol•o•gy *n.* paleontología
pal•ette *n.* paleta
pal•i•sade *n.* palizada
pall *v.* perder su sabor
pal•lid *adj.* pálido
pal•lor *n.* palidez
palm *n.* palma
palm•is•try *n.* quiromancia
pal•pa•ble *adj.* palpable
pal•pi•ta•tion *n.* palpitación
pal•try *adj.* miserable
pam•per *v.* mimar
pam•phlet *n.* folleto
pan *n.* cazuela
pan•a•ce•a *n.* panacea
pan•cake *n.* hojuela
pan•cre•as *n.* páncreas
pan•de•mo•ni•um *n.* pandemónium
pane *n.* hoja de vidrio
pan•el *n.* panel
pang *n.* punzada; dolor
pan•han•dle *v.* mendigar
pan•ic *n.* terror; pánico
pan•o•ram•a *n.* panorama

pan•sy *n.* pensamiento
pant *n., pl.* pantalones
pan•the•ism *n.* panteísmo
pan•ther *n.* pantera
pan•to•mime *n.* pantomima
pan•try *n.* despensa
pa•pa *n.* papá
pa•pa•cy *n.* papado; pontificado
pa•per *n.* papel
pa•pier•ma•che *n.* cartón piedra
pa•poose *n.* crío
pa•py•rus *n.* papiro
par *n.* par
par•a•ble *n.* parábola
par•a•chute *n.* paracaídas
pa•rade *n.* parada
par•a•dise *n.* paraíso
par•a•dox *n.* paradoja
par•af•fin *n.* parafina
par•a•graph *n.* párrafo
par•al•lel *adj.* paralelo
par•a•lyze *v.* paralizar
pa•ram•e•ter *n.* parámetro; límite
par•a•noi•a *n.* paranoia
par•a•pher•nal•ia *n.* arreos
par•a•phrase *n.* paráfrasis
par•a•site *n.* parásito
par•a•troop•er *n.* paracaidista
par•cel *n.* paquete; bulto
parch *v.* secar
parch•ment *n.* pergamino
par•don *n.* perdón; *v.* perdonar
pare *v.* cortar
par•ent *n.* madre; padre
par•en•the•sis *n.* paréntesis
pa•ri•ah *n.* paria
par•ish *n.* parroquia
park *n.* aparcar; *n.* parque
par•ley *v.* parlamentar
par•lia•ment *n.* parlamento
par•lor *n.* sala de recibo
pa•ro•chi•al *adj.* parroquial; estrecho
par•o•dy *n.* parodia
pa•role *n.* libertad bajo palabra
par•ox•ysm *n.* paroxismo
par•rot *n.* loro

par•ry v. parar
par•sley n. perejil
par•son n. clérigo
part v. separar(se); partir(se); n. parte
par•take v. tomar parte
par•tial adj. parcial
par•tial•i•ty n. parcialidad
par•tic•i•pant adj. partícipe
par•tic•i•pate v. participar
par•tic•i•pa•tion n. participación
par•ti•ci•ple n. participio
par•ti•cle n. partícula
par•tic•u•lar adj. particular
par•tic•u•lar•i•ty n. particularidad
part•ing adj. despedida
par•ti•san n. partidario
par•ti•tion n. partición; tabique
part•ner n. socio
par•tridge n. perdiz
par•ty n. fiesta
pass v. aprobar; pasar
pas•sage n. pasaje; travesía; pasadizo
pas•sen•ger n. pasajero; viajero
pas•sion n. pasión
pas•sion•ate adj. apasionado
pas•sive adj. pasivo
pass•port n. pasaporte
pass•word n. santo y seña
past n. pasado
paste n. engrudo; pasta
paste•board n. cartón
pas•teur•i•za•tion n. pasteurización
pas•teur•ize v. pasteurizar
pas•time n. pasatiempo
pas•tor n. pastor
pas•try n. pasteles
pas•ture n. pasto
pat n. golpecito; pastelillo
patch n. pedazo
pat•ent n. patente
pa•ter•nal adj. paterno
pa•ter•ni•ty n. paternidad
path n. senda
pa•thet•ic adj. patético
pa•thol•o•gy n. patología
pa•tience n. paciencia

pa•tient adj. paciente
pa•ti•o n. patio
pa•tri•ar•chy n. patriarcado
pat•ri•mo•ny n. patrimonio
pa•tri•ot n. patriota
pa•trol v. patrullar
pa•tron n. cliente
pat•tern n. patrón
pau•per n. pobre
pause n. pausa
pave v. empedrar; pavimentar
pave•ment n. pavimento
pa•vil•ion n. pabellón
paw v. manosear; n. pata
pawn v. empeñar
pay v. pagar; ser provechoso
pay•roll n. nómina
pea n. guisante
peace n. paz
peace•ful adj. tranquilo
peach n. melocotón
pea•cock n. pavo real; pavón
peak n. pico; cumbre
peal v. repicar
pea•nut n. cacahuete
pear n. pera
pearl n. perla
peas•ant n. campesino
peb•ble n. guijarro
pec•ca•dil•lo n. pecadillo
pe•cu•liar adj. peculiar
pe•cu•li•ar•i•ty n. peculiaridad
ped•al n. pedal
ped•dle v. vender por las calles
ped•dler n. buhonero
ped•es•tal n. pedestal
pe•des•tri•an n. peatón
ped•i•gree n. geneología
peel v. pelar
peer n. par
peg n. clavija; estaca
pel•let n. bolita; pella
pelt n. piel
pel•vis n. pelvis
pen n. pluma
pe•nal adj. penal

penalty

pen·al·ty *n.* pena; castigo
pen·cil *n.* lápiz
pend·ant *n.* pendiente
pend·ing *adj.* pendiente
pen·du·lum *n.* péndulo
pen·e·trate *v.* penetrar
pen·i·cil·lin *n.* penicilina
pen·in·su·la *n.* península
pen·i·tent *n.* penitente
pen·i·ten·tia·ry *n.* presidio
pen·ny *n.* centavo
pen·sion *n.* pensión
pen·sive *adj.* pensativo
pen·ta·gon *n.* pentágono
pe·on *n.* peón
pe·o·ny *n.* peonía
peo·ple *n.* gente; pueblo
pep·per *n.* pimienta; pimiento
pep·per·mint *n.* menta
per *prep.* por
per·ceive *v.* percibir
per·cent *n.* por ciento
per·cent·age *n.* porcentaje
per·cep·tion *n.* percepción
perch *n.* percha; perca
per·di·tion *n.* perdición
per·en·ni·al *adj.* perenne
per·fect *adj.* perfecto
per·fec·tion *n.* perfección
per·fo·rate *v.* perforar
per·form *v.* efectuar; hacer; representar
per·for·mance *n.* representación; función
per·fume *n.* perfume
per·il *n.* peligro
pe·rim·e·ter *n.* perímetro
pe·ri·od *n.* período
pe·ri·od·i·cal *n.* publicación periódica
pe·riph·er·y *n.* periferia
per·i·scope *n.* periscopio
per·ish *n.* perecer
per·jure *v.* perjurar(se)
per·ju·ry *n.* perjurio
per·ma·nent *adj.* permanente
per·mis·sion *n.* permiso
per·mit *v.* permitir; tolerar
per·pen·dic·u·lar *adj.* perpendicular

per·pet·u·al *adj.* perpetuo; continuo
per·plex *v.* confundir
per·se·cute *v.* perseguir
per·se·cu·tion *n.* persecución
per·sist *v.* persistir
per·son *n.* persona
per·son·al·i·ty *n.* personalidad
per·son·nel *n.* personal
per·spec·tive *n.* perspectiva
per·spi·ra·tion *n.* sudor
per·suade *v.* persuadir
per·spire *v.* sudar
per·ver·sion *n.* perversión
pe·ti·tion *n.* petición
phar·ma·cy *n.* farmacia
phi·los·o·phy *n.* filosofía
pho·bi·a *n.* fobia
pho·to·cop·y *n.* fotocopia
pho·to·graph *n.* foto
pho·tog·ra·phy *n.* fotografía
phrase *n.* frase
phys·i·cal *adj.* físico
phy·si·cian *n.* médico
pi·an·o *n.* piano
pick *v.* picar; elegir
pic·ture *n.* foto; cuadro; película
pie *n.* pastel
piece *n.* pedazo
pig *n.* cerdo
pi·geon *n.* paloma
pil·lar *n.* pilar
pine *n.* pino
pink *adj.* rosado
pipe *n.* pipa
pis·tol *n.* pistola
pit·y *n.* lástima
place *v.* poner; *n.* posición; sitio
plac·id *adj.* plácido
plague *n.* plaga
plain *adj., n.* llano
plan *v.* planear; *n.* plano
plane *n.* avión; plano
plan·et *n.* planeta
plas·ma *n.* plasma
plas·tic *n., adj.* plástico
plate *n.* plato

188

play *v.* tocar; jugar; *n.* juego
plea *n.* defensa
plead *v.* suplicar; defender
pleas·ure *n.* placer
plen·ti·ful *adj.* abundante
plen·ty *n.* abundancia
plum *n.* ciruela
plum·age *n.* plumaje
plu·ral *n., adj.* plural
pock·et *n.* bolsillo
po·em *n.* poema
po·et *n.* poeta
po·et·ic *adj.* poético
point *n.* punto
po·lice *n.* policía
po·lit·i·cal *adj.* político
pol·i·ti·cian *n.* político
pol·i·tics *n.* política
pol·lu·tion *n.* polución
pomp·ous *adj.* pomposo
pond *n.* estanque
po·ny *n.* jaca
pool *n.* piscina
poor *n.* pobre
pop·u·lar *adj.* popular
pop·u·late *v.* poblar
pop·u·la·tion *n.* población
port *n.* puerto
por·tion *n.* parte
pose *v.* plantear
po·si·tion *n.* posición
pos·i·tive *adj.* positivo
pos·sess *v.* poseer
pos·ses·sion *n.* posesión
pos·si·bil·i·ty *n.* posibilidad
pos·si·ble *adj.* posible
post *n.* poste; puesto; correo
post·age *n.* porte; franqueo
post·card *n.* tarjeta
post·er *n.* cartel
pos·te·ri·or *adj.* posterior
post·man *n.* cartero
post·mark *n.* matasellos
post·me·rid·i·an *adj.* postmeridiano
post·mor·tem *n.* autopsia
post·pone *v.* aplazar

post·script *v.* postdata
pos·ture *n.* postura
pot *n.* olla; tiesto
po·tas·si·um *n.* potasio
po·ta·to *n.* patata
po·tent *adj.* potente; fuerte
po·ten·tial *adj.* potencial
po·tion *n.* poción
pot·ter·y *n.* alfarería
pouch *n.* bolsa
poul·try *n.* aves de corral
pound *n.* libra
pour *v.* diluviar
pout *v.* hacer pucheros
pov·er·ty *n.* pobreza
pow·der *n.* polvo
pow·er *n.* fuerza; poder
pow·er·ful *adj.* potente; poderoso
prac·ti·cal *adj.* práctico
prac·tice *v.* practicar; ejercer
prag·mat·ic *adj.* pragmático
prai·rie *n.* pradera
praise *v.* alabar
prank *n.* travesura
pray *v.* rezar
prayer *n.* oración
preach *v.* predicar
pre·am·ble *n.* preámbulo
pre·cau·tion *n.* precaución
pre·cede *v.* preceder
prec·e·dent *n.* precedente
pre·cinct *n.* recinto; distrito electoral
pre·cious *adj.* precioso
prec·i·pice *n.* precipicio
pre·cip·i·ta·tion *n.* precipitación
pre·cise *adj.* preciso; exacto
pre·co·cious *adj.* precoz
pre·cur·sor *n.* precursor
pred·e·ces·sor *n.* predecesor
pre·des·ti·na·tion *n.* predestinación
pre·dic·a·ment *n.* apuro
pre·dict *v.* pronosticar
pre·dic·tion *n.* pronóstico
pre·dom·i·nant *adj.* predominante
pref·ace *n.* prólogo; prefacio
pre·fer *v.* preferir

pref•er•ence *n.* preferencia
pre•fix *n.* prefijo
preg•nan•cy *n.* embarazo
preg•nant *adj.* embarazada
pre•his•tor•ic *adj.* prehistórico
prej•u•dice *n.* prejuicio
pre•lim•i•nar•y *n.* preliminar
pre•lude *n.* preludio
pre•med•i•tate *v.* premeditar
pre•miere *n.* estreno
pre•mi•um *n.* prima
pre•mo•ni•tion *n.* presentimiento
pre•oc•cu•pied *adj.* preocupada
prep•a•ra•tion *n.* preparación
pre•pare *v.* preparar(se)
prep•o•si•tion *n.* preposición
pre•pos•ter•ous *adj.* absurdo
pre•req•ui•site *n.* requisto previo
pre•rog•a•tive *n.* prerrogativa
pre•scribe *v.* prescribir
pre•scrip•tion *n.* receta
pres•ence *n.* presencia
pre•sent *adj.* presente; *v.* presentar, *n.* regalo
pres•en•ta•tion *n.* presentación
pre•serv•a•tive *n.* preservativo
pre•serve *v.* preservar; conservar
pre•side *v.* presidir
pres•i•dent *n.* presidente
press *n.* prensa; imprenta
pres•sure *n.* presión; urgencia
pres•ti•dig•i•ta•tion *n.* prestidigitación
pres•tige *n.* prestigio
pre•sume *v.* presumir; suponer
pre•tend *v.* pretender
pre•tense *n.* pretexto
pret•ty *adj.* guapo; bonito; mono
pre•vail *v.* prevalecer; predominar
pre•vent *v.* impedir
pre•vi•ous *adj.* previo
prey *n.* presa
price *n.* precio
price•less *adj.* inapreciable
prick *v.* punzar
pride *n.* orgullo
priest *n.* sacerdote

prim *adj.* estirado
pri•ma•ry *adj.* primario
prime *adj.* primero
prim•i•tive *adj.* primitivo
pri•mo•gen•i•ture *n.* primogenitura
prince *n.* príncipe
prin•cess *n.* princesa
prin•ci•pal *n., adj.* principal
prin•ci•pal•i•ty *n.* principado
prin•ci•ple *n.* principio
print *v.* imprimir
print•ing *n.* imprenta
pri•or *adj.* anterior
pri•or•i•ty *n.* prioridad
pri•or•y *n.* priorato
prism *n.* prisma
pris•on *n.* cárcel
pri•va•cy *n.* soledad
pri•vate *adj.* privado
priv•i•lege *n.* privilegio
prize *n.* premio
prob•a•bil•i•ty *n.* probabilidad
prob•a•ble *adj.* probable
probe *n.* sonda
prob•lem *n.* problema
pro•ce•dure *n.* procedimiento
pro•ceed *v.* proceder
proc•ess *n.* proceso
pro•claim *v.* proclamar
pro•cliv•i•ty *n.* proclividad; inclinación
pro•cras•ti•nate *v.* dilatar; aplazar
pro•cure *v.* obtener; alcahuetear
prod *v.* punzar
prod•i•gal *adj.* pródigo
pro•di•gy *n.* prodigio
pro•duce *v.* producir
prod•uct *n.* producto
pro•fane *adj.* profano
pro•fan•i•ty *n.* profanidad
pro•fes•sion *n.* profesión
pro•fes•sor *n.* profesora; profesor
pro•fi•cien•cy *n.* pericia
pro•file *n.* perfil
pro•fit *n.* ganancia; beneficio
pro•found *adj.* profundo
pro•fuse *adj.* profuso

pro•fu•sion *n.* profusión

prog•e•ny *n.* progenie

prog•no•sis *n.* pronóstico

pro•gram *n.* programa

prog•ress *n.* progreso; desarrollo

pro•gres•sive *adj.* progresivo

pro•hib•it *v.* prohibir

pro•hi•bi•tion *n.* prohibición

pro•ject *n.* proyecto; *v.* proyectar

pro•jec•tile *n.* proyectile

pro•lif•ic *adj.* prolífico

pro•logue *n.* prolongar

prom•i•nent *adj.* prominente

pro•mis•cu•ous *adj.* promiscuo; libertino

prom•ise *v.* prometer; *n.* promesa

prom•on•to•ry *n.* promontorio

pro•mote *v.* promover; fomentar; ascender

pro•mo•tion *n.* promoción

prompt *adj.* puntual; pronto

pro•noun *n.* pronombre

pro•nounce *v.* pronunciar(se)

pro•nounced *adj.* marcado

pro•nun•ci•a•tion *n.* pronunciación

proof *n.* prueba

proof•read•er *n.* corrector de pruebas

prop *n.* apoyo

prop•a•gan•da *n.* propaganda

pro•pel *v.* propulsar

pro•pel•ler *n.* hélice

pro•pen•si•ty *n.* propensión; inclinación

prop•er *adj.* propio; apropiado; decente

prop•er•ty *n.* propiedad

proph•e•cy *n.* profecía

proph•e•sy *v.* profetizar

proph•et *n.* profeta

pro•phy•lac•tic *adj.* profiláctico

pro•pi•tious *adj.* propicio

pro•por•tion *n.* proporción

pro•pose *v.* proponer(se); declararse

prop•o•si•tion *n.* proposición; propuesta

pro•pri•e•tor *n.* propietario

pro•pri•e•ty *n.* corrección; decoro

pro•scribe *v.* proscribir

prose *n.* prosa

pros•e•cute *v.* proseguir

pros•pect *n.* perspectiva

pros•per *v.* prosperar

pros•per•i•ty *n.* prosperidad

pros•ti•tute *n.* prostituta; ramera

pros•trate *v.* postrar(se); derribar

pro•tag•o•nist *n.* protagonista

pro•tect *v.* proteger

pro•tein *n.* proteína

pro•test *n.* protesta; *v.* protestar

pro•to•col *n.* protocolo

pro•ton *n.* protón

pro•to•plasm *n.* protoplasma

pro•trude *v.* salir fuera

proud *adj.* orgulloso; arrogante

prove *v.* probar

pro•verb *n.* proverbio

pro•vide *v.* proveer

prov•ince *n.* provincia

pro•vi•sion *n.* provisión

pro•voc•a•tive *adj.* provocativa; provocador

pro•voke *v.* provocar

prow *n.* proa

prox•y *n.* poder; apoderado

prude *n.* gazmoña

prune *n.* ciruela

pry *v.* meterse; fisgonear

psalm *n.* salmo

pseu•do•nym *n.* seudónimo

psych•e•del•ic *adj.* psiquedélico

psy•chi•a•trist *n.* psiquiatra

psy•chi•a•try *n.* psiquiatría

psy•cho•a•nal•y•sis *n.* psicoanálisis

psy•cho•an•a•lyze *v.* psicoanalizar

psy•cho•log•i•cal *adj.* psicológico

psy•chol•o•gy *n.* psicología

psy•cho•sis *n.* psicosis

pto•maine *n.* ptomaína

pub *n.* taberna

pu•ber•ty *n.* pubertad

pub•lic *n., adj.* público

pub•li•ca•tion *n.* publicación

pub•lish *v.* publicar

pub•lish•er *n.* editor

puck•er *v.* arrugar

pud•ding *n.* pudín

pud•dle *n.* charco

puff *v.* soplar; inflar
pug·na·cious *adj.* pugnaz
puke *v.* vomitar
pull *v.* tirar; arrastrar
pul·ley *n.* polea
pul·mo·nar·y *adj.* pulmonar
pulp *n.* pulpa
pul·pit *n.* púlpito
pulse *n.* pulso
pul·ver·ize *v.* pulverizar
pum·ice *n.* piedra pómez
pump *n.* bomba
pump·kin *n.* calabaza
pun *n.* juego de palabras o vocablos
punch *v.* punzar
punc·tu·al *adj.* puntual
punc·tu·a·tion *n.* puntuación
punc·ture *v.* pinchazo
pun·ish *v.* castigar
pu·ny *adj.* encanijado
pu·pa *n.* crisálida
pu·pil *n.* estudiante; pupila
pup·pet *n.* títere
pur·chase *v.* comprar
pure *adj.* puro
pur·ga·to·ry *n.* purgatorio
pu·ri·fy *v.* purificar
pu·ri·tan *n.* puritano
pur·ple *adj.* purpúreo
pur·pose *n.* fin; propósito; resolución
purr *n.* ronroneo
purse *n.* bolsa
pur·sue *v.* perseguir
pur·suit *n.* perseguimiento; busca;
　　ocupación
pus *n.* pus
push *v.* empujar; apretar
puss·y *n.* gatito
put *v.* meter; poner(se)
pu·tre·fy *v.* pudrir
pu·trid *adj.* podrido
put·ty *n.* masilla
pyr·a·mid *n.* pirámide
pyre *n.* pira
py·thon *n.* pitón

Q

quack *v.* graznar; *n.* graznido
quad·ran·gle *n.* cuadrángulo
quad·rant *n.* cuadrante
quad·rate *adj.* cuadrante
quad·rat·ic *adj.* cuadrático
quad·ri·ceps *n.* cuadriceps
quad·ri·lat·er·al *n., adj.* cuadrilátero
quad·ri·ple·gi·a *n.* cuadriplejia
quad·ri·ple·gic *adj.* cuadripléjico
quad·ru·ple *v.* cuadruplicar(se)
quag·mire *n.* pantano
quail *n.* codorniz
quake *v.* temblar
qual·i·fi·ca·tion *n.* calificación
qual·i·fied *adj.* acreditado; capacitado
qual·i·fi·er *n.* calificativo
qual·i·fy *v.* habilitar
qual·i·fy·ing *adj.* eliminatoria
qual·i·ta·tive *adj.* cualitativo
qual·i·ty *n.* calidad
qualm *n.* duda
quan·ti·ta·tive *adj.* cuantitativo
quan·ti·ty *n.* cantidad
quar·an·tine *n.* cuarentena
quar·rel *n.* riña
quar·rel·er *n.* pendenciero
quar·rel·some *adj.* pendeciero
quar·ry *n.* cantera
quart *n.* cuarto
quar·ter *n.* cuarto
quar·ter·deck *n.* alcázar
quar·ter·ly *adj.* trimestral
quar·tet *n.* cuarteto
quartz *n.* cuarzo
qua·ver *v.* temblar
queen *n.* reina
quench *v.* matar; apagar
quench·a·ble *adj.* apagar
ques·tion *n.* pregunta
quick *adj.* listo; rápido
qui·et *adj.* silencio
quit *v.* dejar; irse
quo·ta·tion *n.* cita

quote *v.* citar

R

rab•bi *n.* rabino
rab•bit *n.* conejo
rab•ble *n.* chusma
rab•id *adj.* rabioso
ra•bies *n.* rabia
rac•coon *n.* mapache
race *v.* correr de prisa; *n.* raza
rac•er *n.* corredor
race•track *n.* pista
ra•cial *adj.* racial
rac•ism *n.* racismo
ra•cist *n.* racista
rack *n.* potro
rack•et *n.* raqueta
rac•y *adj.* picante
ra•dar *n.* radar
ra•di•al *adj.* radial
ra•di•ance *n.* resplandor
ra•di•ant *adj.* radiante
ra•di•ate *v.* radiar; emitir; brillar
ra•di•a•tion *n.* radiación
ra•di•a•tor *n.* radiador
rad•i•cal *n.*, *adj.* radical
rad•i•cle *n.* radícula
ra•di•o *n.* radio
ra•di•o•ac•tive *adj.* radioactivo
ra•di•o•ac•tiv•i•ty *n.* radioactividad
ra•di•o•broad•cast *v.* radiar
ra•di•o•gram *n.* radiograma
ra•di•o•graph *n.* radiografía
ra•di•ol•o•gist *n.* radiólogo
ra•di•ol•o•gy *n.* radiología
rad•ish *n.* rábano
ra•di•um *n.* radio
ra•di•us *n.* radio
ra•don *n.* radón
raff•ish *adj.* ostentoso
raf•fle *n.* rifa
raft *n.* balsa
raft•er *n.* cabrio

rag *n.* trapo
rage *v.* enfurecerse
rag•ged *adj.* desigual
raid *v.* atacar
rail *n.* carril
rail•ing *n.* baranda
rail•road *n.* ferrocarril
rail•way *n.* ferrocarril
rain *v.* llover; *n.* lluvia
rain•bow *n.* arco iris
rain•coat *n.* impermeable
rain•drop *n.* gota de lluvia
rain•fall *n.* precipitación
rain•wear *n.* ropa impermeable
rain•y *adj.* lluvioso
raise *v.* criar; levantar
raised *adj.* repujado
rai•sin *n.* pasa
rake *v.* rastrillar; *n.* rastro
ral•ly *n.* reunión; *v.* reunir(se)
ram *n.* carnero
ram•ble *v.* divagar
ram•bler *n.* vagabundo
ram•bunc•tious *adj.* alborotador
ram•i•fi•ca•tion *n.* ramificación
ramp *n.* rampa
ram•page *n.* alboroto
ramp•ant *adj.* destartalado
ranch *n.* hacienda
ranch•er *n.* hacendado
ran•cid *adj.* rancio
ran•cor *n.* rencor
ran•cor•ous *adj.* rencoroso
ran•dom *adj.* fortuito
range *v.* colocar; alinear
rang•er *n.* guardabosques
rank *n.* rango; fila
rank•ing *adj.* superior
ran•kle *v.* enconarse
ran•sack *v.* saquear
ran•som *v.* rescatar; *n.* rescate
rant *v.* vociferar
rap *v.* golpear
ra•pa•cious *adj.* rapaz
ra•pac•i•ty *n.* rapacidad
rape *v.* violar; *n.* violación

rap•id *adj.* rápido
ra•pid•i•ty *n.* rapidez
rap•ine *n.* rapiña
rap•ist *n.* violador
rap•port *n.* relación
rapt *adj.* absorto
rap•ture *n.* rapto
rap•tur•ous *adj.* extasiado
rare *adj.* poco; raro
rar•e•fied *adj.* refinado
rar•e•fy *v.* enrarecer(se)
rar•ing *adj.* impaciente
rar•i•ty *n.* rareza
ras•cal *n.* bribón
rash *n.* erupción
rash•er *n.* tocino
rasp•ber•ry *n.* frambuesa
rasp•ing *adj.* áspero
rat *n.* rata
rate *v.* tasar; *n.* razón
rath•er *adv.* más bien
rat•i•fy *v.* ratificar
rat•ing *n.* popularidad; clasificación
ra•tio *n.* proporción
ra•ti•o•ci•nate *v.* raciocinar
ra•tion *n.* ración
ra•tion•al *adj.* racional
ra•tion•ale *n.* explicación; razón
ra•tion•al•i•ty *n.* racionalidad
ra•tion•al•i•za•tion *n.* racionalización
ra•tion•al•ize *v.* racionalizar
ra•tion•ing *n.* racionamiento
rat•tle *n.* ruido
rat•trap *n.* ratonera
raun•chy *adj.* sucio
rav•age *v.* destruir; *n.* estrago
rave *v.* delirar
rav•el *v.* deshilar(se)
ra•ven *n.* cuervo
ra•ven•ous *adj.* voraz
ra•vine *n.* barranco
rav•ing *adj.* extraordinario
rav•ish *v.* raptar
rav•ish•ing *adj.* encantador
raw *adj.* novato; crudo
ray *n.* rayo

ray•on *n.* rayón
reach *n.* alcance; *v.* extenderse; alargar
re•act *v.* reaccionar
re•ac•tion *n.* reacción
re•ac•tion•ar•y *n.* reaccionario
re•ac•tor *n.* reactor
read *v.* decir; leer
read•ing *n.* lección
re•ad•just *v.* reajustar
read•y *adj.* pronto; listo
re•al *adj.* real
re•al•i•ty *n.* realidad
re•al•ize *v.* realizar
re•al•ly *adv.* realmente
realm *n.* reino
ream *n.* resma
rea•son *v.* razonar; *n.* razón
rea•son•a•ble *adj.* razonable
reb•el *adj., n.* rebelde
re•bel•lion *n.* rebelión
re•buke *n.* reprimenda
re•call *v.* retirar; hacer
re•cant *v.* retractar(se)
re•cede *v.* retroceder
re•ceipt *n.* ingresos
re•ceive *v.* acoger; recibir
re•cent *adj.* reciente
re•cep•ta•cle *n.* receptáculo
re•cess *n.* nicho
re•ces•sion *n.* retroceso
rec•i•pe *n.* receta
re•cip•ro•cal *adj.* recíproco
re•cit•al *n.* recital
rec•i•ta•tion *n.* recitación
re•cite *v.* recitar
reck•on *v.* considerar
re•claim *v.* reclamar
re•cline *v.* recostar(se)
rec•luse *n.* recluso
rec•og•ni•tion *n.* reconocimiento
rec•om•pense *n.* recompensa
re•con•cile *v.* reconciliar
re•con•struct *v.* reconstruir
re•cord *n.* disco; *v.* registrar
re•course *n.* recurso
re•cov•er *v.* recobrar

re·cruit *n.* recluta

rec·tan·gle *n.* rectángulo

rec·ti·fy *v.* rectificar

re·cu·per·ate *v.* recuperar

re·cu·per·a·tion *n.* recuperación

red *adj.* rojo

red·dish *adj.* rojizo

re·deem *v.* redimir

re·demp·tion *n.* redención

re·do *v.* rehacer

re·duce *v.* disminuir; reducir

re·duc·tion *n.* reducción

reef *n.* escollo

reek *n.* olor

re·fer *v.* referir(se)

ref·er·ee *n.* árbitro

ref·er·ence *n.* referencia

re·fill *v.* rellenar

re·fine *v.* refinar

re·fin·er·y *n.* refinería

re·flect *v.* reflejar

re·flec·tion *n.* reflejo

re·flex *adj.* reflejo

re·flex·ive *adj.* reflexivo

re·form *n.* reforma; *v.* reformarse

re·form·a·to·ry *n.* reformatorio

re·fract *v.* refractar

re·frain *v.* refrenar

re·fresh *v.* refrescar

re·fresh·ment *n.* refresco

re·frig·er·ate *v.* refrigerar

ref·uge *n.* refugio

ref·u·gee *n.* refugiado

re·fund *n.* reembolso

re·fuse *v.* refusar

re·gain *v.* recobrar

re·gard *v.* considerar

re·gen·er·ate *v.* regenerar

re·gent *n.* regente

re·gime *n.* régimen

reg·i·men *n.* régimen

reg·i·ment *n.* regimiento

re·gion *n.* región

reg·is·ter *v.* registrar; *n.* registro

re·gret *n.* sentimiento

reg·u·lar *adj.* regular

reg·u·la·tion *n.* regulación

re·ha·bil·i·tate *v.* rehabilitar

re·ha·bil·i·ta·tion *n.* rehabilitación

re·hearse *v.* ensayar

reign *v.* reinar; *n.* reinado

re·im·burse *v.* reembolsar

rein *n.* rienda

re·in·car·na·tion *n.* reencarnación

re·in·force *v.* reforzar

re·it·er·ate *v.* reiterar

re·ject *v.* rechazar

re·lapse *n.* recaída; *v.* reincidir

re·late *v.* relatar

re·lat·ed *adj.* afín

re·la·tion *n.* relación

re·lax *v.* relajar

re·lease *n.* descargo

re·lent *v.* ceder

re·li·a·ble *adj.* confiable

rel·ic *n.* reliquia

re·lief *n.* alivio

re·lieve *v.* aliviar

re·li·gion *n.* religión

re·lig·ious *adj.* religioso

rel·ish *n.* apetencia; *v.* gustar

re·ly *v.* contar; confiar

re·main *v.* quedar(se)

rem·e·dy *n.* remedio

re·mem·ber *v.* acordarse de

re·mem·brance *n.* recuerdo

re·mind *v.* recordar

rem·i·nis·cence *n.* reminiscencia

re·miss *adj.* descuidado

re·mit *v.* remitir

re·mit·tance *n.* remesa

re·morse *n.* remordimiento

re·mote *adj.* remoto

re·move *v.* apartar(se); quitar(se)

ren·ais·sance *n.* renacimiento

rend *v.* rasgar

ren·der *v.* volver

ren·dez·vous *v.* reunirse

ren·e·gade *n.* renegado

re·new *v.* renovar(se)

re·nounce *v.* renunciar

re·nown *n.* renombre

rent

rent *v.* alquilar; *n.* alquiler
re•pair *v.* remendar; reparar
re•pay *v.* pagar; recompensar
re•peat *v.* repetir(se)
re•pel *v.* repeler
re•per•cus•sion *n.* repercusión
rep•er•toire *n.* repertorio
re•place *v.* reponer
re•ply *v.* respuesta
re•port *v.* informar
rep•re•hen•si•ble *adj.* reprensible
rep•re•sen•ta•tion *n.* representación
re•press *v.* reprimir
rep•ri•mand *v.* reprender
re•proach *n.* reproche
re•pro•duce *v.* reproducir
rep•tile *n.* reptil
re•pub•lic *n.* república
re•pulse *n.* repulsa
rep•u•ta•tion *n.* reputación
re•quest *v.* rogar
re•quire *v.* necesitar; exigir
res•cue *n.* rescate
re•search *v.* investigar
re•sent *v.* resentirse de
res•er•va•tion *n.* reservación
re•serve *v.* reservar
re•side *v.* vivir; residir
res•i•dent *n., adj.* residente
re•sign *v.* resignarse
res•ig•na•tion *n.* resignación
res•in *n.* resina
re•sist *v.* resistir
re•sist•ance *n.* resistencia
res•o•lu•tion *n.* resolución
re•solve *v.* resolver(se)
re•sort *n.* recurso
re•source *n.* recurso
re•spect *n.* respeto
re•spect•a•ble *adj.* respetable
re•spect•ful *adj.* respetuoso
re•spect•ing *prep.* respecto
re•spec•tive *adj.* respectivo
res•pi•ra•tion *n.* respiración
res•pi•ra•tor *n.* respirador
res•pi•ra•to•ry *adj.* respiratorio

re•spire *v.* respirar
res•pite *n.* respiro
re•splen•dent *adj.* resplandesciente
re•spond *v.* responder
re•spon•dent *adj.* resplandesciente
re•sponse *n.* respuesta
re•spon•si•bil•i•ty *n.* responsabilidad
re•spon•si•ble *adj.* responsable
rest *n.* descansar
res•tau•rant *n.* restaurante
rest•ful *adj.* sosegado
res•ti•tute *v.* restituir
res•ti•tu•tion *n.* restitución
rest•less *adj.* inquieto
res•to•ra•tion *n.* restauración
re•store *v.* restaurar
re•strain *v.* refrenar
re•strict *v.* restringir
re•stric•tion *n.* restricción
re•sult *n.* resultado; *v.* resultar
re•sus•ci•tate *v.* resucitar
re•tain *v.* retener
re•tard *v.* retardar
ret•i•na *n.* retina
re•tire *v.* retirarse
re•tract *v.* retractar(se)
re•trieve *v.* recobrar
ret•ro•ac•tive *adj.* retroactivo
re•turn *v.* volver
re•un•ion *n.* reunión
re•veal *v.* revelar
rev•e•la•tion *n.* revelación
re•venge *v.* vengar(se)
re•verse *adj.* inverso
re•view *n.* reseña
re•vise *v.* repasar; revisar
re•vi•sion *n.* revisión
re•vive *v.* revivir
re•voke *v.* revocar
rev•o•lu•tion *n.* revolución
rev•o•lu•tion•ary *n., adj.* revolucionario
re•volve *v.* revolverse
re•volv•er *n.* revólver
re•ward *n.* recompensa
rhap•so•dy *n.* rapsodia
rhe•tor•i•cal *adj.* retórico

rheu•mat•ic *adj.* reumático
rheu•ma•tism *n.* reumatismo
rhyme *v.* rimar; *n.* rima
rhythm *n.* ritmo
rib *n.* costilla
rib•bon *n.* cinta
rice *n.* arroz
rich *adj.* fértil; rico
rid *v.* librar(se)
rid•dle *n.* acertijo
ride *v.* montar
rid•i•cule *v.* ridiculizar
ri•dic•u•lous *adj.* ridículo
ri•fle *n.* rifle
right *adj.* exacto; derecho
rig•id *adj.* rígido
rig•or•ous *adj.* riguroso
rind *n.* piel
ring *v.* sonar; *n.* anillo
rink *n.* pista
rip *v.* arrancar; rasgar
ripe *adj.* maduro
rise *v.* subir; levantarse
risk *n.* riesgo
rite *n.* rito
rit•u•al *n., adj.* ritual
ri•val•ry *n.* rivalidad
riv•er *n.* río
roach *n.* cucaracha
road *n.* camino
roar *v.* rugir

S

Sab•bath *n.* domingo
sa•ber *n.* sable
sa•ble *n.* cebellina
sab•o•tage *v.* sabotear; *n.* sabotaje
sac•cha•rin *n.* sacarina
sack *n.* saco
sac•ra•ment *n.* sacramento
sacred *adj.* sagrado
sac•ri•fice *v.* sacrificar; *n.* sacrificio
sac•ri•lege *n.* sacrilegio

sad *adj.* triste
sad•den *v.* entristecer
sad•dle *n.* ensillar
sad•ism *n.* sadismo
sa•fa•ri *n.* safari
safe *adj.* seguro
safe•ty *n.* seguridad
sag *v.* combar(se)
sa•ga *n.* saga
sage *n., adj.* sabio
sail *v.* navegar; *n.* vela
sail•or *n.* marinero
saint *n.* santo
sake *n.* consideración; motivo
sal•ad *n.* ensalada
sal•a•man•der *n.* salamandra
sal•a•ry *n.* salario
sale *n.* venta
sa•line *n.* salino
sa•li•va *n.* saliva
sal•low *n.* cetrino
sal•ly *n.* salida
salm•on *n.* salmón
sa•lon *n.* salón
sa•loon *n.* salón
salt *n.* sal
sal•u•tar•y *adj.* saludable
sal•u•ta•tion *n.* saludo
sa•lute *v.* saludar
sal•vage *n.* salvamento
sal•va•tion *n.* salvación
salve *n.* ungüento
sal•vo *n.* salva
same *adj.* mismo
sam•ple *v.* probar
san•a•to•ri•um *n.* sanatorio
sanc•ti•fy *v.* santificar
sanc•tion *n.* sanción
sanc•ti•ty *n.* santidad
sanc•tu•ar•y *n.* santuario
sand *n.* arena
san•dal *n.* sandalia
sand•stone *n.* arenisca
sand•wich *n.* bocadillo
sand•y *adj.* arenosco
sane *adj.* sano

san·gui·nar·y *adj.* sanguinario

san·i·tar·i·um *n.* sanatorie

san·i·tar·y *adj.* sanitario

san·i·ta·tion *n.* sanidad; saneamiento

san·i·ty *n.* juicio sano

sap *n.* savia

sa·pi·ent *adj.* sabio

sap·phire *n.* zafiro

sar·casm *n.* sarcasmo

sar·cas·tic *adj.* sarcástico

sar·coph·a·gus *n.* sarcófago

sar·dine *n.* sardina

sa·ri, sa·ree *n.* sari

sash *n.* faja

sas·sy *adj.* descarado

sa·tan *n.* Satanás

sa·tan·ic *adj.* satánico

sate *v.* saciar; hartar

sat·el·lite *n.* satélite

sa·ti·ate *v.* saciar

sat·in *n.* raso

sa·tire *n.* sátira

sat·is·fac·tion *n.* satisfacción

sat·is·fy *v.* satisfacer

sat·u·rate *v.* saturar

Sat·ur·day *n.* sábado

sa·tyr *n.* sátiro

sauce *n.* salsa

sau·cer *n.* platillo

sau·sage *n.* salchicha

sav·age *n., adj.* salvaje

save *v.* ahorrar; salvar

sav·ing *n.* economía

sav·ior *n.* salvador

sa·vor *n.* sabor

saw *n.* sierra

sax·o·phone *n.* saxofón

say *v.* decir

say·ing *n.* dicho

scab *n.* costra

scaf·fold *n.* andamio

scald *v.* escaldar

scale *n.* escala

scal·lop *n.* venera; festón

scalp *n.* pericráneo; cuero cabelludo

scal·pel *n.* escalpelo

scan *v.* escudriñar

scan·dal *n.* escándalo

scan·dal·ize *v.* escandalizar

scant *adj.* escaso

scant·y *adj.* escaso

scape·goat *n.* cabeza de turco

scar *n.* cicatriz

scarce *adj.* escaso

scare *v.* asustar

scare·crow *n.* espantajo; espantapájaros

scarf *n.* bufanda

scar·let *n.* escarlata

scat·ter *v.* esparcir

scav·en·ger *n.* basurero

scene *n.* vista; escena

scen·er·y *n.* paisaje

scent *n.* pista; olor

sched·ule *n.* horario

scheme *v.* intrigar

schism *n.* cisma

schiz·o·phre·ni·a *n.* esquizofrenia

schol·ar *n.* erudito; alumno

schol·ar·ship *n.* erudición; beca

schol·as·tic *adj.* escolar

school *n.* escuela

sci·ence *n.* ciencia

sci·en·tist *n.* científico

scim·i·tar *n.* cimitarra

scis·sors *n.* tijeras

scoff *v.* mofarse

scold *v.* regañar

scoop *n.* paleta

scoot·er *n.* patinete

scope *n.* alcance

scorch *v.* chamuscar

score *n.* cuenta

scorn *n.* desdén

scor·pi·on *n.* escorpión

scotch *n.* frustrar

scoun·drel *n.* canalla

scour *v.* fregar; recorrer

scout *n.* explorador

scowl *v.* poner mal gesto

scraggy *adj.* escarnado

scram·ble *v.* revolver

scrap *n.* fragmento; sobras

scrape *v.* raer

scratch *v.* rayar; rasguñar; rascar

scrawl *n.* garabatos

scream *n.* grito

screen *n.* biombo; pantalla

screw *v.* atornillar; *n.* tornillo

scrib•ble *v.* garabatear

scrim•mage *n.* arrebatiña

script *n.* letra cursiva; guión

scrip•ture *n.* Sagrada Escritura

scroll *n.* rollo de pergamino

scrub *v.* fregar

scru•ple *n.* escrúpulo

scru•ti•nize *v.* escudriñar

scru•ti•ny *n.* escrutinio

scuf•fle *v.* pelear

sculp•tor *n.* escultor

sculp•ture *v.* esculpir; *n.* escultura

scum *n.* espuma

scur•ry *v.* darse prisa

scur•vy *n.* escorbuto

scut•tle *v.* echar a pique

scythe *n.* guadaña

sea *n.* mar

seal *n.* foca

seal *n.* sello; *v.* cerrar

seam *n.* costura

sea•man *n.* marinero

seam•stress *n.* costurera

seam•y *adj.* asqueroso

se•ance *n.* sesión de espiritistas

sea•port *n.* puerto de mar

sear *v.* marchitar; chamuscar

search *v.* buscar

sea•shore *n.* orilla del mar

sea•sick•ness *n.* mareo

sea•son *n.* estación

sea•son•ing *n.* condimento

seat *v.* sentar; *n.* asiento

sea•weed *n.* alga marina

se•clude *v.* aislar

se•clu•sion *n.* retiro

sec•ond *n.* , *adj.* segundo

sec•ond•ar•y *adj.* secundario

sec•ond•hand *adj.* de segunda mano

sec•ond•rate *adj.* inferior

se•cre•cy *n.* secreto

se•cret *n., adj.* secreto

sec•re•tar•y *n.* secretario

se•crete *v.* secretar; ocultar

se•cre•tion *n.* secreción

sect *n.* secta

sec•tion *n.* sección

sec•tor *n.* sector

sec•u•lar *adj.* secular

se•cure *adj.* seguro

se•cu•ri•ty *n.* seguridad

se•date *adj.* sosegado

sed•a•tive sedativo

sed•en•tar•y *adj.* sedentario

sed•i•ment *n.* sedimento

se•di•tion *n.* sedición

se•duce *v.* seducir

se•duc•tion *n.* seducción

see *v.* percibir; ver

seed *n.* semilla; simiente

seed•y *adj.* desharrapado

seek *v.* buscar; solicitar

seem *v.* parecer

seem•ly *adj.* decoroso; correcto

seep *v.* rezumar

se•er *n.* profeta

seg•ment *n.* segmento

seg•re•gate *v.* segregar

seg•re•ga•tion *n.* segregación

seis•mo•graph *n.* sismógrafo

seize *v.* apoderarse de; asir

sei•zure *n.* asimiento

sel•dom *adv.* raramente

se•lect *adj.* selecto; *v.* elegir

se•lec•tion *n.* selección

self *n.* sí mismo

self-cen•tered *adj.* egocéntrico

self-com•mand *n.* dominio de sí mismo

self-con•fi•dence *n.* confianza en sí mismo

self-ev•i•dent *adj.* patente

self-ex•plan•a•to•ry *adj.* evidente; obvio

self-gov•ern•ment *n.* autonomía

self-im•por•tance *n.* presunción

self•ish *adj.* egoísta; interesado

self•less *adj.* desinteresado

self-reliance

self·re·li·ance *n.* confianza en sí mismo
self·same *adj.* mismo
self·suf·fi·cient *adj.* independiente
self·will *n.* terquedad
sell *v.* vender
se·man·tics *n.* semántica
sem·blance *n.* parecido; apariencia
se·men *n.* semen
sem·es·ter *n.* semestre
sem·i·cir·cle *n.* semicírculo
sem·i·co·lon *n.* punto y coma
sem·i·fi·nal *adj.* semifinal
sem·i·nar *n.* seminario
sem·i·nar·y *n.* seminario
sem·i·of·fi·cial *adj.* semioficial
sem·i·pre·cious *adj.* semiprecioso
sem·i·week·ly *adj.* bisemanal
sen·ate *n.* senado
sen·a·tor *n.* senador
send *v.* mandar; enviar
se·nile *adj.* senil
sen·ior *adj.* superior
sen·ior·i·ty *n.* antigüedad
sen·sa·tion *n.* sensación
sense *v.* percibir; *n.* sentido
sense·less *adj.* sin sentido; insensato
sen·si·bil·i·ty *n.* sensibilidad
sen·si·ble *adj.* razonable
sen·si·tive *adj.* delicado
sen·si·tiv·i·ty *n.* delicadeza
sen·so·ry *adj.* sensorio
sen·su·al *adj.* sensual
sen·su·ous *adj.* sensorio
sen·tence *n.* frase
sen·ti·ment *n.* sentimiento
sen·ti·nel *n.* centinela
sen·try *n.* centinela
se·pal *n.* sépalo
sep·a·rate *v.* separar(se)
sep·a·ra·tion *n.* separación
Sep·tem·ber *n.* septiembre
sep·tic *adj.* séptico
sep·ul·cher *n.* sepulcro
se·quel *n.* resultado
se·quence *n.* sucesión
se·ques·ter *v.* separar; aislar

se·ques·tered *adj.* aislado
se·quin *n.* lentejuela
ser·aph *n.* serafín
ser·e·nade *n.* serenata
se·rene *n.* sereno
se·ren·i·ty *n.* serenidad
serf *n.* siervo
se·ri·al *adj.* en serie
se·ries *n.* serie
se·ri·ous *adj.* serio
ser·mon *n.* sermón
ser·pent *n.* serpiente
se·rum *n.* suero
serv·ant *n.* sirviente; servidor
serve *v.* servir
serv·ice *n.* servicio
serv·ice·man *n.* militar
ser·vile *adj.* servil
ses·sion *n.* sesión
set *v.* fijar; poner(se)
set·back *n.* revés
set·ting *n.* engaste
set·tle *v.* arreglar; resolver
set·tle·ment *n.* colonización
set·ler *n.* colono
sev·en *adj.* siete
sev·en·teen *adj.* diecisiete
sev·enth *adj.* séptimo
sev·en·ty *adj.* setenta
sev·er *v.* cortar
sev·er·al *adj.* varios; diversos
se·vere *adj.* severo
sev·er·i·ty *n.* severidad
sew *v.* coser
sew·er *n.* albañal; cloaca
sex *n.* sexo
sex·tet *n.* sexteto
sex·u·al *adj.* sexual
sex·y *adj.* provocativo
shab·by *adj.* raído; en mal estado
shack *n.* choza
shack·le *n.* grillete
shade *v.* sombrear; *n.* sombra
shad·ing *n.* degradación
shad·ow *n.* sombra
shad·ow·y *adj.* umbroso; vago

shad•y *adj.* sombreado

shaft *n.* eje; pozo

shag•gy *adj.* velludo

shake *v.* estrechar; temblar

shak•y *adj.* poco profundo; tembloroso

sham *v.* fingir(se); *adj.* fingido

sham•bles *n.* desorden

shame *n.* vergüenza

shame•less *adj.* desvergonzado

sham•poo *n.* champú

shan•ty *n.* choza

shape *v.* formar; *n.* forma

shape•ly *adj.* bien formado

share *n.* parte

shark *n.* tiburón

sharp *adj.* vivo; cortante

sharp•en *v.* afilar; sacar punta

shat•ter *v.* hacer(se) pedazos

shave *v.* afeitar(se)

shav•er *n.* máquina de afeitar

shawl *n.* chal

she *pron.* ella

shears *n.* tijeras grandes

shed *v.* quitarse; verter

sheen *n.* lustre

sheep *n.* oveja

sheep•ish *adj.* tímido

sheer *adj.* escarpado

sheet *n.* sábana; hoja; lámina

shiek, sheikh *n.* jeque

shelf *n.* estante

shell *n.* cáscara

shel•lac, shel•lack *n.* goma laca

shell•fish *n.* marisco

shel•ter *n.* refugio

shep•herd *n.* pastor

sher•bet *n.* sorbete

sher•iff *n.* aguacil

sher•ry *n.* jerez

shield *n.* escudo

shift *v.* mover(se); cambiar

shil•ly•shal•ly *v.* vacilar

shim•mer *v.* rielar

shin *n.* espinilla

shine *v.* pulir; brillar

shin•gle *n.* tablilla; placa; teja

shin•y *adj.* brillante

ship *n.* barco

ship•ment *n.* embarque; envío

ship•shape *adj.* en buen orden

ship•wreck *n.* naufragio

shirk *v.* evitar; esquivar

shirt *n.* camisa

shiv•er *v.* temblar

shock *n.* susto; choque; postración

shod•dy *adj.* de pacotilla; falso

shoe *n.* zapato

shoe•horn *n.* calzador

shoe•lace *n.* cordón

shoot *v.* espigar; disparar

shoot•ing *n.* tiro; caza con escopeta

shoot•ing star *n.* estrella fugaz

shop *n.* taller; tienda

shop•keep•er *n.* tendero

shore *n.* playa

short *adj.* breve; corto

short•age *n.* deficiencia; escasez

short•com•ing *n.* defecto

short•cut *n.* atajo

short•en *v.* acortar(se)

short•hand *n.* taquigrafía

short•lived *adj.* de breve duración

short•tem•pered *adj.* de mal genio

shot *n.* tiro; tirador

shot•gun *n.* escopeta

should•er *n.* hombro

shout *v.* gritar; *n.* grito

shov•el *n.* pala

show *v.* mostrar(se)

show•er *v.* duchar(se); *n.* ducha

show•man *n.* director de espectáculos

shred *v.* hacer tiras

shrew *n.* arpía

shrewd *adj.* sagaz; prudente

shriek *n.* chillar

shrill *adj.* estridente

shrimp *n.* camarón

shrine *n.* relicario

shrink *v.* encoger(se)

shriv•el *v.* encoger(se); secar(se)

shroud *n.* mortaja

shrub *n.* arbusto

shrub•bery *n.* arbustos
shrug *v.* encogerse de hombros
shud•der *v.* extremecerse
shuf•fle *v.* arrastrar los pies; (cards) barajar
shun *v.* evitar; apartarse de
shut *v.* cerrar(se)
shut•ter *n.* contraventana
shut•tle *n.* lanzadera
shy *adj.* tímido
sic *v.* atacar
sick *adj.* enfermo
sick•en *v.* enfermar(se)
sick•le *n.* hoz
sick•ness *n.* enfermedad
side *n.* partido; lado
side•burns *n.* patillas
side•long *adj.* lateral
side•track *v.* desviar
side•walk *n.* acera
side•ways *adv.* oblicuamente
siege *n.* sitio; cerco
sieve *n.* coladera; tamiz
sift *v.* tamizar
sigh *n.* suspiro; *v.* suspirar
sight *n.* visión; vista
sight•less *adj.* ciego
sight•see•ing *n.* visita de puntos de interés
sign *n.* signo; señal
sig•nal *n.* señal
sig•na•ture *n.* firma
sig•nif•i•cance *n.* significación
sig•ni•fy *v.* significar
si•lence *n.* silencio
si•lent *adj.* silencioso
sil•hou•ette *n.* silueta
sil•i•ca *n.* sílice
sil•i•con *n.* silicio
silk *n.* seda
silk•y *adj.* sedoso
sil•ly *adj.* bobo
si•lo *n.* silo
silt *n.* sedimento
sil•ver *n.* plata
sil•ver•smith *n.* platero

sil•ver•ware *n.* vajilla de plata
sim•i•an *adj.* símico
sim•i•lar *adj.* similar
sim•i•lar•i•ty *n.* semejanza
sim•mer *v.* hervir a fuego lento
sim•per *v.* sonreírse afectadamente
sim•ple *adj.* simple; fácil
sim•pli•fy *v.* simplificar
sim•ply *adv.* sencillamente
sim•u•late *v.* simular
si•mul•ta•ne•ous *adj.* simultáneo
sin *n.* pecado; transgresión
since *conj.* puesto que; *prep.* después; desde
sin•cere *adj.* sincero
sin•cer•i•ty *n.* sinceridad
si•ne•cure *n.* sinecura
sin•ew *n.* tendón
sing *v.* cantar
sing•er *n.* cantante
sin•gle *adj.* único; soltero
sin•gle-hand•ed *adj.* sin ayuda
sin•gu•lar *adj.* singular
sin•is•ter *adj.* siniestro
sink *v.* hundir(se)
sin•ner *n.* pecador
si•nus *n.* seno
sip *n.* sorbo; *v.* sorber
sir *n.* señor
sire *n.* padre
si•ren *n.* sirena
sir•loin *n.* solomillo
sis•ter *n.* hermana
sis•ter-in-law *n.* cuñada
sit *v.* sentar(se)
site *n.* sitio
sit•u•a•tion *n.* situación
six *adj., n.* seis
six•teen *adj., n.* dieciséis
sixth *adj,. n.* sexto
six•ty *adj., n.* sesenta
size *n.* talla
siz•zle *v.* chisporrotear
skate *v.* patinar
skel•e•ton *n.* esqueleto
skep•tic *n.* escéptico
skep•ti•cal *adj.* escéptico

smug

sketch *n.* esbozo; bosquejo
skew•er *n.* broqueta
ski *v.* esquiar
skid *n.* patinazo
skill *n.* destreza; habilidad
skil•let *n.* sartén
skim *v.* espumar; desnatar; hojear
skin *n.* piel
skin•ny *adj.* flaco
skip *v.* saltar; pasar por alto
skir•mish *n.* escaramuza
skirt *n.* falda
skit *n.* parodia
skull *n.* cráneo
skunk *n.* mofeta
sky *n.* cielo
sky•rock•et *n.* cohete
sky•scrap•er *n.* rascacielos
slab *n.* tabla; plancha
slack *adj.* flojo; negligente
slack•en *v.* aflojar
slacks *n.* pantalones
slag *n.* escoria
slam *v.* cerrarse de golpe
slan•der *v.* calumniar; *n.* calumnia
slang *n.* argot
slant *v.* inclinar(se); sesgar(se)
slap *v.* pegar
slash *v.* acuchillar
slat *n.* tablilla
slate *n.* pizarra; lista de candidatos
slaugh•ter *v.* matar
slave *n.* esclavo
slav•er•y *n.* esclavitud
slay *v.* matar
sled *n.* trineo
sleek *adj.* liso; pulcro
sleep *v.* dormir
sleep•y *adj.* soñoliento
sleet *n.* aguanieve
sleeve *n.* manga
sleigh *n.* trineo
slen•der *adj.* delgado
sleuth *n. inf.* detective
slice *v.* tajar; *n.* tajada
slide *v.* deslizarse

slight *adj.* pequeño; de poca importancia
slim *adj.* delgado
slime *n.* lodo; cieno
sling *v.* tirar; suspender
slip *v.* introducir; deslizar(se); resbalar; escaparse
slip•knot *n.* nudo corredizo
slip•per *n.* zapatilla
slip•per•y *adj.* resbaladizo
slip•up *n. inf.* equivocación
slit *v.* cortar
sliv•er *n.* astilla
slob•ber *v.* babear; babosear
slo•gan *n.* mote
slop *v.* verter
slope *v.* inclinar(se); *n.* inclinación
slot *n.* ranura
slov•en•ly *adj.* descuidado; desaseado
slow *adj.* torpe; lento
slow•ly *adv.* despacio
slug *n.* posta
slug•gish *adj.* perezoso; lento
slum *n.* barrio bajo
slump *v.* hundirse; caer
slur *v.* comerse palabras; calumniar
slut *n.* pazpuerca; perra
sly *n.* astuto; disimulado
smack *v.* pegar
small *adj.* pequeño
small•pox *n.* viruelas
smart *adj.* listo; fresco
smash *v.* romper(se)
smear *v.* manchar; untar
smell *v.* oler
smile *n.* sonrisa; *v.* sonreír(se)
smirk *n.* sonrisa afectada
smith *n.* herrero
smock *n.* blusa de labrador
smog *n.* niebla y humo mezclados
smoke *v.* fumar; *n.* humo
smol•der *v.* arder sin llamas
smooch *v. inf.* besar
smooth *adj.* suave
smooth•er *v.* ahogar(se); sofocar(se)
smudge *n.* mancha
smug *adj.* pagado de sí mismo

203

smug•gle v. pasar de (o hacer) contrabando
snack n. merienda
snag n. obstáculo; rasgón
snail n. caracol
snake n. culebra
snap•shot n. foto
snare n. trampa
snatch n. fragmento; trocito
sneak v. moverse a hurtadillas
sneer v. mofarse
sneeze n. estornudo; v. estornudar
sniff v. husmear; oler
snip v. tijeretear
snob n. esnob
snooze v. infin. dormitar
snore n. ronquido; v. roncar
snow v. nevar; n. nieve
snow•ball n. bola de nieve
snow•flake n. copo de nieve
snow•man n. figura de nieve
snub v. desairar
snug•gle v. arrimarse
so conj. por tanto; adv. así; tan
soak v. remojar
soap n. jabón
soar v. remontarse
sob v. sollozar
so•ber adj. sobrio
so•bri•quet, sou•bri•quet n. apodo
so•called adj. llamado; supuesto
soc•cer n. fútbol
so•cia•ble adj. sociable
so•cial adj. social
so•cial•ism n. socialismo
so•cial•ize v. socializar
so•ci•e•ty n. sociedad
so•di•um n. sodio
so•fa n. sofá
soil v. manchar; n. tierra
so•lar adj. solar
sol•dier n. soldado
sole•ly adv. solamente
sol•emn adj. solemne
so•lic•it v. solicitar
sol•id n., adj. sólido
sol•i•dar•i•ty n. solidaridad

sol•i•tar•y adj. solitario
sol•u•ble adj. soluble
so•lu•tion n. solución
solve v. resolver
sol•vent n. adj. solvente
som•ber adj. sombrío
some pron. algunos; adj. alguno
some•bo•dy n. pron. alguien
some•day adv. algún día
some•one pron. alguien
some•thing n. algo
some•times adv. a veces
son n. hijo
song n. canción
son-in-law n. yerno
soon adv. pronto
soothe v. calmar
so•pran•o n. soprano
sor•did adj. vil
sor•ry adj. triste
so•so adv. así así
soul n. alma
sound n. ruido
soup n. sopa
sour adj. agrio
south n. sur
south•east n. sudeste
south•ern adj. del sur
south•west n. sudoeste
sov•er•eign n., adj. soberano
space v. espaciar; n. espacio
spa•cious adj. espacioso
spa•ghet•ti n. espagueti
spasm n. espasmo
spas•mod•ic adj. espasmódico
spas•tic adj. espástico
spat•u•la n. espátula
speak v. decir; hablar
spear n. lanza
spe•cial adj. especial
spe•cial•ist n. especialista
spe•cial•ize v. especializar(se)
spe•cial•ty n. especialidad
spe•cies n. especie
spe•cif•ic adj. específico
spec•i•fy v. especificar

spec•ta•cle *n.* espectáculo

spec•tac•u•lar *adj.* espectacular

speech•less *adj.* mudo

speed *v.* apresurarse; acelerar

spell *n.* deletrear

spell•bind *v.* encantar

spell•ing *n.* ortografía

spend *v.* gastar

sperm *n.* esperma

sperm whale *n.* cachalote

sphere *n.* esfera

spher•i•cal *adj.* esférico

spice *n.* especia

spic•y *adj.* picante

spi•der *n.* araña

spill *v.* verter(se)

spin•ach *n.* espinaca

spi•nal *adj.* espinal

spine *n.* espinazo

spi•ral *adj., n.* espiral

spir•it *n.* espíritu

spir•it•u•al *adj.* espiritual

spir•it•u•al•ism *n.* espiritismo

spit *v.* escupir

spite *n.* rencor

splin•ter *n.* astilla

split *v.* dividir; separarse

spoil *v.* echar(se); estropear(se)

spo•ken *adj.* hablado

sponge *n.* esponja

spon•gy *adj.* esponjoso

spon•ta•ne•i•ty *n.* espontaneidad

spon•ta•ne•ous *adj.* espontáneo

spoon *n.* cuchara

spoon•ful *n.* cucharada

spo•rad•ic *adj.* esporádico

spore *n.* espora

sport *n.* deporte

sports•man *n.* deportista

spot *n.* mancha

spot•ty *adj.* manchado

spouse *n.* esposa; esposo

spread *v.* diseminar

spring *n.* primavera; *v.* saltar

spring•time *n.* primavera

spruce *n.* picea

spu•ri•ous *adj.* espurio

spy *v.* espiar

squad•ron *n.* escuadrón

squal•id *adj.* desaliñado

square *adj.* cuadrado

squeak *n.* chirrido; *v.* chillar

sta•bil•i•ty *n.* estabilidad

sta•ble *adj.* estable

sta•di•um *n.* estadio

stage *n.* etapa

stain *n.* mancha

stair *n.* escalón

stair•way *n.* escalera

stamp *n.* sello

stam•pede *n.* estampida

stand *v.* colocar

stand•ing *adj.* derecho

sta•ple *n.* grapa

sta•pler *n.* grapadora

star *n.* estrella

star•less *adj.* sin estrellas

star•ry *adj.* estrellado

start *v.* comenzar; empezar

state *n.* estado

stat•ic *adj.* estático

sta•tion *v.* estación

sta•tis•tic *n.* estadístico

stat•ue *n.* estatua

stay *v.* quedar(se)

steal *v.* robar

steam *v.* empañar; *n.* vapor

steam•y *adj.* vaporoso

stem *n.* tallo

step *n.* escalera

step•broth•er *n.* hermanastro

step•daugh•ter *n.* hijastra

step•fa•ther *n.* padrastro

step•moth•er *n.* madrastra

step•sis•ter *n.* hermanastra

step•son *n.* hijastro

ste•ril•i•ty *n.* esterilidad

stick *n.* palo

stick•y *adj.* viscoso

stiff *adj.* rígido

still *adj.* tranquilo

stim•u•lant *n.* estimulante

stim•u•late *v.* estimular
stink *v.* hedor
stip•u•late *v.* estipular
stip•u•la•tion *n.* estipulación
stock•ing *n.* media
sto•i•cal *adj.* estoico
stom•ach *n.* estómago
stone *n.* piedra
stop *v.* terminar
stop•light *n.* semáforo
store *n.* almacén; tienda
stork *n.* cigüeña
storm *n.* tempestad
sto•ry *n.* piso; historia
stove *n.* estufa
straight *adj.* directo
strange *adj.* extraño; raro
stra•te•gic *adj.* estratégico
strat•e•gy *n.* estrategia
straw *n.* pajilla
straw•ber•ry *n.* fresa
stream *n.* arroyo
street *n.* calle
strength *n.* vigor; fuerza
strict *adj.* estricto
strike *v.* atacar; golpear
string *n.* cordel
stripe *n.* raya
striped *adj.* rayado
strong *adj.* robusto; fuerte
struc•tur•al *adj.* estructural
stu•dent *n.* estudiante
stu•di•o *n.* estudio
stud•y *v.* estudiar
stu•pen•dous *adj.* estupendo
stu•pid *adj.* estúpido
style *n.* modo; estilo
sub•di•vide *v.* subdividir
sub•ject *adj., n.* sujeto
sub•jec•tive *adj.* subjetivo
sub•lease *v.* subarrendar
sub•let *v.* subarrendar
sub•li•mate *v.* sublimar
sub•li•ma•tion *n.* sublimación
sub•lime *adj.* sublime
sub•lim•it•y *n.* sublimidad

sub•mar•ine *n.* submarino
sub•merge *v.* sumergir(se)
sub•mer•sion *n.* sumersión
sub•mis•sion *n.* sumisión
sub•mis•sive *adj.* sumiso
sub•mit *v.* someter(se); presentar
sub•nor•mal *adj.* anormal
sub•or•di•nate *adj.* subordinado; secundario; dependiente
sub•or•di•na•tion *n.* subordinación
sub•poe•na *n.* citación; compareendo
sub•scribe *v.* subscribir(se)
sub•scrip•tion *n.* subscripción
sub•se•quent *adj.* subsiguiente
sub•ser•vi•ent *adj.* servil
sub•side *v.* bajar; calmarse
sub•sid•i•ar•y *adj.* subsidiario
sub•si•dize *v.* subvencionar
sub•si•dy *n.* subvención; subsidio
sub•sist *v.* subsistir; existir
sub•sis•tence *n.* subsistencia
sub•stance *n.* esencia; substancia
sub•stan•tial *adj.* substancial
sub•stan•ti•a•tion *n.* comprobación; justificación
sub•stan•tive *n.* substantivo
sub•sti•tute *n.* substituto, *v.* substituir
sub•sti•tu•tion *n.* substitución; reemplazo
sub•ter•fuge *n.* subterfugio
sub•ter•ra•ne•an *adj.* subterráneo
sub•ti•tle *n.* subtítulo
sub•tle *adj.* sutil; ingenioso; delicado; astuto
sub•tle•ty *n.* sutileza
sub•tract *v.* substraer
sub•trac•tion *n.* substracción; resta
sub•urb *n.* suburbio
sub•ur•ban *adj.* suburbano
sub•ver•sion *n.* subversivo
sub•ver•sive *adj.* sobversivo
sub•vert *v.* subvertir
sub•way *n.* metro
succeed *v.* suceder
suc•cess *n.* éxito
suc•cess•ful *adj.* próspero; afortunado
suc•ces•sion *n.* sucesión

suc·ces·sor *n.* sucesor
suc·cinct *adj.* sucinto
suc·cor *n.* socorro; auxilio
suc·cu·lent *adj.* suculento
suc·cumb *v.* sucumbir
such *adv.* tan; *pron., adj.* tal
suck *v.* chupar; mamar
suck·er *n.* pirulí
suck·le *v.* lactar; amamantar
suc·tion *n.* succión
suf·fer *v.* sufrir
suf·fer·ance *n.* tolerancia
suf·fice *v.* bastar
suf·fi·cien·cy *n.* suficiencia
suf·fix *n.* sufijo
suf·fo·cate *v.* sofocar; asfixiar
suf·frage *n.* sufragio
suf·fuse *v.* extender; bañar
suf·fu·sion *n.* difusión
sug·ar *n.* azúcar
sug·ar·y *adj.* azucarado
sug·gest *v.* sugerir
sug·ges·tion *n.* sugestión
sug·ges·tive *n.* sugestivo
su·i·cide *n.* suicida
suit *n.* traje
suit·a·ble *adj.* apropiado
suit·case *n.* maleta
suite *n.* juego; serie
sul·fur, sul·phur *n.* azufre
sul·fu·ric ac·id *n.* ácido sulfúrico
sulk *v.* estar de mal humor
sul·len *adj.* hosco
sul·ly *v.* manchar
sul·tan *n.* sultán
sul·tan·ate *n.* sultanato
sul·try *adj.* bochornoso; sensual
sum *v.* sumar; *n.* suma
sum·ma·ry *adj.* sumario
sum·mer *n.* verano
sun *n.* sol
Sun·day *n.* domingo
sun·down *n.* puesta del sol
sun·flow·er *n.* girasol
sun·glass·es *n.* gafas de sol
sun·light *n.* luz del sol

sun·rise *n.* salida del sol
su·per·fi·cial *adj.* superficial
su·per·in·tend *v.* superentender
su·pe·ri·or *n., adj.* superior
su·pe·ri·or·it·y *n.* superioridad
su·per·mar·ket *n.* supermercado
su·per·sti·tion *n.* superstición
sup·er·sti·tious *adj.* supersticioso
su·pine *adj.* supino
sup·per *n.* cena
sup·ple·ment *n.* suplemento
sup·li·cate *v.* suplicar
sup·pose *v.* suponer
sup·pres·sion *n.* supresión
su·prem·a·cy *n.* supremacía
su·preme *adj.* supremo
sure *adj.* seguro
sure·ly *adv.* seguramente
sur·face *n.* superficie
sur·geon *n.* cirujano
sur·ger·y *n.* cirugía
sur·name *n.* apellido
sur·prise *v.* sorprender; *n.* sorpresa
sur·vive *v.* sobrevivir
sus·cep·ti·ble *adj.* susceptible
sus·pend *v.* suspender
sus·pense *n.* incertidumbre
sus·pen·sion *adj.* suspensión
sus·pi·cion *n.* sospecha; sombra
sus·pi·cious *adj.* sospechoso
sus·tain *v.* sustentar
sus·te·nance *n.* sustento
svelte *adj.* esbelto
swab *n.* algodón; tapón
swan *n.* cisne
swap *v.* cambiar
swarm *n.* enjambre
swash·buck·ler *n.* espadachín
swat *v.* matar
sway *v.* bambolearse; inclinar
swear *v.* jurar
swear·word *n.* palabrota
sweat *n.* sudor; *v.* sudar
sweat·y *adj.* sudoroso
sweet *adj.* dulce
sweet·en *v.* azucarar; endulzar

sweet•heart *n.* querida; novia
sweet•meat *n.* dulce
swell *v.* hinchar(se)
swerve *v.* torcer(se); desviar(se)
swift *adj.* veloz
swig *v.* beber a grandes tragos
swill *n.* bazofia
swim *n.* natación; *v.* nadar
swim•mer *n.* nadador
switch *v.* cambiar
swiv•el *n.* alacrán; torniquete; girar
swoon *n.* desmayo
sword *n.* espada
sword•belt *n.* talabarte
sword•fish *n.* pez espada
sword•play *n.* esgrima
swords•man *n.* espadachín
syc•a•more *n.* sicomoro
syc•o•phant *n.* adulador
syl•lab•i•cate *v.* silabear
syl•lab•i•ca•tion *n.* silabeo
syl•lab•i•fy *v.* silabear
syl•a•ble *n.* sílaba
syl•a•bus *n.* resumen; programa
syl•van *adj.* silvestre
sym•bol *n.* símbolo
sym•bol•ic *adj.* simbólico
sym•bol•ism *n.* simbolismo
sym•bol•ize *v.* simbolizar
sym•me•try *n.* simetría
sym•pa•thet•ic *adj.* compasivo; simpático
sym•pa•thy *n.* simpatía
sym•pho•ny *n.* sinfonía
symp•tom *n.* síntoma
syn•a•gogue *n.* sinagoga
syn•chro•nize *v.* sincronizar(se)
syn•di•cate *v.* sindicar
syn•od *n.* sínodo
syn•o•nym *n.* sinónimo
syn•on•y•mous *adj.* sinónimo
syn•op•sis *n.* sinopsis
syn•the•sis *n.* síntesis
syn•thet•ic *adj.* sintético
syph•i•lis *n.* sífilis
sy•ringe *n.* jeringa
sy•rup *n.* jarabe; almíbar

sys•tem *n.* sistema
sys•tem•at•ic *adj.* sistemático
sys•tem•a•tize *v.* sistematizar

T

tab *n.* cuenta
tab•er•nac•le *n.* tabernáculo
ta•ble *n.* mesa
ta•ble•spoon•ful *n.* cucharada
tab•let *n.* tableta
ta•boo, ta•bu *adj.* tabú
tab•u•lar *adj.* tabular
tab•u•late *v.* tabular
tac•it *adj.* tácito
tac•i•turn *adj.* taciturno
tack *n.* tachuela; virada
tack•le *n.* equipo; carga
tact *n.* tacto
tac•tics *n.* táctica
tad•pole *n.* renacuajo
taf•fe•ta *n.* tafetán
taf•fy *n.* caramelo
tag *n.* etiqueta; marbete
tail *n.* cola; rabo
tai•lor *n.* sastre
taint *v.* contaminar(se); corromper(se)
take *v.* coger; tomar; sacar
take•off *n.* despegue
tal•cum pow•der *n.* polvo de talco
tale *n.* cuenta
tal•ent *n.* talento
tal•ent•ed *adj.* talentoso
talk *v.* decir; hablar
talk•a•tive *adj.* hablador
tall *adj.* alto
tal•low *n.* sebo
tal•ly *n.* cuenta
tal•on *n.* garra
tam•bou•rine *n.* pandereta
tame *adj.* domesticado; manso; soso
tam•per *v.* estropear; falsificar
tan *v.* curtir; tostar

tan•dem *adv.* en tándem

tang *n.* sabor fuerte

tan•gent *n.* , *adj.* tangente

tan•ge•rine *n.* naranja mandarina o tangerina

tan•gi•ble *adj.* tangible

tan•gle *v.* enredar(se)

tan•go *n.* tango

tank *n.* tanque

tan•ta•lize *v.* atormentar

tan•ta•mount *adj.* equivalente

tan•trum *n.* rabieta; berrinche

tap *n.* grifo; golpecito

tape *n.* cinta

ta•per *v.* afilar

tap•es•try *n.* tapiz

tape•worm *n.* tenia; solitaria

tap•i•o•ca *n.* tapioca

ta•pir *n.* tapir

tar *v.* alquitranar; embrear

ta•ran•tu•la *n.* tarántula

tar•dy *adj.* tardo; tardío

tar•get *n.* blanco

tar•iff *n.* tarifa

tar•nish *v.* deslustrar(se); empañar

tar•ry *v.* tardar; detenerse

tart *n.* tarta

tar•tar *n.* tártaro

task *n.* tarea; labor

task•mas•ter *n.* capataz

tas•sel *n.* borla

taste *n.* sabor

tast•y *adj.* sabroso

tat•ter *n.* andrajo

tat•tered *adj.* harapiento; andrajoso

tat•too *n.* tatuaje

taunt *n.* mofa; sarcasmo; escarnio

taut *adj.* tieso; tirante

tav•ern *n.* taberna

taw•dry *adj.* charro

taw•ny *adj.* leonado

tax *n.* impuesto; contribución; carga

tax•i *n.* taxi

tax•i•cab *n.* taxi

tea *n.* té

tea•bag *n.* sobre de té; muñeca de té

teach *v.* instruir

teach•er *n.* maestro; profesora; profesor

tea•cup *n.* taza para té

tea•ket•tle *n.* tetera

team *n.* equipo

team•mate *n.* compañero de equipo

team•ster *n.* camionero; camionista

team•work *n.* cooperación

tea•pot *n.* tetera

tear *n.* lágrima

tear *v.* rasgar(se); romper(se)

tease *v.* tomar el pelo; atormentar

tea•spoon *n.* cucharilla

tea•spoon•ful *n.* cucharadita

tech•ni•cal *adj.* técnico

tech•ni•cian *n.* técnico

tech•nol•o•gy *n.* tecnología

te•di•ous *adj.* aburrido; tedioso

tel•e•gram *n.* telegrama

tel•e•graph *n.* telégrafo

te•leg•ra•phy *n.* telegrafía

tel•e•phone *n.* teléfono

tel•e•scope *n.* telescopio

tel•e•vi•sion *n.* televisión

tell *v.* mandar; decir

tem•per•a•men•tal *adj.* temperamental

tem•per•a•ture *n.* fiebre

tem•pes•tu•ous *adj.* tempestuoso

tem•ple *n.* templo

tem•po *n.* tiempo

tem•po•ral *adj.* temporal

temp•ta•tion *n.* tentación

ten *adj., n.* diez

tend *v.* tender

ten•den•cy *n.* tendencia

ten•der•ly *adv.* tiernamente

ten•don *n.* tendón

ten•nis *n.* tenis

tense *v.* tensar; *adj.* tenso

ten•sion *n.* tensión

ter•min•al *adj., n.* terminal

ter•min•ate *v.* terminar

ter•mi•nol•o•gy *n.* terminología

ter•rain *n.* terreno

ter•res•tri•al *adj.* terrestre

ter•ri•ble *adj.* terrible

ter•rif•ic *adj.* terrífico

ter•ror *n.* terror

ter•ror•ism *n.* terrorismo

ter•ror•ist *n.* terrorista

test *v.* examinar; *n.* examen

tes•ti•fy *v.* atestiguar

text *n.* texto

tex•ture *n.* textura

than *conj.* de; que

thanks *n.* gracias

that *adj.* aquella; aquel; esa; ese

the *def. art.* la; le; las; los; lo

the•a•ter *n.* teatro

them *pron.* las; les; los; ellas; ellos

then *adv.* luego; entonces

the•ol•o•gy *n.* teología

the•o•rize *v.* teorizar

the•o•ry *n.* teoría

there *adv.* ahí; allí; allá

ther•mal *adj.* termal

ther•mom•e•ter *n.* termómetro

the•sau•rus *n.* tesauro

these *pron.* éstas; éstos

they *pron.* ellas; ellos

thick *adj.* denso

thief *n.* ladrón

thigh *n.* muslo

thin *adj.* escaso; delgado

thing *n.* cosa

think *v.* creer; pensar

third *adj.* tercero

thirst *n.* sed

thir•teen *n. , adj.* trece

thir•ty *n., adj.* treinta

this *adj.* esta; este; *pron.* esto; ésta; éste

thorn *n.* espina

thorn•y *adj.* espinoso

thor•ough *adj.* completo

though *adv.* sin embargo; *conj.* aunque

thought•ful *adj.* pensativo

thou•sand *n., adj.* mil

threat•en *v.* amenazar

three *n., adj.* tres

throat *n.* garganta

throne *n.* trono

through *prep.* por

throw *v.* lanzar; echar

thumb *n.* pulgar

Thurs•day *n.* jueves

tib•i•a *n.* tibia

tick•le *v.* cosquillear

tide *n.* marea

ti•ger *n.* tigre

till *prep.* hasta

tim•ber *n.* madero

time *n.* hora; tiempo; vez

tim•id *adj.* tímido

tim•id•i•ty *n.* timidez

tip *n.* propina

tire *v.* cansar(se)

tired *adj.* cansado

tire•some *adj.* molesto

tis•sue *n.* tisú

ti•tan•ic *adj.* titánico

tithe *n.* diezmo

ti•tle *v.* titular; *n.* título

tit•ter *v.* reír a medias

tit•u•lar *adj.* titular

TNT, T.N.T. *n.* explosivo

to *adv., prep.* hacia; *prep.* hasta; a

toad *n.* sapo

toad•stool *n.* hongo; hongo venenoso

toast *n.* tostar; brindar

to•bac•co *n.* tabacco

to•bog•gan *n.* tobogán

to•day *n., adv.* hoy

toe *n.* dedo del pie

tof•fee, tof•fy *n.* caramelo

toga *n.* toga

to•geth•er *adv.* juntos

toil *v.* trabajar asiduamente; afanarse

toi•let *n.* retrete; tocado

toi•let•ry *n.* artículo de tocador

to•ken *n.* indicio; prenda; señal

tol•er•a•ble *adj.* tolerable; regular

tol•er•ance *n.* tolerancia

tol•er•ant *adj.* tolerante

tol•er•ate *v.* permitir; tolerar

toll *n.* peaje

to•ma•to *n.* tomate

tomb *n.* tumba

tomb•stone *n.* lápida sepulcral

to•mor•row *adv., n.* mañana
ton *n.* tonelada
tone *n.* tono; tendencia
tongs *n.* tenazas
tongue *n.* lengua
ton•ic *n.* tónico
to•night *adv.* esta noche
ton•nage *n.* tonelaje
ton•sil *n.* amígdala; tonsila
ton•sil•li•tis *n.* amigdalitis
too *adv.* además; también
tool *n.* herramienta
tooth *n.* diente
tooth•ache *n.* dolor de muelas
tooth•brush *n.* cepillo de dientes
top *n.* tapa
to•paz *n.* topacio
top•coat *n.* sobretodo
top•hat *n.* chistera
top•ic *n.* tema
top•i•cal *adj.* tópico
to•pog•ra•phy *n.* topografía
top•ple *v.* venirse abajo
top•sy•tur•vy *adv.* patas arriba
torch *n.* antorcha; hacha
tor•ment *v.* atormentar
tor•na•do *n.* tornado
tor•pe•do *n.* torpedo
tor•rent *n.* torrente
tor•rid *adj.* tórrido
tor•so *n.* torso
tor•toise *n.* tortuga
tor•tu•ous *adj.* tortuoso
tor•ture *v.* torturar
toss *v.* echar
tot *n.* nene; nena
to•tal *n., adj.* total
to•tal•i•tar•i•an *adj.* totalitario
to•tal•ly *adv.* totalmente
tote *v. inf.* llevar
to•tem *n.* tótem
tot•ter *v.* bambolearse
touch *v.* tocar(se)
touch•y *adj.* irritable
tough *adj.* difícil
tough•en *v.* endurecer(se); hacer(se)

tour *n.* viaje; excursión
tour•ism *n.* turismo
tour•ist *n.* turista
tour•na•ment *n.* torneo
tour•ni•quet *n.* torniquete
tou•sle *v.* despeinar
tow *v.* llevar a remolque
to•ward *prep.* cerca de
tow•el *n.* toalla
tow•er *n.* torre
town *n.* pueblo; ciudad
tox•ic *adj.* tóxico
tox•in *n.* toxina
toy *n.* juguete
trace *n.* indicio; huella; rastro
tra•che•a *n.* tráquea
track *n.* vía; pista; senda
tract *n.* extensión; tratado
trac•tor *n.* tractor
trade *v.* comerciar
trade•mark *n.* marca de fábrica; marca registrada
trade un•ion *n.* sindicato
tra•di•tion *n.* tradición
tra•di•tion•al *adj.* tradicional
tra•duce *v.* calumniar
traf•fic *n.* tráfico
trag•e•dy *n.* tragedia
trag•ic *adj.* trágico
trail *v.* arrastrar(se); rastrear
trail•er *n.* remolque
train *n.* tren
trait *n.* característica; rasgo
trai•tor *n.* traidor
tra•jec•to•ry *n.* trayectoria
tramp *n.* andar con pasos pezados
tram•ple *v.* pisotear
trance *n.* arrobamiento; estado hipnótico
tran•quil *adj.* tranquilo
tran•quil•i•ty *n.* tranquilidad
tran•quil•ize *v.* tranquilizar
trans•act *v.* despachar
trans•ac•tion *n.* transacción
tran•scend *v.* sobresalir
tran•scribe *v.* transcribir
tran•script *n.* trasunto

211

tran•scrip•tion *n.* transcripción
trans•fer *v.* transferir; trasladar
trans•fer•ence *n.* transferencia
trans•form *v.* transformar
trans•for•ma•tion *n.* transformación
trans•form•er *n.* transformador
trans•fu•sion *n.* transfusión
trans•gress *v.* traspasar; pecar
trans•gres•sion *n.* transgresión
tran•sient *adj.* transitorio; pasajero
tran•sis•tor *adj., n.* transistor
trans•it *n.* tránsito
tran•si•tive *adj.* transitivo
tran•si•to•ry *adj.* transitorio
trans•late *v.* traducir
trans•la•tion *n.* traducción
trans•lu•cent *adj.* translúcido
trans•mis•sion *n.* transmisión
trans•mit *v.* transmitir
trans•mit•ter *n.* transmisor
tran•som *n.* travesaño
trans•par•ent *adj.* transparente; claro; obvio
tran•spire *v.* transpirar; suceder
trans•plant *v.* trasplantar
trans•port *n.* transporte; *v.* transportar
trans•por•ta•tion *n.* transportación
trans•pose *v.* transponer
trans•verse *adj.* transversal
trap *v.* entrampar
tra•peze *n.* trapecio
trap•e•zoid *n.* trapezoide
trash *n.* basura
tra•uma *n.* trauma
trau•mat•ic *adj.* traumático
trav•el *v.* viajar
trea•son *n.* traición
treas•ure *n.* tesoro
treas•ur•er *n.* tesorero
treas•ur•y *n.* tesoro
treat *v.* tratar
trea•tise *n.* tratado
treat•ment *n.* tratamiento
trea•ty *n.* tratado; pacto
tre•ble *adj.* triple
tree *n.* árbol

trek *v.* caminar
trel•lis *n.* enrejado; espaldera
trem•ble *v.* temblar
tre•men•dous *adj.* tremendo
trem•or *n.* temblor
trench *n.* foso; trinchera
tri•al *n.* prueba
tri•an•gle *n.* triángulo
tri•an•gu•lar *adj.* triangular
tri•bu•nal *n.* tribunal
trib•ute *n.* tributo
trick *n.* truco; trampa; engaño
trick•le *v.* gotear
tri•cy•cle *n.* triciclo
tried *adj.* probado
tri•fle *n.* bagatela
tri•fling *adj.* sin importancia
trig•ger *n.* gatillo
trig•o•nom•e•try *n.* trigonometría
tril•lion *n.* billón
trim *v.* guarnecer
trin•ket *n.* dije
tri•o *n.* trío
trip *n.* viaje
tri•ple *v.* triplicar(se)
trip•let *n.* trillizo
trip•li•cate *v.* triplicar
tri•pod *n.* trípode
trite *adj.* gastado
tri•umph *n.* triunfo
tri•um•phant *adj.* triunfante
triv•i•al *adj.* trivial; frívolo
triv•i•al•i•ty *n.* trivialidad
trol•ley *n.* tranvía
trom•bone *n.* trombón
troop *n.* tropa; escuadrón
troop•er *n.* soldado de caballería
tro•phy *n.* trofeo
trop•ic *n.* trópico
trop•i•cal *adj.* tropical
trot *v.* ir al trote; hacer trotar
trou•ba•dour *n.* trovador
trou•ble *v.* molestar(se)
trou•ble•some *adj.* molesto
trough *n.* abrevadero
troupe *n.* compañía

trou•sers *n.* pantalones
trous•seau *n.* ajuar
trout *n.* trucha
trow•el *n.* paleta; desplantador
tru•ant *n.* novillero
truce *n.* tregua
truck *n.* camión
true *adj.* verdadero
tru•ly *adv.* verdaderamente; realmente
trump *n.* triunfo
trum•pet *n.* trompeta
trun•cate *v.* truncar
trunk *n.* tronco; baúl
truss *v.* empaquetear
trust *v.* esperar; *n.* fideicomiso
trus•tee *n.* fideicomisario
trust•wor•thy *adj.* fidedigno; confiable
trust•y *adj.* seguro
truth *n.* verdad
truth•ful *adj.* veraz
try *v.* probar
try•ing *adj.* difícil; penoso
tryst *n.* cita
T•shirt *n.* camiseta
tub *n.* baño; tina
tu•ba *n.* tuba
tube *n.* tubo
tu•ber•cu•lo•sis *n.* tuberculosis
tuck *v.* alforzar
Tues•day *n.* martes
tuft *n.* copete
tug *v.* tirar con fuerza; remolcar
tug•boat *n.* remolcador
tu•i•tion *n.* enseñanza
tu•lip *n.* tulipán
tum•ble *v.* caer(se)
tum•bler *n.* volteador; vaso
tu•mor *n.* tumor
tu•mult *n.* tumulto
tu•mul•tu•ous *adj.* tumultuoso
tu•na *n.* atún
tun•dra *n.* tundra
tune *n.* aire; afinación
tu•nic *n.* túnica
tun•nel *n.* túnel
tur•ban *n.* turbante

tur•bid *adj.* túrbido
tur•bine *n.* turbina
tur•bu•lence *n.* turbulencia; confusión
tu•reen *n.* sopera
turf *n.* césped
tur•key *n.* pavo
tur•moil *n.* tumulto
turn *v.* volver(se); girar
turn•coat *n.* traidor
tur•nip *n.* nabo
turn•out *n.* concurrencia; producción
turn•pike *n.* autopista de peaje
turn•stile *n.* torniquete
tur•pen•tine *n.* trementina
tur•quoise *n.* turquesa
tur•ret *n.* torrecilla
tur•tle *n.* tortuga
tusk *n.* colmillo
tus•sle *n.* agarrada
tu•te•lage *n.* tutela
tu•tor *n.* tutor
tux•e•do *n.* smoking
TV *n.* televisión
twang *n.* tañido; timbre nasal
tweed *n.* mezcla de lana
twee•zers *n.* bruselas
twelfth *adj.* duodécimo
twelve *adj., n.* doce
twen•ty *adj., n.* veinte
twice *adv.* dos veces
twig *n.* ramita
twi•light *n.* crepúsculo
twill *n.* tela cruzada
twin *adj., n.* gemelo
twinge *n.* dolor agudo
twin•kle *v.* centellear
twirl *v.* girar; piruetear
twist *v.* torcer(se)
twitch *v.* crisparse
twit•ter *v.* gorjear
two *adj., n.* dos
two•faced *adj.* falso; hipócrita
ty•coon *n.* magnate
type *n.* tipo
type•write *v.* escribir a máquina
type•writ•er *n.* máquina de escribir

ty·phoid *n.* fiebre tifoidea
ty·phoon *n.* tifón
ty·phus *n.* tifus
typ·i·cal *adj.* típico
typ·i·fy *v.* simbolizar
typ·ist *n.* mecanógrafo
ty·pog·ra·phy *n.* tipografía
ty·ran·ni·cal *adj.* tiránico; despótico
tyr·an·nize *v.* tiranizar
tyr·an·ny *n.* tiranía

U

u·biq·ui·tous *adj.* ubicuo
u·biq·ui·ty *n.* ubicuidad
ud·der *n.* ubre
ug·li·ness *n.* fealdad
ug·ly *adj.* feo
u·ku·le·le *n.* ukelele
ul·cer *n.* úlcera
ul·cer·ate *v.* ulcerar(se)
ul·cer·ous *adj.* ulceroso
ul·na *n.* cúbito
ul·te·ri·or *adj.* ulterior
ul·ti·mate *adj.* último
ul·ti·ma·tum *n.* ultimátum
ul·tra *adj.* excesivo
ul·tra·mod·ern *adj.* ultramoderno
ul·tra·son·ic *adj.* ultrasónico
ul·tra·sound *n.* ultrasónico
ul·tra·vi·o·let *adj.* ultravioleta
ul·u·late *v.* ulular
um·bil·i·cal *adj.* umbilical
um·bil·i·cus *n.* ombligo
um·brel·la *n.* paraguas
um·pire *n.* árbitro
ump·teen *adj.* muchos
un·a·bashed *adj.* desvergonzado; descarado
un·a·ble *adj.* incapaz
un·a·bridged *adj.* no abreviado
un·ac·cent·ed *adj.* sin acento
un·ac·cept·a·ble *adj.* inaceptable
un·ac·count·a·ble *adj.* inexplicable

un·ac·cus·tomed *adj.* no acostumbrado
un·ac·knowl·edged *adj.* no reconocido
un·a·dorned *adj.* sin adorno
un·a·dul·ter·at·ed *adj.* no adulterado
un·af·fect·ed *adj.* sin afectación
un·a·fraid *adj.* sin terror
un·aid·ed *adj.* sin ayuda
un·am·big·u·ous *adj.* sin ambigüedad
u·nan·i·mous *adj.* unánime
un·an·swer·a·ble *adj.* incontestable
un·ap·proach·a·ble *adj.* inaccesible
un·armed *adj.* desarmado
un·as·sail·a·ble *adj.* inexpugnable
un·as·sist·ed *adj.* sin ayuda
un·as·sum·ing *adj.* modesto; sencillo
un·at·tached *adj.* suelto
un·at·tend·ed *adj.* desatendido
un·at·trac·tive *adj.* inatractivo
un·au·thor·ized *adj.* sin autorización
un·a·void·a·ble *adj.* inevitable
un·a·ware *adj.* ignorante
un·a·wares *adv.* de improviso
un·bal·anced *adj.* desequilibrado
un·beat·a·ble *adj.* invencible
un·beat·en *adj.* invicto
un·be·com·ing *adj.* que sienta mal
un·be·lief *n.* incredulidad
un·be·liev·a·ble *adj.* increíble
un·be·liev·er *n.* descreído
un·be·liev·ing *adj.* incrédulo
un·bend *v.* desencorvar; aflojar
un·bend·ing *adj.* inflexible
un·bi·ased *adj.* imparcial
un·bind *v.* desatar
un·blem·ished *adj.* puro
un·born *adj.* no nacido
un·bos·om *v.* revelar
un·bound·ed *adj.* ilimitado
un·bowed *adj.* recto
un·break·a·ble *adj.* irrompible
un·breath·a·ble *adj.* irrespirable
un·bri·dled *adj.* desenfrenado
un·bro·ken *adj.* inviolado; sin romper
un·buck·le *v.* deshebillar
un·bur·den *v.* descargar
un·but·ton *v.* desabotonar(se)

un•caged *adj.* suelto
un•called•for *adj.* inmerecido
un•can•ny *adj.* extraño; misterioso
un•cap *v.* destapar
un•ceas•ing *adj.* incesante
un•cer•e•mo•ni•ous *adj.* informal
un•cer•tain *adj.* indeciso
un•cer•tain•ty *n.* incertidumbre
un•change•a•ble *adj.* inalterable
un•changed *adj.* inalterado
un•chang•ing *adj.* inalterable
un•chart•ed *adj.* desconocido
un•civ•il *adj.* incivil; descortés
un•civ•i•lized *adj.* incivilizado; inculto
un•clad *adj.* desnudo
un•clasp *v.* separar
un•cle *n.* tío
un•clean *adj.* sucio
un•clear *adj.* confuso
un•clog *v.* sedatascar
un•com•fort•a•ble *adj.* incómodo
un•com•mon *adj.* raro
un•com•un•i•ca•tive *adj.* poco
  comunicativo
un•com•pro•mis•ing *adj.* inflexible
un•con•cern *n.* indiferencia
un•con•nect•ed *adj.* inconexo
un•con•scious *adj.* inconsciente
un•con•sid•ered *adj.* inconsiderado
un•con•trolled *adj.* desenfrenado
un•cooked *adj.* crudo
un•count•ed *adj.* innumerable
un•cross *v.* descruzar
un•de•cid•ed *adj.* indeciso
un•der•es•ti•mate *v.* subestimar
un•der•ground *adj.* subterráneo
un•der•line *v.* subrayar
un•der•neath *adv.* debajo; *prep.* bajo
un•der•wear *n.* ropa interior
un•do *v.* desatar
un•fin•ished *adj.* incompleto
un•fold *v.* extender; abrir
u•ni•form *n.* uniforme
un•ion *n.* unión
u•ni•ted *adj.* unido
u•ni•ver•sal *adj.* universal

un•luck•y *adj.* desdichado
un•rest *n.* inquietud
un•sa•vor•y *adj.* desagradable
un•seem•ly *adj.* indecoroso
un•skilled *adj.* inexperto
un•so•phis•ti•cat•ed *adj.* cándido
un•sta•ble *adj.* inestable
un•stead•y *adj.* inseguro
un•til *prep.* hasta
un•truth•ful *adj.* mentiroso
un•u•su•al *adj.* raro
un•wrap *v.* desenvolver
up *adj.* ascendente; *adv.* acabado; arriba
up•hill *adj.* ascendente
up•hol•ster•y *n.* tapicería
up•on *prep.* sobre; encima de
up•per *adj.* alto
up•per•cut *n.* gancho
up•roar *n.* alboroto
up•set *n.* trastorno; *v.* volcar
up•stairs *adj.* arriba
u•ra•ni•um *n.* uranio
U•ra•nus *n.* Urano
ur•ban *adj.* urbano
urge *n.* impulso; *v.* incitar
ur•gent *adj.* urgente
u•rine *n.* orina
urn *n.* urna
us *pron.* nosotras; nosotros; nos
use *n.* uso; *v.* utilizar; usar
use•less *adj.* inútil
u•su•al *adj.* usual
u•ten•sil *n.* utensilio
u•ter•us *n.* útero
u•til•i•ta•ri•an *n.* utilitario
u•til•i•ty *n.* utilidad
u•til•ize *v.* utilizar
ut•ter•ance *n.* expresión
ux•o•ri•ous *adj.* gurrumino

V

va·can·cy *n.* vacante
va·cant *adj.* vacío
va·ca·tion *n.* vacación
vac·ci·nate *v.* vacunar
vac·ci·na·tion *n.* vacunación
vac·cine *n.* vacuna
vac·il·late *v.* vacilar
vac·il·la·tion *n.* vacilación; fluctuación
va·cu·i·ty *n.* vacuidad
vac·u·um *n.* vacío
va·gar·y *n.* capricho
va·grant *n.* vagabundo
vague *adj.* incierto; vago
vain *adj.* vano
vale *n.* valle
val·e·dic·to·ry *n.* discurso de despedida
val·en·tine *n.* novia o novio en el día de San Valentín
val·id *adj.* válido
val·i·date *v.* validar
va·lid·i·ty *n.* validez
va·lise *n.* maleta
val·ley *n.* valle
val·or *n.* valor; valentía
val·u·a·ble *adj.* valioso; costoso; precioso
val·u·a·tion *n.* valuación; valorización
val·ue *v.* valuar; *n.* valor
valve *n.* válvula
vam·pire *n.* vampiro
van *n.* camión de mudanzas
van·dal *n.* vándalo
van·dal·ism *n.* vandalismo
vane *n.* veleta
van·guard *n.* vanguardia
va·nil·la *n.* vainilla
van·ish *v.* desaparecer
van·i·ty *n.* vanidad
van·quish *v.* vencer; conquistar
van·tage *n.* ventaja; provecho
vap·id *adj.* insípido
va·por *n.* vapor
va·por·ize *v.* vaporizar(se)
va·por·ous *adj.* vaporoso

var·i·a·bil·i·ty *n.* variabilidad
var·i·a·ble *n.*, *adj.* variable
var·i·a·tion *n.* variación
var·i·cose *adj.* varicoso
var·ied *adj.* variado
va·ri·e·ty *n.* variedad
var·i·ous *adj.* variado
var·nish *n.* barniz
var·si·ty *n.* equipo principal de una universidad
var·y *v.* variar; desviarse; cambiar
vase *n.* jarrón
vast *adj.* vasto
veal *n.* ternera
veg·e·ta·ble *n.* legumbre
veg·e·tar·i·an *n.* vegetariano
veg·e·tate *v.* vegetar
veg·e·ta·tion *n.* vegetación
ve·hi·cle *n.* vehículo
vein *n.* vena
ve·lo·ci·ty *n.* velocidad
ve·nal·i·ty *n.* venalidad
vend *v.* vender
ven·er·a·ble *adj.* venerable
ven·er·a·tion *n.* veneración
ve·ni·al *adj.* venial
ven·om *n.* veneno
ven·om·ous *adj.* venenoso
ven·ti·late *v.* ventilar
ven·tral *adj.* ventral
ven·tri·cle *n.* ventrículo
ven·ture·some *adj.* aventurero
Ve·nus *n.* Venus
ve·ra·cious *adj.* veraz
verb *n.* verbo
ver·bal *adj.* verbal
ver·bose *adj.* verboso
ver·bos·i·ty *n.* verbosidad
ver·dict *n.* veredicto
ver·i·fy *v.* verificar
ver·mouth *n.* vermut
ver·nal *adj.* vernal
ver·sa·til·i·ty *n.* adaptabilidad
verse *n.* versículo
ver·sion *n.* versión
ver·te·bra *n.* vértebra

ver•te•brate *adj.* vertebrado
ver•ti•cal *adj.* vertical
ver•y *adj.* mismo; *adv.* muy
ves•sel *n.* vaso
vest *n.* chaleco
vet *n.* veterinario
vet•er•an *adj., n.* veterano
vet•er•i•nar•i•an *n.* veterinario
vet•er•i•nar•y *adj., n.* veterinario
vi•brant *adj.* vibrante
vi•brate *v.* oscilar
vi•bra•tion *n.* vibración
vic•ar *n.* vicario
vi•car•i•ous *adj.* substituto
vice *n.* vicio
vice pres•i•dent *n.* vicepresidente
vice•roy *n.* virrey
vice ver•sa *adv.* viceversa
vi•cin•i•ty *n.* vecindad
vi•cious *adj.* depravado; vicioso; cruel
vic•tim *n.* víctima
vic•tim•ize *v.* hacer víctima
vic•to•ri•ous *adj.* victorioso
vic•to•ry *n.* victoria
view *v.* ver; *n.* escena
vig•i•lance *n.* vigilancia
vig•or *n.* vigor
vig•or•ous *adj.* vigoroso
vil•lage *n.* aldea
vin•di•cate *v.* vindicar
vine *n.* vid
vin•e•gar *n.* vinagre
vi•o•la *n.* viola
vi•o•la•tion *n.* violación
vi•o•lent *adj.* violento
vi•o•let *adj.* violado
vi•o•lin *n.* violín
vir•ile *adj.* viril
vi•ril•i•ty *n.* virilidad
vir•tu•al *adj.* virtual
vir•tu•al•ly *adv.* virtualmente
vir•u•lent *adj.* virulento
vi•rus *n.* virus
vis•cos•i•ty *n.* viscosidad
vis•count *n.* vizconde
vis•count•ess *n.* vizcondesa

vise *n.* tornillo
vis•i•bil•i•ty *n.* visibilidad
vis•i•ble *adj.* visible; conspicuo
vi•sion *n.* visión
vi•sion•ar•y *n.* visionario
vis•it *n.* visita; *v.* visitar
vis•it•a•tion *n.* visitación
vi•sor *n.* visera
vis•u•al *adj.* visual
vis•u•al•ize *v.* representarse en la mente
vi•tal *adj.* vital
vi•tal•i•ty *n.* vitalidad
vi•ta•min *n.* vitamina
vit•re•ous *adj.* vítreo
vit•ri•ol *n.* vitriolo
vi•tu•per•ate *v.* vituperar
vi•va•cious *adj.* vivaz; animado; vivaracho
vi•vac•i•ty *n.* vivacidad; animación
viv•id *adj.* intenso; vivo
vix•en *n.* arpía; zorra
vo•cab•u•lar•y *n.* vocabulario
vo•cal *adj.* vocal
vo•cal•ist *n.* cantante
vo•ca•tion *n.* vocación
vod•ka *n.* vodka
vogue *n.* moda; boga
voice *n.* voz
void *adj.* nulo; vacío
vol•can•ic *adj.* volcánico
vol•can•o *n.* volcán
vo•li•tion *n.* voluntad; volición
vol•ley *n.* descarga; voleo
volt *n.* voltio
volt•age *n.* voltaje
vol•u•ble *adj.* hablador
vol•ume *n.* cantidad; volumen
vol•un•tar•y *adj.* voluntario
vol•un•teer *n.* voluntario
vo•lup•tu•ar•y *n.* voluptuoso
vo•lup•tu•ous *adj.* voluptuoso
vom•it *n.* vómito; *v.* vomitar
vom•it•ing *n.* vómito
voo•doo *n.* vudú
vo•ra•cious *adj.* voraz
vo•ra•ci•ty *n.* voracidad
vor•tex *n.* vórtice

vo•ta•ry *n.* devoto; partidario
vote *v.* votar; *n.* voto
vo•ter *n.* votante
vot•ing *n.* votación
vo•tive *adj.* votivo; exvoto
vouch *v.* afirmar
vouch•er *n.* comprobante
vow•el *n.* vocal
voy•age *v.* viajar; *n.* viaje
vul•gar *adj.* vulgar
vul•gar•ize *v.* vulgarizar
vul•ner•a•ble *adj.* vulnerable
vul•ture *n.* buitre

W

wack•y *adj.* loco; chiflado
wad *n.* fajo; taco; rollo; bolita
wad•dle *v.* anadear
wade *v.* vadear; pasar con dificultad
wag *v.* menear(se)
wage *n.* salario
wag•er *v.* apostar
wag•on *n.* carro
waif *n.* niño abandonado
wail *v.* lamentarse; sollozar
wain•scot *n.* friso de madera
waist *n.* cintura
waist•coat *n.* chaleco
waist•line *n.* talle
wait *n.* espera; *v.* esperar
wait•er *n.* camarero
waive *v.* renunciar a; abandonar
waiv•er *n.* renuncia
wake *v.* despertar(se)
wake•ful *adj.* vigilante
wak•en *v.* despertar(se)
walk *n.* caminata; *v.* caminar; andar
walk•out *n.* huelga
walk•over *n.* triunfo fácil
wall *n.* pared
wall•board *n.* cartón de yeso
wal•let *n.* cartera
wal•lop *v.* zurrar

wal•low *v.* revolcarse
wall•pa•per *n.* papel pintado
wal•nut *n.* nogal
wal•rus *n.* morsa
waltz *n.* vals
wan *adj.* pálido
wan•der•lust *n.* deseo de viajar
wane *v.* disminuir; menguar
want *v.* querer; requerir; desear
want•ing *adj.* deficiente
wan•ton *adj.* lascivo; desenfrenado
war *v.* guerrear; *n.* guerra
war•ble *v.* trinar
war cry *n.* grito de guerra
ward *v.* desviar
war•den *n.* guardián; alcaide
ward•robe *n.* guardarropa; vestuario
ware *n.* mercancías
ware•house *n.* almacén
war•fare *n.* guerra
war•lock *n.* hechicero
warm *v.* calentar(se); *adj.* caluroso; caliente
warm•heart•ed *adj.* afectuoso
war•mon•ger *n.* belicista
warmth *n.* calor
warn *v.* advertir
warn•ing *n.* advertencia; aviso
warp *v.* alabearse; pervertir
war•rant *n.* autorización; garantía
war•ran•ty *n.* garantía
war•ren *n.* conejera
war•ri•or *n.* guerrero
wart *n.* verruga
war•y *adj.* cauteloso
wash *v.* lavar(se)
wash•cloth *n.* paño para lavarse
wash•er *n.* lavadora
wash•ing *n.* lavado
wash•room *n.* lavabo
wash•stand *n.* lavamanos
wash•tub *n.* tina
wasp *n.* avispa
wast•age *n.* desgaste; merma
waste *n.* pérdida; *v.* desperdiciar
wast•rel *n.* derrochador
watch *n.* reloj; *v.* mirar; observar

watch•ful *adj.* vigilante; desvelado
watch•man *n.* vigilante
watch•word *n.* santo y seña
wa•ter *n.* agua
wa•ter•co•lor *n.* acuarela
wa•ter•course *n.* corriente
wa•ter•fall *n.* cascada
wa•ter•fowl *n.* ave acuática
wa•ter•front *n.* terreno ribereño
wa•ter li•ly *n.* nenúfar
wa•ter•logged *adj.* anegado
wa•ter•mark *n.* nivel de agua; filigrana
wa•ter•mel•on *n.* sandía
wa•ter•proof *adj.* impermeable
wa•ter•side *n.* orilla del agua
wa•ter sof•ten•er *n.* ablandador
químico de agua
wa•ter•spout *n.* tromba marina; boquilla
wa•ter•tight *adj.* estanco; seguro
wa•ter•way *n.* canal
wa•ter•y *adj.* insípido
watt *n.* vatio
wave *v.* ondular; *n.* onda
wa•ver *v.* oscilar; vacilar
wav•y *adj.* ondulado
wax *n.* cera
wax•en *adj.* de cera j pálido
wax•work *n.* figura de cera
way *n.* camino; modo; dirección
way•far•er *n.* viajero
way•lay *v.* asaltar
way•side *n.* borde del camino
way•ward *adj.* voluntarioso; travieso
we *pron.* nosotras; nosotros
weak *adj.* débil
weak•en *v.* debilitar(se)
weak•ling *n.* alfeñique
weak•ly *adj.* achacoso
weak•mind•ed *adj.* sin voluntad
weak•ness *n.* debilidad
wealth *n.* riqueza
wealth•y *adj.* rico
wean *v.* destetar
weap•on *n.* arma
weap•on•ry *n.* armas
wear *v.* desgastar(se); llevar

wear•ing *adj.* penoso
wea•ri•some *adj.* fastidioso
wea•ry *adj.* fatigado; aburrido
wea•sel *n.* comadreja
weath•er *n.* tiempo
weath•er•beat•en *adj.* curtido por la
intemperie
weath•er•glass *n.* barómetro
weath•er•man *n.* pronosticador de tiempo
weave *v.* tejido
web *n.* tela
web•bing *n.* cincha
wed *v.* casar(se)
wed•ding *n.* boda
wedge *n.* cuña
wed•lock *n.* matrimonio
Wednes•day *n.* miércoles
wee *adj.* pequeñito
weed *v.* escardar
week *n.* semana
week•day *n.* día laborable o de trabajo
week•end *n.* fin de semana
week•ly *adj.* semanal
weep *v.* llorar
wee•vil *n.* gorgojo
weigh *v.* pesar
weight *n.* pesa
weight•y *adj.* pesado; importante
wel•come *adj.* agradable
weld *v.* soldar
wel•fare *n.* bienestar
well *adv.* pues; *n.* pozo
well-be•ing *n.* bienestar
well-bred *adj.* bien criado
well-dis•posed *adj.* bien dispuesto
well-known *adj.* famoso
well-off *adj.* adinerado
well-read *adj.* leído
well-thought-of *adj.* bien mirado
well-timed *adj.* oportuno
well-to-do *adj.* acaudalado
welt *n.* verduqón
wel•ter revolcar(se)
wench *n.* moza
were•wolf *n.* hombre que puede
transformarse en lobo

west

west *n.* oeste
west•ern *adj.* occidental
wet *v.* mojar(se)
whack *v.* golpear
whale *n.* ballena
whale•bone *n.* ballena
what *pron.* qué; lo que; cuál
what•ev•er *pron.* todo lo que
what•not *n.* estante; juguetero
wheat *n.* trigo
whee•dle *v.* engatusar; halagar
wheel *n.* rueda
wheel•bar•row *n.* carretilla
wheel•chair *n.* silla de ruedas
wheeze *v.* respirar asmáticamente
when *conj.* cuando
whence *adv.* de dónde; de qué
when•ev•er *adv.* siempre que
where *conj., adv.* donde; *adv.* adónde
where•a•bouts *n.* paradero
where•as *conj.* visto que
where•up•on *adv.* con lo cual
wher•ev•er *adv.* dondequiera
wheth•er *conj.* si
whey *n.* suero de la leche
which *pron.* lo que; cuál; la; le
which•ev•er *pron.* cualquiera
whiff *n.* olorcillo
while *conj.* mientras
whim *n.* capricho; lantojo
whim•per *v.* lloriquear
whim•si•cal *adj.* caprichoso
whine *v.* gimotear; gemir
whin•ny *n.* relincho
whip *v.* batir
whir *v.* zumbar; batir
whirl *v.* girar rápidamente
whirl•pool *n.* remolino
whirl•wind *n.* torbellino
whisk•ers *n.* barbas; bigotes
whis•key *n.* whisky
whis•per *n.* cuchicheo; *v.* cuchichear
whis•tle *v.* silbar
white *n., adj.* blanco
white-col•lar *adj.* oficinesco
whit•en *v.* blanquear

white•wash *n.* jalbegue
whith•er *conj.* adonde
whit•tle *v.* cortar poco a poco
whiz *v.* silbar; rehilar
who *pron.* la; el; lo; quién; que
who•ev•er *pron.* quienquiera que
whole *n., adj.* todo
whole•heart•ed *adj.* sincero; incondicional
whole•sale *n.* venta al por menor
whole•some *adj.* saludable
whol•ly *adv.* completamente
whom *pron.* a quién
whom•ev•er *pron.* a quienquiera
whoop *n.* alarido
whore *n.* puta; prostituta
whose *pron.* cuyo
why *adv.* por qué
wick *n.* mecha
wick•ed *adj.* malicioso
wick•er *adj.* de mimbre
wide *adj.* ancho
wide•a•wake *adj.* despabilado
wid•en *v.* ensanchar(se)
wide•spread *adj.* extendido; difuso
wid•ow *n.* viuda
wid•ow•er *n.* viudo
width *n.* anchura
wield *v.* ejercer; mandar; manejar
wife *n.* esposa
wig *n.* peluca
wig•gle *v.* menear(se); cimbrearse
wild *adj.* descabellado
wild boar *n.* jabalí
wil•der•ness *n.* yermo; desierto
wile *n.* ardid
will *v.* querer
will•ful *adj.* voluntarioso; terco; premeditado
will•ing *adj.* dispuesto; complaciente
wil•low *n.* sauce
wil•low•y *adj.* esbelto
wil•ly-nil•ly *adv.* de grado o por fuerza
wilt *v.* marchitar(se)
win *n.* victoria; *v.* lograr; ganar
wince *v.* estremecerse; respingar

wrought

winch *n.* torno
wind *n.* viento
wind *v.* arrollar(se)
wind·fall *n.* ganancia inesperada
wind·mill *n.* molino de viento
win·dow *n.* ventana
win·dow·pane *n.* cristal
wind·shield *n.* parabrisas
wind·y *adj.* ventoso
wine *n.* vino
win·er·y *n.* lagar
wing *n.* ala
wink *v.* guiñar; pestañear
win·ner *n.* ganador
win·ning *n.* ganancias
win·now *v.* aventar
win·some *adj.* atractivo; alegre
win·ter *n.* invierno
win·try *adj.* invernal
wipe *v.* enjugar; secar; borrar
wire *n.* alambre
wire·tap *n.* intervenir
wir·ing *n.* instalación de alambres
wir·y *adj.* nervudo
wis·dom *n.* sabiduría
wise *adj.* acertado; sabio
wise·crack *n.* cuchufleta; pulla
wish *n.* deseo; *v.* desear
wish·ful *adj.* deseoso
wit *n.* ingenio; gracia
witch *n.* bruja
witch·craft *n.* brujería
with *prep.* con
with·draw·al *n.* retirada
with·drawn *adj.* ensimismado
with·er *v.* marchitar(se); secarse
with·hold *v.* retener
with·in *adv.* dentro
with·out *adv.* por fuera
with·stand *v.* resistir
wit·less *adj.* tonto
wit·ness *n.* testigo
wit·ti·cism *n.* dicho gracioso
wit·ty *adj.* salado; ingenioso
wiz·ard *n.* hechicero
wob·ble *v.* bambolear; bailar

woe *n.* aflicción; infortunio
wolf *n.* lobo
wo·man *n.* mujer
wom·an·kind *n.* sexo femenino
womb *n.* matriz
wom·en's rights *n.* derechos de la mujer
won·der *v.* asombrarse
won·der·ful *adj.* maravilloso
woo *v.* cortejar
wood *n.* madera
wood·en *adj.* de madera; sin expresión
wood·land *n.* monte
wood·peck·er *n.* pájaro carpintero
wood·y *adj.* leñoso
wool *n.* lana
wool·ly *adj.* lanudo
word *n.* palabra
work *v.* trabajar; *n.* obra; trabajo
work·book *n.* cuaderno
work·er *n.* trabajador
work·shop *n.* taller
world *n.* mundo
world·ly *adj.* mundano
world·wide *adj.* mundial
worm *n.* gusano
worm·eaten *adj.* carcomido
wormwood *n.* ajenjo
worn *adj.* usado
worrier *n.* aprensivo; pesimista
wor·ry inquietar(se)
wors·en *v.* empeorar
wor·ship *v.* venerar
worth *n.* valor
worth·less *adj.* despreciable
wound *v.* herir
wrap *v.* envolver
wreck *v.* naufragar; *n.* ruina
wrin·kle *v.* arrugar(se); *n.* arruga
wrist *n.* muñeca
write *v.* escribir
writ·er *n.* escritora; escritor
writ·ing *n.* escritura
wrong *adj.* equivocado
wrong·ful *adj.* injusto; falso
wrong·head·ed *adj.* terco
wrought *adj.* forjado; trabajado

wry *adj.* torcido; irónico; mueca

X

x•ray *v.* radiografiar; *n.* radiografía

Y

yank *v.* sacar de un tirón
Yan•kee *n.* yanqui
yard *n.* yarda
yard•goods *n.* tejidos
yard•stick *n.* vara de medir
yarn *n.* hilaza
yar•row *n.* milenrama
yawn *n.* bostezo; *v.* bostezar
ye *pron.* vosotros
yea *adv.* sí
year *n.* año
year•ling *n.* primal
year•ly *adj.* anualmente
yearn *v.* suspirar; anhelar
yearn•ing *n.* anhelo
yeast *n.* levadura
yell *n.* grito; *v.* gritar
yel•low *n., adj.* amarillo
yes *adv.* sí
yes•ter•day *n.* ayer
yet *adv.* todavía
yew *n.* tejo
yield *v.* rendir(se)
yolk *n.* yema
yon•der *adv.* allí; allá
you *n.* pron. vosotras; vosotros; tú
young *adj.* joven
young•ster *n.* jovencito
your *adj.* su(s); tu(s); vuestro(s); vuestra(s)
yours *pron.* deusted(es); el tuyo; elsuyo
your•self *pron.* usted mismo; tú mismo
youth *n.* jóvenes
youth•ful *adj.* juvenil

Z

zeal *n.* ardor
zeal•ous *adj.* celoso
ze•bra *n.* cebra
ze•nith *n.* cenit
ze•ro *n.* cero
ze•ro hour *n.* hora de ataque
zest *n.* gusto
zone *n.* zona
zoo *n.* jardín zoológico
zo•o•log•i•cal *adj.* zoológico
zuc•chi•ni *n.* cidracayote de verano